THE MOST TRUSTED NAME IN TRAVEL: **FROMME**

# FROMMER'S

# SAN FRANCISCO

## 2nd Edition

Van Ness Ave., California
49
& Market Streets

By Erika Lenkert

## FROMMER'S STAR RATINGS SYSTEM

Every hotel, restaurant, and attraction listed in this guide has been ranked for quality and value. Here's what the stars mean:

★ Recommended
★★ Highly Recommended
★★★ A must! Don't miss!

## AN IMPORTANT NOTE

The world is a dynamic place. Hotels change ownership, restaurants hike their prices, museums alter their opening hours, and buses and trains change their routings. And all of this can occur in the several months after our authors have visited, inspected, and written about these hotels, restaurants, museums, and transportation services. Though we have made valiant efforts to keep all our information fresh and up-to-date, some few changes can inevitably occur in the periods before a revised edition of this guidebook is published. So please bear with us if a tiny number of the details in this book have changed. Please also note that we have no responsibility or liability for any inaccuracy or errors or omissions, or for inconvenience, loss, damage, or expenses suffered by anyone as a result of assertions in this guide.

**Harvest time in the Napa and Sonoma wine country brings a brilliant display of autumn colors.**

# CONTENTS

**The iconic Golden Gate Bridge, shrouded in fog against the city skyline.**

# A LOOK AT SAN FRANCISCO

"America's most European city," the tourist brochures insist. And yes, San Francisco is indeed the stuff of postcards. But what brochures all too often overlook is that this city is not just one destination; it's a cornucopia of experiences. Here more than practically anywhere, wherever you go, there you are. Step a block outside of ultra-urban Union Square and you're wandering the colorful maze of Chinatown; a few blocks from there you're immersed in authentically Italian North Beach. Along downtown's Embarcadero waterfront, white-collar workdays pair with glitzy restaurants with spangled Bay Bridge views, while nearby Fisherman's Wharf delivers an oddly compelling flashback to '50s-vintage tourist traps. The gritty-yet-chic Mission District is as crammed with restaurants and boutiques as Pacific Heights is with mansions and billionaires. And tucked into it all, a massive, exceptional park stretches from the center of town to the Pacific Ocean, where wet-suited surfers ride the waves off of a long sand beach. The trick is making sure to get the most out of the City by the Bay—and this book is here to help you do just that.

Alamo Square's Painted Ladies (see p. 137), a hilltop row of pristine Victorian houses, are among the few survivors of San Francisco's 1906 earthquake and fire.

# SAN FRANCISCO'S ICONIC SIGHTS

San Francisco is a city on the rise, as skyscrapers sprout throughout the Financial District (FiDi) and South of Market (SoMa) areas.

A Victorian clock tower anchors Ghirardelli Square (p. 122), the chocolate-factory-turned-shopping-mall near Fisherman's Wharf.

Unfazed by camera-toting tourists, a California sea lion basks in the sun alongside Fisherman's Wharf's Pier 39 (p. 123).

Amid the buzz of Union Square (p. 135), this sculpture offers photo-op proof that "I left my heart in San Francisco."

The everyday bustle of Chinatown (p. 134) gets even more colorful during the annual Autumn Moon Festival.

Golden Gate Park's Conservatory of Flowers (p. 147) houses a world-famous plant collection, from waterlilies to Dracula orchids.

A 1968 gift to San Francisco from Osaka, Japan, the Peace Pagoda sits at the heart of Japantown's shopping malls (p. 141).

Traffic often backs up in the Russian Hill neighborhood as drivers wait their turn to zigzag down steep, twisty Lombard Street (p. 140).

A cultural hub for the Beat Generation writers who colonized North Beach in the 1950s, City Lights Booksellers (p. 194) remains a fascinating store full of hard-to-find titles.

Stranded on a rocky outcrop in the turbulent waters of San Francisco Bay, Alcatraz Prison—accessible only via boat tours (p. 119)—still feels haunted by the ghosts of convicts past

# SAN FRANCISCO LIFE

The bayfront Golden Gate Promenade (p. 152) is the city's most scenic path for runners, walkers, and cyclists.

An all-star line-up of gourmet food shops makes the restored Ferry Building Marketplace (p. 130) an epicurean mecca.

Why ride underground when you can take a spruced-up 1930s F-line streetcar along Market Street from the Embarcadero to the Castro?

Perennial pennant contenders, the San Francisco Giants play ball at AT&T Park (p. 221) in the buzzy SoMa district.

The lush sloping lawns of the Mission District's Dolores Park (see tour p. 184) provide lots of room for picnicking or lounging with a panoramic view.

Cafe culture is alive and well in the North Beach neighborhood, known for its Italian food and beatnik history. Our walking tour (p. 173) suggests plenty of refreshment stops.

Grocery shopping in Chinatown can be an adventure, full of colorful produce, intriguing roots and spices, and briskly haggling locals. Let our walking tour (p. 164) be your guide.

A kitschy relic from the 1960s, the Polynesian-themed Tonga Room at the Fairmont San Francisco (p. 216) charms with its umbrella drinks, Asian fusion food, and fake tropical rainstorms.

Put some campy fun in your weekend with the Sunday's a Drag brunch at the Starlight Room (p. 217), atop the Sir Francis Drake Hotel.

The Beat Era lives on in North Beach's memorabilia-stuffed Vesuvio bar (p. 216), another only-in-San-Francisco experience.

Every June, thousands march down Market Street in the San Francisco LGBT Pride Parade, the nation's largest such celebration.

Psychedelic flourishes on a clothing boutique recall the Summer of Love in Haight-Ashbury (p. 191), once the center of the hippie world.

Held every April, Japantown's Cherry Blossom festival (p. 141) isn't stuck in the tradition-bound past—witness this lively parade float crowded with anime characters.

# DAY TRIPS FROM SAN FRANCISCO

Students chat between classes on the UC Berkeley campus, across the Bay Bridge in Berkeley (p. 223).

Like a soaring cathedral of trees, the coastal redwoods of Muir Woods (p. 236) dwarf human visitors.

Across the Golden Gate Bridge, sunny Sausalito (p. 232) welcomes day-trippers with a string of waterfront cafes and boutiques.

Hiking trails lace Mount Tamalpais State Park (p. 237), one of the Bay Area's favorite outdoor playgrounds.

In the so-called Judgment of Paris in 1976, top honors went to two wines from Napa Valley's Chateau Montelena (p. 248), vaulting California wines to world prominence.

The hilltop Sterling Vineyards estate (p. 249) offers aerial tram rides across a landscape that looks straight out of Tuscany.

In northern Sonoma, the Korbel winery (p. 266), founded by a Czech immigrant in 1882, specializes in sparkling wines.

At smaller family-owned wineries, like Herb Lamb Vineyards, in fall you may be able to watch workers pick, sort, and press grapes.

At the historic Schramsberg winery (p. 249), founded in Calistoga in 1862, visitors can tour 125-year-old caves, where grape juice ferments in oak barrels for up to 10 years.

Movie memorabilia adds extra pizzazz to visits to filmmaker Francis Ford Coppola's Sonoma winery (p. 265), but once you get to the sleek tasting rooms, his wines earn respect in their own right.

Wine country has earned its culinary stars too, with eateries like St. Helena's country-chic Farmstead at Longmeadow Ranch (p. 258).

Sonoma's acclaimed The Girl and the Fig (p. 265) puts a Provençal spin on local ingredients, like this stack of heirloom tomatoes.

Or you can go old-school at the classic Napa Valley burger stand Gott's Roadside (p. 258), originally founded in 1949 as Taylor's Refresher.

The wine country experience includes more than wine tasting—such as bike tours of Napa Valley's gently rolling farmlands.

Charming shopping and dining lines the quaint main street of St. Helena in the Napa Valley.

Sonoma's vintage attraction TrainTown (p. 262) is a great change of pace if you're visiting wine country with kids.

And then there's the almost *de rigueur* thrill of sailing over wine country in a hot air balloon, greeting the dawn with a glass of bubbly. *Bon voyage!*

# THE BEST OF SAN FRANCISCO

San Francisco's reputation as a rollicking city where almost anything goes dates back to the boom-or-bust days of the California Gold Rush. It's always been this way: This city is so beautiful, so exciting and diverse, and so cosmopolitan that you can always find something new to see and do, no matter if it's your first or fiftieth visit. Oh, and bring a warm jacket: Bob Hope once remarked that San Francisco is the city of four seasons—every day.

## THE best ONLY-IN-SAN-FRANCISCO EXPERIENCES

- **Riding the Powell–Hyde Cable Car:** Skip the less-scenic California line and take the Powell–Hyde cable car down to Fisherman's Wharf—the ride is worth the wait. When you reach the top of Nob Hill, grab the rail with one hand and hold your camera with the other, because you're about to see a view of the bay that could make you weep. See p. 126.
- **Doing Time at Alcatraz:** Even if you loathe tourist attractions, you'll dig Alcatraz. Just looking at the Rock from across the bay is enough to give you the heebie-jeebies—and the park rangers have put together an excellent audio tour with narration by former inmates and guards. Heck, even the boat ride across the bay is worth the price. See p. 119.
- **Feasting on a Sourdough Bread Bowl Filled with Clam Chowder:** There is no better way to take the chill off a freezing July day in San Francisco than with a loaf of bread from Boudin Bakery, hollowed out to form a primitive chowder vessel, filled with hot, steamy clam-and-potato soup. See p. 121.
- **Walking Across the Golden Gate Bridge:** Don your windbreaker and walking shoes and prepare for a wind-blasted, exhilarating journey across San Francisco's most famous landmark. It's one of those things you have to do once in your life. See p. 150.
- **Strolling Through Chinatown:** Chinatown is a trip—about as close to experiencing Asia as you can get without a passport.

Skip the camera and luggage stores and head straight for the food markets, where a cornucopia of critters that you'll never see at the grocery store sit, slither, or hop around in boxes waiting for the wok. Better yet, take one of Shirley Fong-Torres's Wok Wiz tours of Chinatown. See p. 158.

o **Laughing Yourself Silly at Beach Blanket Babylon:** Giant hats, over-the-top costumes, and wicked (decidedly liberal) humor are what it's all about at this North Beach classic, the longest-running musical review in the country. See p. 208.

o **Visiting with the California Sea Lions:** These giant, blubbery beasts are probably the most famous residents of the City by the Bay. Though they left en masse for greener pastures—or bluer seas—back in 2009, they are now back in full force, barking, belching, and playing king of the mountain for space on the docks at Pier 39. See p. 123.

# THE best THINGS TO DO FOR FREE (OR ALMOST FREE)

o **Strolling the City:** San Francisco is a walking town, with selfie-worthy vantage points around every corner. If you really want to fall in love with our City by the Bay, put on your walking shoes and get out there. Or, better yet, take one of our walking tours (see chapter 7).

o **Meandering Along the Marina's Golden Gate Promenade and Crissy Field:** There's something about strolling the promenade that just feels right. The combination of beach, bay, boats, Golden Gate views, and clean, cool breezes is good for the soul. Don't miss snacks at the Warming Hut. See p. 152.

o **Crossing the Golden Gate Bridge** (See p. 1.)

o **Browsing the Ferry Building Farmers' Market:** Stroll booth to booth sampling organic food. Buy fresh produce alongside several of the big-name chefs of the Bay Area. People-watch. It is always a party and always free. Held rain or shine every Tuesday, Thursday, and Saturday, this is one of the most pleasurable ways to spend time the city. See p. 130.

o **Pretending You're a Guest of the Palace or Fairmont Hotels:** You may not be staying the night, but you can certainly feel like a million bucks in the public spaces at the **Palace Hotel** (p. 72). The extravagant creation of banker "Bonanza King" Will Ralston in 1875, the Palace Hotel has one of the grandest rooms in the city: the **Garden Court,** where you can have high tea under a stained-glass dome (definitely not free). Running a close second is the magnificent lobby at Nob Hill's **Fairmont San Francisco** (p. 69).

o **Taking a Free Guided Walking Tour:** With over 90 tours to choose from—Murals and the Multi-Ethnic Mission, Castro: Tales of the Village, or Gold Rush City, to name a few—**San Francisco City Guides** offers one of the best deals in town. See p. 157.

o **Touring City Hall:** Come see where, in 2004, ex-Mayor Gavin Newsom made his bold statement to the country about the future of same-sex marriage in this beautiful Beaux Arts building. Free tours are offered to the public. See p. 138.

o **Visiting the Wells Fargo Museum:** Have a look at pistols, mining equipment, an original Wells Fargo stagecoach, old photographs, and other Gold Rush–era relics at the bank's original location. See p. 130.

o **Taking Advantage of Free Culture Days:** Almost every museum in San Francisco opens its doors to the public for free on certain days of the week. See the complete list on p. 139.

o **Hanging Out in Golden Gate Park:** Stroll around Stow Lake, hang out in Shakespeare's Garden, watch disco roller-skaters dancing around the area closed to traffic on Sundays, or just find a sunny patch of grass to call your own. There's tons to do in the city's communal backyard that doesn't cost a cent.

o **Sipping a Cocktail in the Clouds:** One of the greatest ways to view the city is from a top-floor lounge in hotels such as the **Sir Francis Drake** (p. 62) or the venerable **InterContinental Mark Hopkins** (p. 69). Drinks aren't cheap, but considering you're not paying for the view, it almost seems like a bargain.

# THE best OFFBEAT TRAVEL EXPERIENCES

o **A Colorful Old Wise Man Teaching Tea in Chinatown:** No visit to Chinatown is complete without visiting **Uncle Gee** at his tea shop on Grant Street. A San Francisco institution for years, he will give you a Chinese name, offer you some sound advice, and share with you a dizzying array of teas for all that ails you. See p. 169.

o **A Soul-Stirring Sunday Service at Glide Memorial Church:** Every city has churches, but only San Francisco has the Glide. An hour or so with Reverend Cecil Williams (or one of his alternates) and his exuberant gospel choir will surely shake your soul and let the glory out. No matter what your beliefs may be, everybody leaves this Tenderloin church spiritually uplifted and slightly misty-eyed. See p. 135.

o **Cruising Through the Castro:** The most populated and festive street in the city is not just for gays and lesbians (though some of the best cruising in town *is* right here). This neighborhood shows there's truth in San Francisco's reputation as an open-minded, liberal city, where people are free to simply love whomever they want. If you have time, catch a flick and a live Wurlitzer organ performance at the beautiful 1930s Spanish colonial movie palace, the Castro Theatre. See p. 143.

o **Catching Big Air in Your Car:** Relive *Bullitt* or *The Streets of San Francisco* as you careen down the center lane of Gough Street between Ellis and Eddy streets, screaming out "Whooooeee!" Feel the pull of gravity leave you momentarily, followed by the thump of the car suspension bottoming out. Wimpier folk can settle for driving down the steepest street in San Francisco: Filbert Street, between Leavenworth and Hyde streets.

o **Experiencing AsiaSF:** The gender-bending waitresses—mostly Asian men dressed *very* convincingly as hot-to-trot women—will blow your mind with their performance of lip-synched show tunes, which takes place every night. Bring the parents—they'll love it. Believe it or not, even kids are welcome at some seatings. See p. 95.

o **Browsing the Haight:** Though the power of the flower has wilted, the Haight is still, more or less, the Haight: a sort of resting home for aging hippies, ex-Deadheads, homeless kids, and an eclectic assortment of young panhandlers. Think of it as a people zoo, as you walk down the rows of used-clothing stores, hip boutiques, and leather shops. See p. 143.

o **Seeing the Sisters of Perpetual Indulgence:** A leading-edge "Order of queer nuns," these lovely "ladies" got their start in the Castro back in 1979, when a few men dressed up in 14th-century Belgian nuns' habits ("and a teensy bit of make-up so as not to be dowdy on a Friday night") to chase away visiting church officials, in town to preach about the immorality of homosexuality. With their Adam's apples, and sometimes beards, these dames appear at most public events, and have devoted themselves to community outreach, ministry, and helping those on the fringes of society. Amen.

# THE best OUTDOOR ACTIVITIES

o **Spending a Day in Golden Gate Park:** Golden Gate Park is a magical strip of the city that starts in the Haight and stretches down to the beach, with dramatically varying microclimates along the way. Top sights are the **Conservatory of Flowers** (p. 147), the **Japanese Tea Garden** (p. 148), the fabulous **de Young Museum** (p. 148), and its eco-fabulous cross-concourse neighbor, the **California Academy of Sciences** (p. 146). But it's equally fun to walk to the top of Strawberry Hill in the center of **Stow Lake** or rent a pedal boat (p. 149), hang out in Shakespeare's Garden, and scout out the riotously blooming dahlia garden behind the Conservatory of Flowers (in the summer and fall only). The best time to go is Sunday, when main roads in the park are closed to traffic. Toward the end of the day, head west to the beach and watch the sunset. See p. 144.

o **Walking Along the Coastal Trail:** You'll be amazed at how pristine, stunning, and easily walkable the forested **Coastal Trail** is from Cliff House to the Golden Gate Bridge. (The views alone will blow your mind.) Start at the parking lot just above Cliff House and head north. On a clear day, you'll have incredible views of the Marin Headlands and the posh seaside enclave known as Sea Cliff (where Robin Williams used to live), but even on foggy days, it's worth the trek to scamper over old bunkers and relish the cool, salty air. Dress warmly. See p. 153.

o **Going on a Wine Country Excursion:** It'll take you about an hour to get there, traffic permitting, but once you arrive you'll want to hopscotch from one winery to the next, perhaps picnic in the vineyards (and definitely not drive back to the city.) And consider this: When the city is fogged in and cold, especially in summer, Napa and Sonoma can be more than 50° warmer. See chapter 11.

o **Climbing Up or Down the Filbert Street Steps:** San Francisco is a city of stairways, and the crème de la crème of scenic steps is Filbert Street between Sansome Street and the east side of Telegraph Hill, where steep Filbert Street becomes Filbert Steps, a 377-stair descent that wends its way through flower gardens and some of the city's oldest and most varied housing. It's a beautiful walk down from Coit Tower, and great exercise going up.

o **Biking the Golden Gate Bridge:** Go see the friendly folks over at Blazing Saddles in Fisherman's Wharf and ask them to hook you up. Rent a bike and pedal over this San Francisco icon on your own. Take a guided tour over the bridge down into Sausalito, and return to the city by ferry. Heck, they even rent electric bikes—now that is my kind of outdoor adventure. See p. 158.

# THE best MUSEUMS

o **Museum of Modern Art:** A massive, recently completed renovation and expansion resulted in a brand new MoMa, complete with gorgeous living walls; refined dining opportunities; and, most important, far better space for displaying some of the museum's permanent collections and visiting exhibitions. See p. 127.

o **Palace of the Legion of Honor:** Located in a memorial to soldiers lost in World War I, this fine arts museum features Renaissance and pre-Renaissance works—many from Europe—spanning a 4,000-year history. See p. 154.

o **de Young:** Appropriately housed in a modern building in Golden Gate Park (with great photo opportunities from the glass-walled tower), the Legion of Honor's modern art sister, the de Young, features works from more recent times. Both can be entered on the same day with one admission ticket. See p. 148.

o **Contemporary Jewish Museum:** Even if you have absolutely no interest in Jewish culture, history, art, or ideas, go to visit the old-meets-new building, created when New York architect Daniel Libeskind "dropped" shiny steel cubes onto the roof of the 1907 Willis Polk–designed Beaux Arts brick power substation. See p. 127.

o **Asian Art Museum:** Located in a big showy Civic Center space, across the way from City Hall, this is my favorite museum in the city. I never tire of looking at the variety of treasures from countries I had no idea were in fact a part of "Asia." See p. 138.

# THE best ARCHITECTURE

o **The Transamerica Pyramid:** Without this tall, triangular spire gracing its presence, the skyline of San Francisco could be mistaken for almost any other American city. Although you can't take a tour to the top, on the Plaza Level—off Clay Street—there is a Visitor Center with videos and facts, a historical display, and a live feed from the "pyramid-cam" located on the top. Did you know this icon appears white because its facade is covered in crushed quartz? See p. 129.

o **The Palace of Fine Arts:** This Bernard Maybeck–designed stunner of Greek columns and Roman ruins is one of the only structures remaining from the 1915 Panama-Pacific International Exhibition, which was held, in part, to show that San Francisco had risen from the ashes of the 1906 earthquake destruction. See p. 152.

o **Mission Dolores:** Also known as Mission San Francisco de Asís, this was the sixth in a chain of missions ordered built by Father Junipero Serra. Built in 1776, it is the oldest surviving building in the city. See p. 137.

o **Sentinel Building/Columbus Tower:** Real estate is at such a premium in our city, every speck of land has to be used if at all possible. There is no better proof of this than Francis Ford Coppola's triangular-shaped flatiron building, located at the corner of Columbus and Kearny Streets. Under construction in 1906, it was one of the few structures in the city to survive the earthquake and ensuing fires. See p. 129.

o **Recycled Buildings:** San Francisco was the first city in North America to mandate recycling and composting; it only follows we would be good at recycling our old buildings as well. The **Asian Art Museum** (p. 138) was once the city library. The **Contemporary Jewish Museum** (p. 127) was created from an old power substation designed by Willis Polk. Built in 1874 to hold the "diggings" from the Gold Rush, the old U.S. Mint (at 5th and Missions sts.) is currently being recycled and will eventually house the **San Francisco Museum at the Mint.** The **Ferry Building Marketplace** (p. 130) was—surprise—the old ferry building, built between 1895 and 1903, where some 170 ferries docked daily.

o **The Painted Ladies of Alamo Square:** Also known as the Six Sisters, these famous Victorian homes on Steiner Street are among the most photographed sights in the city. The characters from the sitcom *Full House* lived here in TV land. See p. 137.

# THE best PLACES TO STAY

- **Best Service:** The **Ritz-Carlton** is the sine qua non of luxury hotels, offering near-perfect service and every possible amenity. See p. 67.
- **Best Beat Generation Hotel:** The **Hotel Bohème** is the perfect mixture of art, funky style, and location—just steps from the sidewalk cafes and shops of North Beach. If Jack Kerouac were alive today, this is where he'd stay—an easy stagger home from his favorite bar and bookstore. See p. 73.
- **Best Old Luxury:** Hands down, the **Palace Hotel.** Built in 1875, and quickly rebuilt after the 1906 earthquake, the regal lobby and stunning Garden Court atrium—complete with Italian marble columns and elegant chandeliers—will take you back 100 years to far simpler times. See p. 72.
- **Best Newcomer:** Nothing better points to today's San Francisco than the **Proper Hotel.** Located in an historic flatiron building, its vibrant design, posh posturing, and rooftop bar bring a little New York attitude to the up-and-coming, tech-company-heavy mid-Market Street area. See p. 81.
- **Best Hotel in the Woods:** Surrounded by trees in a national park just south of the Golden Gate Bridge, the **Inn at the Presidio** is the perfect place for nature lovers. With a golf course close by, hiking trails out the back door, and a fire pit on the back patio, you may never make it to Fisherman's Wharf. See p. 77.
- **Coolest Doormen:** Nothing can possibly compete with the **Sir Frances Drake Hotel** in this category. The jovial doormen greet guests wearing their signature red Beefeater costumes—complete with frilly white collar, top hat, and tights. The most famous doorman in the city, Tom Sweeney, has been blowing his whistle and handling bags at the Sir Francis Drake for 40 years. Heavy bags are nothing for him; he used to play football with Joe Montana and Dwight Clark. See p. 62.
- **Best for Families:** The **Argonaut Hotel** is set in the heart of Fisherman's Wharf, with sea lions, ice cream sundaes at Ghirardelli's, the beach at Aquatic Park, and the Musée Mechanique, all only a few minutes away. With its cool nautical theme throughout, and a toy-filled treasure box in the lobby that kids can dig into, your tykes may never want to leave. See p. 73.
- **Best Opportunity to Pretend You're a Rich San Franciscan:** Tucked away in the uberwealthy Pacific Heights neighborhood, **Hotel Drisco**'s luxury-home-like accommodations—with all the fixin's—will make you feel part of the multimillionaire set whose mansions crown this exclusive, scenic part of San Francisco. See p. 77.

# THE best PLACES TO EAT

- **The Best of the City's Fine Dining:** Decades have passed since **Restaurant Gary Danko** (p. 102) first opened on the outskirts of Fisherman's Wharf, yet the romantic dining room continues to reign, probably because the chef/owner is still in the kitchen, creating refined French-influenced food accompanied by polished service, an amazing cheese cart, and flambéed finales. For the "foodie" who simply must taste the trendsetters, **Benu** (p. 93) is your best bet; Chef Cory Lee has become one of the city's most revered chefs, and the parade of edible works of art coming out of his flagship dining room show you why.

o **Best Value:** San Franciscans have a serious passion for—and much debate around—the best burritos (and tacos). For less than $10, you can order a super burrito at **Taqueria Cancun** and taste what all the fuss is about—most likely you'll even have leftovers of the gargantuan tortilla tube of fillings to save for your next meal. See p. 111.

o **Best Authentic San Francisco Dining Experience:** Even top local chefs can't get enough of **Swan Oyster Depot,** where patrons have been bellying up to the narrow bar to indulge in fresh crab, shrimp, oysters, and clam chowder since 1912. See p. 98. For a full sit-down dining experience, you can't get more "city" than **Tadich Grill** (p. 91), which has been serving San Franciscans since the Gold Rush and makes a point of ensuring not much has changed since.

o **Best Dim Sum Feast:** At **Ton Kiang** (p. 114), you'll rarely have to wait to get in to be wowed by the variety of dumplings and mysterious dishes.

o **Best-Kept Secret:** Far, far away from Fisherman's Wharf, hidden on a residential street a few blocks from the heart of the Castro, step through the heavy curtain at the front door and enter **L'Ardoise,** which has the look and feel of an old, romantic Paris bistro. See p. 112.

o **Best Water View:** Fog permitting, **The Cliff House** (p. 153) is where to take in the Pacific coastline. Perched high on a cliff above Ocean Beach, it offers an expansive scope of the crashing Pacific Ocean, sunsets, and sea lions out front on the rocks. At the other end of town, **Waterbar** (p. 95) has bayfront tables and an upstairs cocktail area with a patio looking directly onto the Bay Bridge and its nightly twinkling lightshow.

o **Best Out-of-This-World Decor:** Chances are, no matter where you hail from, you have never seen a place like **Farallon,** with its giant hand-blown jellyfish lamps, glass clamshells, kelp columns, and a sea-life mosaic underfoot. You'll feel like you're on the bottom of a beautiful ocean floor while you munch on its inhabitants. See p. 92.

o **Best Urban Vibe:** Restaurant trends come and go, but **Nopa** continually gets our vote for the best energy and crowd, which packs in nightly at the communal table (if you see a seat, grab it!), bar, and split-level open dining room. See p. 106.

# THE most FUN THINGS TO DO WITH KIDS

- **The Exploratorium:** Imagine a hands-on science museum where kids can play for hours, doing cool things like using a microscope to watch miniscule sea creatures attack each other with teeny, tiny claws. Throw in a drinking fountain in a real toilet and you've got the sweetest science museum on the planet. See p. 129.

- **Pier 39 and the California Sea Lions:** Featuring ice cream and candy stores, bungee jumping, a puppet theater, and lots of cool shops, Pier 39 is every kid's dream come true. To top it all off, this pier is home to the famous barking sea lions. See p. 123.

- **Musée Mechanique:** Filled with old fashioned penny arcade games, this is a great place for kids to pop in quarters and experience what their great-great-grandparents did for fun 100+ years ago. See p. 122.

- **Cable Car Museum:** Kids love to learn what makes things work. They'll be fascinated when they enter this cool museum in action, especially if they've just hopped off a cable car. On the main level you can see giant wheels turning the very cables that pull the cars around the city. Below, you might catch a gripper actually grabbing a cable. See p. 132.

- **California Academy of Sciences:** At this 150-year-old institution located in the middle of Golden Gate Park, kids' favorite activities include watching Claude, the cool albino alligator, and learning about the planets while laying back in their chairs at the Morrison Planetarium. See p. 146.

- **Aquarium of the Bay:** Stand on a conveyor belt. Move through a tube in an aquarium while all sorts of sea creatures swim over and around you. Repeat. What's not to love? See p. 121.

# SAN FRANCISCO SUGGESTED ITINERARIES

San Francisco may be only 7 miles squared, but it's got so many dramatically diverse environments and attractions, it's a challenge to put together any "best of" itinerary. I've outlined a good number of the classic must-sees below, along with information about the city's vibrant neighborhoods, almost all of which are worthy of exploration. But don't be afraid to tailor these suggestions to meet your own interests. However you spend your time here, rest assured you'll have an experience that's uniquely San Francisco.

## BEST OF SAN FRANCISCO IN 1 DAY

If you've got only 1 day to explore the city and haven't been here before, follow this whirlwind jaunt of the classic highlights. It starts with a scenic cable car ride, includes a tour of Alcatraz Island (get tickets in advance—it regularly sells out!), and meanders through two of the city's most colorful neighborhoods, Chinatown and North Beach, for lunch, shopping, browsing, cocktails, dinner, cappuccino, and a show. Get an early start and wear comfy walking shoes because you're about to embark on a long, wonderful day in the City by the Bay. *Start: F-Line Streetcar to Union Square.*

### 1 Union Square

Named for a series of pro-Union mass demonstrations staged here on the eve of the Civil War, Union Square is literally that—a square. The epicenter of the city's shopping district, the open space dotted with lingering tourists and pigeons is surrounded by Macy's, Saks, Tiffany & Co., and a sleek new Apple store, along with blocks of other high-end boutiques. Major sales aside, there are few bargains to be found, and even fewer independent retailers. Still, if shopping is your thing, you won't find more places to spend your money than this bustling area. If it's not, you can at least start here for a postcard-perfect take-off on one of the city's most beloved landmarks:

Just 3 blocks down, at Powell and Market streets, is the cable car turnaround where you'll embark on a ride on the nation's only mobile National Historic Landmark. See p. 126.

## 2 Cable Cars & Lombard Street ★★★

Yes, the line of people at the cable car turnaround at Market and Powell streets is long. But the ride is worth the wait. The $7 thrill starts with a steep climb up Nob Hill, and then passes through Chinatown and Russian Hill before clanging its way down Hyde Street to Fisherman's Wharf—all with a picturesque bay backdrop. (*Note:* If you want to check out the famous winding stretch of Lombard Street, hop off the cable car at the intersection of Hyde and Lombard streets; when you've seen enough, either walk the rest of the way down to Fisherman's Wharf or take the next cable car that comes along.) For maximum thrill, stand on the running boards during the ride and hold on Doris Day–style. See p. 126.

## 3 Buena Vista Cafe 🍺 ★

After you've completed your first Powell–Hyde cable car ride, it's a tourist tradition to celebrate with an Irish coffee at the Buena Vista Cafe, located across from the cable car turnaround. It's crowded for sure, but it's a good time, and you can tell your friends you threw one back in the bar that served the first Irish coffees in America in 1952. See p. 103.

To get to Fisherman's Wharf, cross the street and head toward the water for 1 block, to Jefferson Street. Take a right on Jefferson and follow it to Pier 33 to catch the ferry to Alcatraz. (Be sure to buy tickets in advance!)

## 4 Alcatraz Tour ★★★

To tour "the Rock," the Bay Area's famous abandoned prison island, you must first get there—and that's half the fun. The brief but beautiful ferry ride offers captivating views of the Golden Gate Bridge, the Marin Headlands, and the city. Once you're on the island, an excellent audio tour guides you through cellblocks and offers a colorful look at the prison's historic past as well as its most infamous inmates. Book well in advance because these tours consistently sell out. Bring snacks and beverages for the ride (the ferry's food options are limited and expensive, and nothing is available on the island). See p. 119.

From Fisherman's Wharf, hop back onto a cable car to Chinatown, taking either the Powell–Hyde line (PH) or the Powell–Mason line (PM). The PH line is located at Beach and Hyde streets; the PM line at Bay and Taylor streets. Both lines intersect each other. Best place to get off is Washington and Mason streets or Powell and California streets. Walk down a few blocks and you will be in:

## 5 Chinatown ★★

Despite the number of international visitors pounding this small neighborhood's pavement, Chinatown remains its own authentic world. San

Francisco has one of the largest communities of Chinese people in the United States, and more than 15,000 of them are condensed into the blocks surrounding Grant Avenue and Stockton Street. Join the locals and peruse the vegetable and herb markets, restaurants, and shops, and check out the markets along Stockton Street hawking live frogs, armadillos, turtles, and odd sea creatures—all destined for tonight's dinner table. See walking tour on p. 164.

6 China Live 💭 ★
You can't visit Chinatown and not try some of the food. Pop by **China Live** and order some potstickers and perhaps some dry-braised green beans. You can also grab a memento or two here, because who doesn't need a T-shirt that says, "I'm all that and dim sum"? See p. 99.

## 7 North Beach
San Francisco's "Little Italy" celebrates cafe (and bar) culture like no other part of town. Here, dozens of Italian restaurants and coffeehouses brim with activity in what is still the center of the city's Italian community. A stroll along Columbus Avenue will take you past the eclectic cafes, delis, bookstores, bakeries, and coffee shops that give North Beach its Italian-bohemian character. See walking tour on p. 173.

8 Mario's Bohemian Cigar Store 💭 ★
The menu's limited to coffee drinks and a few sandwiches (the meatball is our favorite), but the convivial atmosphere and large windows are perfect for people-watching. It's at 566 Columbus Ave. (📞 **415/362-0536**).

## 9 Dinner in the Neighborhood
You've got a lot of restaurants nearby, so take your pick between dining in Chinatown or North Beach. The best thing about North Beach is its concentration of old-school restaurants—many of them owned by the same family for generations. **Original Joe's** ★ (see p. 100) is a classic, where patrons sit in red leather booths and dine on Italian-American comfort food. Chinatown has its culinary staples, too. Try out the famed crab at **R&G Lounge** ★ (p. 99), or taste the next generation with dinner at **Mr. Jiu's** ★★ (p. 99), ranked one of the best new restaurants in 2016 by *Bon Appétit* magazine.

10 Caffè Greco 💭 ★
By now you should be stuffed and exhausted—which is the exact right time for a cappuccino at **Caffè Greco** (423 Columbus Ave.; 📞 **415/397-6261**). Sit at one of the sidewalk tables and watch the area's colorful citizens come and go.

## 11 Beach Blanket Babylon at Club Fugazi ★★
This whimsical live show is so quintessentially San Francisco, there may be no better way to end the day. Buy tickets in advance and prepare for the outrageous costumes and giant hats of the longest-running musical revue in the country. See p. 208.

# BEST OF SAN FRANCISCO IN 2 DAYS

If you follow the 1-day itinerary above and have a day to spare, use it to get familiar with other famous landmarks around the city. Start with breakfast, a science lesson, and a pleasant bayside stroll in the Marina District. Next, cross the famed Golden Gate Bridge on foot; then take a bus to Golden Gate Park. After exploring the city's beloved park, it's time for lunch and power shopping on Haight Street, followed by dinner and cocktails back in the Marina District. Smashing. **Start:** *Bus nos. 22, 28, 30, 30X, 43, or 76.*

## 1  The Marina District

Long known as one of the most picturesque and coveted patches of local real estate, the Marina area was hard hit in the 1989 earthquake, with televised images of its collapsed mansions grabbing the nation's attention. Today, you'd never know it ever happened. Here, along the northern edge of the city, multimillion-dollar homes back up to the bayfront **Marina,** where flotillas of sailboats and the mighty Golden Gate Bridge make for a magnificent backdrop on a morning stroll.

Start the day with a good cup of coffee on Chestnut Street (see our favorite spot, below); then get some postcard-perfect snapshots at the beautiful neoclassical **Palace of Fine Arts** (p. 152), its columns reflected in a lovely man-made lagoon. Walk from there over to **Crissy Field** (p. 152), with its restored wetlands and beachfront path.

## 2  The Grove 🖵 ★

If you can't jump-start your brain properly without a good cup of coffee, then begin your day at **The Grove** (2250 Chestnut St.; ✆ **415/474-4843**), located in the Marina District—it's as cozy as an old leather couch and has big, killer breakfasts, too. See p. 107.

Follow the beachfront path to historic **Fort Point** (p. 153) and to the southern underside end of:

## 3  The Golden Gate Bridge ★★★

It's one of those things you have to do at least once in your life—walk across the fabled Golden Gate Bridge, the most photographed man-made structure in the world (p. 150). As you would expect, the views along the span are spectacular and the wind a wee bit chilly, so bring a jacket. It takes at least an hour to walk northward to the vista point and back.

When you return to the southern end, board either Muni bus no. 28 or 29 (be sure to ask the driver if the bus is headed toward Golden Gate Park).

## 4  Golden Gate Park ★★★

Stretching from the middle of the city to the Pacific Ocean, 1,017-acre Golden Gate Park is one of the city's best endowments. Since its development in the late 1880s, it has provided San Franciscans with respite from urban life—with dozens of well-tended gardens, museums, a bison

# San Francisco in 3 Days

**BEST IN 1 DAY**
1 Union Square
2 Cable Cars & Lombard Street
3 Buena Vista Cafe ☕
4 Alcatraz Tour
5 Chinatown
6 China Live ☕
7 North Beach
8 Mario's Bohemian Cigar Store ☕
9 Dinner in North Beach 🍽
10 Caffè Grecco ☕
11 Beach Blanket Babylon

**BEST IN 2 DAYS**
1 Marina District
2 The Grove ☕
3 Golden Gate Bridge
4 Golden Gate Park
5 Gordo Taqueria ☕
6 Haight-Ashbury
7 Nopa ☕

**BEST IN 3 DAYS**
1 Ferry Building Marketplace ☕
2 San Francisco Museum of Modern Art
3 Sightglass Coffee ☕
4 Yerba Buena Gardens
5 Super Duper Burgers ☕ ❸
6 The Mission District
7 Foreign Cinema

Golden Gate Bridge

Fort Point

*PACIFIC*

*OCEAN*

Mason St.

101

San Francisco National Cemetery

THE PRESIDIO

Presidio Golf Course

Lincoln Park

California Palace of the Legion of Honor

SEACLIFF

Lake St.

PRESIDIO HEIGHTS

California St.

Laurel St.

Locust St.

Spruce St.

2nd Ave.

Clement St.

Point Lobos Ave.

Geary Blvd.

Anza St.

Arguello Blvd.

Parker Ave.

Stanyan St.

26th Ave.
24th Ave.
22nd Ave.
20th Ave.
18th Ave.
12th Ave.
16th Ave.
Presidio Blvd.
10th Ave.
8th Ave.
6th Ave.
4th Ave.

46th Ave.
44th Ave.
42nd Ave.
40th Ave.
38th Ave.
36th Ave.
34th Ave.
48th Ave.

Balboa St.

RICHMOND

Cabrillo St.

Conservatory of Flowers

32nd Ave.
30th Ave.
28th Ave.

The Panhan

Fulton St.

de Young Museum

John F. Kennedy Dr.

Haight

Spreckels L.

GOLDEN GATE PARK

Stow L.

Calif. Academy of Sciences

Kezar Dr.

Great Hwy.

John F. Kennedy Dr.

Middle Dr. West

Crossover Dr.

Frederick St.
Carl St.

Martin Luther King Jr. Dr.

Lincoln Wy.

17th Ave.
15th Ave.
13th Ave.
11th Ave.
9th Ave.
7th Ave.

Parnassus Ave.

Cole St.
Shrader St.

Irving St.

Judah St.

29th Ave.

La Playa St.

47th Ave.
43rd Ave.
41st Ave.
39th Ave.

Sunset Blvd.

35th Ave.
33rd Ave.
31st Ave.

Kirkham St.

Lawton St.

25th Ave.
23rd Ave.
21st Ave.
19th Ave.

INNER SUNSET

9th Ave.

Clarendon Ave.

SUNSET

45th Ave.

Moraga St.

Noriega St.

27th Ave.

Warren Dr.

Ortega St.

TWIN PEAKS

Golden Gate National Recreation Area

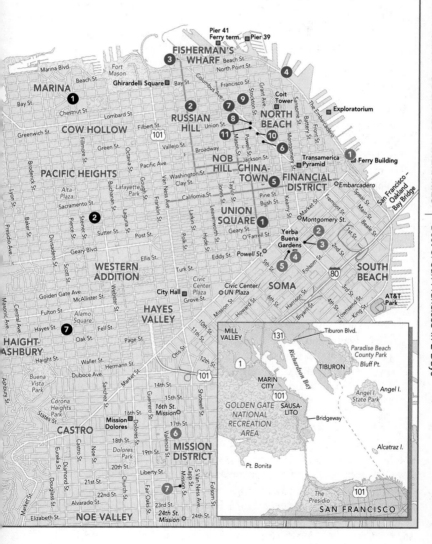

paddock, a Victorian greenhouse, and great grassy expanses prime for picnicking, lounging, or tossing a Frisbee.

Have the bus driver drop you off near John F. Kennedy Drive. Walking eastward on JFK Drive, you'll pass five of the park's most popular attractions: **Stow Lake** (p. 149), the **de Young Museum** (p. 148), the **Japanese Tea Garden** (p. 148), the **California Academy of Sciences** (p. 146), and the **Conservatory of Flowers** (p. 147).

5 Gordo Taqueria 🍵 ★★
By now you're probably starving, so walk out of the park near the Arboretum, up to 9th Avenue at Lincoln Avenue. Continue up 9th to grab an incredible burrito from **Gordo Taqueria** (1239 9th Ave.; ✆ **415/566-6011**), my favorite burrito spot for more than 35 years. Or, if you want a sit-down meal, go across the street to **Park Chow** (1240 9th Ave.; ✆ **415/665-9912**).

Once you're done, walk through the park toward downtown and exit the park on Haight Street.

6 The Haight-Ashbury District ★★★
Despite the overall gentrification of San Francisco, the birthplace of the Summer of Love and Flower Power remains surprisingly gritty. For a several-block-long stretch, Haight Street is lined with inexpensive restaurants and shops popular with young and old nonconformists—as well as plenty of homeless people, who congregate on the sidewalk over beers, bongos, and buds. Spend at least an hour strolling up Haight Street (p. 191), browsing the cornucopia of used-clothes stores, leather shops, head shops, and poster stores. There are some great bargains to be found here, especially for vintage clothing.

At the intersection of Haight and Masonic streets, catch the Muni no. 43 bus heading north, which will take you through the Presidio and back to the Marina District.

7 Dinner & Drinks
After such a full day on your feet, you deserve a memorable San Francisco dinner, and **Nopa** ★★ (p. 106) is a great place to get it. Located nearby but off the tourist path, it's got a vibrant bar scene, killer cocktails, and a fantastic menu offering "urban rustic" food—which translates to contemporary American cuisine with seasonal, farm-fresh influences.

# BEST OF SAN FRANCISCO IN 3 DAYS

There's still so much to see. To cover as much ground as possible, we'll have you hop around a bit today, starting with a beautiful morning nosh at downtown's waterfront stretch, the Embarcadero. From there, you'll take in a little culture in SoMa, before bee-lining to the Mission to browse the district's famous murals, shop vibrant Valencia Street, and get in line for some killer ice cream. Don't forget to wear walking shoes—you'll be on your feet a lot today! *Start: At the foot of Market Street at the Embarcadero.*

## 1 The Ferry Building Marketplace ★★★

As much a locals' destination as an attraction, this long, high-ceilinged renovated historic building is home to so many outstanding restaurants and gourmet food shops (as well as a twice-weekly super-robust farmers' market), it may be hard to choose where to eat. Grab a **Blue Bottle Coffee** and browse the shops, then have breakfast at **Boulette's Larder** (closed Mondays).

From the south end of the Ferry Building, cross the Embarcadero and walk 1 block inland on Don Chee Way to Steuart Street. If you have time, stop in the **San Francisco Railway Museum** at 77 Steuart St. (closed Mon). Catch the nostalgic F line streetcar on the northwestern side of Don Chee Way. Take the F four stops to 3rd and Kearny streets. Walk south on 3rd street for 4 short blocks and you've arrived at:

## 2 Museum of Modern Art ★★★

After its recent expansion, San Francisco's modern art museum (151 Third St. btw. Mission and Howard sts.; sfmoma.org; ✆ **415/357-4000**), is better than ever. Plan to spend a couple of hours checking out its visiting exhibits and impressive permanent collection, as well as an unbelievably lush giant living wall and plenty of places to snack, if desired. See p. 127.

## 3 Sightglass Coffee ☕ ★

Inside the museum, **Sightglass Coffee** is a lovely spot to get a caffeine charge. Grab a little snack, if you must. But hold out for lunch. It's your next stop.

From outside MoMa, cross 3rd Street and walk through:

## 4 Yerba Buena Gardens ★

At the heart of the Yerba Buena Cultural Center (see p. 125), this 5-acre patch of landscape makes a fine place to people-watch and soak up the city's character. Wander through various gardens, and don't miss the **Martin Luther King, Jr. Memorial** water sculpture (p. 128). Then continue to the **Metreon,** the large building in front of you. Inside, on the first floor, you'll find a food court with a variety of options for a quick bite. We recommend:

## 5 Super Duper ☕ ★

This local burger chain (see p. 96) kicks up the comfort-food game with quality ingredients for their salads, burgers, and fries. Order what you want and eat it in the common food-court area. No need to linger over a long lunch (though you can, upstairs, at **Samovar Tea Lounge,** which has a wonderful, healthful selection plus great teas).

At the corner of 5th and Mission streets, catch the 14 bus toward Daly City. Get off at 18th and Mission streets. Walk west up 18th Street to Valencia Street. Get ready to explore:

## 6 The Mission District

There's a reason we include a walking tour dedicated to this neighborhood on p. 184. Follow it in full or in part of ignore the whole thing and simply meander down Valencia Street between 18th Street and 24th Street to browse the dizzying array of places to stop, shop, or taste. It's the city's trendiest neighborhood, and a must-know, especially if you want to scout out which bars to hit later tonight. Hunger should hit again by dinnertime. And good thing, since you're in the epicenter of hot dining spots. There truly are too many choices to list. But one of our favorites is:

### 7 Foreign Cinema ☕ ★★

With incredible indoor-outdoor environs and an ultrafresh menu of expertly prepared California dishes, **Foreign Cinema** (p. 110) has it all. But if you're in snack (or budget) mode, try a burrito from **Taqueria Cancun** ★★ (p. 111)—you really can't come to San Francisco without trying one of our famous burritos.

After dinner, if you have stamina, hit the bars along Valencia and 18th streets—they're always hopping.

# SAN FRANCISCO FOR FAMILIES

Knowing kids have different interests than their folks, we've put together a couple of kid-friendly days to make sure you and your offspring cover some of the "musts" with a bit of time to hang and relax.

## BEST OF SAN FRANCISCO WITH KIDS IN 1 DAY

If you've only 1 day to explore the city, the best place to spend it is around every kid's favorite—Fisherman's Wharf—and The Embarcadero. First stop of the day is a tour to Alcatraz, then a short walk to Pier 39, where you should see the sights, including the sea lions, grab some lunch, and then head to the aquarium. Next stop will be one of the greatest science museums in the world, and then a really cool underwater restaurant for dinner. Finish the night with a cable car ride. *Start: F-Line Streetcar to Pier 33.*

### 1 Alcatraz ★★★

The boat ride over is half the fun. Once on the Rock, if you're lucky, one of the wardens, or even a former prisoner, might be there to greet your boat. Watch a quick movie about the place, and then get your audio tour. Step into a real cell and grab the bars for a photo op. Check out solitary confinement. Look at the dummy masks that three escapees left in their beds to fool the guards. When you feel like leaving, take the ferry back to Pier 33. See p. 119.

Walk a few minutes toward Golden Gate Bridge to Pier 39.

### 2 Pier 39 ★★

Yes, it's touristy and crowded. But with a carousel, nonstop puppet shows and magicians on the stage (behind the carousel), a store with barrel after barrel of candy, cool shops, and bungee jumping, it also happens to be a lot of fun. See p. 122.

### 3 Crepe Café ☕ ★

Why have a healthy lunch when you can have a crepe dripping with melty Nutella instead? OK, have a ham and cheese crepe for lunch, and save the Nutella crepe for dessert. The **Crepe Café** is located about halfway down Pier 39. See p. 103.

Now, sneak out the back door to:

## 4 The California Sea Lions ★★

Watch the sweet-faced swimmers bark, splash, sleep, and fight for space on the docks. If you're lucky, naturalists from the Aquarium of the Bay will be on hand to answer questions. See p. 123.

## 5 Aquarium of the Bay ★

We're not quite done with Pier 39. At yet another "kid favorite" place, you'll be able to see all sorts of sea critters in their near-to-natural habitat. We love the conveyor belt that slowly takes you through a tube under a giant tank filled with sharks and rays; there's also a large otter habitat and an area where you can touch bats and starfish (they're so deep you'll have to roll your sleeve up to your armpit). Located streetside, where Pier 39 meets the Embarcadero. See p. 121.

Now, walk back toward Pier 33 and continue down the Embarcadero for 15 minutes (you can also take that historic F-Line streetcar) to Pier 15.

## 6 The Exploratorium ★★★

Originally housed in the Marina District's Palace of Fine Arts, the Exploratorium—one of the best science museums in the world—moved in 2013 to these new waterfront digs. It tends to be crowded as all get-out, and on busy days lines in the cafeteria can be long, but that's only because so many kids *love* this multi-room, multimedia, hands-on experience. It could easily captivate them for an entire day. See p. 129.

Continue down the Embarcadero for another 10 minutes, or hop on the F-Line streetcar, to:

### 7 Dinner at The Ferry Building Marketplace ☕ ★★

You've had a long day exploring and it is time to take a break. Luckily, you're close to one of the top stops for delicious downtown eats. Inside the Ferry Building, you'll find gourmet burgers and shakes at Gott's Roadside, famous upscale Vietnamese at the Slanted Door, ridiculously good Japanese takeout at Delica (come early; they close most days by 6pm), healthy Mexican food at Mijita, and much, much more. See p. 94.

# The Best of San Francisco with Kids

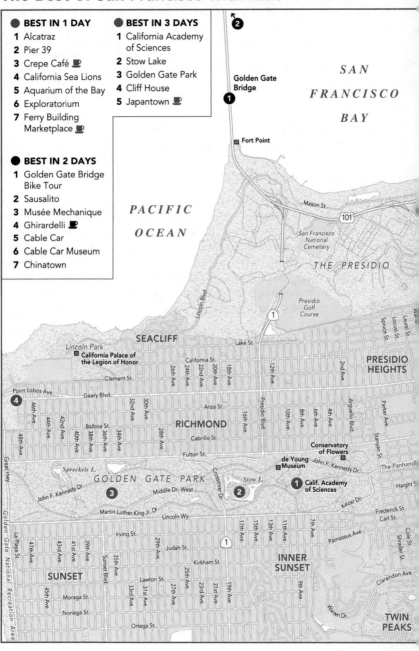

● **BEST IN 1 DAY**
1 Alcatraz
2 Pier 39
3 Crepe Café ☕
4 California Sea Lions
5 Aquarium of the Bay
6 Exploratorium
7 Ferry Building Marketplace ☕

● **BEST IN 2 DAYS**
1 Golden Gate Bridge Bike Tour
2 Sausalito
3 Musée Mechanique
4 Ghirardelli ☕
5 Cable Car
6 Cable Car Museum
7 Chinatown

● **BEST IN 3 DAYS**
1 California Academy of Sciences
2 Stow Lake
3 Golden Gate Park
4 Cliff House
5 Japantown ☕

Golden Gate Bridge

Fort Point

*SAN FRANCISCO BAY*

*PACIFIC OCEAN*

Mason St.

101

San Francisco National Cemetery

*THE PRESIDIO*

Presidio Golf Course

Lincoln Blvd

1

Lincoln Park

California Palace of the Legion of Honor

SEACLIFF

Lake St.

California St.

PRESIDIO HEIGHTS

Clement St.

Point Lobos Ave.

Geary Blvd.

Anza St.

RICHMOND

Cabrillo St.

Fulton St.

Balboa St.

Presidio Blvd.

Arguello Blvd

Parker Ave.

Stanyan St.

Conservatory of Flowers

The Panhandle

de Young Museum

John F. Kennedy Dr.

Haight S

*Spreckels L.*

*GOLDEN GATE PARK*

John F. Kennedy Dr.

Middle Dr. West

*Stow L.*

Calif. Academy of Sciences

Kezar Dr.

Frederick St.

Carl St.

Martin Luther King Jr. Dr.

Lincoln Wy.

Crossover Dr.

Cole St.

Shrader St.

Irving St.

Judah St.

1

Parnassus Ave.

INNER SUNSET

Kirkham St.

SUNSET

Lawton St.

Moraga St.

Noriega St.

Ortega St.

Sunset Blvd.

Golden Gate National Recreation Area

La Playa St.

Great Hwy.

Warren Dr.

Clarendon Ave.

TWIN PEAKS

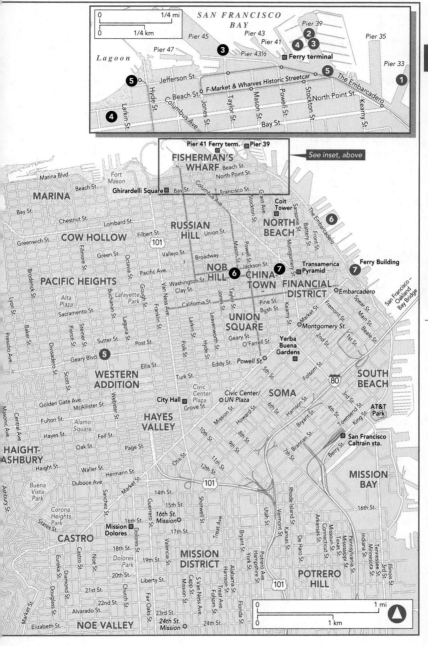

# BEST OF SAN FRANCISCO WITH KIDS IN 2 DAYS

On Day 2, it's time to leave Fisherman's Wharf and get familiar with a couple of the other famous spots in the city. Start with a tour over that big orange bridge, lunch in Sausalito, and a ferry ride across the bay. Next, stop to play a few old-fashioned video games, and then it's off to a working museum. End your tour at the crowded, colorful world that is Chinatown. **Start:** *Historic F-Line streetcar to Fisherman's Wharf.*

## 1 Guided Golden Gate Bridge Bike Tour

The perfect way to start your day is a pedal across one of the most recognized landmarks in the world. Don't worry, you are not alone! You'll have a great guide from one of the Fisherman's Wharf–area bike shops (p. 158) to show you the way.

Bring a jacket and meet a few minutes early for a safety briefing. Follow your guide up and over the bridge, then down into Sausalito.

## 2 Sausalito ★

Say goodbye to your guide and stop for lunch or refreshments anywhere along Bridgeway (the main drag through Sausalito). Two of my favorites are **Barrel House Tavern** ★★ (660 Bridgeway; barrelhousetavern.com; ✆ **415/729-9593**), which has spectacular bayfront patio seating, and the beachside bocce ball and fire pits at **Bar Bocce** ★ (1250 Bridgeway; barbocce.com; ✆ **415/331-0555**). Explore the town, and then take the ferry from Sausalito back to the city. It's a quick ride from the ferry back to the bike shop to ditch the bikes.

Walk 3 blocks to the corner of Taylor and the Embarcadero at Pier 45.

## 3 The Musée Mechanique ★★

Give the kids a roll of quarters and let them run free at this antique penny arcade where everything works. Capture the moment in black-and-white at the classic photo booth. See p. 122.

Walk 2 blocks inland, then turn right and go 4 blocks west on Beach Street. .

## 4 Ghirardelli for Ice Cream ★

Aptly located in historic Ghirardelli Square, this ice cream parlor of the same name is embarrassingly pricy, but it's one of the best places to grab a sweet treat in the city. See p. 122.

Retrace your steps 1 block on Beach Street, turn left onto Jefferson Street, and walk 1 block to the corner of Jefferson and Hyde streets.

## 5 Powell–Hyde Cable Car to Nob Hill ★★★

Take a cling-clang over the hills; it's a thrill for kids of all ages. Stay on long enough and the spot they've been dying to sit or stand in is sure to open up. See p. 126.

Hop off at the corner of Washington and Mason streets on Nob Hill, for the:

## 6 Cable Car Museum ★★

After riding these moving landmarks, kids will love this quick museum that shows how the cable cars work. The actual cables that pull all the cars through the city are right here, spinning on giant wheels. See p. 132.

Walk a few blocks downhill on Washington Street. By the time you get to Stockton Street, you'll be in:

## 7 Chinatown ★★★

The perfect way to end the day is a stroll through this very colorful neighborhood. Kids will love the shops selling everything from air guns to kites to fireworks to live animals. For a detailed tour itinerary, see p. 164. When it's time for dinner, the possibilities are endless (see box on p. 99).

# BEST OF SAN FRANCISCO WITH KIDS IN 3 DAYS

If you are lucky enough to have 3 full days in San Francisco with your kids, head to the other side of town on Day 3 and hit Golden Gate Park. There you'll visit a science museum, go for a boat ride, wander through the park some more, then go relax at the beach, and have yummy shabu shabu for dinner. **Start:** *Bus nos. 5, 28, or 44.*

## 1 California Academy of Sciences ★★★

Anchored in Golden Gate Park is this family-favorite spot where you can visit a planetarium, find an albino alligator, climb through a tropical rainforest, learn about earthquakes, see penguins splash about, and check out jellyfish and other sea creatures. Grab a gourmet snack at the surprisingly good cafe if hunger hits. See p. 146.

Walk west for a few minutes until you reach Stow Lake.

## 2 Rent a Boat on Stow Lake ★

Frogs, ducks, seagulls, strolling residents, pretty much everyone loves this picturesque little lake with a walkable center island called Strawberry Hill. Rent a pedal boat, a rowboat, or a low-speed electric boat at the **Boathouse** (p. 161) and take in a classic San Francisco experience.

Wander at will around this vast city park (see map p. 144 to get your bearings).

## 3  More Golden Gate Park ★★★

By now the kids are probably tired of having an agenda—enjoy this beautiful park. Maybe the **Japanese Tea Garden** (p. 148)? Perhaps the **Conservatory of Flowers** (p. 147)? There's even a fantastic and elaborate **children's playground** complete with a carousel. For a list of things to do, see p. 144.

Either walk or hop on a bus and head west to the beach. Use 511.org to figure out which bus to take, depending on where you are in the park. At the end, where the streets all stop, is Ocean Beach (see p. 161). At its north end, on Point Lobos Avenue, you'll find:

## 4  Cliff House ★

Stop in the famous **Cliff House** (see p. 153) for a drink and a bathroom break. Look at the pictures all over the walls showing what this area looked like 100 years ago. Once refreshed, head outside and look for wildlife on Seal Rocks. Walk to the right and climb around the ruins of the Sutro Baths. Go relax on the beach and take a nap, or dig a hole. Do not go swimming here; the currents are dangerous.

## tips FOR GETTING AROUND

Here are a few strategies for making your way around the city:

1. **San Francisco is really a small city.** If you're in reasonably good shape, and you leave your stilettos at home, you can hoof it quite easily between many of the sights we suggest in this book, without stressing about taxis, buses, cable cars, and such.

2. **If you only remember the "F-Line" historic streetcar, you will be able to get almost anywhere you want to go in the eastern half of the city.** The F-Line starts at the Castro, close to Mission Dolores in the Mission District, and runs northwest "up" Market Street to within a couple of blocks of City Hall, the Asian Arts Museum, and many of the performing arts venues in the Civic Center area. The route continues along Market Street to the Union Square area and the Yerba Buena District, through the Financial District, and on to the historic Ferry Building. Then the F-Line turns left, running along the Embarcadero past the Exploratorium, past streets leading to Coit Tower in North Beach, and on to Pier 39 and the rest of Fisherman's Wharf, where the route ends. Add in the no. 5 Fulton bus, which runs east-west from downtown to the ocean, and you have most of the city covered with only two routes to remember.

3. **If all else fails, use your smart phone to search 511.org.** You can input your current and desired addresses and this foolproof site will give you all your public transportation options—and tell you when the next vehicle will be along to save you.

Take bus no. 38 to the corner of Geary and Fillmore streets.

5 Japantown for Dinner 🍴 ★
Chinese last night—how about Japanese tonight? Fun options inside the Japan Center mall include perennial kid favorite **Benihana** (1737 Post St.; ⓒ **415/563-4844;** reserve in advance!) and **Isobune Sushi** (in Japan Center, 1737 Post St.; ⓒ **415/563-1030;** drop-in okay), where you'll pluck plates of surprisingly affordable sushi off of little boats floating around a circular centerpiece stream. See p. 106.

# CITY LAYOUT

San Francisco occupies the tip of a 32-mile-long peninsula between San Francisco Bay and the Pacific Ocean. Its land area measures about 46 square miles, although the city is often referred to as being 7 square miles. At more than 900 feet high, towering **Twin Peaks** (which are, in fact, two neighboring peaks), mark the geographic center of the city and make a great place to take in a vista of San Francisco.

**MAIN ARTERIES & STREETS** **Market Street** is downtown San Francisco's main thoroughfare. Most of the city's buses travel this route on their way to the Financial District from the outer neighborhoods to the west and south. The tall office buildings clustered downtown are at the northeast end of Market; 1 block beyond lies the Embarcadero and the bay.

With lots of one-way streets, San Francisco might seem confusing at first, but it will quickly become easy to navigate. The city's downtown streets are arranged in a simple grid pattern, with the exceptions of Market Street and Columbus Avenue, which cut across the grid at right angles to each other. Hills appear to distort this pattern, however, and can disorient you. As you learn your way around, the hills will become your landmarks and reference points.

The **Embarcadero**—an excellent strolling, skating, and biking route—curves along San Francisco Bay from south of the Bay Bridge near the Giants' home at AT&T Park to the northeast perimeter of the city. It terminates at the famous tourist-oriented Fisherman's Wharf. Aquatic Park, Fort Mason, and Golden Gate National Recreation Area are on the northernmost point of the peninsula.

From the eastern perimeter of Fort Mason, **Van Ness Avenue** runs due south, back to Market Street. This area forms a rough triangle, with Market Street as its southeastern boundary, the waterfront as its northern boundary, and Van Ness Avenue as its western boundary. Within this triangle lie most of the city's main tourist sights.

Another main artery, which is less on the tourist track, is **Geary Boulevard,** which stretches from Union Square, through the bedroom-community Richmond District, and all the way out to Ocean Beach.

**FINDING AN ADDRESS** Because most of the city's streets are laid out in a grid pattern, finding an address is easy when you know the nearest cross street. Numbers start with 1 at the beginning of the street and proceed at the rate of 100 per block. When asking for directions, find out the nearest cross street and your destination's neighborhood, and the rest should be straightforward. *Note:* Be careful not to confuse numerical avenues with numerical streets. Numerical avenues (Third Avenue and so on) are in the Richmond and Sunset districts in the western part of the city. Numerical streets (Third Street and so on) are south of Market Street in the east and south parts of town.

## Major Neighborhoods in Brief

See the "San Francisco Neighborhoods" map on p. 28.

**Union Square** Union Square is the bustling retail hub of San Francisco. Most major hotels and department stores are crammed into the area surrounding the actual square, which was named for a series of violent pro-Union rallies staged here on the eve of the Civil War. A plethora of upscale boutiques, mediocre restaurants (soon to be improving), and art galleries occupy the spaces tucked between the larger buildings. A few blocks west is the **Tenderloin** neighborhood, a patch of poverty and blight brimming with drug addicts and homeless people. While most keep to themselves, this is definitely a place to keep your wits about you. The **Theater District,** also populated by down-on-their-luck residents, is 3 blocks west of Union Square.

**The Financial District** East of Union Square, this area is sometimes referred to as FiDi. Bordered by the Embarcadero and by Market, Third, Kearny, and Washington streets, it is the city's business district and home to many major corporations. The triangular spire-topped Transamerica Pyramid at Montgomery and Clay streets is the district's most conspicuous architectural feature. To its east sprawls the Embarcadero Center, an 8½-acre complex housing offices, shops, and restaurants. Farther east still at the water's edge is the old Ferry Building, the city's pre-bridge transportation hub. Ferries to Sausalito and Larkspur still leave from this point. However, a renovation in 2003 made the building an attraction all its own; today it's packed with outstanding restaurants and gourmet food- and wine-related shops. Several days a week, it's also surrounded by an outstanding farmers' market that attracts not only residents but also top chefs looking to fill their kitchens' fridges.

**Nob Hill & Russian Hill** Bounded by Bush, Larkin, Pacific, and Stockton streets, Nob Hill is a genteel, well-heeled district occupied by the city's power brokers and the neighborhood businesses they frequent. A cluster of grande dame luxury hotels also preside atop Nob Hill. North and west of Nob Hill, the Russian Hill neighborhood extends north from Pacific to Bay streets, between Polk and Mason streets. Here you'll find steep streets—among them the fabled "twisty Lombard Street"—lush gardens, and high-rises occupied by both the moneyed and the bohemian. See walking tour p. 180.

**Chinatown** A large red-and-green gate on Grant Avenue at Bush Street marks the official entrance to Chinatown. Beyond lies a 24-block labyrinth, bordered by Broadway, Bush, Kearny, and Stockton streets, filled with restaurants, markets, temples, shops, apartment buildings, and a substantial percentage of San Francisco's Chinese residents. Chinatown is a great place for exploration all along Grant and Stockton streets, Portsmouth Square, and the alleys that lead off them, like Ross and Waverly. Chinatown's incessant traffic and precious few parking spots mean you shouldn't even consider driving around here. See walking tour p. 164.

**North Beach** This Italian neighborhood, which stretches from Montgomery and Jackson streets to Bay Street, is one of the best places in the city to grab a coffee, pull up a cafe chair, and do some serious people-watching. At night, the restaurants, bars, and clubs along Columbus and Grant avenues attract folks from all over the Bay Area. Down Columbus Avenue toward the Financial District are the remains of the city's Beat

Generation landmarks, including Ferlinghetti's City Lights Booksellers. Broadway Street—a short strip of sex joints—cuts through the heart of the district. Telegraph Hill looms over the east side of North Beach, topped by Coit Tower, one of San Francisco's best vantage points. See walking tour p. 173.

**Fisherman's Wharf** North Beach gives way to Fisherman's Wharf, which was once the busy heart of the city's great harbor and waterfront industries. Today it's a popular tourist area with little authentic waterfront life, except for a small fleet of fishing boats and some noisy sea lions. What it does have going for it are activities for the whole family, with honky-tonk attractions and museums, restaurants, trinket shops, and beautiful views everywhere you look.

**The Marina District** Created on landfill—actually rubble from the 1906 earthquake—for the Panama Pacific Exposition of 1915, the Marina District boasts some of the best views of the Golden Gate, as well as plenty of grassy fields alongside San Francisco Bay. Elegant Mediterranean-style homes and apartments, inhabited by well-to-do singles and wealthy families, line the streets. Here, too, you'll find the architectural icon the Palace of Fine Arts, the art-centric warehouses of Fort Mason (see walking tour p. 180), and a dog- and jogger-lover's paradise, Crissy Field. The main street is Chestnut, between Franklin and Lyon streets, which abounds with shops, cafes, and boutiques. Because of its landfill foundation, the Marina was among the hardest-hit districts in the 1989 quake.

**Cow Hollow** Located west of Van Ness Avenue, between Russian Hill and the Presidio, this flat area supported 30 dairy farms in 1861. Today, Cow Hollow is largely residential, a magnet for post-collegiate young professionals. Its two primary commercial thoroughfares are Lombard Street, known for its relatively cheap motels, and Union Street, an upscale shopping sector filled with restaurants, pubs, cafes, and boutiques.

**Pacific Heights** The ultra-elite, such as the Gettys and Danielle Steel—and those lucky enough to buy before the real-estate boom—reside in the mansions and homes in this neighborhood. When the rich meander out of their fortresses, they wander down to the neighborhood's two posh shopping and dining streets—Fillmore or Union—and join the pretty people who frequent their chic boutiques and lively neighborhood restaurants, cafes, and bars.

**Japantown** Bounded by Octavia, Fillmore, California, and Geary streets, Japantown actually shelters only a small percentage of the city's Japanese population (for more on its history, see p. 141), but it remains a focal point for Japanese culture in San Francisco. At its epicenter is Japan Center, a dated but fun 2-block indoor mall featuring Japanese knickknack shops, bookstores, noodle restaurants, and more. Duck inside one of the photo booths and take home a dozen Hello Kitty stickers as a souvenir.

**Civic Center** Although millions of dollars have gone toward brick sidewalks, ornate lampposts, and elaborate street plantings, the southwestern section of Market Street can still feel a little sketchy, due to the large number of homeless people who wander the area. The Civic Center, however, which is situated near the intersection of Market Street and Van Ness, is a stunning beacon of culture and refinement. This large complex of buildings includes the domed and dapper City Hall, the Opera House, Davies Symphony Hall, the new SFJAZZ building, and the Asian Art Museum. The landscaped plaza connecting the buildings is the staging area for San Francisco's frequent demonstrations for or against just about everything.

**SoMa** This expansive flatland area within the triangle of the Embarcadero, Highway 101, and Market Street is characterized by wide, busy streets and old warehouses and industrial spaces, where you'll find a few scattered underground nightclubs, restaurants, and shoddy patches of residential areas. But over the past 2 decades, the area has changed significantly, with the arrival of the Museum of Modern Art, Yerba Buena Gardens, the Jewish and African Diaspora museums, Metreon, and AT&T Park, home to the San Francisco Giants baseball team. Almost inevitably, offices for major companies like Twitter followed. All this has infused the

# San Francisco Neighborhoods

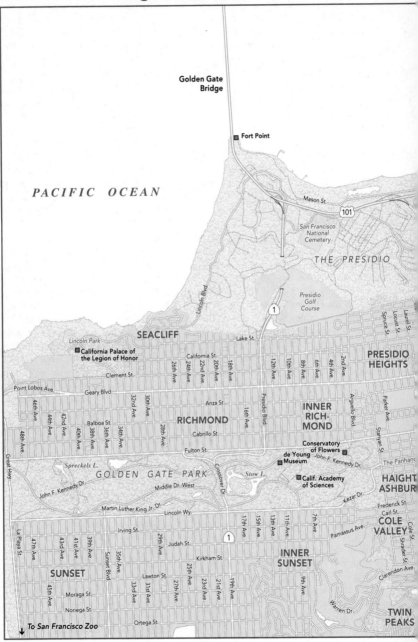

PACIFIC OCEAN

Golden Gate
Bridge

Fort Point

Mason St.

101

San Francisco
National
Cemetery

THE PRESIDIO

Presidio
Golf
Course

SEACLIFF

Lincoln Park

California Palace of
the Legion of Honor

Clement St.

Lake St.

Lincoln Blvd.

California St.

PRESIDIO
HEIGHTS

Spruce St.

Locust St.

Laurel St.

Point Lobos Ave.

Geary Blvd.

Anza St.

INNER
RICH-
MOND

Parker Ave.

Arguello Blvd.

2nd Ave.

4th Ave.

6th Ave.

8th Ave.

10th Ave.

12th Ave.

18th Ave.

20th Ave.

22nd Ave.

24th Ave.

26th Ave.

28th Ave.

30th Ave.

32nd Ave.

34th Ave.

36th Ave.

38th Ave.

40th Ave.

42nd Ave.

44th Ave.

46th Ave.

48th Ave.

RICHMOND

Balboa St.

Cabrillo St.

Fulton St.

Presidio Blvd.

16th Ave.

Staryan St.

Conservatory
of Flowers

de Young
Museum

John F. Kennedy Dr.

The Panhandle

Spreckels L.

GOLDEN GATE PARK

Stow L.

Calif. Academy
of Sciences

HAIGHT
ASHBURY

John F. Kennedy Dr.

Middle Dr. West

Crossover Dr.

Kezar Dr.

Frederick St.

Carl St.

Martin Luther King Jr. Dr.

Lincoln Wy.

COLE
VALLEY

Irving St.

Parnassus Ave.

Clarendon Ave.

Shrader St.

Cole St.

Judah St.

1

Kirkham St.

INNER
SUNSET

La Playa St.

47th Ave.

45th Ave.

43rd Ave.

41st Ave.

39th Ave.

35th Ave.

Sunset Blvd.

33rd Ave.

31st Ave.

29th Ave.

27th Ave.

25th Ave.

23rd Ave.

21st Ave.

19th Ave.

17th Ave.

15th Ave.

13th Ave.

11th Ave.

7th Ave.

9th Ave.

SUNSET

Lawton St.

Moraga St.

Noriega St.

Ortega St.

Warren Dr.

TWIN
PEAKS

Great Hwy.

To San Francisco Zoo

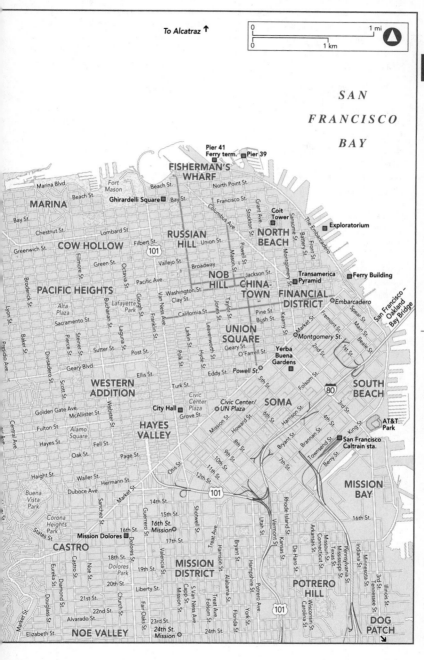

To Alcatraz ↑

0                  1 mi
0                  1 km

*SAN*

*FRANCISCO*

*BAY*

Pier 41
Ferry term.   Pier 39
FISHERMAN'S
WHARF

Beach St.     North Point St.
Marina Blvd.     Fort
Mason    Ghirardelli Square   Bay St.
MARINA     Beach St.     Francisco St.
Bay St.     Columbus Ave.     Grant Ave.    Coit    Exploratorium
Chestnut St.    Lombard St.     Stockton St.    Tower
COW HOLLOW    Filbert St.    RUSSIAN    NORTH
Greenwich St.    101    HILL    BEACH
Green St.    Vallejo St.    Union St.    Powell St.    The Embarcadero
Octavia St.    Broadway    Battery St.    Ferry Building
Pacific Ave.    NOB    Jackson St.    Transamerica    Front St.
PACIFIC HEIGHTS    HILL    CHINA-    Pyramid
Alta    Lafayette    Washington St.    TOWN    FINANCIAL    Embarcadero
Plaza    Park    Clay St.    DISTRICT
Sacramento St.    Franklin St.    California St.    Pine St.    Kearny St.
Buchanan St.    Van Ness Ave.    Bush St.    Market St.
Laguna St.    Larkin St.    UNION    Montgomery St.    Fremont St.
Steiner St.    Pierce St.    Gough St.    Leavenworth St.    SQUARE    Main St.    Beale St.
Sutter St.    Geary St.    2nd St.    1st St.
Geary Blvd.    Post St.    O'Farrell St.    Yerba
Divisadero St.    Ellis St.    Hyde St.    Buena    Folsom St.
WESTERN    Polk St.    Eddy St.    Powell St.    Gardens    SOUTH
ADDITION    Turk St.    5th St.    80    BEACH
Scott St.    Webster St.    Civic    3rd St.
Golden Gate Ave.    Center    Civic Center/    SOMA    AT&T
McAllister St.    City Hall    Plaza    UN Plaza    4th St.    Park
Fulton St.    Alamo    Grove St.    6th St.
Hayes St.    Square    HAYES    Mission St.    Harrison St.    King St.
Fell St.    VALLEY    Howard St.    Bryant St.    Townsend St.    San Francisco
Oak St.    Page St.    8th St.    7th St.    Brannan St.    Berry St.    Caltrain sta.
Haight St.    Waller St.    Hermann St.    9th St.    10th St.
Buena    Duboce Ave.    Sanchez St.    Market St.    11th St.    MISSION
Vista    12th St.    BAY
Park    Otis St.    101
Corona    14th St.    Rhode Island St.    16th St.
Heights    15th St.    Vermont St.    Kansas St.    Utah St.
Park    States St.    Guerrero St.    16th St.    Mission Dolores    16th St.    Mission    Shotwell St.    De Haro St.
17th St.    Dolores St.
CASTRO    Castro St.    18th St.    Dolores    MISSION    Bryant St.    POTRERO
Eureka St.    Noe St.    Park    Valencia St.    DISTRICT    Alabama St.    HILL
Diamond St.    19th St.    Treat Ave.    Florida St.    York St.    Pennsylvania St.
Douglass St.    20th St.    Liberty St.    Capp St.    Hampshire St.    Potrero Ave.    Mississippi St.    Missouri St.
21st St.    Church St.    Fair Oaks St.    S. Van Ness Ave.    Folsom St.    Texas St.    Wisconsin St.    Indiana St.
Market St.    22nd St.    101    Carolina St.    Minnesota St.
Alvarado St.    23rd St.    24th St.    Tennessee St.    3rd St.
Elizabeth St.    NOE VALLEY    24th St.    Mission    DOG    Illinois St.
PATCH

Lyon St.    Baker St.    Broderick St.    Divisadero St.    Central Ave.    Presidio Ave.    Fillmore St.    Taylor St.    Mason St.    Jones St.    Hyde St.    Sansome St.    Grant Ave.

San Francisco –
Oakland
Bay Bridge

gritty area with multimillion-dollar lofts, fancy high-rise residences, and a bevy of new businesses, hotels, restaurants, and nightclubs. Soon, a new stadium for the Golden State Warriors basketball team will open here as well, which will only add to SoMa's popularity.

**Mission District** First Irish and later Mexican and Latin American populations made this area home, with their cuisine, traditions, and art creating a vibrant cultural area. Today, however, the Mission is home to San Francisco's hipsters and hippest restaurants. Some parts of the neighborhood are still poor and sprinkled with the homeless, gangs, and drug addicts, but young urbanites have declared the place their own, lured by the endless oh-so-hot restaurants and bars that stretch from 16th and Valencia streets to 25th and Mission streets. Less adventurous tourists may just want to duck into Mission Dolores (San Francisco's oldest building), cruise past a few of the 200-plus amazing street murals, and head back downtown. But anyone who's interested in hanging with the cool kids and experiencing the sizzling restaurant and bar scene should definitely beeline it here. See walking tour on p. 184.

**The Castro** One of the liveliest districts in town, the Castro is practically synonymous with San Francisco's gay community, who moved here en masse back in the 1970s, turning this once Irish working-class neighborhood into a bustling hotbed of shops, bars, and restaurants. Its heart is the intersection of Market Street, 17th Street, and Castro Street, officially named Harvey Milk Plaza after the pioneering gay city supervisor of the 1970s. The Castro offers a thoroughly entertaining dose of street theater, and while most businesses cater to the gay community, it's more than welcoming to open-minded straight people.

**Haight–Ashbury** Part trendy, part nostalgic, part funky, the Haight, as it's most commonly known, was the soul of the psychedelic free-loving 1960s and the center of the counterculture movement. Today, thanks to a never-ending real estate boom, the gritty neighborhood straddling upper Haight Street on the eastern border of Golden Gate Park is more gentrified, but the commercial area still harbors all walks of life. You don't need to be groovy to enjoy the Haight—the ethnic food, trendy shops, and bars cover all tastes. From Haight Street, walk south on Cole Street for a more peaceful neighborhood experience.

**Richmond & Sunset Districts** San Francisco's suburbs of sorts, these are the city's largest and most populous neighborhoods, consisting mainly of small homes, shops, cafes, and neighborhood restaurants. Although they border Golden Gate Park and Ocean Beach, few tourists venture into "the Avenues," as these areas are referred to locally, unless they're on their way to the Cliff House, zoo, beach, or Palace of the Legion of Honor Museum.

# SAN FRANCISCO IN CONTEXT

Often referred to as America's most European city, regularly topping travel magazine favorite cities lists, and famed for its postcard-perfect vistas, San Francisco is indeed, as John Steinbeck described, "a golden handcuff with the key thrown away." But it's more than topography that makes the City by the Bay one of the top places for 25.5-million-plus visitors to leave their hearts each year. Molded politically, socially, and physically by its history, and refined by a variety of natural and manmade events, the city's character is like no other.

## SAN FRANCISCO TODAY

During the past 2 decades, California's fourth-largest city has weathered the wild ride of two boom-or-bust economies. The first, in the late 1990s, was the famed "Dot-com boom," which, when it went bust in the early 2000s, left the city's residents, businesses, and real estate market reeling from economic whiplash. The second, which is underway now, has seen even more growth and influx of new wealth, and it seems there's no end in sight. The Bay Area is the epicenter of the now-established Internet industry, and San Francisco has become the most compelling crash pad for young entrepreneurs and tech workers (who have access to big luxurious private buses that shuttle them to Silicon Valley). All this has made the face of the city change at wireless Internet speed.

Already the state's most densely populated city, with 864,000 residents (it's also the second most densely populated in the nation, behind New York), San Francisco has been strained even further by a nearly 10% population increase in the last 7 years—while ethnic diversity has diminished. Teardown homes in nice neighborhoods are selling for upward of $2 million. Room rentals in shared homes regularly go for more than $1,200. Once-desolate industrial areas are now being developed into multi-use communities teeming with glistening new luxury condos, chic restaurants, and trendy businesses.

In updating this guide, I repeatedly ran up against shocking evidence of just how ritzy our city has become. You can see it most clearly in the restaurant scene, which mirrors the great divide our city and nation is experiencing: While there are lots of expensive new restaurants opening, where entrees cost $30 or more, and there are plenty of supercheap grab-and-go places to eat, there are fewer and fewer "middle class" restaurants—which used to be one of our most abundant attributes—and those that survive seem very much like relics from another time.

Not surprisingly, there's backlash. Reports show that middle-income residents are moving out of San Francisco at rates much faster than others are moving in. Not only is this a problem for restaurants, hotels, and other businesses, who struggle to find and keep lower-pay-grade workers, it has also meant fewer of the colorful, offbeat residents that used to be a significant part of the city's bohemian culture. In the fall of 2011, the Occupy SF movement—itself part of Occupy Wall Street—brought the city's economic struggles front and center, as hundreds camped out and protested in San Francisco, Oakland, and throughout the Bay Area. (A legitimate question heard from the encampment in Justin Herman Plaza: Why can't everyone who works in San Francisco afford housing in or near San Francisco?)

And, of course, there are still the typical big-city problems: While crime is generally down over the past couple of years, drug abuse is up, and despite efforts to curb the ubiquitous problem of homelessness and panhandling, it's still a thorny—and shockingly visible—issue.

Still, you can't help but feel San Francisco is the place to be right now. Its convention halls are fully booked, hotels and restaurants are opening around every corner, and San Franciscans eagerly line up for hot clubs and nightspots, theaters and film festivals. It's hard to predict just how much the continued flood of privileged new residents will affect its tolerant, alternative soul, but so far, San Francisco continues to embrace diverse lifestyles and liberal thinking. While it may never relive its glory days as King of the West Coast, San Francisco will undoubtedly retain the title of Everyone's Favorite California City.

## California's New Cannabis Laws

In November 2016, California voters passed Proposition 64, legalizing the sale and possession of recreational marijuana (for persons age 21 or older) after January 1, 2018. But before you jump on a plane and head to the Golden State looking for a quick legal high, know that each locality still has to decide on how much local tax to impose and how to license cannabis retailers and distributors, not to mention regulating cannabis growers. You won't find the streets of San Francisco lined with pot boutiques for a while. Until then, the only marijuana that can be legally sold is medical marijuana, to holders of a medical marijuana card. Which, in practice, is not that hard to obtain (see p. 211), but still. . . .

# LOOKING BACK AT SAN FRANCISCO

## In the Beginning

Born as an out-of-the-way backwater of colonial Spain and blessed with a harbor that would have been the envy of any of the great cities of Europe, San Francisco boasts a story that is as varied as the millions of people who have passed through its Golden Gate.

**THE AGE OF DISCOVERY**   After the "discovery" of the New World by Columbus in 1492, legends of the fertile land of California were discussed in the universities and taverns of Europe, even though no one really understood where the mythical land was. (Some evidence has been unearthed of arrivals in California by Chinese merchants hundreds of years before Columbus's landing, although few scholars are willing to draw definite conclusions.) The first documented visit by a European to northern California, however, was by the Portuguese explorer João Cabrilho, who circumnavigated the southern tip of South America and traveled as far north as the Russian River in 1542. Nearly 40 years later, in 1579, Sir Francis Drake landed on the northern California coast, stopping for a time to repair his ships and to claim the territory for Queen Elizabeth I of England. He was followed several years later by another Portuguese explorer, Sebastian Cermeño, "discoverer" of Punta de los Reyes (King's Point) in the mid-1590s. Ironically, all three adventurers completely missed the narrow entrance to San Francisco Bay—maybe because it was enshrouded in fog, or, more likely, because they simply had no idea there was anything to look for there. (Believe it or not, the bay's entrance is nearly impossible to see from the open ocean.)

# DATELINE

1542   Juan Cabrillo sails up the California coast.

1579   Sir Francis Drake lands near San Francisco, missing the entrance to the bay.

1769   Members of the Spanish expedition led by Gaspar de Portolá become the first Europeans to see San Francisco Bay.

1775   The *San Carlos* is the first European ship to sail into San Francisco Bay.

1776   Captain Juan Bautista de Anza establishes a presidio (military fort); San Francisco de Asís Mission opens.

1821   Mexico wins independence from Spain and annexes California.

1835   The town of Yerba Buena develops around the port; the United States tries unsuccessfully to purchase San Francisco Bay from Mexico.

1846   Mexican-American War.

1847   Americans annex Yerba Buena and rename it San Francisco.

1848   Gold is discovered in Coloma, near Sacramento.

continues

It would be another two centuries before a European actually saw the bay that would eventually extend Spain's influence over much of the American West. **Gaspar de Portolá,** a soldier sent from Spain to meddle in a rather ugly conflict between the Jesuits and the Franciscans, accidentally stumbled upon the bay in 1769, en route to somewhere else. Even so, he did not realize the importance of his discovery, but stoically plodded on to his original destination, Monterey Bay, more than 100 miles to the south. Six years later, **Juan Ayala,** while on a mapping expedition for the Spanish, actually sailed into San Francisco Bay and immediately realized the enormous strategic importance of his find.

Colonization quickly followed. **Juan Bautista de Anza** and around 30 Spanish-speaking families marched through the deserts from Sonora, Mexico, arriving after many hardships at the northern tip of modern-day San Francisco in June 1776. They immediately claimed the peninsula for Spain. (Coincidentally, their claim of allegiance to Spain occurred only about a week before the 13 English-speaking colonies of North America's eastern seaboard, a continent away, declared their independence from Britain.) The settlers' headquarters was an adobe fortress, the Presidio, which they built on the site of today's park with the same name. Their church, built a mile to the south, was the first of five Spanish missions later developed by **Franciscan priests** around the edges of San Francisco Bay. The name of the church was officially Nuestra Señora de Dolores, but the Franciscans dedicated it to their patron, St. Francis of Assisi, and the mission became known as San Francisco. Eventually, the name began to be applied to the entire bay.

In 1821, Mexico broke away from Spain, secularized the Spanish missions, and abandoned all interest in converting the Indian natives to Catholicism. Freed of Spanish restrictions, California's ports were suddenly opened to trade. The region around San Francisco Bay supplied large numbers of hides

| | |
|---|---|
| 1849 In the year of the Gold Rush, San Francisco's population swells from about 800 to 25,000. | 1906 The Great Earthquake strikes, and the resulting fire levels the city. |
| 1850 Congress swiftly grants California statehood, in hopes that the U.S. can control Gold Rush profits. | 1915 The Panama Pacific International Exposition celebrates San Francisco's restoration and the completion of the Panama Canal. |
| 1851 Lawlessness becomes acute before attempts are made to curb it. | 1936 The Bay Bridge is built. |
| 1857 California's first winery, Buena Vista, was founded in Sonoma by Hungarian-born "Count" Agoston Haraszthy. | 1937 The Golden Gate Bridge is completed. |
| | 1945 The United Nations Charter is drafted and adopted by the representatives of 50 countries meeting in San Francisco. |
| 1869 The transcontinental railroad reaches San Francisco. | 1950 The Beat Generation moves into the bars and cafes of North Beach. |
| 1873 Andrew S. Hallidie invents the cable car. | |

and tallow, which ships could then transport around Cape Horn to the tanneries and factories of New England and New York. Such prospects for prosperity persuaded an English-born sailor, **William Richardson,** to jump ship in 1822 and settle on the site of what is now San Francisco. To impress the commandant of the Presidio, whose daughter he loved, Richardson converted to Catholicism and established the beginnings of what would soon became a thriving trading post and colony.

Richardson named his trading post **Yerba Buena** (or "good herb"), because of a species of wild mint that grew there, near the site of today's Montgomery Street. (The city's original name was recalled with endless mirth 120 years later during San Francisco's hippie era.) Richardson conducted a profitable hide-trading business, and eventually he became harbormaster and the city's first merchant prince. By 1839, the place was a veritable town, with a mostly English-speaking populace and a saloon of dubious virtue.

Throughout the 19th century, armed hostilities had continued to erupt from time to time between English-speaking settlers from the eastern seaboard and the Spanish-speaking colonies of Spain and Mexico, in various places as widely scattered as Texas, Puerto Rico, and along the frequently shifting United States–Mexico border. In 1846, a group of U.S. Marines from the warship *Portsmouth* boldly seized the sleepy main plaza of Yerba Buena, ran the U.S. flag up a pole, and declared California an American territory. The Presidio (occupied by about a dozen unmotivated Mexican soldiers) surrendered without a fuss. The first move made by the citizenry of the new territory—most of whom were Yankees anyway—was to officially adopt the name of the bay as the name of their town.

**THE GOLD RUSH** The year 1848 was one of the most pivotal years in European history, with unrest sweeping through Europe and widespread economic disillusionment troubling the east coast of the United States. Stories

1967 A free concert in Golden Gate Park attracts 20,000 people, ushering in the Summer of Love and the hippie era.

1974 BART's high-speed transit system opens the tunnel linking San Francisco with the East Bay.

1976 "The Judgment of Paris" puts Napa Valley on the world's wine map when two Napa wines—a Chardonnay and a Cabernet Sauvignon—beat out the French competition in a blind tasting in Paris.

1978 Harvey Milk, a city supervisor and America's first openly gay politician, is assassinated, along with Mayor George Moscone, by political rival Dan White.

1989 An earthquake registering 7.1 on the Richter scale hits San Francisco during a World Series baseball game, as 100 million watch on TV; the city quickly rebuilds.

1991 Fire rages through the Berkeley/Oakland hills, destroying 2,800 homes.

1993 Yerba Buena Center for the Arts opens.

1995 New San Francisco Museum of Modern Art opens.

continues

about the golden port of San Francisco and the agrarian wealth of the American West filtered slowly east, attracting potential settlers. Ex-sailor Richard Henry Dana extolled the virtues of California in his best-selling novel *Two Years Before the Mast* and helped fire the public's imagination about the territory's bounty, particularly that of the Bay Area.

The first overland party had already crossed the Sierra and arrived in California in 1841. After that, San Francisco grew steadily, reaching a population of approximately 900 by April 1848, two years after the "conquest" of Yerba Buena. Still, nothing hinted at the population explosion that was to follow.

Historian Barry Parr has referred to the California Gold Rush as the most extraordinary event to ever befall an American city in peacetime. In time, San Francisco's winning combination of raw materials, healthful climate, and freedom would have attracted thousands of settlers even without the lure of gold. But the gleam of the soft metal is said to have compressed 50 years of normal growth into less than 6 months. In 1848, the year gold was first discovered (see "The Rise of Gold Fever," facing page), the population of San Francisco jumped from under 1,000 to 26,000 in less than 6 months. As many as 100,000 more passed through San Francisco in the space of less than a year on their way to the rocky hinterlands where the gold was rumored to be.

A world on the brink of change responded almost frantically: The Gold Rush was on. News of the gold strike spread like a plague through every discontented hamlet in the known world. Shop owners hung GONE TO THE DIGGINGS signs in their windows. Flotillas of ships set sail from ports throughout Europe, South America, Australia, and the East Coast, sometimes nearly sinking with the weight of mining equipment. Townspeople from the Midwest headed overland, and the social fabric of a nation was transformed almost overnight. Not since the Crusades of the Middle Ages had so many people been mobilized in so short a period of time.

1996 Former Assembly Speaker Willie Brown becomes San Francisco's first African-American mayor.

2000 Pacific Bell Park (now AT&T Park), the new home to the San Francisco Giants, opens.

2004 Thirty-six-year-old supervisor Gavin Newsom becomes the city's 42nd mayor and quickly makes headlines by authorizing City Hall to issue marriage licenses to same-sex couples. Six months later, the state supreme court invalidates 3,955 gay marriages.

2005 The new, seismically correct $202-million de Young Museum opens in Golden Gate Park.

2006 The 100-year anniversary of the Great Earthquake and fire of 1906, the greatest disaster ever to befall an American metropolis, is commemorated.

2008 The California Supreme Court overturns the ban on same-sex marriage, touching off short-lived celebrations at San Francisco City Hall. The ban is reinstated in an election later that year, added to the ballot as "Proposition 8."

2009 The economic downturn puts San Francisco in a financial tailspin. Although tourism dollars keep pouring in, small businesses

## The Rise of Gold Fever

When small particles of gold were first discovered in January 1848—at a sawmill that he owned on the bank of the American River near Coloma, California—Swiss-born John Augustus Sutter intended to keep the discovery quiet. It was his employee, John Marshall, who leaked word of the discovery to friends. It eventually appeared in local papers, and smart investors on the East Coast took immediate heed. The rush did not really start, however, until Sam Brannan—a Mormon preacher and famous charlatan—ran through the streets of San Francisco shouting, "Gold! Gold in the American River!" Just before making the announcement heard around the world, however, the crafty Brannan had already bought up all the harborfront real estate he could get and cornered the market on shovels, pickaxes, and canned food.

Although other settlements were closer to the gold strike, San Francisco was the famous name, and therefore, where the gold-diggers disembarked. Daily business stopped; ships arrived in San Francisco and were almost immediately deserted by their crews. Tent cities sprang up, and demand for virtually everything skyrocketed. Although some miners actually found gold, the people who really got rich quick were enterprising merchants, who profited hugely by servicing the thousands of miners who arrived ill-equipped and ignorant of the lay of the land. Prices soared. Miners, faced with staggeringly inflated prices for goods and services, barely scraped a profit after expenses.

Most prospectors failed, many died of hardship, others committed suicide at the alarming rate of 1,000 a year. Yet despite the tragedies, graft, and vice associated with the Gold Rush, within mere months San Francisco was forever transformed from a tranquil Spanish settlement into a roaring, boisterous boomtown.

struggle, battling high rents and a cash-strapped public.

2010 The San Francisco Giants baseball team wins the World Series against the Texas Rangers; thousands of fans fill Civic Center Plaza for the parade and celebration.

2011 Ed Lee is elected San Francisco's 43rd mayor.

2012 The San Francisco Giants beat the Detroit Tigers to win the World Series, again.

2013 California Governor Jerry Brown instructs county clerks to begin issuing same-sex marriage licenses after the U.S. Supreme Court strikes down "Prop 8."

2014 The San Francisco Giants win the World Series. Yes, again.

2017 Dry conditions and extremely high winds contribute to the deadliest wildfires in California history, primarily tearing through Napa and Sonoma counties. The weeklong firestorm destroyed more than 245,000 acres, 8,400 structures, and killed at least 42 people. As this book went to press, the cause of the fires had yet to be determined.

**BOOMTOWN FEVER**   By 1855, most of California's surface gold had already been panned out, leaving only the richer but deeper veins of ore, which individual miners couldn't retrieve without massive capital investments. By that time, San Francisco had already evolved into a vast commercial magnet, sucking into its warehouses and banks whatever riches the overworked newcomers had dragged, ripped, and distilled from the rocks, fields, and forests of western North America.

Investment funds were being lavished on more than mining. Speculation on the newly established San Francisco stock exchange could make or destroy an investor in a single day, and several noteworthy writers (including **Mark Twain**) were among the young men forever influenced by the boomtown spirit. In 1861, the American Civil War found California firmly in the Union camp, and after the war San Francisco was ready, willing, and able to receive hordes of disillusioned soldiers fed up with the war-mongering eastern seaboard.

In 1869, the boom got a huge boost when the **transcontinental railway** linked the eastern and western seaboards of the United States. The railways shifted economic power bases, however. Now cheap manufactured goods from the east were readily available, undercutting the high prices that merchants had been able to charge for goods shipped around the tip of South America. Ownership of the newly formed Central Pacific and Southern Pacific railroads was almost completely controlled by the "Big Four"—Leland Stanford, Mark Hopkins, Collis P. Huntington, and Charles Crocker—all iron-willed capitalists whose ruthlessness was legendary. Their fortunes were rivalled only by the so-called Bonanza Kings (see p. 133), who'd made a killing in the mining industry. Meanwhile, thousands of Chinese immigrants arrived in overcrowded ships at San Francisco ports, fleeing starvation and unrest in Asia to provide bone-crushing labor for the railway, at wages so low that few Americans would have accepted the work.

During the 1870s, just as the flood of profits from the Comstock Lode in western Nevada diminished to a trickle, a cycle of droughts wiped out part of California's agricultural bounty. Discontented workers blamed their woes on the now-unwanted hordes of Chinese workers, who by preference and for mutual protection had congregated into teeming all-Asian communities. As the 19th century came to a close, the monopolistic grip of the railways and robber barons became more obvious, and civil unrest became more frequent.

Despite these downward cycles, the city enjoyed other bouts of prosperity around the turn of the 20th century. First came the **Klondike Gold Rush** in Alaska, starting in 1896. Long accustomed to making a buck off gold fever, San Francisco managed to position itself as a point of embarkation for supplies bound for Alaska. During the **Spanish-American War** in 1898, San Francisco was a major port serving warships bound for the Philippine Islands. Also during this time emerged the **Bank of America,** which eventually evolved into the largest bank in the world. Founded in North Beach in 1904, Bank of America was the brainchild of Italian-born A. P. Giannini, who later

## The Barbary Coast

In the lawless San Francisco of the Gold Rush, a red-light district quickly sprang up in the waterfront area near Portsmouth Square. Inhabited by prostitutes, drunkards, pickpockets, vicious gangs, visiting sailors, and small-time prospectors with gold dust to be squandered, it seemed like a city unto itself, centered along a notorious stretch of Pacific Street. Saloons, brothels, dance-halls (some with performers in drag), opium dens, and dark alleys beckoned. In the 1860s, residents began to refer to it as the Barbary Coast, after the notorious pirate haven in North Africa. Even as law and order prevailed in the rest of the growing city, the Barbary Coast continued to thrive on its own free-wheeling terms throughout the latter 19th century and on into the early 20th century. After it was wiped out by the 1906 earthquake and fire, city fathers rebuilt it as a respectable entertainment district, Terrific Street. Some say, however, that the spirit of the old Barbary Coast lives on in San Francisco's countercultural bent.

funded part of the construction for a bridge that many critics said was preposterous: the Golden Gate.

**THE BIG ONE, PART 1: THE GREAT FIRE**   On the morning of April 18, 1906, San Francisco changed for all time. The city has never experienced an earthquake as destructive as the one that hit at 5:13am. (Scientists estimate its strength at 8.1 on the Richter scale.) All but a handful of the city's 400,000 inhabitants lay fast asleep when the ground beneath the city went into a series of convulsions. As one eyewitness put it, "The earth was shaking . . . it was undulating, rolling like an ocean breaker." The quake ruptured every water main in the city, and simultaneously started a chain of fires that rapidly fused into one gigantic conflagration. The fire brigades were helpless, and for 3 days, San Francisco burned.

Militia troops finally stopped the flames from advancing by dynamiting entire city blocks, but not before more than 28,000 buildings lay in ruins. Minor tremors lasted another 3 days. The final damage stretched across a path of destruction 450 miles long and 50 miles wide. In all, 497 city blocks were razed, or about one-third of the city. As Jack London wrote in a heart-rending newspaper dispatch, "The city of San Francisco is no more."

The earthquake and subsequent fire so decisively changed the city that post-1906 San Francisco bears little resemblance to the town before the quake. Out of the ashes rose a bigger, healthier, and more beautiful town, though latter-day urbanologists regret that the rebuilding that followed the San Francisco earthquake did not follow a more enlightened plan. So eager was the city to rebuild that the old, somewhat unimaginative gridiron plan was reinstated, despite the opportunities for more daring visions that the aftermath of the quake afforded.

In 1915, in celebration of the opening of the Panama Canal and to prove to the world that San Francisco was restored to its full glory, the city hosted the **Panama Pacific International Exhibition,** a world's fair that exposed hundreds of thousands of visitors to the city's unique charms. The fair was even built on landfall created by post-earthquake rubble—a beautiful bayfront area between the Presidio and Fort Mason, today known as the Marina District (see p. 30). The sole surviving building of that fair, the Palace of Fine Arts (see p. 152), gives you an idea of the exposition's elegant ambitions.

In the years following World War I, there was a frenzy of civic boosterism in San Francisco, and investments reached an all-time high. Despite Prohibition, speakeasies did a thriving business in and around the city. Building sprees were as high-blown and lavish as the profits on the San Francisco stock exchange, which survived the stock-market crash of 1929 with surprising strength.

**WORLD WAR II** The Japanese attack on Pearl Harbor on December 7, 1941 mobilized the United States into a massive war machine. Many shipyards were strategically positioned along the Pacific Coast, including in San Francisco. Within less than a year, several shipyards were producing up to one new warship per day, employing hundreds of thousands of people working in 24-hour shifts. (The largest, Kaiser Shipyards in Richmond, employed more than 100,000 workers alone.) In search of work and the excitement of life away from villages and cornfields, workers flooded into the city from virtually everywhere, forcing an enormous boom in housing. Hundreds found themselves separated from their small towns for the first time in their lives and reveled in their newfound freedom.

After the hostilities ended, many soldiers remembered San Francisco as the site of their finest hours and returned to live there permanently. The economic prosperity of the postwar years enabled massive enlargements of the city, including freeways, housing developments, a booming financial district—and pockets of counterculture enthusiasts.

**THE 1950S: THE BEATS** San Francisco's reputation as a rollicking place where anything goes dates from the Barbary Coast days (see box p. 39). Its more modern role as a haven for the avant-garde began in the 1950s, with a group of young writers, philosophers, and poets who challenged the materialism and conformity of American society. Embracing anarchy and Eastern philosophy, they expressed their notions in poetry and jazz music. They adopted a uniform of jeans, sweaters, sandals, and berets, called themselves Beats, and hung out in North Beach where rents were low and cheap wine was plentiful. The famous *San Francisco Chronicle* columnist Herb Caen—to whom their philosophy was totally alien—dubbed them **beatniks,** and the name stuck.

Allen Ginsberg, Gregory Corso, and Jack Kerouac had begun writing at Columbia University in New York, but it wasn't until they came west and hooked up with Lawrence Ferlinghetti, Kenneth Rexroth, Gary Snyder, and others that the movement gained national attention. The bible of the Beats was Ginsberg's long poem "Howl," which he first read at the Six Gallery on October 13, 1955. By the time he finished reading, Ginsberg was crying, the audience was chanting, and his fellow poets were announcing the arrival of an epic bard. In 1956 Ferlinghetti published "Howl," and an obscenity trial soon followed; when the court ruled that the book had redeeming social value, it was hailed as a landmark victory for the right of free expression. The group's other major work, Jack Kerouac's *On the Road*, was published in 1957 and instantly became a bestseller. (He had written it as one long paragraph in 20 days in 1951.) The freedom and sense of possibility that this book conveyed became the bellwether for a generation.

While the Beats gave poetry readings and generated controversy, two clubs in North Beach were making waves, notably the hungry i and the Purple Onion, where everyone who was anyone (or became anyone) on the entertainment scene appeared—Mort Sahl, Dick Gregory, Lenny Bruce, Barbra Streisand, and Woody Allen all worked here. Maya Angelou appeared as a singer and dancer at the Purple Onion. The cafes of North Beach were the center of bohemian life in the '50s: the Black Cat, Vesuvio, Caffe Trieste, Tosca Cafe, and Enrico's Sidewalk Café. When the tour buses started rolling in, however, rents went up, and Broadway turned into strip-club row in the early 1960s. Thus ended an era, and the Beats moved on. The alternative scene shifted to Berkeley and the Haight.

**THE 1960S: THE HAIGHT**    The torch of freedom had been passed from the Beats and North Beach to Haight-Ashbury and the hippies, but it was a radically different torch. The **hippies** replaced the Beats' angst, anarchy, negativism, nihilism, alcohol, and poetry with love, communalism, openness, drugs, rock music, and a back-to-nature philosophy.

Although the scent of marijuana wafted everywhere—on the streets, in the cafes, in Golden Gate Park—the real drugs of choice were LSD (a tab of good acid cost $5) and other hallucinogens. Timothy Leary experimented with its effects and exhorted youth to turn on, tune in, and drop out. Instead of hanging out in coffeehouses, the hippies went to concerts at the Fillmore or the Avalon Ballroom to dance.

The first Family Dog Rock 'n' Roll Dance and Concert, "A Tribute to Dr. Strange," was given at the Longshoreman's Hall in fall 1965, featuring Jefferson Airplane, the Marbles, the Great Society, and the Charlatans. At this event, the first major happening of the 1960s, Beat poet Allen Ginsberg led a snake dance through the crowd. In January 1966, the 3-day Trips Festival, organized by rock promoter Bill Graham, was also held at the Longshoreman's Hall. The climax came with Ken Kesey and the Merry Pranksters Acid Test show, which used five movie screens, psychedelic visions, and the sounds of the Grateful Dead and Big Brother & the Holding Company.

The **"be-in"** followed in the summer of 1966 at the polo grounds in Golden Gate Park, when an estimated 20,000 heard Jefferson Airplane perform and Ginsberg chant, while the Hell's Angels acted as unofficial police. It was followed by the **Summer of Love** in 1967 as thousands of young people streamed into the city in search of drugs and free love.

The '60s Haight scene was very different from the '50s Beat scene. The hippies were much younger than the Beats had been, constituting the first youth movement to take over the nation. (Ironically, they also became the first generation of young, independent, and moneyed consumers to be courted by corporations.) Ultimately, the Haight and the hippie movement deteriorated from love and flowers into drugs and crime, drawing a fringe of crazies like Charles Manson and leaving only a legacy of sex, drugs, violence, and consumerism. As early as October 1967, the Diggers, who had opened a free shop and soup kitchen in the Haight, symbolically buried the dream in a clay casket in Buena Vista Park.

The end of the Vietnam War and the resignation of President Nixon took the edge off politics. The last fling of the mentality that had driven the 1960s occurred in 1974, when heiress Patty Hearst was kidnapped from her Berkeley apartment by the Symbionese Liberation Army, participating in their bank-robbing spree before surrendering in San Francisco in 1975.

**THE 1970S: GAY RIGHTS**   The homosexual community in San Francisco was essentially founded at the end of World War II, when thousands of military personnel were discharged back to the United States via San Francisco. A substantial number of those men were homosexual, and they decided to stay on in tolerant, open-minded San Francisco. A gay community began to coalesce along Polk Street between Sutter and California streets. Later, the larger community moved into the **Castro,** where it remains today.

The modern-day gay political movement is usually traced to the 1969 Stonewall raid and riots in Greenwich Village. But although the political movement started in New York, California had already given birth to two major organizations for gay rights: the Mattachine Society, founded in 1951 by Henry Hay in Los Angeles, and the Daughters of Bilitis, a lesbian organization founded in 1955 in San Francisco. After Stonewall, the Committee for Homosexual Freedom was created in spring 1969 in San Francisco; a Gay Liberation Front chapter was organized at Berkeley.

As the movement grew in size and power, debates on strategy and tactics occurred, most dramatically between those who wanted to withdraw into separate ghettos and those who wanted to enter mainstream society. The most extreme proposal was made in California by Don Jackson, who proposed establishing a gay territory in California's Alpine County, just south of Lake Tahoe, with a totally gay administration, civil service, university, museum— everything. (The residents of Alpine County were not pleased with the proposal.) Before the situation turned ugly, Jackson's idea was abandoned because of lack of support in the gay community. In the end, the movement would concentrate on integration and civil rights, not separatism. They would seek to elect politicians sympathetic to their cause, and celebrate their new identity by establishing National Gay Celebration Day and Gay Pride Week, first celebrated in June 1970 with 1,000 to 2,000 marchers in New York, 1,000 in Los Angeles, and a few hundred in San Francisco.

By the mid-1970s, the gay community craved a more central role in San Francisco politics. **Harvey Milk,** owner of a camera store in the Castro, decided to run as an openly gay man for the board of supervisors. He won,

# WE'RE queer AND WE'RE here

In the dawn of the gay rights movement, gay rights activists in San Francisco fed a groundswell of seminal protests.

In fall 1969, *San Francisco Examiner* columnist Robert Patterson referred to homosexuals as "semi males, drag darlings," and "women who aren't exactly women." On October 31 at noon, a group began a peaceful picket of the *Examiner*'s offices. Peace reigned—until someone threw a bag of printer's ink from an *Examiner* window. Someone else wrote "F--- the Examiner" on the wall, and the police moved in to clear the crowd, clubbing them as they went. The remaining pickets retreated to Glide Methodist Church (see p. 135) and then marched on City Hall. Unfortunately, the mayor was away. Unable to air their grievances, the protesters started a sit-in that lasted until 5pm, when they were ordered to leave. Most did, but three remained and were arrested.

Later that year, an anti-Thanksgiving rally was staged, at which gays protested against several national and local businesses: Western and Delta airlines, the former for firing lesbian flight attendants, the latter for refusing to sell a ticket to a young man wearing a Gay Power button; KFOG, for its anti-homosexual broadcasting; and also some local gay bars for exploitation.

The following spring, on May 14, 1970, a group of gay rights activists joined women's liberationists in invading the convention of the American Psychiatric Association in San Francisco to protest the reading of a paper on aversion therapy for homosexuals, forcing the meeting to adjourn.

Later that summer, at the National Gay Liberation conference held in August 1970 in the city, Charles Thorp, chairman of the San Francisco State Liberation Front, called for militancy and issued a challenge to come out with a rallying cry of "Blatant is beautiful." Decrying the fact that homosexuals were kept in their place at the three B's—the bars, the beaches, and the baths—Thorp also argued for the use of what he felt was the more positive, celebratory term *gay* instead of *homosexual*.

becoming the first openly gay person to hold a major public office. He and liberal mayor George Moscone developed a gay rights agenda, but in 1978 both were killed by former supervisor Dan White, who shot them after Moscone refused White's request for reinstatement. (White, a Catholic and former police officer, had consistently opposed Milk's and Moscone's more liberal policies.) At his trial, White successfully pleaded temporary insanity caused by his fast-food diet—the "Twinkie defense," as the media dubbed it. The charges against White were reduced to manslaughter. Angry and grieving, the gay community rioted, overturning and burning police cars in a night of rage. To this day, a candlelight memorial parade is held each year on the anniversary of Milk's death; the intersection at the heart of the Castro is now officially Harvey Milk Plaza.

The emphasis in the gay movement shifted abruptly in the 1980s when the AIDS epidemic struck the gay community. AIDS has had a dramatic impact on the Castro. While it's still a thriving and lively community, it's no longer the constant party that it once was. The hedonistic lifestyle that had played out in the discos, bars, baths, and streets changed as the seriousness of the epidemic sunk in and the number of deaths increased. Political efforts shifted away from enfranchisement and toward demanding money for social services. The gay community has developed its own organizations, such as Project Inform and Gay Men's Health Crisis, to publicize information about AIDS, treatments available, and safe sex. Though new cases of AIDS within the gay community are on the decline in San Francisco, it still remains a serious problem.

**THE 1980S: THE BIG ONE, PART 2**　　The '80s may have arrived in San Francisco with a whimper (compared to previous generations), but they went out with quite a bang. At 5:04pm on Tuesday, October 17, 1989, as more than 62,000 fans filled Candlestick Park for the third game of the World Series—and the San Francisco Bay Area commute moved into its heaviest flow—an earthquake of magnitude 7.1 struck. Within the next 20 seconds, 63 lives would be lost, $10 billion in damage would occur, and the entire Bay Area community would be reminded of its humble insignificance. Centered about 60 miles south of San Francisco within the Forest of Nisene Marks, the deadly temblor was felt as far away as San Diego and Nevada.

Scientists had predicted an earthquake would hit on this section of the San Andreas Fault, but that was little help, as even structures that had been built to withstand such an earthquake failed miserably. The most catastrophic event was the collapse of the elevated Cypress Street section of I-880 in Oakland, where the upper level of the freeway literally pancaked the lower level, crushing everything. Other structures heavily damaged included the San Francisco–Oakland Bay Bridge, which was shut down for months after a section of the roadbed collapsed; San Francisco's Marina district, where several multimillion-dollar homes collapsed on their weak, shifting bases of landfill and sand; and the Pacific Garden Mall in Santa Cruz, which was completely devastated.

President George H. W. Bush declared a disaster area for the seven hardest-hit counties, where 63 people died, at least 3,700 people were reported injured, and more than 12,000 were displaced. More than 18,000 homes were damaged and 963 others destroyed. Although fire raged within the city and water supply systems were damaged, the major fires sparked within the Marina district were brought under control within 3 hours, due mostly to the heroic efforts of San Francisco's firefighters.

After the rubble had finally settled, it was unanimously agreed that San Francisco and the Bay Area had pulled through miraculously well—particularly when compared to the more recent earthquake in northeast Japan, which killed thousands. After the San Francisco quake, a feeling of esprit de corps swept the city. Neighbors helped each other rebuild and donations poured in from all over the world. Though it's been over 2 decades since, the city is still feeling the effects of the quake. That another "big one" will strike is inevitable: It's the price you pay for living on a fault line. But if there is ever a city that is prepared for a major shakedown, it's San Francisco.

**THE 1990S: THE DOT-COM BUBBLE**   In the early 1990s, the nation-wide recession did not spare San Francisco. Yet even then, there were quiet rumblings of the new frontier in Silicon Valley, happening largely under the radar. By the middle of the decade, San Francisco and the surrounding areas were the site of a new kind of gold rush—the birth of the Internet industry.

Not unlike the gold fever of the 1850s, this era saw people flocking to the western shores to strike it rich—and they did. In 1999, the local media reported that each day 64 Bay Area residents were gaining millionaire status. Long before the last year of the millennium, real estate prices went into the stratosphere. The city's gentrification financially squeezed out many of those residents who didn't mean big business (read: alternative and artistic types, seniors, and minorities who made the city colorful). New businesses popped up everywhere—especially in SoMa, where start-up companies jammed warehouse spaces.

As the most popular post-education destination for MBAs and the leader in the media of the future, San Francisco was no longer a beacon to everyone looking for the legendary alternative lifestyle—unless he or she could afford a $1,000 studio apartment and $20-per-day fees to park the car.

Y2K jitters aside, San Francisco's new elite looked forward to the new millennium with bubbly in hand, foie gras and caviar on the linen tablecloth, and seemingly everyone in the money. New restaurants charging $35 per entree were all the rage, hotels were renovated to luxury standards, the new bayfront ballpark was packed, and stock market tips were as plentiful as million-dollar SoMa condos and lofts. Though there were whispers of a stock market correction, and inklings that venture capital might dry up, San Franciscans were too busy raking in the dough to heed the writing on the wall.

**THE MILLENNIUM**   When the city woke up from the dot-com party, San Franciscans found themselves suffering from a millennium hangover. In the early 2000s, dot.coms became "dot.bombs" faster than you could say "worthless stock options," with companies shuttering at a rate of several per day. The crash of the Internet economy brought with it a real estate exodus, and scads of empty live-work lofts opened up in SoMa.

But from the ashes of the collapse grew the seeds of innovation. By mid-decade, San Francisco was back on the cutting edge with a little search engine called Google, headquartered in nearby Mountain View, California. Wikipedia, YouTube, and new skyscrapers followed, holding steady even as Wall Street and big banks fell around their feet in 2008. It was an undeniable testament to the resilience and mettle of San Franciscans, who always seem to have an ace in the hole, even when things seem at their worst.

**THE 2010S: BUBBLE 2.0**   Over the past seven years, San Francisco has seen more dramatic change, as the Internet and tech industries yet again raise the prices of, well, everything. Only this time, rather than residents briefly achieving millionaire status based on their volatile (and short-lived) company stock valuations, San Franciscans are cash rich—and showing as much by snatching up multimillion-dollar homes *in cash,* and often paying hundreds of

# A BRIEF HISTORY OF wine country

Like most everything else around San Francisco, the Northern California wine industry began with the 1849 Gold Rush. It took a bunch of European immigrants—most of whom originally came seeking gold—to discover that the hilly countryside north of San Francisco offered a perfect climate for viticulture. Hungarian nobleman Agoston Haraszthy imported some 300 different vines from Europe for his Buena Vista winery, founded near the town of Sonoma in 1857; the next year, 1858, Bavarian winemaker Jacob Gundlach opened another winery nearby which is still in business today (see p. 261). Meanwhile, in Napa Valley to the east, Englishman John Patchett began planting vines in 1854, opening a winery in 1858; Prussian immigrant Charles Krug, who'd worked for both Patchett and Haraszthy, founded his own winery in St. Helena in 1861. (Today it's owned by the Mondavi family.) Fellow Germans quickly followed—Jacob Schram with his Schramsberg winery (see p. 249) in 1862, and former Krug cellarmaster Jacob Benziger (see p. 260) in

1876—along with Finnish-born Captain Gustave Niebaum, who began making Bordeaux-style wines at his Inglenook Winery in 1879 (now part of Francis Ford Coppola's wine empire—see p. 265). In 1862, Gold Rush millionaire Samuel Brannan launched Napa Valley tourism by building a spa town around the natural hot springs of Calistoga.

Through the 1870s and 1880s, the American wine industry burgeoned, surviving an invasion of the native *phylloxera* bug (accidentally introduced to Europe in the 1860s, where it nearly wiped out the continent's vineyards—giving American wines an edge in the market for a couple of decades). In 1889, when Inglenook wines won gold medals at the Paris World's Fair, the American wine industry really became a world player.

All of this came crashing to a halt in 1920 when Prohibition made alcoholic beverages illegal. Production fell by a whopping 94%, with only a few winemakers hanging on by making communion wines, which were exempt. By the time Prohibition was repealed in 1933,

thousands of dollars over asking for the privilege. Teslas are the car du jour—even though most people Lyft or Uber everywhere anyway, and $750 VIP wristbands for massive weekend music concerts sell out faster than you can say, "I'm with the band."

In stark contrast, tent cities have popped up under overpasses, acting as the only refuge for many of our less-fortunate citizens. In the Tenderloin, Mission, and SoMa, it's not uncommon to see a homeless, drugged-out, or just plain crazy person defecating or urinating in the middle of the sidewalk in broad daylight, completely oblivious to passersby. I'd like to think these are growing pains—we have gained around 70,000 residents in the past 7 years, which is a dramatic uplift from the prior 800,000 residents. But honestly, in the 50 years I've lived in or around the city, I've never seen transformation as great as this. The City truly is undergoing yet another Gold Rush–style evolution, and it's changing the face of the city forever (just look up at SoMa's mammoth new skyscraper—Salesforce Tower—to see what I mean). But real estate brokers are bracing for the inevitable softening of the market and the economy in general, and we all know it will come. What it will leave in its the California wine industry had collapsed. For various social and cultural reasons, Americans had switched from wine to cocktails and beer. The few wineries that survived flooded the market with cheap, low-quality wines.

A new wave of California winemakers in the early 1960s, however, began to focus on quality. Led by Robert Mondavi, who opened his Oakville winery in 1965 (see p. 251), these vintners began marketing their wines with varietal names (Pinot Noir, Chardonnay, Chablis) instead of the place names of European wines (such as Burgundy or Bordeaux). As gourmet chefs like Julia Child and James Beard promoted fine dining in the later 1960s, Americans aspired to drink wine again—but not domestic wines, which still were considered inferior. All that changed in 1976, when a highly publicized blind taste testing in Paris— presided over by French wine experts— stunned the world by awarding top honors to two California wines, a Chardonnay by Chateau Montelena (see p. 248) and a Cabernet Sauvignon by

Stag's Leap Wine Cellars, both from Napa Valley. The stigma of California wines vanished seemingly overnight. Between 1980 and 1989 in Sonoma County, grapes went from being the fourth-largest agricultural product to being its top crop.

And along with the wine boom came something new: enotourism. Napa Valley began to market itself as a tourist destination for wine lovers in 1975. Spurred by their efforts, wineries opened sleek tasting rooms and developed tours of their cellars and wine-making facilities, while luxury resorts opened all around the valley. By the mid-1990s, it had become a culinary destination as well, with Thomas Keller's famed French Laundry restaurant in Yountville opening in 1994 and a branch of the Culinary Institute of America opening in 1995 in St. Helena. Neighboring Sonoma County, with more small, family-owned wineries, was quick to jump onto the enotourism bandwagon as well, offering a more laidback alternative to Napa (see "Deciding Between Napa or Sonoma," p. 246).

wake is anyone's guess, but history has proven that if any city can ride out the changing of tides and still come out on top, it's San Francisco.

# SAN FRANCISCO & THE ARTS

Getting acquainted with San Francisco through the work of authors and filmmakers will provide an extra dimension to your trip—including the thrill of happening upon a location you recognize from a favorite movie or novel.

For a great introduction to the city, check out *San Francisco Stories: Great Writers on the City,* edited by John Miller and published by San Francisco's own Chronicle Books. This collection of short pieces covers the personal and the political as recalled by acclaimed authors including Mark Twain, Jack Kerouac, Tom Wolfe, and Amy Tan.

## San Francisco in Film

As one of the loveliest spots on the planet, San Francisco has been a favorite of location scouts since the beginning of the film industry. Hundreds of

# SOUNDS OF THE '60s

During its heyday in the 1950s and 1960s, San Francisco was *the* place to be for anyone who eschewed the conventional American lifestyle. From moody beatniks to political firebrands, the city attracted poets, writers, actors, and a bewildering assortment of free thinkers and activists. Thousands of the country's youth—including some of America's most talented musicians—headed west to join the party. What culminated in the 1960s was San Francisco's hat trick of rock legends: It was able to lay claim to three of the rock era's most influential bands—the Grateful Dead, Janis Joplin's Big Brother & the Holding Company, and Jefferson Airplane.

**The Grateful Dead**   Easily the most influential band spawned from the psychedelic movement of the 1960s, the Grateful Dead was San Francisco's hometown band of choice. Described as the "house band for the famous acid tests that transformed the City by the Bay into one endless freak-out," the Dead's cerebral, psychedelic music was played simultaneously (and loudly) on so many stereo systems that it almost felt like one enormous, citywide jam session. More than any other band of the 1960s, the Grateful Dead were best appreciated during live concerts, partly due to the love-in mood that percolated through its drug-infused

audiences. In the 1980s and 1990s, they marketed repetitive permutations of their themes, delighting their core base while often baffling or boring virtually everyone else. The group disbanded in 1995 after the death of its charismatic lead vocalist, Jerry Garcia, but its devoted fans had already elevated the Grateful Dead to cult empire status, and several of the band's original members still tour in various incarnations. (Most recently, mega-hot guitarist John Mayer has been touring with a reconstituted version of the Dead.) Tie-dyed "Deadheads" (many of whom followed the band on tour for decades) can still be found tripping within the Haight, reminiscing about the good old days. If you're looking for an album that best expresses the changing artistic premises of San Francisco, look for its award-winning retrospective *What a Long Strange Trip It's Been* at any of the city's record stores.

**Big Brother & the Holding Company and Janis Joplin**   In the fertile musical landscape of 1960s San Francisco, Texas-born Janis Joplin honed her unique vocal technique: a rasping, gravel-y, shrieking voice that expressed the generational angst of thousands. Her breakthrough style was first embraced by audiences at the Monterey Jazz Festival in 1967, where *Billboard* magazine characterized her sound as composed of equal portions of

movies and television shows have been shot or placed in San Francisco, making the hills and bridges among the most recognized of backgrounds.

It may be difficult to locate, but the 1936 Clark Gable/Jeanette MacDonald romance *San Francisco* (1936) is lauded for its dramatic reenactment of the 1906 earthquake. It'll be easier to find the classic film *The Maltese Falcon* (1941), based on Dashiell Hammett's detective story, with Humphrey Bogart starring as Sam Spade. This movie includes shots of the Bay Bridge, the Ferry Building, and Burrit Alley (above the Stockton Tunnel). John's Grill, mentioned in the novel, continues to flog its association with Hammett's hero from its location at 63 Ellis St. (btw. Stockton and Powell sts.).

An obvious choice on the list of great San Francisco films, Alfred Hitchcock's *Vertigo* (1958), starring James Stewart and Kim Novak, is always honey, Southern Comfort, and gall. She was backed up during her earliest years by Big Brother & the Holding Company, a group she eventually outgrew. Though specialists warned that her vocal technique would ruin her larynx before she was 30, Janis continued to wail, gasp, growl, and stagger over a raw, vivid blues repertoire. Stories of her substance abuse, sexual escapades, and general raunchiness litter the emotional landscape of modern-day San Francisco. Contemporary photographs show a ravaged body and a face partially concealed behind aviator's goggles, long hair, and a tough but brittle facade. Described as omnisexual—and completely comfortable with both male and female partners—she once (unexpectedly) announced to a group of nightclub guests her evaluation of the sexual performance of two of the era's most visible male icons: football quarterback Joe Namath (not particularly memorable) and TV talk-show host Dick Cavett (absolutely fantastic). Promoters frantically struggled to market (and protect) Janis and her voice for future artistic endeavors but, alas, her talent was simply too huge for her to handle. The star died of a heroin overdose at the age of 27, a tragedy still mourned by her thousands of fans, who continue to refer to her by her nickname, "Pearl."

**Jefferson Airplane**   In the San Francisco suburbs of the late 1960s, hundreds of bands dreamed of stardom. Of the few that succeeded, none expressed the love-in ethic of that time better than the soaring vocals and ferocious guitar-playing of Jefferson Airplane. Singers Grace Slick and Marty Balin—as well as bass guitar player Jack Casady—were considered at the top of their profession by their peers. Most importantly, all members of the band, especially Paul Kantner and Jorma Kaukonen, were songwriters. Their fertile mix of musical styles and creative energies led to songs that still reverberate in the minds of anyone who owned an AM radio during the late 1960s. Intense and lonely songs such as "Somebody to Love" and "White Rabbit" became musical anthems, as American youth explored a psychedelic consciousness within the catalytic setting of San Francisco. In 1989 the group reassembled its scattered members for a swan song renamed Jefferson Starship, but the output was a banal repetition of earlier themes; the energy of those long-faded summers of San Francisco in the late 1960s was never recovered. As Jefferson Airplane, however, the band is still inextricably linked to the Bay Area's epoch-changing Summer of Love.

worth viewing. Stewart plays a former detective hired to tail a woman who he thinks is the wife of an old college friend; Stewart becomes obsessed with his prey as they make their way around the Palace of the Legion of Honor, Fort Point, Mission Dolores, and the detective's apartment at 900 Lombard St.

The city is also a major character in the 1968 thriller *Bullitt,* starring Steve McQueen, famous for its hair-raising car chases over many hills. Along the way you'll see the Bay Bridge from a recognizable point on the Embarcadero, Mason Street heading north next to the Fairmont Hotel, the front of the Mark Hopkins Hotel, Grace Cathedral, and the fairly unchanged Enrico's Sidewalk Café. Close on its heels came 1971's Clint Eastwood classic *Dirty Harry,* where Eastwood's rogue cop Harry Callahan sleuths his suspect at such photo-op spots as Marina Green, Alamo Square, and City Hall.

Another of cinema's all-time classic car chase scenes appears in the very funny romantic comedy *What's Up, Doc?* (1972) with Barbra Streisand and Ryan O'Neal. Watch for shots of Lombard Street, Chinatown, and Alta Plaza Park in Pacific Heights. The mood darkens with Francis Ford Coppola's engrossing 1978 thriller *The Conversation,* which stars Gene Hackman as a surveillance expert obsessively combing for clues in a surreptitious video shot in Union Square.

If you have kids to rev up, the 1993 comedy *Mrs. Doubtfire,* starring Sally Field and San Francisco favorite son Robin Williams, shows off the city with blue skies and refreshingly uncrowded cable cars. In case you care to gawk, the house where the character's estranged wife and children live is located in Pacific Heights at 2640 Steiner St. (at Broadway St.).

Finally, the 2005 documentary *24 Hours on Craigslist* covers a day in the life of the Internet community bulletin-board phenom. The filmmaker posted an ad on Craigslist, followed up with a handful of volunteers—an Ethel Merman impersonator seeking a Led Zeppelin cover band; a couple looking for others to join a support group for diabetic cats; a single, older woman needing a sperm donor—and sent film crews to cover their stories. While other films display the physical splendors of San Francisco, *24 Hours on Craigslist* will give you a sense of the city's psyche, or at least offer an explanation of why non–San Franciscans think the place is populated with . . . um . . . unusual types.

## San Francisco in Fiction

One of the more famous and beloved pieces of modern fiction based in San Francisco is Armistead Maupin's *Tales of the City.* Whether or not you've seen the miniseries, this is a must-read for a leisurely afternoon—or bring it with you on the plane. Maupin's 1970s soap opera covers the residents of 28 Barbary Lane (Macondry Lane on Russian Hill was the inspiration), melding sex, drugs, and growing self-awareness with enormous warmth and humor.

For a vividly depicted look at San Francisco during the Gold Rush, read *Daughter of Fortune,* by acclaimed novelist and Marin County resident Isabel Allende.

# WHEN TO GO

If you're dreaming of convertibles, Frisbee on the beach, and tank-topped evenings, change your reservations and head to Los Angeles. Contrary to California's sunshine-and-bikini image, San Francisco's weather is "mild" (to put it nicely) and can often be downright bone-chilling because of the wet, foggy air and cool winds. **Summer,** the most popular time to visit, is often the coldest time of year, with damp, foggy days; cold, windy nights; and crowded tourist destinations. A good bet is to visit in spring or, better yet, autumn. Just about every **September,** right about the time San Franciscans mourn being cheated (or fogged) out of another summer, something wonderful happens:

## In a Fog

San Francisco's infamous coastal fog is caused by a rare combination of water, wind, and topography. The fog lies in wait off the coast; rising air currents pull it in when the land heats up. Held back by coastal mountains along a 600-mile front, the low clouds seek out any passage they can find. And where's the easiest access? It's the slot where the Pacific Ocean penetrates the continental wall—also known as the Golden Gate.

The thermometer rises, the skies clear, and the locals call in sick to work and head for the beach. It's what residents call "Indian summer." The city is also delightful during **winter:** the opera and ballet seasons are in full swing, hotel prices dip because there are fewer tourists, and downtown bustles with holiday cheer.

San Francisco's temperate, marine climate usually means relatively mild weather year-round. In summer, chilling fog rolls in most mornings and evenings, and if temperatures top 70°F (21°C), the city is ready to throw a celebration. Even when autumn's heat occasionally stretches into the 80s (upper 20s Celsius) and 90s (lower 30s Celsius), you should still dress in layers, or by early evening you'll learn firsthand why sweatshirt sales are a great business at Fisherman's Wharf. In winter, the mercury seldom falls below freezing and snow is almost unheard of, but that doesn't mean you won't be whimpering if you forget your coat. Still, compared to most of the state's weather conditions, San Francisco's are consistently pleasant, and even if it's damp and chilly, head north, east, or south 15 minutes and you can usually find sun again.

If you're heading up to the **wine country,** you'll find that summertime is ludicrously busy, with endless traffic on the counties' two-lane roads. Still, the scenery is gorgeous then, with grapes hanging heavy on the vine, and it's also the season for garden tours. Grapes are harvested and squeezed in the fall and, alas, this time can also be maddening, because people flock here to witness the action involved in harvest and the resulting winemaking. I'm a fan of visiting in winter: Tourists tend to stay away then, so you'll get much more attention and education from the vintners, hotel prices (notoriously expensive) are way down, and it's easier to get restaurant reservations. Plus it's extremely romantic then, with the nip of winter, the dormant grapevines, and twinkle lights illuminating various nooks and crannies. Spring is a close second, when the area bursts with the green and yellow of mustard flowers. It's never terribly cold—wine country everywhere, by definition, has mostly enviable weather, because that's what makes it good for grape growing.

## Travel Attire

Even if it's sunny out, don't forget to bring a jacket and dress in layers; the weather can change almost instantly from sunny and warm to windy and cold—especially as you move between microclimates. Also bring comfortable walking shoes or your feet will pay the price.

## San Francisco's Average Temperatures (°F/°C)

|  | JAN | FEB | MAR | APR | MAY | JUNE | JULY | AUG | SEPT | OCT | NOV | DEC |
|---|---|---|---|---|---|---|---|---|---|---|---|---|
| Avg. High | 57/14 | 60/16 | 61/16 | 63/17 | 64/18 | 66/19 | 66/19 | 67/22 | 72/23 | 69/21 | 64/17 | 57/13 |
| Avg. Low | 46/8 | 48/9 | 49/9 | 50/10 | 51/11 | 53/12 | 54/12 | 55/13 | 56/13 | 55/13 | 51/11 | 47/8 |

# Holidays

Banks, government offices, post offices, and many stores, restaurants, and museums are closed on the following legal national holidays: January 1 (New Year's Day), the third Monday in January (Martin Luther King, Jr. Day), the third Monday in February (Presidents' Day), the last Monday in May (Memorial Day), July 4 (Independence Day), the first Monday in September (Labor Day), the second Monday in October (Columbus Day), November 11 (Veterans Day/Armistice Day), the fourth Thursday in November (Thanksgiving Day), and December 25 (Christmas). The Tuesday after the first Monday in November is Election Day, a federal government holiday in presidential-election years (held every 4 years).

# San Francisco–Area Calendar of Events

For more information on San Francisco events, visit **www.onlyinsanfrancisco.com** for an annual calendar of local events, as well as **http://events.frommers.com**, where you'll find a searchable, up-to-the-minute roster of what's happening in cities all over the world.

## FEBRUARY

**Chinese New Year, Chinatown.** Public celebrations spill onto every street in Chinatown, beginning with the "Miss Chinatown USA" pageant parade, and climaxing a week later with a celebratory parade of marching bands, rolling floats, barrages of fireworks, and a block-long dragon writhing in and out of the crowds. The action starts at Market and Second streets and ends at Kearny Street. Arrive early for a good viewing spot on Kearny Street. You can purchase bleacher seats online starting in December; for dates and information, call $\textcircled{C}$ **415/680-6297** or visit www.chineseparade.com.

## MARCH

**St. Patrick's Day Parade, Union Square, and Civic Center.** Everyone's an honorary Irish person at this festive affair, which starts at 11:30am at Market and Second streets and continues to City Hall. But the party doesn't stop there. Head down to the Civic Center for the post-party, or venture to the Embarcadero's Harrington's Bar & Grill (245 Front St.) and celebrate with hundreds of Irish-for-a-day yuppies as they gallivant around the closed-off streets and numerous pubs. Sunday before March 17.

## APRIL

**Cherry Blossom Festival, Japantown.** Meander through the arts-and-crafts and food booths lining the blocked-off streets around Japan Center and watch traditional drumming, flower arranging, origami making, and a parade celebrating the cherry blossoms and Japanese culture. Call $\textcircled{C}$ **415/563-2313** or visit sfcherryblossom. org for information. Mid- to late April.

**San Francisco International Film Festival.** Begun in 1957, this is America's longest running film festival, with screenings at the Sundance Kabuki Cinemas (Fillmore and Post sts.), and at many other locations. It features close to 200 films and videos from more than 50 countries. Tickets are relatively inexpensive, and screenings are accessible to the public. Entries include new films by beginning and established directors, and star-studded tributes. For a schedule and to purchase tickets, visit **sffilm.org**. Early April.

## MAY

**Cinco de Mayo Festival, Mission District.** As the Latino community celebrates the victory of the Mexicans over the French at Puebla in 1862, mariachi bands, dancers, food, and revelers fill the streets of the Mission. The celebration is usually on Valencia Street between 21st and 24th streets. Contact the Mission Neighborhood Center for more information at © **415/206-7752** or mncsf.org/sfcincodemayo.

**Bay to Breakers Foot Race, the Embarcadero through Golden Gate Park to Ocean Beach.** Even if you don't participate, you can't avoid this giant, moving costume party (which celebrated its 106th year in 2017) that goes from downtown to Ocean Beach. More than 75,000 participants gather—many dressed in wacky, innovative, and sometimes X-rated costumes—for the approximately 7½-mile run. If you don't want to run, join the throng of spectators who line the route. Sidewalk parties, bands, and cheerleaders of all ages provide a good dose of true San Francisco fun. For more information, call © **415/231-3130**, or check their website, baytobreakers.com. Third Sunday of May.

**Carnaval Festival, Harrison Street between 16th and 23rd streets.** The Mission District's largest annual event, held from 9:30am to 6pm and celebrating 40 years of fun in 2018, is a weekend of festivities that includes food, music, dance, arts and crafts, and a parade that's as sultry and energetic as the Latin American and Caribbean people behind it. It's one of San Franciscans' favorite events, with more than half a million spectators lining the parade route; samba musicians and dancers continue to entertain on 14th Street, near Harrison, at the end of the march, where you'll find food and craft booths, music, and more revelry. Call © **415/206-0577** for more information. Celebrations are held Saturday and Sunday of Memorial Day weekend, but the parade is on Sunday morning only. See **carnavalsf. org** for more information.

**Bottle Rock Napa Valley, Napa.** Held over Memorial Day weekend, this multi-day music, food, and wine festival draws tens of thousands to see the likes of Stevie Wonder, Foo Fighters, Maroon 5, Warren G, Death Cab for Cutie, and dozens of other bands, who perform on multiple stages backed by an awesome array of gourmet foods (and appearances by famed chefs) and local wines. Not surprising, accommodations in the area are wildly expensive during this time, but those in the crowd say the fun-in-the-sun-loving weekend is worth the expense. Held Memorial Day weekend. For more information see bottlerocknapavalley. com.

JUNE

**Union Street Art Festival, Pacific Heights along Union Street from Steiner to Gough streets.** This outdoor fair celebrates San Francisco with gourmet food booths, music, entertainment, and a juried art show featuring works by more than 250 artists. It's a great time and a chance to see the city's young well-to-dos partying it up. Call the **Union Street Association** (© **415/441-7055**) for more information or see unionstreetfestival.com. First weekend of June.

**Haight-Ashbury Street Fair, Haight-Ashbury.** A far cry from the froufrou Union Street Fair (see above), this grittier fair features alternative crafts, ethnic foods, rock bands, and a healthy number of hippies and street kids whooping it up and slamming beers in front of the blaring rock-'n'-roll stage. The fair usually extends along Haight Street between Stanyan and Ashbury streets. For details, visit haightashburystreetfair.org. Second Sunday of June.

**North Beach Festival, Grant Avenue, North Beach.** In 2018, this party celebrates its 64th anniversary; organizers claim it's one of the oldest outdoor festivals in the country. More than 100,000 city folk meander along Grant Avenue, between Vallejo and Union streets, to eat, drink, and browse the arts-and-crafts booths, poetry readings, swing-dancing venue, and *arte di gesso* (sidewalk chalk art). The most enjoyable parts of the event? Listening to music and people-watching. Visit sresproductions.com/events/north-beach-festival.

**Stern Grove Music Festival, Sunset District.** Pack a picnic and head out early to join the thousands who come here to lie in the grass and enjoy free world-class classical, jazz, and ethnic music and dance in the grove, at 19th Avenue and Sloat Boulevard. The free concerts take place every Sunday at

2pm between mid-June and August. Show up with a lawn chair or blanket. There are food booths if you forget snacks, but you'll be dying to leave if you don't bring warm clothes—the Sunset District can be one of the coldest parts of the city. Call ✆ **415/252-6252** for listings or go to sterngrove.org. Sundays, mid-June through August.

**San Francisco Lesbian, Gay, Bisexual, Transgender Pride Parade & Celebration, downtown's Market Street.** This prideful event draws up to one million participants who celebrate all of the above—and then some. The parade proceeds west on Market Street until it gets to the Civic Center, where hundreds of food, art, and information booths are set up around several soundstages. Call ✆ **415/864-0831** or visit sfpride.org for information. Usually the third or last weekend of June.

## JULY

**Fillmore Jazz Festival, Pacific Heights.** July starts with a bang, when the upscale portion of Fillmore closes to traffic and the blocks between Jackson and Eddy streets are filled with arts and crafts, gourmet food, and live jazz from 10am to 6pm. For more information visit **fillmorejazzfestival.com**. First weekend in July.

**Fourth of July Celebration & Fireworks, Fisherman's Wharf.** This event can be something of a joke—more often than not, fog comes into the city, like everyone else, to squelch the festivities. Sometimes it's almost impossible to view the million-dollar pyrotechnics from Pier 39 on the northern waterfront. Still, it's a party, and if the skies are clear, it's a darn good show.

**San Francisco Marathon, San Francisco and beyond.** One of the largest marathons in the world starts and ends at the Ferry Building at the base of Market Street, winds 26-plus miles through virtually every neighborhood in the city, and crosses the Golden Gate Bridge. For entry information, visit **thesfmarathon.com**. Usually the last weekend in July.

## AUGUST

**Outside Lands, Golden Gate Park.** This annual music event draws about 70,000 people to a vast, fenced-off expanse in Golden Gate Park where multiple stages host 3 days and nights of awesome contemporary music (and comedy) artists, while food and drink stands ensure everyone has every reason to stay for the long haul—as if Metallica, The Who, St. Lucia, and more aren't enough. Tickets are expensive and sell out quickly, so if you're planning to go, buy in the second tickets go on sale. See sfoutsidelands.com for more information. Usually in mid-August.

## SEPTEMBER

**Sausalito Art Festival, Sausalito.** A juried exhibit of more than 20,000 original works of art, this festival includes music—usually provided by known, old-school jazz, rock, and blues performers from the Bay Area and beyond—and international cuisine, enhanced by wines from some 50 Napa and Sonoma producers. Parking is difficult; make it easier and take the ferry (blueandgoldfleet.com) from Pier 41 to the festival site. For more information, call ✆ **415/332-3555** or log on to sausalitoartfestival.org. Labor Day weekend.

**Opera in the Park.** Usually in Sharon Meadow, Golden Gate Park. Each year, the San Francisco Opera launches its season with a free concert featuring a selection of arias. Call ✆ **415/861-4008** or visit sfopera.com to confirm the location and date. Usually the Sunday after Labor Day.

**Folsom Street Fair,** along Folsom Street between 7th and 12th streets, the area south of Market Street (SoMa, 11am–6pm). This is a local favorite for its kinky, outrageous, leather-and-skin gay-centric blowout celebration. It's hardcore, so only open-minded and adventurous types need head into the leather-clad and partially dressed crowds. For info visit folsomstreetfair.org. Last Sunday of September.

## OCTOBER

**Hardly Strictly Bluegrass, Golden Gate Park** in Hellman Hollow (formerly Speedway Meadows), Lindley, and Marx meadows. This free annual music event (see box p. 145) lures thousands into Golden Gate Park for 3 days of awesome music, beer drinking, and pot smoking. It's about as groovy, happy-go-lucky San Francisco as it gets. Visit **hardly strictlybluegrass.com** for info.

**Fleet Week, Marina and Fisherman's Wharf.** Residents gather along the Marina Green, the Embarcadero, Fisherman's Wharf, and other vantage points to watch incredible (and loud!) aerial performances by the Blue Angels and other daring stunt pilots, as well as the annual parade of ships. Call ☎ **415/306-0911** or visit **fleetweeksf.org** for details and dates.

**Artspan Open Studios, various San Francisco locations.** Find an original piece of art to commemorate your trip, or just see what local artists are up to by grabbing a map to over 800 artists' studios that are open to the public during weekends in October and May. Visit artspan.org for more information.

**Castro Street Fair, the Castro.** Celebrate life in the city's most famous gay neighborhood. Call ☎ **800/853-5950** or visit castro streetfair.org for information. First Sunday in October, from 11am to 6pm.

**Italian Heritage Parade, North Beach and Fisherman's Wharf.** In 2017, for the 149th year in a row, the city's Italian community leads festivities around Fisherman's Wharf celebrating Columbus's landing in America with a parade along Columbus Avenue. But for the most part, it's a great excuse to hang out in North Beach and people-watch. For more information, visit **sfcolumbusday.org**. Observed the Sunday before Columbus Day.

**Halloween, the Castro.** This once-huge street party has been tamed down by city officials in the past decade to curb violence and prevent the increasing influx of out-of-towners into the neighborhood. Castro denizens still whoop it up with music and drag costume contests, but if you go to gawk, you may be disappointed. October 31.

## NOVEMBER

**Napa Valley Film Festival.** Held in intimate venues throughout Napa County, this 5-day festival features 100-plus films and an abundance of food, wine, and music festivities. Tickets range from single screenings starting at $20 to event passes that start at $295 and go up to $2,500 for VIP access. Visit nvff.org for information. Usually the second week of November.

## DECEMBER

**The Nutcracker, War Memorial Opera House, Civic Center.** The **San Francisco Ballet** (☎ **415/865-2000**) performs this Tchaikovsky classic annually. (It was actually the first ballet company in America to do so, in 1944.) Order tickets to this holiday tradition well in advance. Visit sfballet.org for information.

**SantaCon, various San Francisco locations.** Get into the holiday spirit and join thousands of wannabe Santas as they booze their way across the city. Dress up as Santa, Mrs. Claus, an elf, or your own interpretation for a full day of drinking, singing, and being merry. This is an adults-only pub crawl that, true to San Francisco style, includes nudity. The time, date, and location change annually and the details are released only a few days before the event, so follow SantaCon on twitter or check out the website at **santa-con.info/San_Francisco-CA**.

# WHERE TO STAY

From luxury resorts to funky motor inns to charming B&Bs, San Francisco is more than accommodating to its 24 million annual guests. Many of the city's 200-plus hotels are downtown, but smaller, independent gems are scattered throughout. Stay close to Union Square for easy access to shopping and museums, near Fisherman's Wharf for the more touristy attractions, or shack up in the city's quieter residential neighborhoods for a more authentic experience. Whatever you do, the city's small size means you'll have easy access to everything you want to do and see. While there are multiple transportation options, you may find that hoofing it is the best way to see the sights—at least by day.

## HOW TO GET THE BEST DEAL

There are many ways to find the best hotels for the best prices. The rates we list in this chapter showcase the low and high end of each hotel's price structure. Since there is no way of knowing what the offers will be when you're booking, consider these general tips if you want to get the best prices:

**Choose your season carefully.** Room rates can vary dramatically—by hundreds of dollars in some cases—depending on the time of year you'll be visiting. Winter, from November through March, is best for bargains, excluding Thanksgiving, Christmas, and New Year's, of course—though the days between Christmas and New Year's can sometimes offer amazing deals, and these just happen to be some of the best shopping days all year in Union Square. Occupancy rates hover around 90% from June through October, and rates adjust upward accordingly.

Oddly, when the city fills up, lesser-quality hotels will often charge prices that are equal to or even higher than what the luxury hotels are asking, so it's important to *never* assess the quality of a hotel by the price it's asking. Instead, read reviews carefully and compare the prices you're being quoted to make sure you're not getting taken. Trip Advisor and Yelp are good review sources, but be sure to focus on reviews from the past few months and not ones that were made a year ago or more. Also, look for hotels' responses to negative reviews—did they acknowledge and try to fix the

## The Price You'll Pay

With the average price for a double room topping $200 per night, occupancy rates increasing up to 90% in peak season, and $400 hotel rooms going for $125 through Priceline on an off night, getting a good deal on a bed in this city is a bit like playing roulette—you never know what the winning number will be. If you have your heart set on a particular neighborhood or hotel, by all means book it. But you're likely to save money if you shop around, check the discount hotel sites, and stay in neighborhoods less central than Union Square. *Tip:* If you visit a hotel booking site and then leave and return later, you may be offered a better price, and the same goes for individual hotels' websites.

problem? Such responses are indications that the hotel cares about the guest experience. It's also important to factor in the extras. Most folks simply look at the price when booking a room, without considering the value of the extras thrown in with a slightly more expensive place. Hotel Drisco is a perfect example (see p. 77). Many people might not even consider booking a room at this gorgeous and peaceful hotel because its rates start at about $400 per night. But when you factor in the extras—free parking (about a $50 value if you're hoping to park a car downtown), free weekday chauffeur service downtown (up to $20), free breakfast (they call it "continental" but the ample gourmet buffet with made-to-order espresso drinks is worth at least $40 per couple), excellent wine and hot appetizers in the evening (easily another $20 per couple), free bikes on loan, and free Wi-Fi—all of a sudden it's as if you're only paying around $200 for the room itself. For one of the finest boutique hotels in the country, that's an excellent deal. Whenever possible, we've tried to focus on hotels that offer free breakfast, cocktails, nibbles, parking, and Wi-Fi—it adds up.

**Stay in a hotel away from Fisherman's Wharf**—or SoMa, Nob Hill, or Union Square, for that matter. The advantages of staying in the popular tourist locations are overrated, particularly so when money is an issue. Muni buses and, especially, the historic F-line streetcars, can take you to most tourist sites in minutes. Your daily ride up and down Market Street on these old beauties will likely be a lovely lasting memory of your visit; even if you stay as far away as The Castro, you can be at the ferry launch for Alcatraz in about half an hour. You'll not only get the best value for your money by staying outside the tourist areas in the residential neighborhoods, you'll have a better overall experience: You won't be fighting crowds, you'll have terrific restaurants nearby, and you'll see what life in the city is really like. Lodgings in the Castro, Haight-Ashbury, Civic Center, the Marina, and Japantown offer particularly good savings.

**Visit over a weekend.** If your trip includes a weekend, you might be able to save big. Business hotels tend to empty out, and rooms that go for $400 or more Monday through Thursday can drop dramatically in cost, to as low as

4

WHERE TO STAY

How to Get the Best Deal

$200 or less, once the execs have headed home. These deals are especially prevalent in SoMa. Also, you'll find that Sunday nights are the least expensive throughout the city, except Fisherman's Wharf. Check hotels' websites for weekend specials, or just call and ask.

**Do what they do in Europe, and share a bathroom.** San Francisco is often said to be one of the most European-feeling cities in the U.S., so it's perhaps no surprise that several of its hotels have layouts that expect some guests to share bathrooms. What is the value of a private loo? In San Francisco, it's at least $100 per night. If the thought of sharing brings back dreaded memories of the high school locker room scene, don't worry; "sharing" usually means you can lock the door to the bathroom—as you would when visiting a friends' house. The bathroom simply won't be in your room, it will be down the hall, and will be used by fellow guests.

**Try the chains.** Since you probably know what you'll get with a Hyatt, Hilton, or Holiday Inn, in this chapter we have focused primarily on smaller, unknown, independent properties with character and a good local feel. That said, the big brand names are usually in good locations, and, depending on how booked they are, can offer great deals since they have loads of rooms. Most chain hotels let kids stay with parents for free using existing bedding and they accept loyalty points. Ask for every kind of discount; if you get an unhelpful reservation agent, call back, and try calling the local number. For your convenience, we have listed all of the major chains—including neighborhood, website, address, and local phone number, on p. 63.

**Avoid excess charges and hidden costs.** Little things add up big in hotels. If you're cash-conscious (and who isn't?) consider these strategies: Skip the minibar's drinks and snacks; use your cellphone or prepaid phone cards instead of pricy hotel phones; and look for hotels that offer free Wi-Fi. (And, if you use the hotel's Wi-Fi, make sure your smartphone is on it so you don't rack up excess data usage. For information about free Wi-Fi throughout the city, see p. 283.) When booking, ask hotels whether the quoted valet parking price includes tax, and whether larger vehicles rate an extra fee. If you decide not to use hotel parking, investigate parking rates—downtown rates are as high as $60 a day, and you may find better rates through parking websites (just search for "cheap San Francisco parking") than through hotels. Also, if a hotel insists upon tacking on an "energy surcharge" that wasn't mentioned at check-in, you can often make a case for getting it removed.

**Buy a money-saving package deal.** A travel package that combines your airfare and your hotel stay for one price may just be the best bargain of all. In some cases, you'll get airfare, accommodations, transportation to and from the airport, plus extras—maybe an afternoon sightseeing tour or restaurant and shopping discount coupons—for less than the hotel alone had you booked it yourself. Most airlines and many travel agents, as well as the usual booking websites (Priceline, Orbitz, Expedia, Travelocity) offer good packages to San Francisco.

# ALTERNATIVE ACCOMMODATIONS

**Consider private accommodations.** Thanks to companies like Airbnb, there are more and more varied options on where to stay than ever before. Now you can easily rent a bed, a room, or a whole house or apartment from a private owner. This type of accommodation is usually much cheaper than a hotel room, it allows you to meet a friendly local, and it places you in a residential neighborhood. One of the best companies to use for this type of booking is Airbnb.com, though many also turn to homeaway.com, flipkey.com, or bedandbreakfast.com. Be sure to read recent reviews; before booking, get all details in writing, including number (and type) of beds and an exact price for

---

## FINDING HOTEL DISCOUNTS online

Turn to the Internet to get deep discounts on hotels—and when you do, be sure to use the best hotel search engine. They're not all equal, as we at Frommers.com learned in 2017 after putting the top 20 sites to the test in 20 cities (including NYC) around the globe. We found that **Booking.com** found the lowest rates for hotels in the city center, and in the under-$200 range, 16 out of 20 times. And Booking.com includes all taxes and fees in its results (not all do, which can make for a frustrating shopping experience). For high-end properties, again in the city center only, both Priceline.com and HotelsCombined.com came up with the best rates, tying at 14 wins each.

There are three types of online deals to look out for:

1. **Extreme discounts on sites where you bid for lodgings without knowing which hotel you'll get.** You'll find these on such sites as **Priceline.com** and **Hotwire.com**, and they can be money-savers, particularly if you're booking within a week of travel (that's when the hotels resort to deep discounts to get beds filled). As these companies use only major chains, you can rest assured that you won't be put up in a dump. Before you bid, visit

**BiddingTraveler.com**, where actual travelers spill the beans about what they bid on Priceline.com and other sites and which hotels they got. You'll be surprised by the quality of many of the hotels that are offering these "secret" discounts.

2. **Discounts on a specific hotel's website.** Most hotels now reserve special discounts for travelers who book directly through the hotels' websites. These are usually the lowest rates on the hotels in question, though discounts can range widely, from as little as $1 to as much as $50. Our advice: Search for a hotel that's in your price range and ideal location and check the hotel website for deals before going to the general booking sites.

3. **Last-minute discounts.** Booking last-minute can be a great savings strategy, as prices sometimes drop in the week before travel as hoteliers scramble to fill their rooms. But you won't necessarily find the best savings through companies that claim to specialize in last-minute bookings. Instead, use the sites recommended above.

It's a lot of surfing, I know, but in the hothouse world of hotel pricing, this sort of diligence can pay off.

the stay, including applicable taxes and fees. And if you have pet allergies, be sure to ask if the room or house you'll be staying in has had canine or feline visitors.

**Try a home exchange.** There are three types of home exchanges: simultaneous (you stay in someone's house while they stay in yours), non-simultaneous (you stay at someone's home, no one stays in yours), and a hospitality exchange (you stay in someone's home while they are there). Sound like a weird new trend? **Homelink** (homelink.org), one of the premier home-exchange companies, has been in business for over 60 years. You can take a look for free, but once you're ready to join there is a membership fee of $50 to $152,

| Price Categories |
| --- |
| **Expensive:** $250 and up |
| **Moderate:** $150–$250 |
| **Inexpensive:** Under $150 |

depending on length of membership and whether you want to travel internationally. You'll be instantly connected with homeowners around the world.

I have never done a home exchange, but friends have, and they swear by it. They say that by the time the exchange happens, they have emailed and spoken on the phone with their exchange partners so often, they feel like old friends. Two more companies specializing in exchanges are **HomeExchange** (homeexchange.com), and **Intervac** (intervac.com). Most experts warn against using **Craigslist** for swaps due to problems with scammers. The clubs that charge a fee—and all those listed above do—are able to weed out the ne'er-do-wells with their screening processes.

# UNION SQUARE

While the actual "square" is a single block, bordered by Powell, Post, Stockton, and Geary streets, the name also refers to the immediate neighborhood, so a "Union Square hotel" may be a few blocks away from the square itself. The draw to this area is multifold: As the heart of bustling downtown San Francisco, it boasts the city's largest number of hotels and the highest concentration of department stores and boutiques. It's also convenient to a lot of interesting neighborhoods, including SoMa, Chinatown, and North Beach (as well as Fisherman's Wharf and the less-intriguing, workaday Financial District). While most of the area's restaurants aren't exciting enough to lure locals, they are in abundance. One undesirable factor that comes with a downtown stay is exposure to a lot of homeless people lingering outside shops, asking for change, and perhaps muttering to themselves or doing hard drugs. That's a saddening factor of urban life, but these people tend to be harmless.

## Expensive

**Hotel Triton ★** This hotel has just as much funky character and personality as San Francisco itself. Wild, colorful murals cover the lobby, employees

# Union Square, Nob Hill & SoMa Hotels

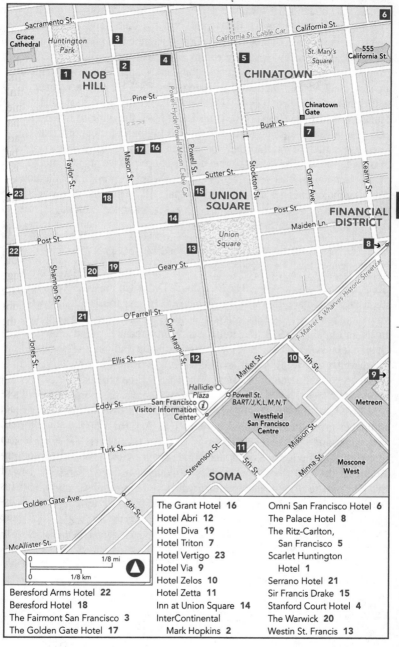

The Grant Hotel **16**
Hotel Abri **12**
Hotel Diva **19**
Hotel Triton **7**
Hotel Vertigo **23**
Hotel Via **9**
Hotel Zelos **10**
Hotel Zetta **11**
Inn at Union Square **14**
InterContinental
   Mark Hopkins **2**

Omni San Francisco Hotel **6**
The Palace Hotel **8**
The Ritz-Carlton,
   San Francisco **5**
Scarlet Huntington
   Hotel **1**
Serrano Hotel **21**
Sir Francis Drake **15**
Stanford Court Hotel **4**
The Warwick **20**
Westin St. Francis **13**

Beresford Arms Hotel **22**
Beresford Hotel **18**
The Fairmont San Francisco **3**
The Golden Gate Hotel **17**

wear their own clothes instead of uniforms, and the evening wine reception occasionally features poetry and tarot card readings. Using bright colors and an eclectic collection of furniture, Hotel Triton does a good job making you forget that the rooms are a little small and the bathrooms positively tiny. Entertainers such as comedian Kathy Griffin and the late great musician Jerry Garcia designed a few specialty rooms, complete with original watercolors painted by Garcia. Another specialty room, the Häagen-Dazs Sweet Suite, has an ice-cream theme, including a custom-designed ice-cream cabinet filled with pints of assorted flavors. The location, on the border of chic Union Square and historic Chinatown, is also a draw at this vibrant hotel. On one side you have the upscale luxury shops and high-end restaurants that Union Square is famed for; on the other, through the gates and under the red lanterns of old Chinatown you'll find simple noodle shops and tea stands and old men mixing ancient recipes with Chinese herbs. *Note:* At press time, the hotel is planning major changes and renovations that will be put into effect in 2018.

342 Grant Ave. (at Bush St.). hoteltriton.com. ✆ **415/394-0500.** 140 units. $179–$359 double; $289–$559 suite. Rates include morning tea and coffee and an evening wine reception in the lobby. Parking $58. Pets welcome ($100). Bus: 3, 8, 30, 35. Streetcar: All Market St. lines. Cable car: All 3 lines. **Amenities:** Cafe; restaurant; 24-hr. fitness center; business center; room service; concierge; free Wi-Fi.

### Sir Francis Drake ★★

The Sir Francis Drake isn't just a luxurious hotel, it's a city landmark that's as much beloved by the locals for its sweeping views and retro-swanky bars as it is by visitors for the royal treatment it offers. In operation since 1928, the Renaissance architecture, grand lobby, ornate chandeliers, swirling staircases, and British pomp and circumstance seem to pre-date the city itself. Upon arrival, the fully costumed Beefeater doormen will help you with your bags, setting the tone for the type of service you can expect at this regal hotel. As with most vintage hotels, the rooms are small and well-loved, but they're also filled with rich wood furnishings, and the striped wallpaper gives them a plush, European feel. Ask for a higher floor for the best views and quieter rooms. Even if you don't stay here, the hotel is still worth a visit. Pop in for a drink and gorgeous city views from **The Starlight Room** on the 21st floor. The Starlight's totally awesome "Sunday's a Drag Brunch," where drag queens perform while you sip mimosas and nibble on omelets, is also a classic San Francisco experience worth looking into.

450 Powell St. (at Sutter St.). sirfrancisdrake.com. ✆ **415/392-7755.** 416 units. $205–$400 double; $400–$1,200 suite. Rates include evening social hour in the lobby. Valet parking $59. Pets free. Bus: 2, 3, 8, 30. Streetcar: All Market St. lines. Cable car: Powell-Hyde and Powell-Mason. BART: Powell St. **Amenities:** 2 restaurants; bar; concierge; fitness center; free Wi-Fi.

### Westin St. Francis ★

If you're looking for a hotel exuding classic San Francisco elegance, the Westin St. Francis delivers, with its massive lobby, crown molding, marble columns, and iconic Magneta Grandfather Clock. Built in 1904 by railroad magnate Charles Crocker and his wealthy friends

# NAME-BRAND hotels

Because this is a pocket guidebook with limited space, I've focused on independent hotels that offer uniquely San Francisco experiences (or really great deals). On the other hand, many readers alleviate the cost of travel with free stays through hotel loyalty programs, so you'll find the following list of name-brand hotels, in all price ranges (here I list an average rate, but you may often be able to find a lower price). Just so you know, the hotels in the Civic Center, while indeed centrally located, are in an area that has a large homeless population. Check online reviews before you book so you know what to expect.

**Hyatt** (hyatt.com)
- Hyatt Regency **FiDi** ($379), 5 Embarcadero Center, ℂ **415/788-1234**
- **Fisherman's Wharf** ($399), 555 North Point St., ℂ **415/563-1234**
- **Union Square** Grand Hyatt ($289), 345 Stockton St., ℂ **415/398-1234**

**Marriott** (marriott.com)
- Courtyard **Downtown** ($249), 299 Second St., ℂ **415/947-0700**
- **Fisherman's Wharf** ($279), 1250 Columbus Ave., ℂ **415/775-7555**
- Courtyard **Fisherman's Wharf** ($299), 580 Beach St., ℂ **415/775-3800**
- Marquis **SoMa** ($199), 780 Mission St., ℂ **415/896-1600**
- JW Marriott **Union Square** ($279), 515 Mason St., ℂ **415/771-8600**
- **Union Square** ($249), 480 Sutter St., ℂ **415/398-8900**

**Starwood** (starwoodhotels.com)
- Le Meridien **Embarcadero** ($339), 333 Battery St., ℂ **415/296-2900**
- Sheraton **Fisherman's Wharf** ($299), 2500 Mason St., ℂ **415/362-5500**

- St. Regis **SoMa** ($545), 125 Third St., ℂ **415/284-4000**
- W San Francisco **SoMa** ($359), 181 Third St., ℂ **415/777-5300**
- The Park Central (**SoMa**) ($237), 50 Third St., ℂ **415/974-6400**
- Westin St. Francis **Union Square** ($300), 335 Powell St., ℂ **415/397-7000**

**Hilton** (hilton.com)
- **FiDi** ($275), 750 Kearney St., ℂ **415/433-6600**
- **Union Square** ($269), 333 O'Farrell St., ℂ **415/771-1400**

**Holiday Inn** (holidayinn.com)
- **Civic Center** ($207), 50 Eighth St., ℂ **415/626-6103**
- Express **Fisherman's Wharf** ($227), 550 North Point St., ℂ **415/409-4600**
- **Fisherman's Wharf** ($247), 1300 Columbus Ave., ℂ **415/771-9000**
- SF- **Golden Gateway** ($174), 1500 Van Ness Ave., ℂ **415/441-4000**

**Travelodge** (travelodge.com)
- SF Central (**Castro**) ($158), 1707 Market St., ℂ **415/621-6775**
- **Fisherman's Wharf** ($179), 1201 Columbus Ave., ℂ **415/776-7070**
- By the Bay (**Fort Mason**) ($184), 1450 Lombard St., ℂ **415/673-0691**
- **Presidio** ($233), 2755 Lombard St., ℂ **415/931-8581**

**Days Inn** (daysinn.com)
- **Civic Center** ($167), 465 Grove St., ℂ **415/864-4040**
- **Lombard/Marina** ($170), 2358 Lombard St., ℂ **415/922-2010**

(see "The Big Four & the Bonanza Kings," p. 133), the St. Francis has hosted a who's who of world-famous celebrities including Helen Keller, Charlie Chaplin, Douglas Fairbanks, Mary Pickford, Queen Elizabeth, Mother Teresa, and a number of U.S. presidents. The Westin comprises two buildings:

The historic Landmark Building fronts the square, while the 32-story Tower Building, built in 1972, features larger rooms and bathrooms with a sleeker aesthetic. Floor-to-ceiling windows offer views of the city on higher floors. The St. Francis is especially lovely around the holidays, when executive pastry chef Jean-Francois Houdre unveils an elaborate sugar castle or an entire village, and Union Square's Christmas tree can be viewed from most rooms. While you'll find the best food elsewhere, there's something for everyone at this hotel's restaurants, from casual fare in the lobby at Caruso's to the classic American menu at the Oak Room. You'll also find creative cocktails and gourmet bar bites at Clock Bar and wine tasting at Chateau Montelena.

335 Powell St. (btw. Geary and Post sts.). westinstfrancis.com. ℂ **415/397-7000.** 1,195 units. $199–$699 double; $299–$4,999 suite. Children stay free w/parents when using existing beds. Valet parking $62 and up. Bus: 2, 3, 8, 30, 45. Streetcar: All Market St. lines. Cable car: Powell-Hyde and Powell-Mason. BART: Powell St. Pets under 40 lb. welcome. **Amenities:** 2 restaurants; concierge; fitness studio; room service, Wi-Fi ($15 per day).

## Moderate

**Hotel Abri** ★★ Originally an apartment building, this hotel is more than 100 years old, but the interior is pure 21st century, making this boutique one of the best spots for anyone seeking a stylish urban crash pad central to Union Square shopping. Public areas are inviting, with architectural art and lounge music in the lobby, a relaxed bar, and a sitting area with high-backed mid-century leather chairs and a fireplace, although they seem to be more quick stopovers than places people actually linger. Still, rooms feel posh, and the updated bathrooms allow you to enjoy tons of storage space as well as new bathtubs. Suites include a sitting area with a pullout sofa bed and a desk. Alas, you won't find all the big-hotel amenities here, such as room service or a fitness center, but right next door there's **Puccini & Pinetti,** a lively, family-friendly, just-okay restaurant and bar that serves Italian food (with a great happy-hour deal from 3–6pm) in a spacious, comfortable setting. As with all hotels in this area, guests should exercise caution at night, as the area can get a little dicey.

127 Ellis St. (btw. Cyril Magnin and Powell sts.). hotelabrisf.com. ℂ **415/392-8800.** 91 units. $169–$299 double; $299–$399 suite. Rates include morning coffee and tea. Valet parking $60. Bus: 38, 27, 45. Streetcar: All Market St. lines. Cable car: Powell-Hyde and Powell-Mason. BART: Powell St. **Amenities:** Business center; restaurant; free Wi-Fi.

**Hotel Diva** ★★ Despite a modest entryway, this cute boutique hotel will pleasantly surprise you, with decorative touches such as custom shades featuring burlesque images, and sleek, steel headboards that set a hip, modern tone. Adults can enjoy signature cocktail shots every evening, while kids will go wild for the one-of-a-kind Little Divas Suite—a completely tricked-out room featuring bunk beds, a computer, toys, games, and more. (Parents stay in the adjoining room.) Restaurants, galleries, and high-end stores are all close by, as are the cable cars and historic F-line streetcars.

440 Geary St. (btw. Mason and Taylor sts.). hoteldiva.com. ✆ **415/885-0200.** 116 units. $199–$470 double; $470–$700 suite. Valet parking $55 and up. Dogs welcome ($50). Bus: 2, 3 8, 27, 38, 45. Streetcar: All Market St. lines. Cable car: Powell–Mason and Powell–Hyde lines. BART: Powell St. **Amenities:** Concierge; restaurant; 24-hr. fitness center; 24-hr. business center; free Wi-Fi.

**Hotel Vertigo** ★   Hitchcock buffs might recognize this small, mid-range hotel from his movie *Vertigo*—it was here that Kim Novak's character stood gazing out the bay window in her green dress. Today, the hotel embraces its cinematic history, with both rooms and lobby featuring mid-century furnishings, the signature tangerine-and-white colors from the movie's promotional materials, and wall art inspired by *Vertigo*'s dizzying spiral motif. The film plays on a loop in the lobby, so you're sure to catch a glimpse of the fabulous Kim Novak, as the object of Jimmy Stewart's obsession. If you're not into the ornate aesthetic of many Victorian hotels in the area, you'll appreciate Vertigo's bold simplicity.

940 Sutter St. (btw. Leavenworth and Hyde sts.). hotelvertigosf.com. ✆ **415/885-6800.** 110 units. $149–$499 double; $224–$650 suite. Rates include morning coffee and tea in lobby. Parking available in 2 garages 1 block away. Bus: 2, 3, 27, 38. Cable car: All lines. **Amenities:** Fitness center; business center; free Wi-Fi.

**Inn at Union Square** ★★   Completely renovated in 2017 and now boasting a sleek, updated 1950s mod-style, this small boutique hotel sits right next to Union Square. It also offers all of the amenities you'd expect from a large hotel combined with the personal attention of an inn small enough for the staff to actually remember your name. If you're feeling flush, book the Alma Spreckels Suite, designed in honor of the late, great (she was over 6 ft. tall!) San Francisco philanthropist who was the model for the Goddess of Victory statue atop the Dewey Monument in Union Square. Morton's Steak House, located next door, provides the room service. A complimentary continental breakfast and hosted evening wine hour are just two of the perks found here.

440 Post St. (btw. Powell and Mason sts.). unionsquare.com. ✆ **415/397-3510.** 30 units. $209–$300 double; $289–$399 junior suite, $349–$600 suite. Rates include continental breakfast and evening wine and cheese reception. Valet parking $53 and up. Bus: 2, 3, 8, 30, 45. Streetcar: All Market St. lines. Cable car: Powell-Hyde and Powell-Mason. BART: Powell St. **Amenities:** Room service from Morton's Steak House; access to Active fitness center ($18/day); free Wi-Fi.

**Serrano Hotel** ★★   Located at the intersection of tourist action and local hangouts, this beautifully appointed hotel bathed in warm gold and red boasts amenities and luxury not usually available at a boutique urban hotel. The stunning lobby is a registered historic landmark and features intricately painted and carved ceilings and the original 1926 chandeliers. At press time, plans were on track for a full (but gradual—the hotel won't close) renovation to be completed in early 2018. Request a room with a view—rooms on higher floors boast views from Union Square to Twin Peaks. While there is no room service, the adjoined Jasper's Corner Tap & Kitchen offers breakfast, lunch, and dinner. It's a fun place to grab a beer—they have 18 on tap—or dinner, where upscale bar bites and progressive American cuisine are served tapas-style. There's even a late-night menu, so you surely won't go hungry, especially if you indulge in their Mighty Duck Poutine.

405 Taylor St. (at O'Farrell St.). serranohotel.com. ✆ **415/885-2500.** 236 units. $159–$300 double; $349–$1,000 suite. Rates include morning coffee and tea in lobby. Valet parking $58 and up. Pets welcome. Bus 2, 3, 27, 38, 45. Streetcar: All Market St. lines. Cable car: Powell–Mason and Powell–Hyde lines. BART: Powell St. **Amenities:** Restaurant; 24-hr. business center; 24-hr. fitness center; free Wi-Fi.

**The Warwick** ★ A reliable choice in the theater district, which is still very close to Union Square, this boutique hotel upped its understated-opulence game with a complete makeover, from its rooms to its restaurant, and you can see why its motto is "authentic history, modern hospitality." The hotel has magically maintained its sense of timeless luxury with furnishings that combine turn-of-the-century and modern styles. Attractive accommodations in a blue-and-grey palette feature new everything, including the suites' spacious bathrooms with walk-in marble showers. Downstairs, the hotel's bar and lounge, The European, is a fun place to start your night with a craft cocktail in front of the fireplace, and the hotel' restaurant, BOTA, features Spanish tapas and paella. *Tip:* Book directly with the hotel, instead of a third party, to get the best rates.

490 Geary St. (btw. Mason and Taylor sts.). warwicksf.com. ✆ **415/928-7900.** 74 units. $199–$399 double; $249–$1,299 suite. Parking $52 and up. Bus: 2, 3, 27, 30, 38, 45. Streetcar: All Market St. lines. Cable car: Powell–Hyde and Powell–Mason. BART: Powell St. **Amenities:** Restaurant; bar; access to nearby health club ($15/day); room service; free Wi-Fi.

## Inexpensive

**Beresford Arms Hotel** ★★★ As a low-cost hotel in the stylish Nob Hill neighborhood, the Beresford Arms is an especially good choice for large families or groups: A family of up to seven can stay in a two-bedroom suite with a full kitchen, including a complimentary continental breakfast, afternoon wine, cheese, and cookies, for around $210—a practically unheard-of deal. Listed on the National Register of Historic Places, the public areas have a '20s feel, complete with parlor furniture, white columns, elegant chandeliers, and a grandfather clock. The regular rooms are also large, and all suites—not just the two-bedrooms—have a kitchenette or wet bar. The downsides: It's a little dated, a little noisy, there's no air-conditioning (although in San Francisco you'll almost never need it), and the beds are not the most comfortable. The property's sister hotel, **Beresford Hotel ★,** at 635 Sutter St. (beresford.com; ✆ **415/673-9900;** $89–$165 double, extra person $15), is another budget option in an old Victorian serving free continental breakfast, but the rooms there are downright tiny and basic. Still, if all you're looking for is a crash pad, the price is right.

701 Post St. (at Jones St.). beresford.com. (C) **415/673-2600.** 95 units. $159–$209 double. Parlor suite $210. Rates include continental breakfast, afternoon wine and tea. Valet parking $40 and up. Pets welcome ($25), dependent on availability. Bus: 2, 3, 27, 30, 38, 45. Cable car: Powell–Hyde and Powell–Mason. **Amenities:** Access to nearby health club ($10/day); free Wi-Fi.

# NOB HILL

Topping out at 376 feet, Nob Hill is the tallest hill in downtown San Francisco, surpassing Telegraph and Russian hills by nearly 100 feet. Railroad and mining barons began to build their mansions on the hill in the late 1870s, and the area has been posh ever since. A few very steep blocks away from Union Square, it's also where most of the city's finer veteran hotels are perched. (See "The Historic Hotels of Nob Hill," p. 68.)

## Expensive

**The Ritz-Carlton, San Francisco ★★★**   Superior service, stately environs, an abundance of amenities, and the Ritz reputation make this luxury stalwart the premier choice for most dignitaries and celebrities. Rooms are spacious and well appointed, although bathrooms in some of the smaller accommodations are surprisingly basic. Guest amenities include an outstanding fitness center and spa. The casual restaurant, **Parallel 37,** offers decent farmers' market–driven American cuisine. The **Lounge** is the place to be during spring and winter holidays for legendary afternoon tea service, and for a drink or a quick bite year-round. If you're here in December with a tot in tow, don't miss the teddy bear tea. The price is steep, but the experience—and the free plush bear—make it worthwhile.

600 Stockton St. (at California St.). ritzcarlton.com. (C) **415/296-7465.** 336 units. Doubles from $335–$668; $359–$1,100 suite. Buffet breakfast $39. Parking $65. Pet-friendly for dogs under 10 lb. Bus: 8, 30, 45. Cable car: California St. **Amenities:** 2 restaurants; 2 bars; concierge; fitness center; spa; room service; in-room Wi-Fi $15 per day, free in bar and lobby areas.

## Moderate

**Omni San Francisco Hotel ★**   Italian marble, crystal chandeliers, and rich wood paneling in the lobby set the elegant tone in this award-winning hotel. Flanked by city skyscrapers, it's located at the base of Nob Hill near the Financial District on iconic California Street, where cable cars roll up the steep incline. The hotel boasts ballrooms, a health center, and a popular steakhouse, and has all the trappings of a luxury Omni hotel—spacious rooms, sheets with a high thread count, all the expected amenities. However, its location gears it a bit more to the business trip rather than the family vacation or

# THE HISTORIC HOTELS OF nob hill

When writer and poet Robert Louis Stevenson visited the city in 1879, he dubbed San Francisco's Nob Hill "the Hill of Palaces," and that has remained an apt description to this day. The grand hotels that sit atop Nob Hill today were born of the fierce competition between millionaire businessmen (see "The Big Four & the Bonanza Kings" on p. 133) to see who could build the largest, most lavish mansion—all of which burned to the ground after the 1906 fire and earthquake. Their names live on, however, in these luxury lodgings.

On the site where railroad president Leland Stanford erected his mansion, you'll find the **Stanford Court Hotel** ★ (905 California St. at Powell St.; stanfordcourt.com; ℂ **415/989-3500;** 393 units; $204–$556.) Compared to its luxury-minded Nob Hill neighbors below, the Stanford Court describes itself as a hotel where "high-tech meets high style," appealing to business travelers with a newly renovated business center in 2017. There is also complimentary Wi-Fi and a 24-hour fitness center. There is no room service, but this hotel is a comfortable option in a great location.

Stanford's wheeler-dealer partner Colis P. Huntington had his home where Huntington Park now stands, at California and Taylor streets, but he also has a Nob Hill hotel named in his honor: the **Scarlet Huntington Hotel** ★ (1075 California St. btw. Mason and Taylor sts.; huntingtonhotel.com; ℂ **415/474-5400;** 134 units; $329–$629), which added "Scarlet" to its name after a $15-million renovation in 2014. The makeover lent a much-needed modernization to the guest rooms, complete with new bathrooms adorned with hand-carved vanities and marble showers, and made improvements to the public spaces with Asian-inspired touches and a new color scheme featuring rich jewel tones accented with gold. Rooms are large and tastefully decorated; the lobby is small and elegant. The hotel restaurant, suitably named **The Big Four** (big4restaurant.com; ℂ **415/474-5400**), is a veritable museum commemorating the railroad barons who so grandly settled Nob Hill; its upscale chicken pot pie seems designed to please any ravenous railroad barons who decide to drop in for a bite.

At the former address of railroad's treasurer Mark Hopkins, you can sleep at the

romantic getaway. But families are certainly welcome; when they arrive, kids receive complimentary backpacks filled with art supplies and other surprises.

500 California St. (at Montgomery St.). omnihotels.com/FindAHotel/sanfrancisco.aspx. ℂ **415/677-9494.** 362 units. $189–$799 double; $399–$1,500 suite. Valet parking $55 and up. Dogs up to 20 lb. welcome ($100 fee). Bus: 1, 3, 8, 30, 41. Streetcar: All Market St. lines. Cable car: California St. **Amenities:** Restaurant and bar; 24-hr. health club; business center; in-room fitness kits and treadmills (select rooms); free guided walking tour every Sat; kid's program with free milk and cookies; 24-hr. room service; Wi-Fi in room $15/day.

## Inexpensive

**The Golden Gate Hotel** ★ Staying at this homey, tranquil spot is like visiting Grandma's house—quaint, friendly, and filled with antiques. There's

**InterContinental Mark Hopkins** ★★ (1 Nob Hill at California and Mason sts.; intercontinentalmarkhopkins.com; *C* 415/392-3434; $199–$500; pets up to 25 lb. welcome for $50). The lobby is part French chateau, part Italian Renaissance, with high ceilings, light-drenched sitting areas, and ornate chandeliers. The rooms and suites, all with city views, feature rich woods and fine fabrics, though they are on the smaller side thanks to the Victorian architecture style. While steeped in history, the hotel has added modern touches to its farm-to-table restaurant and lounge, **Nob Hill Club,** which offers a self-serve espresso bar that uses touch screens to deliver the goods. Enjoy grab-and-go pastries from the bakery or sit down to a daily breakfast buffet amid the aubergine-colored walls, high-backed chairs, and gold details. The hotel's real jewel, however, is the famous **Top of the Mark** restaurant on the 19th floor, where locals and visitors alike go to soak in the 360-degree views. *Tip:* Go for the champagne brunch on Sundays, when the food (and service) tends to be a bit more on point.

Last but not least is the **Fairmont San Francisco** ★★★ (950 Mason St. at California St.; fairmont.com/sanfrancisco; *C* **415/772-5000;** 606 units; $399–$899). Originally built to honor mining magnate James Fair, it was extensively rebuilt after the quake. Perched atop Nob Hill a steep but quick jaunt from Union Square and Chinatown, the majestic Fairmont is the hotel of choice if you're looking for classic San Francisco elegance and flavor. After a $21-million refreshment of its rooms in 2014, the decor is contemporary and fresh with custom furnishings and hand-blown glass lamps (the large marble bathrooms are still intact). But it's the common areas that make this hotel extra special. The lobby, with its vaulted ceilings and gold-trimmed Corinthian columns, begs to be your selfie background, especially during the winter holidays when it adds a neck-craning Christmas tree, kid-friendly tea service, and walk-thru gingerbread house. Downstairs, no one (including us) can get enough of the hotel's kitschy-fabulous **Tonga Room & Hurricane Bar** (p. 216), where Asian fusion food, umbrella drinks, tiki huts, and the occasional "thunder storm" surround a centerpiece pool with a live band playing on a little pontoon boat floating in its middle.

even a ginger cat on staff that goes by the titles "Feline Overlord" and "Room Service Cuddle Provider." Rooms are tiny, decorated with floral curtains and wallpaper, but there's a European charm to this B&B. Coffee, tea, juice, and croissants are served in the parlor each morning and homemade cookies each afternoon. The family-run staff is helpful, and it's an easy walk to Union Square, Chinatown, and Nob Hill.

775 Bush St. (btw. Powell and Mason sts.). goldengatehotel.com. *C* **415/392-3702.** 23 units. Double from $150 (w/shared bathroom), from $225 (w/private bathroom). Rates include continental breakfast, afternoon tea and cookies. Parking $30. Pets allowed, with fee. Bus: 2, 3, 8, 30, 45. Cable car: All 3 lines. **Amenities:** Concierge; free Wi-Fi.

**The Grant Hotel** ★  Choose this lower Nob Hill crash pad if all you care about is an awesome location and basic but clean accommodations. Minutes away from Union Square yet far from Tenderloin sketchiness, the Grant is a rare find. Its bedspreads are dated, the bathrooms are tiny, and there's no air-conditioning (though that's almost never an issue in this temperate town). But the price is right, especially if you're here to enjoy the city, not the room. Complimentary continental breakfast is served in the lobby, where there is a spacious seating area. There's a 24-hour front desk person, but don't expect him to be your travel agent. This is bare bones at its best.

753 Bush St. (btw. Mason and Powell sts.). granthotel.net. ✆ **415/421-7540.** 76 units. $129–$200 double. Rates include continental breakfast. Children under 18 stay free if using existing beds. Garage parking across street $26/night with hotel validation. Bus: 2, 3, 8, 30, 45. Cable car: Powell–Hyde and Powell–Mason. Streetcar: All Market St. lines. **Amenities:** Free Wi-Fi.

# SOMA & SOUTH BEACH

SoMa, which stands for South of Market, starts only a few blocks away from Union Square, stretches for several long blocks toward the Mission District, and gives way to what is now called South Beach, the newest happening area located just north of Third Street toward the bay. Both areas offer an eclectic mix of lodgings, from some of the highest thread counts in the city to budget motels. Hotels are generally located near the Moscone convention center, the Museum of Modern Art, the Yerba Buena Center for the Arts, and AT&T Park.

## Expensive

**Hotel Via** ★★  This sleek, brand-new-from-the-ground-up boutique hotel has a lot to offer. For one thing, it's directly across the street from AT&T Park, home to the San Francisco Giants and host to performances by Beyoncé, Lady Gaga, James Taylor, and more. The rooftop bar, reserved for guests of the hotel (that may change once they've been open for a while), offers 360-degree views of the ballpark, bay, and downtown and ultra-modern yet comfy chaise lounges and seating areas, with fire pits placed strategically throughout. The rooms are bright and comfortable, with modern, custom-designed furniture and amenities, although there's not a lot of privacy with the sliding glass bathroom door (when fully closed, it still leaves a gap of about an inch or so). While families are welcome, this hotel is definitely geared more toward a young, hip crowd looking to catch a game and a cocktail, either on the rooftop or at Bar Via on the ground floor, which serves signature cocktails, small bites, and floor-to-ceiling windows so you can see and be seen. Breakfast is available in the brightly lit basement cafe each morning from 6:30 to 10am, but with so many excellent restaurants and coffeehouses nearby, you might prefer to explore. Be sure to ask for a room with a view of the ballpark.

138 King St. (btw. 2nd and 3rd sts.). hotelviasf.com. ✆ **415/200-4977.** 159 units. $209–$400 double; $350–$749 suite. Valet parking $55 and up. Bus: 10, 30, 45, 47. Streetcar: T. **Amenities:** Restaurant; bar; 24-hr. fitness center; business center; room service; free Wi-Fi.

# THE most FAMILY-FRIENDLY HOTELS

**Argonaut Hotel** (p. 73)   Close to all the funky kid fun of Fisherman's Wharf and the National Maritime Museum, this bayside hotel also has kid-friendly perks like board games, PG movies, a Wii system in the lobby, and the chance for each child to grab a gift from the hotel's "treasure chest."

**Beresford Arms Hotel** (p. 66)   The Parlor Suite can sleep up to a family of seven and comes with a full kitchen and dining room—all for around $299. The Junior Suite sleeps six and costs around $259. Located a few blocks from Union Square, this Victorian charmer is perfect for families on a budget wanting a little extra space.

**Fairmont San Francisco** (p. 69)   While the glamorous lobby and spectacular Nob Hill city views delight parents, the whole family will be thrilled by the hotel's **Tonga Room,** a fantastically kitsch tropical bar and restaurant where "rain" falls every 30 minutes.

**Hotel Del Sol** (p. 78)   It's as colorful as a box of crayons, but tots are more likely to be impressed by the VIP treatment they'll receive. With a lending library, toys and movies, evening cookies and milk, a heated pool, and a nearby park, what's not to love?

**Hotel Diva** (p. 64)   The sleek, mod Diva has all sorts of fun, kid-friendly perks.

Check out SF's version of the Walk of Fame right outside the door, and definitely ask about their two-room Little Divas Suite, with bunk beds, drawing tables, and a TV loaded with kids' movies.

**Ritz-Carlton** (p. 67)   The Ritz's Very Important Kid program offers a kid-size in-room tent, coloring books, and milk and cookies at turndown.

**Seal Rock Inn** (p. 78)   The Seal Rock's setting—surrounded by parks, across the street from the beach, and just a few minutes from the San Francisco Zoo (see p. 155)—is a real draw, as are the hotel's suites with kitchenettes.

**Stanyan Park Hotel** (p. 84)   Plenty of elbow room and a half-block walk to Golden Gate Park's Children's Playground make this admittedly dated hotel in the Haight a prime budget spot for crashing family-style. The biggest bonuses are the suites, which come with one or two bedrooms, a full kitchen, and a dining area.

**Westin St. Francis** (p. 62)   A classic San Francisco hotel down to its hospitality, the Westin welcomes little ones with gifts and toys, including coloring books and crayons. Kids love riding in the glass elevators, and the bustle of Union Square is right outside the front door.

## Moderate

**Hotel Zelos** ★★   Formerly Hotel Palomar, this boutique property may have changed its name but it hasn't changed its star attraction—Dirty Habit, a hip bar/restaurant tucked away on the fifth floor, boasting a cool terrace with heat lamps and a fire pit, craft cocktails, and fresh, seasonal menus for breakfast and dinner (it's closed for lunch, but available for private functions midday). The great location is just minutes away from Union Square (though technically South of Market), close to the convention center, museums, and tons of shopping, and it draws visitors traveling for both business and pleasure. The hotel itself was remodeled in 2014, which gave the lobby an elegant chandelier, Art Deco touches, and modern art. Rooms are on the large size for the area and bathrooms offer plenty of counter space. If you plan on sleeping in, avoid rooms on the fifth floor as they pick up the restaurant noise.

12 4th St. (at Market St.). hotelzelos.com. ℭ **415/348-1111.** $189–$500 double; $300–$1,200 suite. Rates include morning coffee and tea in lobby. Valet parking $55 and up. Pets stay free. Bus: 8, 27, 30, 45. Streetcar: All Market St. lines. Cable car: Powell–Hyde or Powell–Mason. **Amenities:** Restaurant; fitness center; business center; in-room spa services (surcharge); free Wi-Fi.

**Hotel Zetta ★** Sleek, masculine, and trendy, with an L.A. sensibility, this hotel embodies the "work hard, play hard" ethic of San Francisco's young professionals, providing a proverbial adult playground for the tech crowd. For starters, it has a highly interactive lobby, complete with a Plinko Game and a playroom featuring a pool table, shuffleboard, and video games—and if you need to really get away, step into Exit Reality, a virtual reality booth. Guest rooms start at a spacious 250 square feet and feature large butcher-block desks, pillow-top mattresses, smart TVs, and illy espresso machines; the roomy bathrooms feature mosaic-tiled walk-in showers. The sexy lobby bar and comfy-cool Cavalier restaurant are both worth a visit (try the potted Dungeness crab).

55 5th St. (btw. Minna and Market sts.). viceroyhotelgroup.com/en/zetta. ℭ **415/543-8555.** 116 units. $249–$399 double; $449–$699 suite. Valet parking $62 and up. Pets welcome ($75). Bus: 8, 14, 27, 45. Streetcar: All Market St. lines. Cable car: Powell–Hyde or Powell–Mason **Amenities:** Restaurant; bar; fitness center; game room; free Wi-Fi.

**The Palace Hotel ★★★** Enter the Palace Hotel and its stunning Garden Court and you might think you've stepped into a Parisian castle. Marble columns and massive chandeliers, crowned by an atrium of over 80,000 panes of stained glass, will take your breath away. While completely rebuilt after the 1906 earthquake, its history dates back to 1875 when it was considered the largest, most expensive hotel in the world. For a historic hotel, the rooms are a good size (even the least expensive standard rooms have enough space for a comfy chair to relax in and a desk set). The surprisingly high ceilings help give the illusion that rooms are a little larger. A stately hotel of this magnitude wouldn't be complete without plenty of options to eat and imbibe, and the Palace delivers. Enjoy breakfast, lunch, or afternoon tea on Saturdays (Mon–Sat btw. Thanksgiving and Christmas), and Sunday brunch in the Garden Court, which doubles as the only indoor historic landmark in the city. Or cozy up to the swanky Pied Piper, where you can sip an expertly crafted classic cocktail or dine on upscale American cuisine, while gazing at the $3-million Pied Piper mural that hangs behind the bar.

2 New Montgomery St. (at Market St.). sfpalace.com. ℭ **415/512-1111.** 556 units. $249–$799 double; $449–$5,000 suite. Parking $59 and up. Pets up to 80 lb. welcome ($100). Bus: 30, 45. Streetcar: All Market St. lines. **Amenities:** 2 restaurants; 2 bars; health club w/pool and Jacuzzi; 24-hr. room service; concierge; Wi-Fi (free in lobby, $20/day in-room).

# NORTH BEACH & FISHERMAN'S WHARF

The birthplace of the Beat Generation, North Beach is where Little Italy meets and mixes with neighboring Chinatown. You'll find an energetic mix of authentic Italian trattorias, bakeries, and delicatessens on one side, and bars, historic bookstores, and topless clubs (mostly on one block, at the northern edge of the area) on the other. It also borders the busy Fisherman's Wharf area, with all its kitschy-fun "attractions" and activities.

## Expensive

**Argonaut Hotel ★★★**  If you want to stay in a beautiful, historic building and walk right out your door into the heart of Fisherman's Wharf action—and are willing to pay for the privilege—this nautical-themed hotel is perfect for you. Located in the historic Haslett warehouse and cannery built in 1908, guest rooms are done up in navy and beige and decorated with tasteful maritime knickknacks. Kids love the treasure chest at the front desk and the Wii game system in the lobby, plus Ghirardelli ice cream is just around the corner. You'll find the lobby lounge warm and welcoming, with a fireplace, plush red chairs, and all sorts of naval paraphernalia mounted on the walls, such as maps, compasses, and wooden steering wheels. The nautical theme carries over to the Blue Mermaid Restaurant, which underwent a full renovation in 2017. You don't even need to leave the hotel to soak up San Francisco's seafaring past— located off the lobby is an interactive museum that both kids and adults will love, a feature that has made this spot a historical national landmark since the '70s.

495 Jefferson St. (at Hyde St.). argonauthotel.com. ✆ **415/563-0800.** 252 units. $179–$379 double; $358–$649 suite. Parking $59 and up. Pets welcome ($75). Bus: 30 or 47. Streetcar: F. Cable car: Powell–Hyde. **Amenities:** Restaurant; bar; 24-hr. fitness center; business center; concierge; in-room spa services; room service; free Wi-Fi.

## Moderate

**The Hotel Bohème ★**  Located in the center of North Beach restaurant and cafe activity, this historic boutique hotels harnesses the bohemian culture that dominated North Beach back when Beat poet Allen Ginsberg hung his hat at this very hotel. This sweet spot with rooms up a flight of stairs (no elevator) is painted in colorful '50s colors and adorned with black-and-white photographs of Beat Generation greats. Accommodations and bathrooms are tiny, but what the rooms lack in space, they make up for in European charm, and the smell of fresh cannoli wafting up from **Stella Pastry & Café** downstairs adds to the cozy feel. Sit at the cabaret table in your shabby-chic room while you enjoy complimentary sherry (served in the lobby each evening) to

# San Francisco Hotels

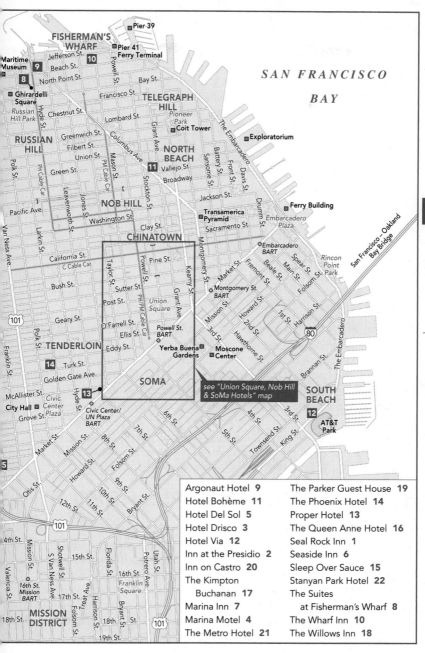

FISHERMAN'S WHARF

Pier 39
Pier 41
Ferry Terminal

Maritime Museum **9**
**10**
Jefferson St.
Beach St.
North Point St.

**8**
Ghirardelli Square
Russian Hill Park

Francisco St.

SAN FRANCISCO BAY

TELEGRAPH HILL
Pioneer Park
Coit Tower

RUSSIAN HILL
Greenwich St.
Filbert St.
Union St.
Green St.

Chestnut St.
Lombard St.

NORTH BEACH
**11** Vallejo St.
Broadway

Exploratorium

Jackson St.

Pacific Ave.

NOB HILL
Washington St.
Clay St.

Transamerica Pyramid
Sacramento St.

Ferry Building
Embarcadero Plaza

California St.
C Cable Car

CHINATOWN
Pine St.

Embarcadero BART

Rincon Point Park

Bush St.

Sutter St.
Post St.

Union Square

Montgomery St. BART

Beale St.
Spear St.
Main St.
Folsom St.

San Francisco – Oakland Bay Bridge

**4**

WHERE TO STAY | North Beach & Fisherman's Wharf

Geary St.
O'Farrell St.
Ellis St.
Eddy St.

Powell St. BART

Mission St.
Howard St.
2nd St.
Hawthorne St.
1st St.
Harrison St.

**80**

TENDERLOIN
**14** Turk St.
Golden Gate Ave.

Yerba Buena Gardens
Moscone Center

SOMA

see "Union Square, Nob Hill & SoMa Hotels" map

SOUTH BEACH
**12**
AT&T Park

McAllister St.
City Hall
Grove St.

Civic Center Plaza
**13** Civic Center/ UN Plaza BART

6th St.
4th St.
3rd St.

**101**

Market St.
Mission St.
Howard St.
Folsom St.
9th St.
Bryant St.

Townsend St.
King St.

**5**

Otis St.

10th St.
11th St.
12th St.

MISSION DISTRICT
16th St. Mission BART
Franklin Square

15th St.
16th St.
17th St.
18th St.
19th St.

**101**

| | |
|---|---|
| Argonaut Hotel **9** | The Parker Guest House **19** |
| Hotel Bohème **11** | The Phoenix Hotel **14** |
| Hotel Del Sol **5** | Proper Hotel **13** |
| Hotel Drisco **3** | The Queen Anne Hotel **16** |
| Hotel Via **12** | Seal Rock Inn **1** |
| Inn at the Presidio **2** | Seaside Inn **6** |
| Inn on Castro **20** | Sleep Over Sauce **15** |
| The Kimpton | Stanyan Park Hotel **22** |
| Buchanan **17** | The Suites |
| Marina Inn **7** | at Fisherman's Wharf **8** |
| Marina Motel **4** | The Wharf Inn **10** |
| The Metro Hotel **21** | The Willows Inn **18** |

75

experience the hotel as Ginsberg likely did, or meander next door in either direction for a taste of North Beach's cafe culture.

444 Columbus Ave. (btw. Vallejo and Green sts.). hotelboheme.com. ✆ **415/433-9111.** 15 units. $199–$295 double. Rates include afternoon sherry. Parking at nearby garages $30–$35. Bus: 12, 30, 41, or 45. Cable car: Powell–Mason. **Amenities:** Concierge; free Wi-Fi.

### The Suites at Fisherman's Wharf ★★

Set right on the Hyde–Powell cable car line, a block away from Aquatic Park and the famous Buena Vista Restaurant, this posh and surprisingly residential-feeling hotel offers a home-away-from-home right in the middle of the tourist action. Choose between a one- or two-bedroom suite with an upscale apartment vibe—you'll get perks such as a pullout couch, two flatscreen TVs, and a full kitchen. Rooms facing the bay also have a balcony where you can watch the cable cars roll by and see the lights of the famous Ghirardelli Square sign. While the lobby and rooms are clean and tasteful, the thing you'll be writing home about is the roof deck, which offers views of both bridges, Alcatraz, and the neighboring Victorian houses (weather permitting). Do as San Franciscans do and bring a bottle of wine to the deck around sunset for your very own happy hour.

2655 Hyde St. (at North Point St.). https://www.shellvacationsclub.com/club/resorts/suites_fisherman/index.page. ✆ **415/771-0200.** 24 units. $250–$399 double. Bus: 19, 30, 47. Cable car: Powell–Hyde. **Amenities:** Limited on-site parking $20/day; coin-op laundry; 24-hr. front desk; free Wi-Fi.

### The Wharf Inn ★

Though this small hotel is a little dated (a partial room renovation was under way in late 2017), the Wharf Inn is the rare example of a good deal right in the heart of Fisherman's Wharf. Pier 39, the cable car turnaround, and Boudin Bakery are all just steps away. Guest rooms are clean and basic. The helpful staff, free parking, and free coffee, tea, and hot chocolate all day in the lobby help most guests enjoy their stay, despite the lack of frills.

2601 Mason St. (at Beach St.). wharfinn.com. ✆ **415/673-7411.** 51 units. $199–$275 double. Rates include hot beverages all day in the lobby. Bus: 30, 47. Streetcar: F. Cable car: Powell–Mason. **Amenities:** Free parking; free Wi-Fi.

# THE MARINA, PACIFIC HEIGHTS & THE PRESIDIO

The Marina is an upscale, lively neighborhood full of young residents, Victorian houses, apartments, and some jaw-dropping luxury homes facing the Marina and bay. Unlike the neighborhood's residences, many of its visitor accommodations are 1950-and-later motor inns that have been updated for the modern traveler. Up on the hill, Pacific Heights boasts old-money mansions (such as those belonging to the Gettys and Danielle Steel), quiet streets, and outrageous views. And for the nature-lover, the Presidio will make you forget that you're just minutes from the urban hustle.

# Expensive

**Hotel Drisco ★★★**   If you're looking for thoughtful luxury, exceptional service, and lovely views without the clamor of crowds downtown, stay at this just-renovated, elegant yet understated hotel nestled among the multimillion-dollar mansions of swanky Pacific Heights. What looks from the outside like an upscale apartment building is actually *the* place for guests seeking discreet, high-class service and amenities, mercifully free of pomp and pretension. The hotel's complimentary "continental" breakfast is more like a full gourmet meal—it includes more baked goods than one person can possibly choose from, local organic sheep's milk yogurt, a selection of meats and cheeses, lox, eggs, and espresso drinks made to order. The evening wine reception allows guests to socialize in the renovated parlor while noshing on cheese, charcuterie, and hot hors d'oeuvres. Room service is available 24 hours a day and while the menu is limited, the food is tasty and the prices surprisingly reasonable. Boutique shopping and great restaurants (without the tourists) on Fillmore, Union, and Chestnut streets are short scenic walks away. You can also hop on the 1 bus to be in the heart of Chinatown or the Financial District in less than 30 minutes, or take advantage of the hotel's free weekday morning chauffeur service. With all of these amenities, the price of a stay seems quite reasonable. ***Hint:*** If you're lucky enough to be there when Shay is working, ask her about the history of the hotel or for recommendations of any sort—she's a veritable encyclopedia of knowledge.

2901 Pacific Ave. (at Broderick St.). hoteldrisco.com. © **415/346-2880.** 48 units. $389–$900, doubles and suites. Rates include breakfast, afternoon tea and cookies, and evening wine reception. Free street parking available. Bus: 1, 3, 24. **Amenities:** Concierge; exercise room and free pass to YMCA; room service; free bikes to borrow; free Wi-Fi.

**Inn at the Presidio ★★**   If you prefer nature to the traffic, crowds, and skyscrapers of a big city, this former officers' quarters, converted to an inn in 2011, was created just for you. Set on over 1,400 acres of coastal dunes, forests, and prairie grasslands, this stately red-brick Georgian Revival–style building puts you in the middle of San Francisco's natural beauty—as well as a flashback to the U.S. Army days when the Presidio played an important role defending the new territories on the West Coast. Though Pershing Hall, as the inn was formerly called, is on the National Register of Historic Places, it's anything but a musty old boys club. Rooms are modern and elegant, featuring high ceilings and original moldings; most are suites with fireplaces and many have views of the bay. At almost 300 square feet, even the basic queen rooms are large by San Francisco hotel standards. Public spaces are warm and inviting; guests enjoy complimentary continental breakfast and an evening wine and cheese reception. The inn has been such a success that in the summer of 2013, Funston House—a Victorian-style home that used to house officers and their families—opened as a four-bedroom cottage that can be rented per room or as a whole. If you want to see the city sights, the PresidioGo shuttle offers daily rides (free with a pass from the inn) downtown. But with miles of hiking trails just outside your door, a fire pit out back, and rocking chairs on the porch, you might not make it to Fisherman's Wharf. *Note:* Make sure you don't confuse this elegant inn for the more basic Presidio Inn, located on Lombard Street.

Main Post, 42 Moraga Ave. (at Funston Ave.). innatthepresidio.com. ✆ **415/800-7356.** 26 units. $295–$500 double and suites. Rates include continental breakfast, evening wine reception. Self-parking $8. Bus: 28, 43, or PresidioGo shuttle bus. Pets welcome ($40). **Amenities:** Access to Presidio YMCA gym; free Wi-Fi.

## Moderate

**Hotel Del Sol** ★★   Funky, colorful Hotel del Sol is strategically located in the family-friendly Marina District, just a couple of blocks from the bustling thoroughfare of Lombard Street. Children will be thrilled to know they are not far from the Disney Museum and the hiking trails of the Presidio, as well as the noise and excitement of Fisherman's Wharf. When little ones tire of touring, they can cool off in the hotel's sparkling outdoor heated pool, which is thoughtfully stocked with beach balls and pool toys, while tired parents can lounge in the hammocks and chaises. Family suites include a queen and two trundle beds, and kids are always treated like VIPs—they'll have access to books, toys, and kid-friendly movies. Rooms are light and airy, with colorful decor—think more 1970s funk than old-world Victorian (like most of the city). Although it's built in the style of a mid-century motor lodge, it has all the style and amenities of a boutique hotel.

3100 Webster St. (at Greenwich St.). jdvhotels.com/hotels/california/san-francisco-hotels/hotel-del-sol/. ✆ **415/921-5520.** 57 units. Double from $150–$250; suite $199–$300. Rates include continental breakfast. Self-parking $35. Pets up to 35 lb. welcome. Bus: 22, 28, 30, 43. **Amenities:** Outdoor pool; discount pass to nearby Crunch Fitness; free Wi-Fi.

## seaside SLEEPS

Established in 1959, the **Seal Rock Inn** ★★, 545 Point Lobos Ave. at 48th Avenue (sealrockinn.com; ✆ **415/752-8000**), is San Francisco's only oceanfront motor inn. The perfect spot for a family stay, the inn is surrounded by parks and trails and sits across the street from the beach—great for exploring, though don't expect a sun-filled beach outing, as this part of San Francisco is often nestled in fog. Unless you've got a wetsuit and are an accomplished surfer, it's best not to swim here; there is a nasty current. But the **San Francisco Zoo** (p. 155) and **Golden Gate Park** (p. 144) are just a few minutes away and filled with family-friendly activities. The motel's restaurant is popular among locals and serves a great brunch. Rooms are large, and some feature kitchenettes or fireplaces; all have fridges, free Wi-Fi, and access to free parking. Doubles go for $170 to $202 per night, with a 2-night minimum on weekends and holidays; it's $10 per night for additional guests 16 and older, $5 for guests under 16.

With parking fees averaging $45 to $65 (plus tax) a night at most hotels, if you're arriving in San Francisco with a car you might want to consider staying at one that offers free parking:

o **Hotel Drisco,** Pacific Heights (lots of free street parking; p. 77)

o **Inn on Castro,** Castro District (free street parking; p. 83)

o **Marina Motel,** Marina District/Cow Hollow (below)

o **Phoenix Hotel,** Civic Center (p. 82)

o **Seal Rock Inn,** Richmond District (facing page)

o **Seaside Inn,** Marina District (p. 80)

o **The Wharf Inn,** North Beach/ Fisherman's Wharf (p. 76)

o **The Willows Inn,** Castro District (free street parking; p. 83)

## Inexpensive

**Marina Inn** ★  Here's a decent option for the traveler on a budget who doesn't mind a busy street. Set in a 1920s Victorian building, the rooms, updated in 2017, still have a Victorian feel, with patterned wallpaper and dark paneling; rooms with bay windows are especially nice. (If you're traveling alone, however, steer clear of the single-bed rooms, as they're a bit stark.) Unless you're a sound sleeper, things can get noisy if your room is close to busy Lombard Street, so ask for a room in the back. With prices as low as $50 for a double, it's hard to find a better deal in the city, but drivers take heed—the inn doesn't offer parking and street parking in the neighborhood is generally limited to 2 hours.

3110 Octavia St. (at Lombard St.). marinainn.com. (C) **415/928-1000.** 40 units. $50–$219 double. Rates include continental breakfast. Bus: 28, 30, 43, 47, 49. **Amenities:** Concierge; barber shop; hair and nail salon; free Wi-Fi.

**Marina Motel** ★  If you're looking for simple, convenient accommodations, the Marina Motel is one of your best bets. Guests enter the property on a cobblestone driveway, and pull their cars into a courtyard with cascading flowers, reminiscent of a European inn. They then park in their own private garage—unheard of at most San Francisco hotels, and, for that matter, most San Francisco houses, too. Rooms are small and clean, though a little noisy if they front Lombard Street. (Ask for a room in the back if you're a light sleeper.) All rooms have fridges and complimentary coffee, tea, and hot chocolate. Some of the units have fully equipped kitchens, making this a great choice for extended stays and families. This sweet and simple "auto courtyard" motel was built to celebrate the opening of the Golden Gate Bridge in 1939, and has been owned by the same Gold Rush–era pioneer family ever since. Trendy restaurants and shops on Chestnut and Union Streets are just a few blocks away.

2576 Lombard St. (btw. Divisadero and Broderick sts.). marinamotel.com. (C) **415/921-9406.** 39 units. $149–$229 double; $269–$369 suite. Dogs welcome ($25 for 1st night, $10 each additional night). Bus: 28, 30, 43, 45. **Amenities:** Free parking; free Wi-Fi.

**Seaside Inn** ★   What this motor inn lacks in ambience, it makes up for in its friendly staff, walkability in a lively neighborhood, and bargain price point. Though it's not much to look at from the outside, its proximity to the Golden Gate Bridge and great bars and eateries makes it a worthy contender for the budget traveler. Rooms and bathrooms are just a step above basic, but they were completely renovated in 2012, so they're still in decent shape with desks, entertainment units, smart black-and-white furnishings, and perks like mini-fridges, microwaves, and coffeemakers. Free parking, free Wi-Fi, and continental breakfast add to the very good deal.

1750 Lombard St. (btw. Octavia and Laguna sts.). sfseasideinn.com. ☏ **415/921-1842.** 20 units. $90–$179 double. Rates include continental breakfast. **Amenities:** Limited free parking; free Wi-Fi.

# JAPANTOWN & ENVIRONS

Whether you're drawn to the area for its Japanese culture and eateries or its relative peace and quiet compared to other parts of the city, the 6-block area that comprises Japantown and its neighboring community offer a very different kind of experience that is still very San Francisco. With Japan Center in the middle and the high-end shopping street of upper Fillmore to the north, there's plenty of shopping, sightseeing, and eating to be had—all within walking distance. And if you stay in April, you may be lucky enough to take in the sights, sounds, and culture of the week-long Cherry Blossom Festival.

## Moderate

**The Kimpton Buchanan** ★★   Located in the footprint of the former Hotel Tomo, the Buchanan is the elegant result of a nearly 2-year complete renovation, highlighting a soft, modern style that's at once welcoming, playful (check out the cheeky statements on the backs of the armchairs in the lobby), and hip. Expect unexpected touches, like in-room yoga mats and lawn games and the daily 5pm hosted wine and sake hour. You can even buy a s'mores kit in the lobby and head out to the courtyard fire pit to prepare them. Rooms are bright, with simple, stylish furnishings—pick a balcony queen or king room for the views and outdoor seating, or go for the "Spa King" and soak in the Japanese deep spa tub. Pets are welcome at no charge, but don't worry if you're allergic—there's a dedicated pet-free floor. Room service isn't available, but with so many options nearby—Japanese ramen shops, sushi bars, and upscale haunts featuring seasonal California cuisine, plus Mum's, an on-property Japanese restaurant serving traditional shabu-shabu—you won't go hungry. (At press time, Mum's is undergoing a remodel slated to complete by the end of 2017.)

1800 Sutter St. (at Buchanan St). thebuchananhotel.com. ☏ **415/921-4000.** 131 units. $185–$400 double. Rates include daily wine and sake reception. Parking $38. Pets welcome. Bus: 2, 3, 22, 38. **Amenities:** Restaurant, fitness center, business center; free Wi-Fi.

**The Queen Anne Hotel** ★  Visitors are certain this historic Victorian mansion is haunted by a Miss Mary Lake, the former headmistress of the school that occupied this building more than 100 years ago. Her office was in room 410, and experts swear there is paranormal activity in the area. But don't be scared away by the ghost rumors. This "haunted hotel" is one of the best values in the city for those looking for unusually large guest rooms and loads of ornate decor. Rooms are furnished in beautiful period antiques, and some have fridges. In the morning, guests enjoy a free full breakfast including sausage and eggs; when evening rolls around, complimentary tea and cookies invite guests to congregate in the common area.

1590 Sutter St. (btw. Laguna and Webster sts.). queenanne.com. ℭ **415/441-2828.** 48 units. $125–$250 double; $169–$350 quad; $350–$459 suite. Rates include breakfast, afternoon tea and sherry, morning newspaper. Parking $30. Bus: 2, 3, 38. **Amenities:** 24-hr. concierge; complimentary local town car service weekday am; discounted airport shuttle; free Wi-Fi.

# CIVIC CENTER/TENDERLOIN

This area is another one of those locations where you get more bang for your buck. However, the area has a large and very visible homeless population, as well as drug addicts and dealers, and you can expect to weave your way past them if you walk the neighborhood, especially if you meander down Market Street between 6th and 10th streets. But, like everywhere else in the city, the area is rapidly becoming gentrified, and these denizens are used to tourists and tend to go about their business. Plus, with the Asian Art Museum, the opera, ballet, symphony, SFJAZZ venue, Hayes Valley shopping, and lots of restaurants and bars all close by, you'll rarely find yourself alone.

## Expensive

**Proper Hotel** ★★  Occupying the entire flatiron-style building at Market, McAllister and 7th streets, Proper, which opened in September 2017, is an ambitious endeavor from top to bottom. Luxury interior designer Kelly Wearstler created the hotel's eclectic style—think Art Deco chic mixed with futuristic Art Moderne plus high-tech 21st-century amenities. The stunning rooms have such unexpected features as bold contrasting wallpaper, a decorative Vifa bluetooth speaker for streaming music, and a "curated" mini-bar stocked with cocktail and snack offerings. Proper is home to three restaurants: Villon, offering contemporary American cuisine; La Bande, a cafe with outdoor seating; and Charmaine's, the rooftop bar with views up and down Market Street. Geared more toward the ultra-hip urbanite than the traveling family, Proper is a sight to see—you'll want to explore this building and sample the food and drink even if you don't stay here.

1100 Market St. (btw. McAllister and 7th sts). properhotel.com/hotels/san-francisco/. ℭ **415/735-7777.** 131 units. $300–$800 double; $600–$1,500 suite. Valet parking $65. Pets allowed ($300 refundable deposit). Bus: 5, 19. Streetcar: All Market Street lines. **Amenities:** 3 restaurants; bar; concierge; fitness center; free Wi-Fi.

## Moderate

**The Phoenix Hotel** ★   Welcome to the unofficial rock-and-roll sleeping hall of fame, where the likes of Moby, Joan Jett, and the Red Hot Chili Peppers crashed when it first opened decades ago. Stay here and you just may sleep in the room that was once accidentally assigned (simultaneously) to both Debbie Harry and JFK, Jr., unbeknownst to them. As this book goes to press, a gradual renovation is slated to begin early 2018, but we expect rooms to stay colorful (and a little noisy); all face the pool in the courtyard where visiting entertainers, bands, and regular guests gather around to swim and swap stories around the fire pits. Chambers, the ultra-cool bar and restaurant, is also a big draw for guests and locals. Funky mid-century furnishings, walls of vintage records, and sexy corners and booths recall a hip L.A. vibe. Added perk: Guests get free weekday passes to **Kabuki Springs & Spa** (p. 142)—check the Kabuki website to see which days are co-ed or restricted to men- or women-only.

601 Eddy St. (at Larkin St.). thephoenixhotel.com. ℂ **415/776-1380.** 44 units. $149–$389 double; $429–$749 suite. Rates include continental breakfast. Free parking. Bus: 19, 31, 47, 49. Streetcar: All Market St. lines. BART: Civic Center/UN Plaza. **Amenities:** Restaurant; bar; outdoor pool; free Wi-Fi.

## Inexpensive

**Sleep Over Sauce** ★   Not quite a B&B, and much too hip to call itself a boutique hotel, Sleep Over Sauce is something all its own. The three brothers who run it call it an urban guesthouse for those seeking the comforts of home and friendly neighborhood living. It consists of eight cozy rooms (with comfortable beds and fresh bathrooms) and a living room complete with a fireplace over the award-winning restaurant Sauce. Located in the center of the city, the hotel makes a great base for visitors who want to see more than Fisherman's Wharf. Most of the city's performing arts venues, as well as the fabulous Asian Art Museum, are a short walk away. The Mission District, Japantown, Castro, and Haight-Ashbury neighborhoods can be reached by Muni in a few minutes, and the historic F-line will take guests to Union Square and Fisherman's Wharf. Don't look for a front desk—guests check in at the bar.

135 Gough St. (at Lily St.). sleepsf.com. ℂ **415/621-0896.** 8 units. $155–$195 double; $235–$300 suite. Some dates have 2-night minimum. Bus: 6, 7, 21. Streetcar: All Market St. lines. **Amenities:** Restaurant; bar; business center; free Wi-Fi.

# CASTRO

Most businesses here cater to LGBTQ customers, but everyone is welcome in this lively neighborhood. Though located a few miles from most of the traditional tourist action, the Castro is centrally located for visiting the more hip neighborhoods, such as the Mission and Hayes Valley, and public transportation makes for an easy ride straight to the tourist-centric meccas of Union Square, Fisherman's Wharf, and the Ferry Building. Another perk of this area is that while most of the city is blanketed in fog, chances are it'll be sunny and warm(er) in this colorful, walkable neighborhood filled with some of the city's nicer (and well-maintained) Victorian and Edwardian homes. And if you need anything at all, visit **Cliff's Variety** (479 Castro St.; cliffsvariety. com), a treasure trove of a variety store that manages to be both silly and practical, selling everything from office supplies to hardware to unicorn snot.

## Moderate

### The Parker Guest House ★★★

Rated one of the city's top guest-houses by gay travel sites such as Spartacus and Purple Roofs, this lovely 1909 Edwardian B&B in the heart of the Castro is the perfect oasis to return to after a long day of sightseeing. Sip a glass of wine outside by the garden fountain at the daily complimentary social, or lounge by the fireplace or in the library. Spacious, newly renovated rooms feature down comforters, terry robes, and a modern feel. Located in one of San Francisco's sunniest neighborhoods, it's an ideal launch pad for exploring the Mission, Hayes Valley, and Mid-Market neighborhoods. Pretend you've been here for ages and head to local favorites Philz Coffee and Dolores Park a few blocks away.

520 Church St. (btw. 17th and 18th sts.). parkerguesthouse.com. ✆ **415/621-3222.** 20 units. $189–$289 double and junior suite. Minimum stays weekends and events. Rates include continental breakfast and evening wine reception. Limited self-parking $28. Bus: 22, 33. Streetcar: J. **Amenities:** Concierge; gardens; free Wi-Fi.

## Inexpensive

### Inn on Castro ★

If living like a local is your thing when traveling to a new city, this inn is a great option. Guests have two choices when it comes to sleeping arrangements. The first is one of the two apartments (a 10-min. walk from the inn), which sleep up to four people comfortably and feature a full kitchen. Mollie Stone's Market is just a short walk away, as are some of the city's best eateries, like **Starbelly** ★ (p. 112) and **L'Ardoise** ★★ (p. 112). The second choice is a room in the full-service B&B, located in a restored Edwardian building filled with fresh flowers and original artwork. Contemporary furnishings make this old building feel modern and hip. Bathrooms are shared or private, depending on which room you choose. Guests of the B&B rooms enjoy a complimentary full breakfast each morning. Expect friendly and personal hospitality from the small, knowledgeable staff.

321 Castro St. (at Market St.). innoncastro.com. ✆ **415/861-0321.** 8 units, 2 w/shared bathroom. From $135 single w/shared bathroom; $205 w/private bathroom; $245 2-bedroom apartment w/kitchen. B&B room rates include breakfast. Free street parking. Bus: 24, 33, 35. Streetcar: F, K, L, M, and T. **Amenities:** Complimentary decanter of brandy in B&B rooms; free Wi-Fi.

### The Willows Inn ★

If you don't mind sharing a bathroom and enjoy a friendly, social setting, the Willows is an excellent choice. Housed in an old Edwardian building in the heart of the Castro, this is a favorite among LGBTQ guests, but all are welcome. Rooms feature bent wicker headboards, antique dressers or armoires, and cozy, colorful duvets. Though no rooms have a private bathroom, each has a vanity sink and some have chaise lounges or bay windows. Guests enjoy complimentary continental breakfast including eggs, juice, yogurt, fruit, and coffee. Evening cocktails are also hosted, encouraging guests to mingle and relax.

710 14th St. (near Church and Market sts.). willowssf.com. © **415/431-4770.** 12 units, all w/shared bathroom. Room rates from $130–215. Rates include continental breakfast and evening cocktails. Free street parking. Bus: 22, 37. Streetcar: F, J, K, L, M, N, and T. **Amenities:** Free Wi-Fi.

# HAIGHT-ASHBURY

San Francisco's summers of love are long gone, but open-minded folks wanting to escape the tourist scene and embrace eccentricity will dig the Haight. With Golden Gate Park (p. 144) right next door, an eclectic selection of tasty eateries, and unique and unusual shopping options (Fluevog fans—you know who you are—will make a beeline to John Fluevog Shoes at 1697 Haight Street; fluevog.com), this is yet another neighborhood in which to lose oneself.

## Moderate

**Stanyan Park Hotel ★** This historic Victorian B&B's main draw is its location—right across the street from Golden Gate Park's eastern entrance. However, the property is old and shows some wear—think peeling paint in some spots and weathered furniture. Don't expect modern luxury or a ton of space (the rooms vary in size); instead, set your sights on clean, cozy rooms decorated with Victorian furnishings. The hotel also has several one- and two-bedroom apartments, which feature full kitchens, dining rooms, and living rooms. In addition to the complimentary breakfast buffet, there's afternoon tea with freshly baked cookies and a weekday evening wine and cheese reception.

750 Stanyan St. (at Waller St.). stanyanpark.com. © **415/751-1000.** 36 units. From $180–$499. Rates include continental breakfast, afternoon tea, and evening wine reception. Off-site parking $20. Bus: 6, 7, 43. Streetcar: N. **Amenities:** 24-hr. front desk; free Wi-Fi.

## Inexpensive

**The Metro Hotel ★** Family-run since it opened in 1985, the Metro is by no means fancy, but it's got a warm, welcoming staff and clean, basic rooms, making it perfect for people seeking nothing more than a safe, comfy, centrally located place to crash. Front desk staff is happy to help with suggestions for things to do, see, and eat in Haight-Ashbury and beyond, and the artwork sprinkled throughout the hotel is original and painted by family members. There's a pleasant garden area with benches in the back, and around the corner from the main entrance is the property's studio with a kitchenette, living room, and a private entrance. For travelers looking to spend time in an area with a different kind of history—more 1960s hippie counterculture, less 1850s Gold Rush and railroad boom—the Metro Hotel is a solid budget bet. You may be able to find street parking, but be aware that many streets in the area have 2-hour time limits for non-residents, and parking violations are expensive.

319 Divisadero St. (btw. Oak and Page sts.). metrohotelsf.com. © **415/861-5364.** 24 units. $120–$180 double; $190 studio annex. Rates include coffee and tea in lobby. Bus: 6, 7, 24. **Amenities:** Free Wi-Fi.

# WHERE TO EAT

During the Gold Rush, immigrant miners hungry for a taste of home created a demand—and the supply—for small kitchens serving classic dishes from all over the globe. And just like that San Francisco's restaurant culture was born. Add in year-round access to an unparalleled bounty of local organic produce, seafood, free-range meats, and wine, along with restaurant-obsessed residents and a vibrant chef community, and you've got one of the world's top foodie destinations. It's virtually impossible to get in and out of San Francisco without having some kind of gastronomic epiphany—or at least a few dining experiences that make you feel that you've left your stomach, as well as your heart, in San Francisco.

**5**

With more than 4,400 restaurants within its 7 square miles, San Francisco has more dining establishments per capita than any other U.S. city—which creates a heck of a lot of competition. With the rising costs of doing business and staying "relevant" in this trend-conscious city, dining rooms are now finding it harder and harder to keep their doors open (which is why those who survive are charging higher menu prices than ever before). Still, there's far more to enjoy than you'll be able to tackle on even a month-long visit here.

While this guide barely scratches the surface of the city's culinary delights, I've included can't-miss favorites across a wide range of cuisines, price ranges, and neighborhoods (one of the best ways to get to know a city is to sample its neighborhood restaurants). Some are new, yet already earning coveted awards; others have been around forever—for good reason. They range from white-tablecloth establishments that present their culinary masterpieces with warm formality, to others so casual they practically toss you your food, a paper plate, and a napkin.

## PRACTICAL INFORMATION

Although dining in San Francisco is usually a hassle-free experience, here are a few things to keep in mind:

- **If you want a table at the restaurants with the best reputations,** you probably need to **book 6 to 8 weeks in advance** for weekends, and a few weeks ahead even for weekdays.

The restaurants listed below are classified first by area, then by price, using the following categories: **Expensive,** dinner for $50 or more per person; **Moderate,** dinner from $35 per person; and **Inexpensive,** dinner less than $35 per person. These categories reflect prices for an appetizer, a main course, a dessert, and a glass of wine.

- **If you can't get a reservation** at your desired restaurant, don't hesitate to put your name on a **waiting list.** I have received "that call" from popular places. Just make sure to call back quickly—they mean business.
- **If there's a long wait for a table, ask if you can order at the bar,** which is often faster and more fun.
- **Don't leave** *anything* **visible in your car** while dining, particularly in or near high-crime areas such as the Mission, downtown, or Fisherman's Wharf. (Thieves know tourists with nice cameras and trunks full of mementos are headed there.)
- **No smoking.** It is against the law to smoke in any restaurant in San Francisco, even if it has a separate bar or lounge area. You're welcome to smoke outside; make sure to stay 20 feet away from any entryway.
- **Plan on dining early.** This ain't New York. Most restaurants close their kitchens around 10pm.
- **If you're driving to a restaurant, add extra time to your itinerary for parking,** which can be an especially infuriating exercise in areas like the Mission, downtown, the Marina, and, well, pretty much everywhere. Expect to pay anywhere from $12 to $20 for valet service, *if* the restaurant offers it.
- **If you have to find parking, check out sfpark.org** (more on p. 278).

# FINANCIAL DISTRICT

While it may seem a concrete jungle, Union Square's neighboring district is home to many corporate entities and business hotels, which partially explains the number of destination-worthy restaurants here.

## Expensive

**Kokkari ★★** GREEK/MEDITERRANEAN    A perfect choice for a date or large party, this upscale Mediterranean stalwart with cozy-chic environs never disappoints. Exposed wood, earthen pottery, soft lighting, an open kitchen, and a large rotisserie fireplace give it a warm, chic, Mediterranean feel. Reliably superb food completes the experience. Try such Hellenic classics as *horiatiki* (traditional Greek salad), *dolmathes* (stuffed grape leaves), baked feta cheese, *moussaka* (eggplant, potato, lamb, yogurt béchamel), or any dish with lamb. Into Greek coffee? Ask your server to take you back by the kitchen

# San Francisco Restaurants

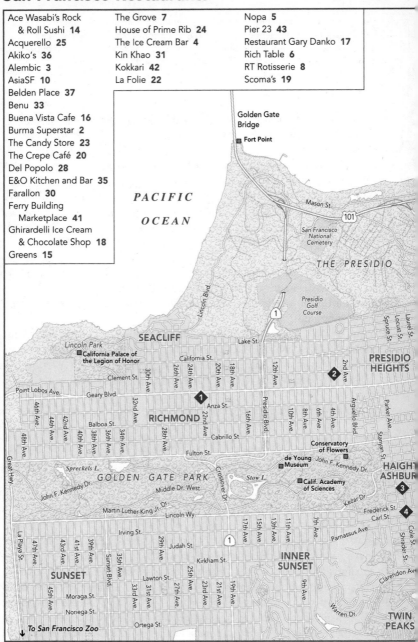

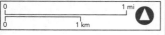

The Slanted Door **41**
SoMa StrEat Food Park **9**
Sons and Daughters **29**
SPQR **12**
State Bird Provisions **11**
Super Duper **34**
Swan Oyster Depot **26**
Swensen's Ice Cream **21**

Tacolicious **13**
Tadich Grill **40**
Tommy's Joynt **27**
Ton Kiang **1**
Waterbar **38**
Westfield
  San Francisco Centre **32**
Yank Sing **39**

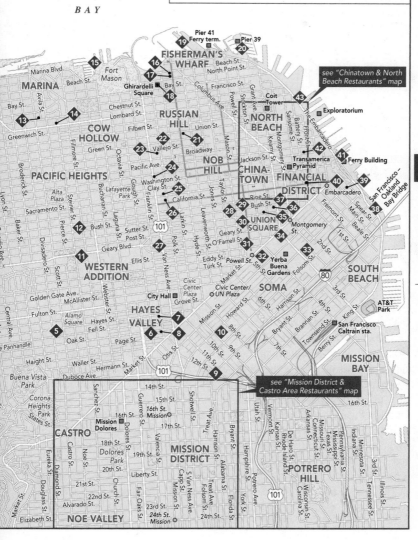

**5**

# online resources FOR DINING

Want to book your reservations online? Go to **opentable.com**, where you can reserve seats in real time.

Marcia Gagliardi's local food blog **Tablehopper** (tablehopper.com) posts smart, gourmand observations every Tuesday and Friday. To see what else is hot during your visit, check **Eater SF** (sf. eater.com).

For an epic culinary scavenger hunt, see **7x7.com**'s annual Big Eat list, which shows photos of specific dishes to hunt for. Also don't miss the *San Francisco Chronicle*'s annual Top 100 Restaurants list (sfchronicle.com), which will point you to a diverse selection of local flavors.

Food truck fans should check out **Off the Grid,** a daily gathering of a half dozen or so trucks, usually from 11am to 2pm and 5 to 9pm, occasionally with live music. Check offthegridsf.com/markets for information. They also line up trucks for **Presidio Picnic,** held on summer Sundays around a grassy expanse in the—you guessed it—Presidio. If it's a sunny day, there's no better place to be, especially given trucks like Nopalito (a fantastic Mexican restaurant with California flair, serving up amazing tacos) and the glistening bay as the backdrop. Otherwise, **Roaming Hunger** (roaming hunger.com) lists locations of food trucks, based on Twitter feeds.

Menus here generally tend to offer good vegetarian options, and in the listings below we've singled out a few restaurants that are exclusively vegetarian. For vegan eats, consult **Happy Cow** (happycow.net). Gluten-free is also big here, too.

to show you how it's made: in an *ibrik,* and slowly heated in hot sand. Best seat in the house for two is just to the right of the fireplace.

200 Jackson St. (at Front St.). kokkari.com. ✆ **415/981-0983.** Entrees $19–$35 lunch, $26–$48 dinner. Mon–Thurs 11:30am–10pm; Fri 11:30am–11pm; Sat 5–11pm, Sun 5–10pm. Valet parking (dinner only). Bus: 1, 12. Streetcar: All Market St. lines.

**The Slanted Door ★★** VIETNAMESE    Considered by many to be the best Vietnamese restaurant in America, the Slanted Door has become one of the most well-known must-tries when visiting the City by the Bay. The draw? Gorgeously fresh and refined interpretations of Southeast Asian classics made from local, organic ingredients and served in a bright and bustling contemporary space in the Ferry Building, overlooking the bay and twinkling Bay Bridge. Don't miss the grass-fed estancia shaking beef, crab with glass noodles, crispy imperial rolls, or pho—all conceived of by self-taught chef/owner Charles Phan, a long-beloved darling of San Francisco's fickle restaurant scene. Celebrity fans including Mick Jagger, Keith Richards, Quentin Tarantino, Luke Wilson, and Gwyneth Paltrow have been known to sneak in for a bite.

1 Ferry Building (at the Embarcadero and Market St.). slanteddoor.com. ✆ **415/861-8032.** Lunch entrees $12–$36; dinner entrees $18–$45; fixed-price lunch $48 and dinner $53–$65 (parties of 7 or more only). Lunch Mon–Sat 11am–2:30pm, Sun 11:30am–3pm. Afternoon tea daily 2:30–4:30pm. Dinner daily 5:30am–10pm. Bar menu 2:30–5:30pm. Bus: All Market St. buses. Streetcar: All Market St. lines.

## Moderate

**Tadich Grill** ★ SEAFOOD   California was not even a state when Tadich Grill opened in 1849. It's the oldest continuously-run restaurant in San Francisco, owned by the Buich family since 1928. When you walk through the door, time stands still. From the dark wood, brass fixtures, long bar, and private booths, you get the feeling you are in an old boys club and expect to see deals being made under the haze of cigar smoke. If you can only try one dish here, know that people come from all over the world for Tadich's *cioppino:* a red stew chockful of scallops, clams, prawns, mussels, fish, and crab, served with garlic bread for dipping. Another specialty is the Hangtown Fry, a mélange of eggs, bacon, and deep-fried oysters, scrambled together to make a dish the late Herb Caen—*Chronicle* journalist, unofficial mayor, and recipient of a Pulitzer Prize for being the "voice and conscience" of San Francisco—loved almost as much as the city itself. This special fry has been served continuously since the Gold Rush days, when miners who struck it rich would come in to enjoy one of the most expensive meals in the city. Finish your trip down memory lane with the simple rice pudding—the recipe has not changed in over 100 years.

240 California St. (btw. Battery and Front sts.). tadichgrill.com. ✆ **415/391-1849.** Entrees $15–$38. Mon–Fri 11am–9:30pm; Sat 11:30am–9:30pm. No reservations. Bus: All Market St. buses. Streetcar: All Market St. lines. BART: Embarcadero.

## Inexpensive

**Pier 23** ★ SEAFOOD   When the occasion calls for a casual, let-your-hair-down kind of place where you'll want to throw back a few cocktails, indulge in straightforward grub, and perhaps dance it up with tipsy locals after happy hour—all backed by an awesome view of the bay—this is where to go. Up front, the tables in the small, loud dining room are accessories to the long bar and band area, while out back—a favorite afternoon spot on sunny days—the patio flanked by the bay allows for salt-kissed alfresco dining. Ask to be seated out back, then dig into heavenly fish and chips, or a juicy Black Angus burger, while watching the boats sail by. A hearty brunch, served on weekends, features a variety of dishes like huevos rancheros, whole roasted Dungeness crab, and a smoked salmon plate. Even the little ones will be happy; the kids menu offers all the usual faves—grilled cheese, chicken strips, and more.

Pier 23 (on Embarcadero). pier23cafe.com. ✆ **415/362-5125.** Entrees $15–$28. Weekdays 11:30am–10pm, Sat 11am–10pm, Sun 10am–8pm. Streetcar: F.

# UNION SQUARE/TENDERLOIN

Perhaps it's the captive tourist audience that keeps mediocre restaurants flourishing in this area. Whatever the cause, there aren't as many great dining rooms in San Francisco's premier hotel and shopping hub as I'd like. On the bright side, this will hopefully encourage you to get out of downtown and into the city's vibrant neighborhoods, where you can taste more of the local flavor of the City by the Bay.

# Expensive

**Farallon** ★★ SEAFOOD   If you're looking for seafood, this dramatically decorated, festive restaurant is one of your best bests. Even before looking at the menu, you'll get the point: Giant jellyfish lamps float overhead from an arched mosaic ceiling, their dangling tentacles lighting the way to your table. Amber-hued kelp columns rise from the floor, amid 8-foot sea urchins and a giant clamshell. Owner/designer Pat Kuleto and owner/chef Mark Franz (who are also both behind seafood shrine **Waterbar** ★★, p. 95) worked together to create this unique underwater fantasy in the former Elks Club building. Food sticks to the sea, too—picks might range from buttermilk-poached petrale sole with Dungeness crab to grilled scallops with chickpea risotto—but a few land offerings are always available, such as a dry-aged rib-eye with bone-marrow Bordelaise, horseradish cream, and sourdough onion rings. Desserts, like the French cruller doughnut with grape jelly and peanut butter ice cream, or the chocolate mousse with hazelnut crumble and pomegranate compote, also rate.

450 Post St. (at Powell St.). farallonrestaurant.com. ℂ **415/956-6969.** Main courses $37–$45. Dinner Sun 5:30–9pm, Mon–Thurs 5:30–9:30pm, Fri–Sat 5:30–10pm. Reservations recommended. Cable car: Powell–Mason or Powell–Hyde line. BART: Powell St.

# Moderate

**Akiko's** ★★ SUSHI   It's been around for more than 20 years, but after a smart recent renovation of the sushi bar and cozy, narrow dining room, this family-owned Union Square spot came out of the dining shadows to be recognized as one of the city's best. If you want the chefs to blow your mind, order the omakase menu (be prepared; it's about $100 per person), or tell the chefs how much you want to spend and let them craft a menu; or stick with a la carte options, which are reasonably priced for fish flown in fresh from Tokyo's fish market. If you're hungry for something more substantial, there are a few cooked specials, including ramen. *Note:* Don't confuse this restaurant with the unrelated Akiko's Sushi nearby on Mason Street; that other place is nowhere near as good.

431 Bush St (btw. Kearny St. & Grant Ave.). akikosrestaurant.com. ℂ **415/398-2318.** Sushi $7–$14. Mon–Fri 11:30am–2:30pm and 5:30–9pm, Sat 5:30–9pm. Bus: 2, 3, 30, 45, 76X, 91. Streetcar: All Market Street lines.

**Kin Khao** ★★ THAI   In a town with plenty of good Thai food, it takes a lot to rise to the top. But owner Pim Techamuanvivit has won Michelin-star status by combining a modern, handsome dining room, the traditional foods of her homeland, and the use of seasonal produce and sustainable seafood and meat. The concise menu always includes the fan favorite, "pretty hot" wings and "chicken fat rice" with ginger-poached chicken, but pretty much everything is worth trying here (a good thing, because portions aren't as generous as at most Thai dining rooms). Another step up from traditional Thai—there's a full cocktail menu. Just be warned: Fancier Thai food and prime downtown positioning result in surprisingly upscale prices.

55 Cyril Magnin St. (at corner of Mason and Ellis sts.). kinkhao.com. ⓒ **415/362-7456.** Main courses $9–$50. Sun–Thurs 11:30am–2pm and 5:30–10pm; Fri–Sat 11:30am–2pm and 5:30–11pm. Cable car: Powell–Mason or Powell–Hyde line. BART: Powell St.

## Inexpensive

**E&O Kitchen and Bar** ★ PAN-ASIAN    When I have to meet friends in Union Square for an affordable bite, I head to this atmospheric, cavernous three-story dining room serving Asian share plates (think chicken satay, Chinese chicken salad, dry-fried green beans). It's got so many seats, there's almost never a wait, even for larger parties. Despite reasonable prices, the bill climbs quickly, especially if you indulge in the full bar, so if you're on a budget, consider coming for happy hour (Mon–Sat 3–6pm), when certain cocktails and wine are $6, beer is $4, oysters are a buck each, and snacks, like beef short-rib sliders, are $1 to $4.

314 Sutter St. (btw. Grant and Stockton sts.). eosanfrancisco.com. ⓒ **415/693-0303.** Main courses $9–$38. Mon–Thurs 11:30am–10pm, Fri–Sat 11:30am–11pm, Sun 5–9:30pm. Cable car: Powell–Mason or Powell–Hyde. BART: Powell St.

# SOMA

A massive expanse of long industrial streets stretching from the bay to the Mission, SoMa is the opposite of a walkable neighborhood, but it's got plenty of museums, bars, clubs, and restaurants, not to mention the game day crowds swarming into AT&T Park.

## Expensive

**Benu** ★★ ASIAN FUSION    Housed in a heritage building in the heart of SoMa, a few minutes' walk from MoMa and other cultural attractions, Benu is one of the world's rare three-Michelin-star restaurants. Although it has no dress code, no tablecloths, and no stuffy servers, it is unquestionably a luxury culinary adventure, with all that that entails: more courses than you can count, bite-size servings, custom-created porcelain, wine pairings (if desired; there's an $80 corkage fee if you BYOB), and a $285 charge per person, plus

# graze ANATOMY

If you're downtown and can't decide what you want to eat—or find yourself hungry and without reservations—head to any of these dining smorgasbords, with multiple options all under one roof or along one street. Your toughest decision will be which establishment you want to try.

A litany of spectacular tastes await at the **Ferry Building Marketplace ★★★** (ferrybuildingmarketplace.com), the city's top culinary destination, overlooking the bay on the Embarcadero at the foot of Market Street. You'll need a reservation to dine at **Slanted Door ★★** (p. 90), but there are many other dining options in this long marketplace flanked with incredible food—perhaps you'll settle down for oysters, wine, and more at a patio table at **Hog Island Oyster Co.**, or dive a fork into exceptional, unexpected Japanese "deli" items at counter-service-only **Delica.** Any respectable burger, fries, and shake craving is conquered at **Gott's Roadhouse,** while gluten-free diners may actually cry tears of joy over the sandwiches—or just the unbelievably bread-like bread—at **Mariposa Baking Company.** Grab picnic provisions from various shops selling cheese, caviar, wine, dessert (try **Dandelion Chocolate!**), and other foods. The best part?

With so many options, every budget and taste are accommodated here. Open Monday through Friday 10am to 7pm, Saturday 8am to 6pm, and Sunday 11am to 5pm.

Just a few blocks from Union Square, the Financial District's charming, foot-traffic-only street **Belden Place ★** is flanked with European restaurants and sidewalk seating, making it an appealing place to loll away the afternoon, perhaps with a chilled bottle of white wine and a bowl of mussels (with a side of fries, of course), or some paella. The food is hit-and-miss, but in a pinch, you're sure to find a seat and something to eat. Restaurant hours vary but most are open for lunch and dinner. See the website (belden-place.com) for details.

When I find myself hungry while shopping in Union Square, I always head to the basement food court at the **Westfield San Francisco Centre ★** (westfield.com/sanfrancisco). Along with plenty of junky fast-food options, you'll find everyday-sustenance sure-things like Chipotle, Loving Hut Vegan Cuisine, and Starbucks. But my favorite stop is the gourmet grocer, Bristol Farms, which has incredible hot and cold prepared foods ranging from pizza to sushi to pasta. Open daily 10am to 8:30pm.

20% service charge. If you're a fan of this type of dining, you won't be disappointed by the culinary wizardry of chef/owner Corey Lee (formerly of the famed French Laundry, see p. 260). Lee's eclectic menu might include such wildly creative choices as potato salad with anchovy; thousand-year-old quail egg with ginger and nasturtium; monkfish liver on brioche; or salt and pepper squid—none of which look like they sound. Lee excels at daring combinations such as faux shark-fin soup with black truffle custard, or charcoal-grilled lamb belly with quinoa, pear, and sunflower. Plan to spend upwards of 3 hours basking in a top-quality dining experience in minimalist, serene surroundings. *Note:* Young children not allowed unless they "partake in the tasting menu."

22 Hawthorne St. (at Howard St.). benusf.com. © **415/685-4860.** Tasting menu $285. Tues–Sat 5:30–9pm. Valet parking $20. Bus/streetcar: All Market St. lines.

**Waterbar** ★★ SEAFOOD   Waterbar delivers just about everything a San Francisco visitor—or local—could want. A contender for the "Best Views" award, it has unparalleled front-row seats for the Bay Bridge and its perpetual evening light show. It's got a bar with a sexy vibe and an outdoor patio; two floor-to-ceiling fish tanks in the middle of the dining room teem with eels, fish, and other Pacific Ocean critters; you can feast on $1 oysters from 11:30am to 5:30pm daily; and there's a fab weekend brunch (the exotic Bloody Mary comes with smoked bacon and jumbo prawns). Even more impressive, the food rises to the occasion, with creative seafood dishes such as Kampachi sashimi with tempura-fried peach, *gochujang* aïoli, white soy, and lemon verbena; or miso-glazed halibut with black bean sauce, puffed wild rice, *katsuobushi,* and summer squash. The menu offers a wide variety of fresh, ethically sourced, seasonal seafood, but it also has a steak and more for culinary landlubbers.

399 Embarcadero (at Harrison St.). waterbarsf.com. ✆ **415/284-9922.** Entrees $36–$44. Lunch Mon–Fri 11:30am–2pm, brunch Sat–Sun 11:30pm–2:30pm; dinner Sun–Mon 5:30–9:30pm, Tues–Sat 5:30–10pm. Valet parking $20. Bus: 1, 12, 14, or 41. BART: Embarcadero.

## Moderate

**AsiaSF** ★ ASIAN/CALIFORNIAN   Food is not the point at this theatrical dinner-and-show destination featuring a multicourse meal and transgender stars. A popular spot for bachelorette and birthday parties, dates, and curious tourists, this joint on a gritty stretch of SoMa gets you in and out with enough time to digest a so-so meal, while watching bar-top lip-sync performances and dancing by truly gifted talents. (Despite the high kicks and sashays on a min-iscule space, owner Skip Young says only two girls have fallen off the bar in the venue's 19-year history.) For small groups, the *ménage a trois* menu gets you three dishes from a list, including tamarind chicken satay, miso glazed salmon served over black "forbidden" rice, truffled soba noodles, and "baby got back" ribs. It's a lot of fun and, believe it or not, kids are welcome at the first seating. *Note:* You must dine to see the show.

201 Ninth St. (at Howard St.). asiasf.com. ✆ **415/255-2742.** Dinner $39–$79; Wed a la carte menu $25/person minimum. Sun, Wed–Thurs 7–10pm; Fri 7pm–2am; Sat 5pm–2am; cocktails/dancing until 2am Fri–Sat. Bus/streetcar: All Market St. lines. BART: Civic Center.

**Yank Sing** ★ DIM SUM   Not much has changed at this banquet-room-style restaurant since I was a kid. And that's fine by me, because I always know what I'm going to get—ultra-fresh, expertly made, not-greasy dump-lings and other little-plate delicacies carted around the carpeted dining room for me to pick and choose as I like. The childhood favorites—stuffed crab claw, *har gau,* taro root dumplings, and Peking duck—still do the trick, along-side about 60 other temptations that make an appearance each day. A down-side, if there is one, is the price: You'll pay double what you'd spend in the

Richmond District or Chinatown, where dim sum is an everyday part of delicious San Francisco life.

101 Spear St. (at Mission St.). yanksing.com. © **415/781-1111.** Dishes $6–$27. Mon–Fri 11am–3pm, Sat–Sun 10am–4pm. Bus: 14. BART: Embarcadero.

## Inexpensive

**SoMa StrEat Food Park** ★★ FOOD TRUCK  The first permanent food truck plaza in San Francisco, SoMa StrEat Food Park established itself as one of the best places to sample a variety of outstanding foods. Each day eight or so trucks, from a pool of about 30 rotating vendors, roll in and serve lunch; on weekends the fun continues through dinner. Choose from among vendors such as Curry Up Now, Seoul on Wheels, Adam's Grub Truck, and Chairman Bao—you're sure to find something you like, no matter when you show up. The food is high quality, the trucks are clean, and there's covered seating, music, flatscreen TVs, restrooms, and free Wi-Fi. With no tourist attractions close by, but easy public transportation access, this place is a destination in itself; it feels like one big party, where you can hang out and eat with locals. Most vendors take credit cards; there's also an ATM on-site.

428 11th St. (at Division St.). somastreatfoodpark.com. Entrees $5–$19. Mon–Fri 11am–3pm; Sat 11am–9pm; Sun 11am–5pm. Bus: 9, 12, 27, or 47.

**Super Duper** ★ BURGERS  A step above your average greasy spoon, this outpost of the local boutique burger chain is one of the most satisfying affordable options downtown. Its burgers are made with humanely raised beef and cushioned between freshly baked buns—and served with house-made pickles, if desired. Even soft-serve gets a makeover here; it's created with cream from Bay Area's revered Straus Family Creamery. You can find breakfast here, too, though the menu's limited to breakfast sandwiches, hash browns, and addictive onion-ring-shaped donuts, with Blue Bottle Coffee, if desired. (What's not to like?) Order at the counter and pull up a seat, once one comes available. There are two other downtown locations: in the Metreon at 783 Mission St. (btw. 4th and Yerba Buena) and in the Financial District at 346 Kearny St. (btw. Bush and Pine sts.; closed Sun).

721 Market St. (btw. 3rd and 4th sts.). superduperburgers.com. © **415/538-3437.** Mon–Wed 8am–11pm, Thurs–Fri 8am–11:30pm, Sat 10:30am–11:30pm, Sun 10:30am–10pm. Breakfast items $3.75–$7.50, lunch & dinner items $5.50–$7.75. Cable car: Powell–Mason or Powell–Hyde line. BART: Powell St.

# NOB HILL/RUSSIAN HILL

In these two neighboring residential districts, upscale locals help to keep quality restaurants afloat.

## Expensive

**Acquerello** ★★★ ITALIAN  A perfect special-occasion restaurant, this hidden gem has somehow remained "hidden" for decades, while offering the city's most delicious, refined contemporary Italian fare in an elegant and intimate setting. Don't let its obscure location off somewhat gritty Polk Street fool you. Inside, it's classic fine-dining luxury, from polite request for proper attire (jackets for men, equivalent for women) to the surprisingly spacious dining room (you can actually hear your dinner companion), to attentive service and a Michelin-starred menu and wine list (and don't miss the cheese cart!). Owners Giancarlo Paterlini and chef Suzette Gresham-Tognetti have been here since 1989, and continue to ensure a most special experience. For a quiet, memorable meal, this is your place. Best of all, you won't leave feeling overindulged, as is so often the case with fancy multicourse meals.

1722 Sacramento St. (btw. Polk & Van Ness sts.). acquerello.com. © **415/567-5432.** 3-course menu $105; 4-course menu $130; 5-course menu $150. Tues–Thurs 5:30–9:30pm, Fri–Sat 5:30–10pm. Bus: 47, 49.

**House of Prime Rib** ★★ PRIME RIB   The name tells part of the story—the focus here is indeed on epic prime rib, as it has been since 1949. What it doesn't say is that this veteran establishment on a nondescript strip of Van Ness Avenue offers one spectacular retro dining experience, as recently featured by Anthony Bourdain on his TV show *No Reservations.* The restaurant hits every note: the masculine English club decor, the stiff and generous drinks, the formally dressed waiters who mix Caesar salads tableside and cut slabs of meat to order, after wheeling them over on stainless steel–domed carts. Add sides of creamed spinach and Yorkshire pudding and you're in carnivore heaven.

1906 Van Ness Ave. (btw. Jackson and Washington sts.). houseofprimerib.net. © **415/885-4605.** Dinner $3–$60. Mon–Thurs 5:30–10pm, Fri 5–10pm, Sat–Sun 4–10pm. Bus: 19, 47, 49.

**La Folie** ★ FRENCH   A Russian Hill fixture since 1988, this intimate, chic, yet relaxed restaurant is a prime pick if you're looking for a classic French meal. Chef/owner Roland Passat was born in the Rhône–Alpes in France and honed his craft at cooking school in Lyon; his food is anchored in French tradition, yet contemporary and seasonal (hence the vegetarian menu offered)—and unlike many celebrity chefs, this local legend is still in the kitchen every night, ensuring consistent quality. Diners choose among three-, four-, and five-course menus, which may feature such indulgences as stunningly presented frog legs and snail ragout; lobster and mushroom risotto bathed in lobster broth with leeks; or duck breast coq au vin with rhubarb marmalade and duck liver mousse. As a final performance, do not miss the baked Alaska, and the Edam cheese soufflé. Portions are generous, so if you're trying to decide which menu to pick, you may want to go with fewer courses. *Note:* There's a dress code here, specifying no "athletic wear," sports shoes, beachwear, flip flops, slippers, casual shorts, or caps. Makes you wonder what inspired it!

2316 Polk St. (btw. Green and Union sts.). lafolie.com. © **415/776-5577.** 3-course menu $110; 4-course menu $130; 5-course menu $150; chef's tasting menu $160. Mon–Sat 5:30–10pm. Valet parking $15. Bus: 12, 19, 27, 45, and 47.

**Sons and Daughters** ★★ AMERICAN   Michelin-starred chef/owner Teague Moriarty and chef de cuisine Alex Jackson keep this tiny Nob Hill restaurant full, with a perfect combination of cozy atmosphere and a delicious, seasonal, beautifully presented nine-course tasting menu (which includes knockout desserts by award-winning pastry chef Robert Hac). It's a charming place to celebrate a birthday or anniversary, as you sit by the fireplace and enjoy an evening of culinary delights. The set tasting menu is the only option here: Recent luscious offerings include Hamachi crudo with white miso and a pear, turnip, and marigold salad; roasted squab with stewed eggplant and golden raisins; and sunflower-seed custard with peach sorbet, sumac, and raspberries (intriguing, right?). The exceptionally friendly staff know the dishes well and are happy to accommodate any food allergies or dislikes. *One last note:* Don't even think of trying to park a car on the street around here. If you must drive, the Sutter/Stockton garage a block away is a good bet.

708 Bush St. (at Powell St.). sonsanddaughterssf.com. ℭ **415/391-8311.** Tasting menu $175; pairings $100. Wed–Sun 5–9:30pm. Bus: 1, 2, or 30. Cable car: Powell–Hyde or Powell–Mason.

## Moderate

**Swan Oyster Depot** ★★ SEAFOOD   Historic Swan Oyster Depot— the city's most popular raw and seafood bar—opened in its current building in 1912, and little has changed since. Pull on a fish-shaped brass door handle, step across the cracked mosaic floor, slide onto one of the 18 barstools in the narrow room, and get whisked back in time. There's no website, no computer system, no reservations on Open Table. You won't find over-the-top haute cuisine here, either, just a beautifully simple winning formula: wonderfully fresh and barely adulterated seafood served by a friendly member of the San-cimino Family—owners since 1946—at a worn marble counter, along with paper napkins to wipe the crab juice off your mug. Recipes are no-fuss—think steamed, raw or fried seafood, with terrific house-made cocktail sauce—the prices are very reasonable, and the service gruffly charming. Eating here is a fun, old-timey experience—and needs to be, as there's usually an hour or two wait to get in! If you're starving and tired of waiting, you can call in a take-out order while standing in line. Only cash and local checks accepted.

1517 Polk St. (btw. California and Sacramento sts.). ℭ **415/673-1101.** Entrees $6–$45. Mon–Sat 10:30am–5:30pm. No reservations. Bus: 1, 12, 19, 47, or 49. Cable car: California St.

## Inexpensive

**Del Popolo** ★★ PIZZA   Wood-fired Neapolitan-inspired pizza is the star at this casual Nob Hill joint, an outgrowth of owner Jon Darsky's wildly popular food truck of the same name. The menu goes way beyond the expected, however: Roasted mushrooms with toasted hazelnuts and aged gouda make a

# CHINATOWN—SO MANY choices!

San Francisco's **Chinatown** is the largest Chinese enclave outside of China, so it follows that we have lots of Chinese restaurants, most of them in the inexpensive category. It's hard to know which place to try. Some look clean and inviting, with bright colored photos of yummy delicacies posted outside; others have sun-faded menus peeling off of dirty windows—but looks can be deceiving. So how do you choose? We think the following restaurants stand out from the pack.

**Brandy Ho's Hunan Food** ★, 217 Columbus Ave. (brandyhos.com; ✆ **415/788-7527**), is rightly known for its Three Delicacies—a main dish of scallop, shrimp, and chicken seasoned with ginger, garlic, and wine. Most dishes are served hot and spicy; just ask if you want the kitchen to tone it down.

**R&G Lounge** ★, 631 Kearny St. (rnglounge.com; ✆ **415/982-7877**), is a very popular—and pricy—three-story restaurant with plenty of room for large and small parties; best on the menu are the salt-and-pepper crab, and R&G special beef.

**Great Eastern** ★, 649 Jackson St. (greateasternsf.com; ✆ **415/986-2500**), specializes in dim sum, as well as fresh seafood pulled from tanks lining the walls—Prez Obama stopped in here for takeout.

At **House of Nanking** ★★, 919 Kearny St. (houseofnanking.net; ✆ **415/421-1429**), abrupt and borderline-rude waiters—half the fun of Chinatown—serve vegetarian dishes as well as perfect sesame chicken. The fish soup is stellar too, though you have to ask for it specially, as it's not on the English-language menu.

**Hunan Home's** ★★, 622 Jackson St. (✆ **415/982-2844**), is popular with locals for its wicked hot-and-sour soup, and "Succulent Bread"—baked and then slightly deep fried.

The delicious, wonderfully spicy Sichuan dishes at **Z & Y Restaurant** ★★, 655 Jackson St. (zandyrestaurant.com; ✆ **415/981-8988**) top all the food critics' hit lists. Expect a long wait to taste why.

One of the hottest recent restaurant openings, **Mr. Jiu's** ★★, 28 Waverly Place (misterjius.com; ✆ **415/857-9688**) combines Chinese flavors and cooking sensibilities with California's farm-to-table practices to create an elegant, must-try menu offered in a modern, streamlined dining room.

Another newsworthy recent opening, casual and loud **Market Restaurant** at **China Live** ★, 644 Broadway (chinalivesf.com; ✆ **415/788-8188**), is connected to a Chinese gourmet emporium. The well-priced dishes served in moderate portions tend to be on the sweet side . . . kind of like a gourmet P.F. Chang's.

great start to any meal, as do the heirloom tomatoes with avocado and seeded crackers. Heck, add an order of mussels and you could make a meal of it before even sinking your teeth into a slice of margherita or house-made sausage pizza. But that would be a mistake: Don't miss out on those gourmet pizzas.

855 Bush St. (btw. Taylor and Mason sts.). delpopolosf.com. ✆ **415/589-7940.** Antipasti $6–$14, pizzas: $12–$19. Sun and Tues–Thurs 5:30–10pm; Fri–Sat 5:30–11pm.

# NORTH BEACH/TELEGRAPH HILL

A popular nightlife destination, North Beach is known for old-school Italian restaurants, sidewalk cafes, a smattering of strip clubs, and vintage bars where Beat writers once hung out—but it's got a few trendy, upscale surprises as well.

## Expensive

**Coi** ★★ CALIFORNIAN   An intimate beacon of refinement on bawdy Broadway, Coi (pronounced "kwa," an Old French word meaning tranquil) offers one of the city's top iterations of haute cuisine with molecular gastronomy influence. A tiny spot divided into two wood-on-wood dining rooms (it feels somewhere between a luxury double-wide and a modern cabin—in a good way), Coi was founded by self-taught two-Michelin-star–ranked chef Daniel Patterson; new chef Matthew Kirkley continues Patterson's minimalist yet perfectionistic approach. Each evening Coi offers only one tasting menu with 8 to 11 courses based on what is fresh and available. Selections might include abalone with Bartlett pear, sea lettuce, and celery; skate wing with sweetbreads, green apple, and chive; black bass with spot prawn Finocchiona and cucumber; or a stunning sculptural praline with crémeux and mandarin orange.

373 Broadway (at Montgomery St.). coirestaurant.com. ✆ **415/393-9000.** Tasting menu $250. Thurs–Mon 5:30–9:30pm. Valet parking $15. Bus: 1, 8, 10, or 12.

**Quince** ★★ CALIFORNIAN/ITALIAN   Chef Michael Tusk's formula for success is straightforward: Make friends with the best farmers, ranchers, and fishermen in the region, ensure they reserve the best of the best for you, then lovingly combine your ingredients into superb, seasonally focused dishes. Tusk, who honed his skills at Chez Panisse (the iconic Bay Area restaurant that pioneered California's farm-to-table cooking style), takes this concept to the highest level, allowing ingredients to star on a plate without much distraction. Such preciousness doesn't come cheap: Diners choose between a multicourse dinner menu in the dining room or a caviar menu plus a handful of a la carte entrees in the Salon, with wine pairings available for an additional (steep) fee. Many of the dishes are Italian in origin (like the *garganelli*—lobster with lemon verbena and English peas); meaty entrees also shine (Watson Farm lamb with olive, fava bean, and allium). Leave room for dessert—along with stunning edible works of sweet art, you're presented a selection of chocolates.

470 Pacific Ave. (at Montgomery St.). quincerestaurant.com. ✆ **415/775-8500.** Tasting menu $250, Salon entrees $32–$44; bar menu $12–$60. Mon–Sat 5:30–10pm. Valet parking $12. Bus: 1, 10, 12, or 30.

## Moderate

**Original Joe's** ★ ITALIAN   This San Francisco institution claims it has served everyone from "the head politician to the head prostitute"—presumably not at the same time, though you never know. Founded by Tony Rodin in 1937, during the Great Depression, the restaurant is now run by his grandkids, John Duggan and his sister Elena, and they haven't changed it much. The

# Chinatown & North Beach Restaurants

TELEGRAPH HILL

Pioneer Park ■ Coit Tower

Filbert Steps

Filbert St.

Grant Ave.

Washington Square

Jasper Pl.

Union St.

Kearny St.

Green St.

Green St. Stairs

Front St.

**12**

**11**

Vallejo St.

Vallejo St. Stairs

Columbus Ave.

NORTH BEACH

Broadway

Montgomery St.

**10**

Battery St.

**8**

**7**

**9**

Stockton St.

Pacific Ave.

**6**

**5**

Jackson St.

Sansome St.

**3** **4**

Kearny St.

CHINATOWN

Washington St.

Powell St.

Grant Ave.

Waverly Pl.

Portsmouth Square

■ Chinese Culture Center

Transamerica Pyramid

Clay St.

Leidesdorff St.

**2**

Commercial St.

Sacramento St.

**1**

Powell/Hyde/Powell-Mason Cable Car

Wells Fargo History Museum ■

Halleck St.

California St.

California St. Cable Car

FINANCIAL DISTRICT

Kearny St.

Pine St.

Montgomery St.

Bush St.

Sutter St.

Brandy Ho's Hunan Food **7**
Coi **10**
Golden Boy Pizza **11**
Great Eastern **4**
House of Nanking **6**
Hunan Home's **5**
Market Restaurant at China Live **8**

Mister Jiu's **1**
Original Joe's **12**
Quince **9**
R&G Lounge **2**
Z & Y Restaurant **3**

0 ———— 1/8 mi
0 ———— 200 m

menu still features a large selection of typical Italian comfort food in generous portion sizes, and at reasonable prices in vintage surroundings. By the way, this is not quite the original "Original Joe's": That one was located in the Tenderloin from 1937 until it was destroyed by fire in 2007. The current Original Joe's opened in North Beach in 2012, and their loyal clientele followed. Once you've had the Parmigiana here, you'll understand why.

601 Union St. (at Stockton St.). originaljoessf.com. ✆ **415/775-4877.** Entrees $11–$44. Mon–Fri 11:30am–10pm, Sat–Sun 10am–10pm. Bus: 30, 41, or 45.

### Inexpensive

**Golden Boy Pizza ★ PIZZA**   Even 30 years ago, it was a tradition to stop by this sliver of a restaurant to grab a fresh square of focaccia-style pizza to help soak up the beer consumed at the myriad Grant Avenue bars around the corner. The tradition continues. But you needn't be buzzed or closing the bars to find satisfaction—you can grab a to-go slice or plunk yourself down on a barstool to devour slices or whole sheets of cheese, pepperoni, sausage, clam and garlic, pesto, or combo pizza—not to mention wash it down with beer or wine.

542 Green St. (btw. Jasper and Bannan Place). goldenboypizza.com. ✆ **415/982-9738.** Slices $2.75–$3.75; sheets $35–$41. Sun–Thurs 11:30am–11:30pm; Fri–Sat 11:30–2:30am. Bus: 8, 30, 41.

# FISHERMAN'S WHARF

The myriad restaurants along this northeastern edge of town cater primarily to tourists, who happily pay top dollar for the ease and privilege of eating seafood overlooking the bay. While most of these spots are overpriced and not necessarily that good (though even an average bowl of chowder served in a sourdough bowl from a streetside stand is pretty darned tasty), there are several worth seeking—including one of the city's most highly revered restaurants.

### Expensive

**Restaurant Gary Danko ★★★ FRENCH**   If there is one place to splurge in San Francisco, this is it. The sophisticated cuisine of chef/owner Gary Danko eschews over-the-top molecular gastronomy pomp to focus instead on expertly prepared dishes influenced by global ingredients and French technique. Over the 2-plus decades that Chef Danko's sleek, art-filled dining room has been an "it" destination, he's garnered plenty of prestige—Michelin stars, a five-star Mobil rating, the James Beard Award for Best New Restaurant and Best Chef in California. But the real win is that diners continue to rank his dining room at the top, despite an ongoing rush of contenders. The portions are generous, the service is unparalleled, and there's not a hint of pretention—as it should be.

800 North Point St. (at Hyde St.). garydanko.com. ✆ **415/749-2060.** Entrees $28–$39. 3-course menu $76; 4-course $96; 5-course $111; wine pairing $76. Daily 5:30–10pm. Valet parking $20. Bus: 30, 47, or 49. Streetcar: All Embarcadero lines. Cable car: Powell–Hyde.

## Moderate

**Buena Vista Cafe** ★ AMERICAN    Serving breakfast all day, along with a variety of fat burgers, sandwiches, salads, pasta, steaks, and crab cakes, the Buena Vista has become a tourist destination in its own right. Buena Vista means "good view" in Spanish, and this classic spot right by the cable-car turnaround certainly lives up to its name. Converted from a boarding house to a saloon in 1916, it provided a perfect setting for fishermen and dockworkers to take a break while watching the bay, literally, "for their ships to come in." When the fishing boats arrived, they could chug their drinks and quickly run down the hill to get back to work. Grab an empty space at one of the large, round communal tables and laugh as long-time waitress Katherine flings napkins at you and scowls if, heaven forbid, you dare *not* order their famed Irish coffee—a "national institution," for it was here, in 1952, that the first Irish coffee in the U.S. (inspired by a similar drink served in Ireland's Shannon Airport) was crafted by owner Jack Koeppler and Pulitzer Prize–winning travel writer Stanton Delaplane.

2765 Hyde St. (at Beach St.). thebuenavista.com. ☏ **415/474-5044.** Breakfast & lunch $12–$16; dinner entrees $15–$22. Mon–Fri 9am–2am, weekends 8am–2am, no food or children after 9:30pm. Bus: 47. Streetcar: All Embarcadero lines. Cable car: Powell–Hyde.

**Scoma's** ★★ SEAFOOD    Hidden on a tranquil pier between the bay and Fisherman's Wharf's bustling main shopping street, this old-school San Francisco seafood restaurant would be worth visiting even if it didn't offer free valet parking(!) in the middle of Fisherman's Wharf. It's even more worthwhile since the menu got a makeover a few years back. Plates piled high with crispy fried calamari, fish and chips, cioppino, and Dungeness crab Thermidor all showcase the restaurant's "pier to plate" commitment to bring you native seafood caught by small local fishermen. It's got lots of dining nooks and interesting views of the city's workaday bayfront; there's also a reasonably priced kids menu of classics (think chicken nuggets). For lunch on the wharf, this is always my first choice. Bonus: A renovation of the bar and dining room a few years ago kept the 1960s vintage vibe, which is a very good thing.

1965 Al Scoma Way, Pier 47. scomas.com. ☏ **415/771-4383.** Lunch entrees $17–$23, dinner $18–$40. Sun–Thurs 11:30am–10pm; Fri–Sat 11:30am–10:30pm. Bus: 76. Streetcar: F.

## Inexpensive

**Crepe Café** ★ FRENCH    What started as a food cart in touristy Ghirardelli Square has become a favorite in a permanent location on Pier 39. The cafe serves up all the usual crepe toppings, both sweet (sugar, Nutella, strawberries) and savory (ham, eggs, or chicken), but it also gets creative with unusual choices like pesto and avocado. People in the know take their crepes out the back door and find a seat on the wooden benches to watch chubby sea lions bark and fight for space on the docks.

Pier 39 (at Embarcadero). the-crepe-cafe.com. ☏ **415/318-1494.** Entrees $6–$12. Free valet parking. Daily 9am–10pm. Bus: 47. Streetcar: All Embarcadero lines.

# THE MARINA/PACIFIC HEIGHTS/ COW HOLLOW

These picturesque communities feature a plethora of charming vintage apartment complexes, seriously stunning multimillion-dollar homes, and a few shopping streets, where restaurants (and plenty of bars) are always abuzz with convivial, young, and well-heeled residents.

## Expensive

**Greens ★★ VEGETARIAN**  Greens was, arguably, the first restaurant in the U.S. to take a gourmet approach to vegetarian food, with an ambitious menu, extensive wine list, and a serene decor of hand-carved wood and oversize windows offering up one of the best water views in the city. (The restaurant is in a former warehouse at Fort Mason.) Its status remains untouched. Come here even if you're a devoted carnivore: The food is delicious and jumps continents with ease, offering terrific veggie takes on Moroccan, Mexican, Asian, and Italian foods. Or opt for the "Greens to Go" menu (daily 9am–4pm) if you'd like to take a picnic on the Marina Green.

Bldg. A, Fort Mason Center. greensrestaurant.com. ✆ **415/771-6222.** Entrees $17–$28; brunch $15–$20. Lunch Tues–Fri 11:45am–2:30pm; brunch Sat 11am–2:30pm; brunch Sun 10:30am–2pm. Dinner nightly 5:30–9pm (until 9:30 Fri–Sat). Bus: 28 or 30.

## Moderate

**Ace Wasabi's Rock & Roll Sushi ★ SUSHI/JAPANESE**  This hopping neighborhood restaurant frequented by a casual, younger set infuses affordable, creative sushi with moody brick-walled environs and '80s hits that make you want to hang out for a while. Locals go for the nigiri, specialty rolls, salads, and cooked appetizers such as whole grilled calamari, tuna poke tostadas, and grilled short ribs. Delicious, affordable—and fun. Weekday happy hour from 5:30 to 6:30pm is a great deal, too.

3339 Steiner St. (btw. Chestnut & Lombard sts.). acewasabisf.com. ✆ **415/567-4903.** Sushi $6–$16, appetizers $3–$14. Mon–Wed 5:30–10pm, Thurs 5:30–10:30pm, Fri–Sat 5:30–11pm, Sun 5–10pm. Bus: 47, 49, 30.

**SPQR ★★ ITALIAN/CALIFORNIAN**  Of the many reasons to visit the upscale shopping stretch of upper Fillmore, this perpetually crowded small restaurant tops my list. Locals flock here for the fine cooking of executive chef (and 2014 *Food & Wine* Best New Chef) Matthew Accarrino, paired with the exceptional Italian wine list crafted by award-winning wine director and owner Shelley Lindgren. Order an array of plates to share, definitely including a pasta—perhaps corn raviolini with *huitlacoche* butter, chive, smoked chanterelle mushroom, and goat cheddar; or bacon-wrapped rabbit with eggplant, cherry tomato, and basil—and sample 3-ounce wine tastes, mixing and matching your way through a perfect San Francisco meal.

1911 Fillmore St. (btw. Bush and Pine sts.). spqrsf.com. ✆ **415/771-7779.** Lunch entrees $17–$34; dinner $31–$42. Mon–Fri 5:30–10:30pm; Sat 11am–2:30pm and 5:30–10:30pm; Sun 11am–2:30pm and 5:30–10pm. Bus: 22.

# family-friendly **RESTAURANTS**

San Francisco's trendiest culinary adventures—3+ hours for a multicourse farm-to-table feast—may be beyond your scope, when traveling with little ones who want nothing more a quick bowl of buttered noodles. Still, San Francisco is one of the best cities in the world to visit with children, and we have lots of places where you can painlessly expand their culinary horizons.

Kids and adults can both be satisfied at the Richmond District's **Ton Kiang** (p. 114), a dim sum restaurant where lazy susans in the center of the table make it extra fun to access your pork bun; simple dishes like fried rice can be ordered off the menu, and when all else fails, there's always a big bowl of fresh fruit at the ready. Downtown, more expensive **Yank Sing** delivers the same style of deliciousness and fun, though it's in a much larger and more posh environment.

**Farallon** (p. 92), with its jellyfish lamps and kelp rising from the floor, is an underwater fantasy perfect for budding marine biologists and *Little Mermaid* fans; ordering from the a la carte menu means dinner does not have to be a 3-hour affair. Or, for more old-school seafood options, both **Scoma's** (p. 103) and **Pier 23** (p. 91) offer handy kids menus.

**SoMa StrEat Food Park** (p. 96) is a happening place to grab lunch with the kids, with a variety of food trucks guaranteeing something for even the pickiest tot. Let them run free amongst the local dot-com geniuses lunching here. Who knows? Maybe they will make a few future connections.

Kids like getting up close to the sea creatures displayed in the **Swan Oyster Depot** (p. 98) window. Plus it's so small, loud, and crowded, if your child accidentally drops a bowl of chowder on the floor, no one will even notice.

One last thought for kids: Take them to one of our city's colorful Chinese restaurants—see **"Chinatown—So Many Choices"** on p. 99.

**Tacolicious ★ MEXICAN**   This crowded, festive spot is popular for its delicious gourmet tacos and strong cocktails. With high ceilings, modern lighting, and warm green jewel tones on the walls, there's nary a Mexican flag in sight; the only clue you've entered a Mexican restaurant—and it's a big one—is the 120 types of tequila offered at the bar. Trying to fit into the micro-miniskirt that seems de rigueur for women customers here? Order the Marina Girl Salad, featuring avocado, cucumber, pumpkin seeds, cotija cheese, and jalapeno vinaigrette. Or follow SF Giants pitcher Tim Lincecum, who's all about the *carnitas,* which he enjoys with his Giants teammates on occasion. We're guessing they go for the tacos, which are made with a variety of fillings including summer squash, filet mignon, and the house specialty, guajillo-braised beef short ribs. This place is so popular that the owners have opened two more city locations, in North Beach (1548 Stockton St.) and in the Mission (741 Valencia St.), plus two more in the South Bay.

2250 Chestnut St. (at Avila St.) tacolicious.com. ℭ **415/346-1966.** Entrees $9–$18. Mon–Wed 11:30am–11pm; Thurs–Fri 11:30am–midnight; Sat 11am–midnight; Sun 11am–11pm. No reservations. Bus: 22, 30, or 43.

# JAPANTOWN/WESTERN ADDITION

Abutting each other in the middle of the city, these two districts are relatively easy to reach, lying just east of the Civic Center and south of Pacific Heights. Western Addition is a somewhat gritty, nondescript area, with most of its action along or around the Divisadero Street thoroughfare, while Japantown (see p. 141 for its history) is little more than a pair of indoor malls. Nevertheless, there are some restaurant gems here.

## Moderate

**Nopa** ★★ CALIFORNIAN   A poster child for the gestalt of the San Francisco restaurant scene, large and airy Nopa combines seasonal "urban rustic" and "organic wood-fired" cuisine, served in high-ceilinged industrial-chic environs with a hopping bar scene. Make a reservation well in advance or wait to pounce on a barstool or a seat at the big, first-come-first-served communal table. You'll enjoy artisan libations, one of the city's best grass-fed burgers, and plenty of veggie-, meat-, and fish-centric dishes that celebrate the region's bounty. Don't worry—the rather precious "taste from the kitchen" (perhaps a single radish with salt or some other tease) isn't indicative of the regular portions, which are hearty. Another reason to visit: It's in an up-and-coming stretch of the city rarely explored by tourists, conveniently near **The Independent** (p. 212), where, if you're lucky, you can catch an awesome live show.

560 Divisadero St. (at Hayes St.). nopasf.com. ⓒ **415/864-8643.** Entrees $19–$32, brunch $7–$16. Daily 6pm–midnight (until 1am Fri–Sat); Sat–Sun brunch 11:30am–2:30pm. Reservation recommended. Bus: 21, 24.

**State Bird Provisions** ★★★ CALIFORNIAN   One of the hottest destinations since its December 2011 opening (and still nearly impossible to get into, thanks to online reservations that are never available), State Bird snared a James Beard Award right out of the gate—a nearly unheard-of occurrence. Chef Stuart Brioza's creative, fresh, internationally influenced small plates are wheeled around on carts and carried on trays—just like at your favorite Chinese dim sum restaurant—and they are impossibly good. In the casual, friendly dining room with a shockingly tiny open kitchen, everything comes easily—perhaps too much so; you need only point to what you want as it passes by. The enthusiastic staff might offer you Nova Scotia oysters with spicy kohlrabi kraut and sesame seeds, or croquettes created from rabbit and fontina cheese; you can also order from a small menu of standards, which includes savory pancakes. Whatever the case, you're bound to have a meal to remember. Reservations are necessary up to 60 days in advance. If you don't have one, stand in line at 4:30pm, and wait for the doors to open at 5:30pm—you will eventually get seated; one third of the restaurant is set aside for walk-ins, including the chefs' counter where you get the best view of the cooks in action.

1529 Fillmore St. (at O'Farrell St.). statebirdsf.com. ⓒ **415/795-1272.** Dishes $3–$22. Mon–Thurs 5:30–10pm, Fri–Sat 5:30–11pm. Reservations recommended. Bus: 1, 22, or 38.

# CIVIC CENTER/HAYES VALLEY

Hayes Valley, which is just a few blocks from the Civic Center, is one of the hippest shopping areas in town. It's also lined with restaurants that cater to the area's discerning clientele, as well as those en route to or returning from the symphony, opera, or ballet, which are all within walking distance.

## Expensive

**Rich Table** ★ CALIFORNIAN  Owners/chefs Evan and Sarah Rich have some serious kitchen cred behind them, with years of combined experience at gold-star San Francisco restaurants Michael Mina, Quince, and Coi. When they launched their own restaurant in 2012, they wanted an open kitchen and California casual decor to make people feel they've been invited into their home. It works. Employees have a laidback but attentive style of service, fitting for the whole *mi-casa-su-casa* theme. The menu changes regularly depending on what's available and the whims of the chefs, but you can usually find the house-favorite sardine chips (one of 7×7 magazine's 100 bucket-list dishes) and dried porcini mushroom doughnuts served with raclette. Entrees may include such crowd pleasers as tagliatelle with pork sausage, manila clams, and pizza crust, or Douglas Fir pierogis with roasted apple and brown butter. You can also leave it up to the chefs for $95 per person.

199 Gough St. (at Oak St.). richtablesf.com. ✆ **415/355-9085.** Entrees $17–$36, chef tasting menu $95. Daily 5:30–10:30pm. Bus: 5, 9, 38, 47, or 49. Streetcar: Any Market St. line.

## Inexpensive

**The Grove** ★ AMERICAN  Though not a destination in itself, this comfy outpost of a popular local cafe chain is the right place to come in Hayes Valley for a fortifying, generous "healthy-ish" meal at a great price. Here's the drill: Order at the counter, find a table or a cushy armchair, and set up camp until your order comes to your table. I almost always get one of the gargantuan salads (they have about 10 fully loaded types), but you'll also find bacon-wrapped dates, ribs, potpie, and sandwiches; there's a kids menu, and, in the morning, a full breakfast. Additional locations include two in SoMa (one at Yerba Buena, 690 Mission St., and another in the Design District at 1 Henry Adams St.) and one tucked amid Upper Fillmore shopping at 2016 Fillmore St.

301 Hayes St. (at Franklin St.). thegrovesf.com. ✆ **415/624-3953.** Entrees $10–$14. Mon–Wed 8am–10pm; Thurs–Fri 8am–10:45pm; Sat 8:30am–10:45pm; Sun 8:30am–10pm. Bus: 5, 9, 38, 47, or 49. Streetcar: Any Market St. line.

**RT Rotisserie** ★★ ROTISSERIE  "Fast-casual" is quickly becoming the new norm for San Francisco restaurateurs as they seek to offset the soaring costs of doing business in this city. Still, it's pretty awesome to come to this casual counter-service joint (by the team behind high-end **Rich Table**, see above), where you can order outstanding rotisserie chicken by the whole or half (with an eclectic mix of optional sauces) or grab a sandwich or soup or salad for under $12. (Don't miss the cauliflower.) Not surprising, the sides are a step up from the norm—think fries dusted with porcini and rice powder, or charred cabbage with almonds. Grab a Mexican Coke or some wine or beer and finish with a soft serve, all of which can be enjoyed at one of the wood tables or taken to go.

101 Oak St. (at Franklin St.). rtrotisserie.com. ℰ **415/829-7086.** Entrees $9–$12. Daily 11am–9pm. Bus: 7. BART: Van Ness.

**Tommy's Joynt** ★ AMERICAN    This San Francisco institution is a love-it-or-loathe-it kind of place, where vibrant murals outside and flea–market decor inside set the perfect scene for ultracasual cafeteria-style dining and drinking. To me, the point is the price; it's getting harder and harder in the city to find well-priced food options, and they don't get much more affordable than this for a rib-sticking meal. Grab a tray and order the likes of corned beef, buffalo stew, or roast beef (plus every heavy, delicious side you can imagine) from the heat-lamp-warmed counter, then settle into a seat to devour your heaping helping of comfort food. And if you want to do some serious drinking, Tommy's offers a variety of almost 100 beers and ciders from over 30 different countries.

11011 Geary Blvd. (at Van Ness Ave.). tommysjoynt.com. ℰ **415/775-4216.** Entrees $10–$16. Daily 11am–1:40am (bar opens 10am). Bus: 38 or 90.

# MISSION DISTRICT

Concrete, urban, gritty, and colorful, the oh-so-trendy Mission District is a hotbed for restaurant hunters, who come here for everything from a humongous, unbelievably delicious to-go burrito to an unforgettable and elegant sit-down meal.

## Expensive

**Central Kitchen** ★ CALIFORNIAN    This is the epitome of California-chic dining in the trendy Mission District, brought to you by Thomas McNaughton, of upscale pizzeria **flour + water** fame (another worthy dining option; it's at 2401 Harrison St.). A covered garden patio provides alfresco dining space year-round; meanwhile, in the open kitchen, you can watch McNaughton create such delectables as halibut crudo with chili, melon rind, avocado, and shiso; basil pappardelle with braised duck, squash, and pistachio-and-squash-blossom pesto; or smoked short ribs with charred eggplant, harissa, and mint. The entrance is set back from the street, to the left of the McNaughton-owned market/cafe, **Salumeria,** at the same address.

3000 20th St. (at Florida St.). centralkitchensf.com. ℰ **415/826-7004.** Entrees $19–$29, tasting menu $65, pairings $45. Mon–Sat 5:30–10pm, Sun 5:30–9pm. Bus: 22, 27, or 33.

## Moderate

**Delfina** ★★ ITALIAN    This super-urban, relatively casual neighborhood restaurant has been one of the city's top Italian restaurants for nearly 20 years. James Beard Award–winning chef and owner/chef Craig Stoll is known for simple, rustic cuisine done right, while his wife, Annie, ensures the relaxed,

# Mission District & Castro Restaurants

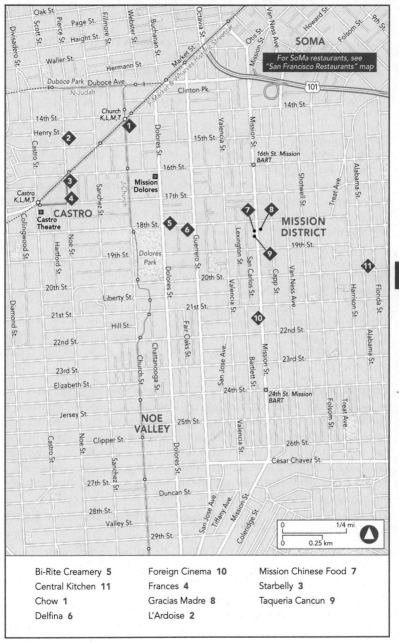

| | | |
|---|---|---|
| Bi-Rite Creamery **5** | Foreign Cinema **10** | Mission Chinese Food **7** |
| Central Kitchen **11** | Frances **4** | Starbelly **3** |
| Chow **1** | Gracias Madre **8** | Taqueria Cancun **9** |
| Delfina **6** | L'Ardoise **2** | |

knowledgeable service is equally pro. Yes, there are pastas here. But you'll find just as much satisfaction in other simple pleasures, such as grilled octopus, or roasted chicken with mushrooms and olive oil mashed potatoes. An outdoor patio open mid-March through October provides more space for diners. More casual and less expensive is neighboring **Pizzeria Delfina** (3611 18th St.; pizzeriadelfina.com; ✆ **415/437-6800**), and a second pizzeria in Pacific Heights at 2406 California St. (✆ **415/440-1189**).

3621 18th St. (btw. Dolores and Guerrero sts.). delfinasf.com. ✆ **415/552-4055.** Entrees $17–$30. Mon–Thurs 5:30–10pm; Fri–Sat 5:30–11pm; Sun 5–10pm. Bus: 14 or 22. Streetcar: J.

**Foreign Cinema** ★★ CALIFORNIAN   One of the first hot spots during the late '90s dot-com boom, this culinary (and still cool) stalwart in the Mission remains at the top of my list for its one-two punch of fantastic food and stunning atmosphere. Chef/owners Gayle Pirie and John Clark are on hand nightly, presiding over the daily-changing menu, which is dictated by the freshest finds at the morning's farmers' market and their own parade of purveyors. Always available are raw-bar specialties (oysters, crab, and more), and, if you're lucky, showstopping appetizers like baked fromage d'Affinois in a fig leaf, Mission figs, olivada, new potatoes, crudité, and baguette crostini. But there's so much more, you really need to try for yourself—and I recommend you do. Whether you eat inside the windowed, industrial-chic dining room or on the atrium patio where foreign and indie flicks play on the side of a neighboring building, it's a magical experience.

2534 Mission St. (btw. 21st and 22nd sts.). foreigncinema.com. ✆ **415/648-7600.** Entrees $12–$31. Daily 5:30–10pm (until 11pm Thurs–Sat); brunch Sat–Sun 11am–2:30pm. Bus: 14.

**Gracias Madre** ★ VEGAN/MEXICAN   San Francisco is so famous for its Mexican food, no resident within city limits lacks an opinion on where to find the best tacos or burrito. For vegans, this one often tops the list. Soft corn tacos laden with garlicky greens or grilled eggplant manage to be satisfying and surprisingly light—as well as fresh, since many of the vegetables are grown at the restaurateur's own farm. Get here early; there's always a line out front. Organic beer, wine, and cocktails are also available, and there's a happy hour Monday through Thursday from 3 to 6pm.

2211 Mission St. (at 19th St.). gracias-madre.com. ✆ **415/683-1346.** Entrees $11–$16. Daily 11am–11pm. Bus: 14 or 22.

**Mission Chinese Food** ★ CHINESE   For many foodies, eating at now-famous James-Beard-Award–winning chef Danny Bowien's original restaurant is a rite of passage. While the Chinese food is indeed inventive (Kung Pao pastrami, for example, or the pork mapo burrito), some people argue that it's overrated, and I tend to agree. Still, others can't get enough. Regardless, the cramped bustling dining space—confusingly identified out front as "Lung

Shan Restaurant"—is affordably priced and always a fun time. Portions are large and great for sharing. BYOB.

2234 Mission St. (at 18th St.). missionchinesefood.com. ℂ **415/863-2800.** Entrees $13–$25. Lunch Thurs–Mon 11:30–3pm, dinner daily 5–10:30pm. Bus: 14 or 22.

## Inexpensive

**Taqueria Cancun** ★★ MEXICAN    After a night on the town, visitors and locals looking for mouth-watering, cheap Mexican food walk, stagger, stumble, and shuffle into this tiny Mission *taqueria,* open nightly until the wee hours. Green, yellow, and red plastic cut-outs cover the ceiling; beer flags, guitars, and the Virgin Mary hang on bright yellow walls—and the clientele is as decorated and colorful as the restaurant, ranging from hipsters sporting seriously complex tattoos to slightly tipsy button-down finance guys. When you grab a table, chances are the previous diner's yellow plastic food basket will still be sitting there—you'll wait a long time for someone to clear it; just take a seat and push it aside. If the line to order is long, don't worry, it moves quickly; this place is used to crowds. No wonder—the food is delicious. The Carne Asada Super Burrito for $9 is huge, juicy, and full of flavor, its steak charred to perfection. What a surprise—they only take cash. No reservations.

2288 Mission St. (btw. 18th and 19th sts.). ℂ **415/252-9560.** Entrees $5–$9. Daily 10:30am–12:30am. Bus: 14 or 22.

# ANYONE FOR sweet nothings?

After strolling across the Golden Gate Bridge, hiking up to Coit Tower, or walking through 6,000 years of history at the Asian Art Museum, you might feel the need for a sweet treat—here are a few places sure to satisfy.

**Bi-Rite Creamery,** 3692 18th St. (birite creamery.com; ℂ **415/626-5600**) uses organic ingredients to create mouthwatering ice cream with flavors like roasted banana and toasted coconut. Bonus: They're open until 10pm!

**The Candy Store,** 1507 Vallejo St. (thecandystoresf.com; ℂ **415/921-8000**), is a candy boutique in Russian Hill featuring confections from around the world and nostalgic, old-fashioned treats.

Right in the thick of Fisherman's Wharf action at Pier 39, **The Crepe Café** (p. 103; the-crepe-cafe.com; ℂ **415/318-1494**) purveys delicious dessert crepes loaded with Nutella, caramel, strawberries, bananas, and whipped cream.

**Ghirardelli** (p. 122), 900 North Point St. at Ghirardelli Square (ghirardelli.com; ℂ **415/474-3938**), is an ice cream parlor and chocolate shop that's been serving up sweet treats for the last 160 years.

Out in Cole Valley, **The Ice Cream Bar** (815 Cole St. btw. Frederick and Carl sts.; theicecreambarsf.com; ℂ **415/742-4932**) does double duty, dispensing both sundaes and craft cocktails in a retro ice-cream parlor setting (see p. 113).

The original **Swensen's Ice Cream,** 1999 Hyde St. (swensens.com; ℂ **415/775-6818**), opened here in 1948—pure old-school indulgence.

# THE CASTRO & NOE VALLEY

As the epicenter of San Francisco's gay community since the late 1960s and 1970s, the Castro has for years supported some excellent restaurants. Directly to the south, the neighborhood of Noe Valley has more recently begun to attract foodies, particularly along a strip of 24th Street west of Church Street.

## Expensive

**Frances** ★★ CALIFORNIAN   With only 37 seats, this tiny neighborhood restaurant with a tiny menu consistently delivers a huge dining experience. Ever since it opened in 2009, Melissa Perello's baby has remained a top place in the city. Its eclectic menu includes choices as varied as seared king salmon with creamed corn, English peas, black garlic, and charred shishito pepper; or Liberty duck confit with ricotta dumpling, grilled broccolini, and habañero stone fruit jam. Don't miss the applewood-smoked bacon beignets—you dip them in crème fraîche with maple and chive. For dessert, the lumberjack cake—apple, kumquat, Medjool dates, and maple ice cream—is a crowd pleaser, as is the clever idea of selling house red and white wines for the bargain price of $1.80 an ounce. Make a reservation up to 60 days in advance, or walk in and sit at the bar.

3870 17th St. (at Pond St.). frances-sf.com. ℂ **415/621-3870.** Entrees $18–$29. Daily except Mon, 5–10pm (Fri–Sat until 10:30pm). Reservations recommended. Bus: 22, 24, or 33. Streetcar: Any Market St. line.

## Moderate

**L'Ardoise Bistro** ★★ FRENCH   Pronounced "lard wazz"—French for the large chalkboard listing the daily specials—this hidden Castro gem feels like an old Parisian bistro, with rich burgundy walls, plush carpet, heavy curtains, and dark wood. The mood is romantic, and the food a bit more special than usual. Escargots are served *en gueusaille*—in fried potato cups—with garlic and parsley cream sauce. Favorite entrees are just as Gallic; think coq au vin in red wine sauce with potato puree, bacon, and pearl onions; or roasted rack of lamb with *pomme frites,* garlic, and parsley butter. Add a bottle from the selective wine list and a cheese plate to finish, and your evening will be *parfait.*

151 Noe St. (at Henry St.). ardoisesf.com. ℂ **415/437-2600.** Entrees $17–$34. Tues–Thurs 5:30–10pm; Fri–Sat 5–10:30pm. Bus: 24. Streetcar: Any Market St. line.

**Starbelly** ★ CALIFORNIAN   American classics and a sweet cafe atmosphere make this small, laid-back post with an outdoor patio a favorite. Burgers with house-cut fries, potpies, steaks, and a variety of thin-crust pizzas are complemented by microbrew beers, some imported from Belgium and Canada, others produced by local artisan breweries. Dessert here is anything but a second thought: Try the salted caramel pot de crème with rosemary cornmeal cookies, or warm toffee cake drenched in caramel sauce and served with Medjool dates and mascarpone cheese.

3583 16th St. (at Noe and Market sts.). starbellysf.com. ℂ **415/252-7500.** Entrees $11–$24. Mon–Thurs 11:30am–11pm; Fri 11:30am–midnight; Sat 10:30am–midnight; Sun 10:30am–11pm. Bus: 22. Any Market St. light rail or streetcar.

## Inexpensive

**Chow** ★ AMERICAN   This casual neighborhood restaurant chain—an affordable local favorite, with crowds to match—features a slew of comfort foods as well as wholesome options to satisfy every palate. It's just the place to go when you're hungry and want a menu that's sure to have something you want, with that kind of all-day breakfast feel. Expect upscale versions of such classics as a BLT, Cobb salad, chicken noodle soup, spring pesto lasagna, grilled catch of the day, or beef pot roast. The hearty weekend brunch is popular, as is the weekday breakfast. Beer and wine are available. There's usually a line to get in, but you can call the same day to put your name on the list; reservations are only accepted for groups of eight or more.

215 Church St. (near Market St.). chowfoodbar.com. ⓒ **415/552-2469.** Entrees $9–$16. Sun–Thurs 8am–10pm; Fri–Sat 8am–10:30 pm. Bus: 22 or 37. Streetcar: Any Market St. line.

# COLE VALLEY/HAIGHT-ASHBURY

Though a few short blocks away from each other, Cole Valley and the Haight are like distant cousins. While Cole Valley is a charming hamlet with 3 short blocks of restaurants, cafes, and shops, Haight-Ashbury can be distinctly grungy and utterly urban.

## Moderate

**Alembic** ★★ NEW AMERICAN   What started out as a casual-yet-refined cocktail escape from the grungy Haight Street vibe is now known as a great place to eat. Plunk yourself at a window seat for fantastic people-watching, or gather at one of the cozy tables in the pub-like front bar/dining area or the adjoining dining room. Either way, you're privy to the cooking mastery of chef Rachel Aronow, who focuses her menu on seasonal, vegetable-forward snacks, shared plates, and entrees, often starring underutilized cuts of meat, like hog tail or beef heart. (Traditionalists, never fear: There's also darn fine fried chicken and a snazzy bourbon-brined grilled pork tenderloin.) The kitchen takes a rest on Monday, but the bar is open 7 days a week.

1725 Haight St. (btw. Cole and Schrader sts). alembicsf.com. ⓒ **415/666-0822.** Entrees $16–$27. Tues 4pm–midnight; Wed–Fri 4pm–2am; Sat 2pm–2am; Sun 2pm–midnight. Bus: 6, 7, 33, 43.

**The Ice Cream Bar** ★★ ICE CREAM   Mixology and nostalgia collide at this 1930s-style soda fountain. Add in locally sourced, organic ingredients and you've got a quintessential "new San Francisco" establishment—and perhaps the only bar that can satisfy both kids and adults in one delightfully retro space. While kids can choose from the unique ice cream flavors, sundaes, and floats made in-house daily, adults can imbibe on adult-sweet treats, like Dublin Honey, a float made with Guinness and port. There's also a wide selection of beer, wines, and artisanal cocktails (made with liquors and syrups that the staff infuses on site), plus dessert and food items like pulled pork sandwiches. Don't plan on lingering over a meal too long, though—there are only a few seats.

815 Cole St. (btw. Frederick and Carl sts.). theicecreambarsf.com. © **415/742-4932.** Sun–Thurs noon–10pm, Fri–Sat noon–11pm. Bus: 6. Streetcar: N.

# RICHMOND/SUNSET DISTRICTS

Yes, it's a haul from downtown to "the Avenues," but these restaurants make it worth the trip out to these quiet neighborhoods with quaint shopping streets.

## Inexpensive

**Burma Superstar** ★★ BURMESE    Despite the perpetual line to get in, this is one of my favorite restaurants—its authentic Burmese cuisine is just that good. So do what we do: Either arrive 15 minutes before the place opens to be seated first, or leave your cellphone number with the host and browse the interesting shops on Clement Street until they give you a jingle. Once you're seated in the somewhat loud, upbeat dining room, the menu may at first seem baffling, as Burmese food is influenced by so many other cuisines: Indian, Chinese, Laotian, Thai. Trust me: It's all good. Don't miss the tea leaf salad or the fried yellow-bean tofu appetizers—dishes you may swear you could live on—then try the clay-pot chicken, chili lamb with coconut rice, or any of the curries. If you don't want to wait, the waiter may direct you to their sister restaurant down the street. It's not as good and the atmosphere is so-so, but it serves many of the same items (and has fantastic happy-hour food prices).

309 Clement St. (at Fourth Ave.). burmasuperstar.com. © **415/387-2147.** Entrees $8–$16. Daily 11:30am–3pm and 5–9pm (Fri–Sat until 10pm). No reservations. Bus: 2, 38, or 44.

**Ton Kiang** ★★ CHINESE/DIM SUM    My family and I have been coming to this basic, somewhat tired-looking two-story dining room for decades to dine on dim sum. While there are hipper places to go these days, I still end up here because it's easier to get a seat than it is at the hot spots—and because the dim sum offerings, paraded out on trays during peak dining hour, are still delicious. Browse the passing dishes of potstickers, deep-fried taro root, and dumplings filled with every imaginable combination of mushrooms, peas, spinach, cabbage, shrimp, scallops, pork, and crab; simply say "yes" to anything you want. The *dai dze gao* (scallop and shrimp dumplings with cilantro), and *gao choygot* (green chives and shrimp dumpling) are so crunchy, light, and perfect, you will inhale them and keep asking for more. If dim sum is not your style, you can order from the regular menu, filled with delicacies from southeastern China, including clay-pot casseroles and Peking duck.

5821 Geary Blvd. (btw. 22nd and 23rd aves.). tonkiangsf.com. © **415/752-4440.** Dim sum $4–$8; main courses $12–$30. Mon–Tues 10:30am–9pm; Thurs 10:30am–9pm; Fri 10:30am–9:30pm; Sat 9:30am–9:30pm; Sun 9am–9pm. Closed Wed. Bus: 5 or 38.

# EXPLORING SAN FRANCISCO

Like its many microclimates, San Francisco is constantly changing. Although it is a fairly small city (just over 47 sq. miles), it's packed with well-defined, diverse neighborhoods, each with a completely different personality and a wide variety of indoor and outdoor activities and attractions, sprinkled all across the city map. There's literally something for everyone, whether you're a history buff, a foodie, a culture maven, an artist, a thrill-seeker or a laid-back wanderer. In this chapter, you'll find everything from structured tours and walking itineraries to suggestions for kid-friendly activities and the best spots for you to rest and rejuvenate. Spend time in world-famous tourist destinations or discover the city's lesser-known gems—either way you're bound to discover why millions of visitors leave their hearts in San Francisco.

## FISHERMAN'S WHARF

Once known as Meiggs' Wharf and extending 200 feet farther out into the bay than it does now, the pier was built by developer Henry Meiggs as part of his get-rich-quick plan to draw business from the lumber shipping trade and further develop what is now North Beach. Unfortunately, Meiggs' Wharf wasn't built with the currents and tides in mind, and he soon discovered that most ships preferred to dock closer to shore, in calmer waters. To avoid financial ruin, Meiggs foolishly tried to steal from city funds and wound up fleeing to Chile in 1854 to escape arrest. In 1856, the Cobweb Palace Saloon Eatery opened at the foot of the wharf and fishing boats began docking close by, laden with delicious local Dungeness crab.

Today, Fisherman's Wharf (fishermanswharf.org; © **415/674-7503;** for parking info go to visitfishermanswharf.com/parking) is a lot more Disney than Steinbeck, as it has been for decades. Even with the crowds of 15-plus million annual tourists that visit (as well as longtime residents like me, who relish its kitschy fun and appreciate that it's more "authentic" than most of the city), it's a spot with plenty to do and see, along one of the city's most famed postcard-perfect backdrops.

Asian Art Museum **25**
AT&T Park **17**
The Bay Lights **15**
Cable Car Museum **10**
California Palace of the
  Legion of Honor **2**
The Castro Theater **29**
Children's Creativity
  Museum **18**
Chinatown Gate **13**
City Hall **26**
Coit Tower **6**
Contemporary Jewish Museum **21**
Dolores Park **31**
The Exploratorium **7**
Ferry Building Marketplace **8**
The GLBT History Museum **28**

Glide Memorial United Methodist Church **23**
Golden Gate Bridge **3**
Golden Gate Fortune Cookie Factory **9**
Grace Cathedral **12**
Haas-Lilenthal House **11**
Japan Center **24**

**3** Golden Gate Bridge

Fort Point

Mason St.

101

San Francisco
National
Cemetery

**4**

THE PRESIDIO

*PACIFIC*

*OCEAN*

Presidio
Golf
Course

1

SEACLIFF

Lake St.

**2** Lincoln Park

California St.

Spruce St.
Locust St.
Laurel St.

PRESIDIO
HEIGHTS

Clement St.

Point Lobos Ave.

Geary Blvd.

30th Ave.
26th Ave.
24th Ave.
20th Ave.
18th Ave.

12th Ave.

2nd Ave.

Anza St.

46th Ave.
44th Ave.
42nd Ave.

32nd Ave.

22nd Ave.

16th Ave.

Presidio Blvd.

10th Ave.
8th Ave.
6th Ave.
4th Ave.

Arguello Blvd.

Parker Ave.

RICHMOND

Balboa St.

48th Ave.
40th Ave.
38th Ave.
36th Ave.
34th Ave.

28th Ave.

Gabrillo St.

Fulton St.

John F. Kennedy Dr.

Stanyan St.

The Panhan

HAIGHT
ASHBUR

Spreckels L.

GOLDEN GATE PARK

Stow L.

Crossover Dr.

Middle Dr. West

John F. Kennedy Dr.

Martin Luther King Jr. Dr.

Lincoln Wy.

Kezar Dr.

Frederick St.
Carl St.

*see "Golden Gate Park" map*

Irving St.

17th Ave.
15th Ave.
13th Ave.
11th Ave.
7th Ave.

Parnassus Ave.

Cole St.
Shrader St.

Great Hwy.

Judah St.

1

29th Ave.

35th Ave.

25th Ave.
23rd Ave.
21st Ave.
19th Ave.

9th Ave.

INNER
SUNSET

Kirkham St.

SUNSET

La Playa St.

47th Ave.
45th Ave.
43rd Ave.
41st Ave.

39th Ave.

Sunset Blvd.

Lawton St.

33rd Ave.
31st Ave.
27th Ave.

Clarendon Ave.

Moraga St.

Noriega St.

Warren Dr.

TWIN
PEAKS

Ortega St.

1

Lombard Street **5**
Mission Dolores **30**
The Painted Ladies of Alamo Square **27**
Pier 24 Photography **16**
Precita Eyes Mural Arts Center **32**
San Francisco Museum of Modern Art ( SFMOMA) **19**

San Francisco Zoo **1**
Walt Disney Family Museum **4**
Wells Fargo History Museum **14**
Yerba Buena Center
  for the Arts **20**
Yerba Buena Gardens **22**

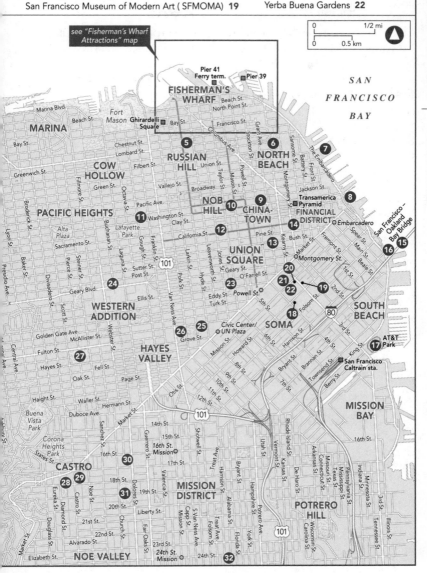

see "Fisherman's Wharf Attractions" map

Unless you come early in the morning to watch the few remaining fishing boats depart, you won't find many traces of traditional waterfront life here; the primary draw of Fisherman's Wharf is the sprawl of shops and entertainment venues stretching from Ghirardelli Square at the west end to Pier 39 at the east. Two marinas flanking Pier 39 house sightseeing ferry fleets, including the ferries to Alcatraz and Angel islands (see p. 159). The most famous residents of Fisherman's Wharf are the hundreds of **California sea lions** (p. 123) that hang out, barking on the docks at Pier 39.

Perennially popular sights at the Wharf are the **Ripley's Believe It or Not! Museum** at 175 Jefferson St. (ripleys.com/sanfrancisco; © 415/202-9850) and the street performers who convene on the stage at Pier 39. In the summer of 2014, two more cheesy attractions opened at 145 Jefferson Street: **The San Francisco Dungeon** (http://sanfrancisco.thedungeons.com; © 855/753-9999; see website for show times), where costumed character actors take visitors through 200 years of colorful San Francisco history; and **Madame Tussauds** (madametussauds.com/SanFrancisco; © 866/223-4240; daily 10am–9pm), the world-famous gallery of wax statues that features legends like Lady Gaga,

## which discount CARD SHOULD YOU BUY?

Several outfits in town will try to sell you a card that grants you discounts at a variety of attractions and restaurants; some throw in transportation, too. They really *do* give what they promise, but there's a problem with most of these cards: They usually include deals on stuff you'd never normally want to see or have time to cram in. Visiting extra attractions in an effort to make a "discount card" purchase pay off is a classic way to derail your vacation out of a sense of obligation.

Our advice? Don't buy a discount card without first mapping out the plans you have for your visit's days, because you will likely discover you'd spend more money obtaining the card than you'll make back in touring. Never buy a discount card, here or in any other city, on the spur of the moment.

That being said, some may pay off, especially those that allow you to skip the lines—they offer real value in terms of time saved. Here are the two we recommend:

**CityPass** (citypass.com) is a Muni and cable car pass with unlimited rides for 3

consecutive days. It also allots users 9 consecutive days to visit four top sights (five if you opt for the de Young Museum and Legion of Honor choice): California Academy of Sciences, Blue & Gold Fleet Bay Cruise Adventure, Aquarium of the Bay, and the Exploratorium or the de Young Museum. The attractions alone have a retail value of more than $150 for an adult—compare that to the CityPass price of $89 ages 12 and up, and $66 for ages 5 to 11. We think this is likely the better of the two options, as it only includes the sights most visitors would already want to see.

The **Go San Francisco Card** (smart destinations.com) can be purchased for 1 to 5 days. The price varies accordingly and does not include Muni transportation. However, Alcatraz is an option *if* you buy a "Build-Your-Own" pass. For those interested in tours (including a tour of wine country; see chapter 11) or traveling with children (it includes many sights that will interest them) it *might* be a worthwhile buy.

Alcatraz Island **14**

Alcatraz Landing
at Pier 33 **13**

Aquarium of the Bay **10**

Boudin at the Wharf **6**

Cable Car Turnaround **3**

California Sea Lions **12**

Ghirardelli Square **2**

Madame Tussaud's
Wax Museum **8**

Musée Mechanique **5**

Pier 39 **11**

Ripley's Believe It Or Not!
Museum **7**

San Francisco Dungeon **9**

San Francisco Maritime
National Historical Park **1**

USS *Pampanito* **4**

Johnny Depp, Martin Luther King, Jr., and—get this—Mark Zuckerberg. While the wax museum is perfect for all ages, some 10-year-olds might find the Dungeon frightening, and parents may find some of its content inappropriate for children under 13. Check both websites for ticket prices, which include advance purchase discounts and combo packages if you visit both attractions.

Alongside these sorts of attractions, there are still some traces of old-school San Francisco character here to enjoy. In fact, now more than ever, as the rest of the city rapidly gentrifies, Fisherman's Wharf's bric-a-brac shops, restaurants, and overall vibe remain the same as they have been for decades. Make sure to check out the convivial seafood street vendors who dish out piles of fresh Dungeness crab and sourdough bread bowls full of clam chowder from their steaming, stainless-steel carts. And, yes, you can hop on a boat and go fishing.

**Alcatraz Island** ★★★ HISTORIC SITE   If you can only take one tour in San Francisco, make it Alcatraz. Probably the most famous prison in America, if not the world, this was where the worst of the worst criminals were marooned to suffer and freeze. The building has barely changed from its days as a "grey-bar hotel." It's like stepping into the past.

In 1775, Juan Manuel Ayala was the first European to set foot on the island, naming it after the many *alcatraces,* or pelicans, that nested here. From the 1850s to 1933, Alcatraz became the site of a U.S. Army fortress and prison. Then, in 1934, the federal government converted the buildings of the military outpost into a maximum-security civilian penitentiary. It soon became known as one of the roughest places in history to be incarcerated. Inmates suffered psychologically and emotionally. The wind howled through the windows, the concrete was chilly and dank, and everything good and right in the world seemed an unreachable distance away. Worst of all, given the island's sheer cliffs, treacherous tides and currents, and frigid water temperatures, it was believed to be totally escape-proof.

Over the next 30 years, among the famous gangsters who occupied cell-blocks A through D were Al Capone; Machine Gun Kelly; Robert Stroud, the so-called Birdman of Alcatraz (an expert in ornithological diseases); and Alvin "Creepy" Karpis, a member of Ma Barker's gang. It cost a fortune to keep them imprisoned there, however, because all supplies, including water, had to be shipped in. In 1963, after an apparent escape in which no bodies were recovered, the federal government decided to close the prison. The prison complex moldered, abandoned, until 1969, when a group of Native Americans chartered a boat to the island and symbolically reclaimed Alcatraz Island for "Indians of All Tribes." They occupied the island until 1971—the longest occupation of a federal facility by Native Americans to this day—but eventually were forcibly removed by the government. (See www.nlm.nih.gov/nativevoices/timeline/520.html for more information on the Native American occupation of Alcatraz.) The next year the island was given over to the National Park Service, natural habitats were restored, and the wildlife that had been driven away during the prison years began to return. Today, you can see black-crested night herons and other seabirds here on a trail along the island's perimeter.

Admission to the island includes a fascinating audio tour, "Doing Time: The Alcatraz Cellhouse Tour," narrated by actual former convicts, who are less grizzled than you might guess. Don't be shy about pausing the recording with the stop button—otherwise it rushes you along a bit too quickly. And don't be afraid to break away after your first pass through Broadway (the main corridor) so that you can explore the recreation yard. Wear comfortable shoes (the National Park Service notes that there are a lot of hills to climb) and be sure to wear plenty of warm layers, because even when the sun's out, it's cold and windy on Alcatraz. Although there is a beverage-and-snack bar on the ferry, the options are limited and expensive; you might want to bring your own snacks for the boat. Only water is allowed to be carried onto the island.

*Note:* The excursion to Alcatraz is very popular and space is limited, so purchase tickets as far in advance as possible (up to 90 days) via the **Alcatraz Cruises** website at alcatrazcruises.com. You can also purchase tickets in person at the Hornblower Alcatraz Landing ticket office at **Pier 33.** The first departure, called the "Early Bird," leaves at 8:45am, and ferries depart about every half-hour afterward until 4pm. For a wonderfully spooky experience, try one of the night tours, or if you're looking for the extreme Alcatraz experience, take the 5-hour "Behind the Scenes" tour, which lets you explore areas previously closed to the public.

Pier 33, Alcatraz Landing near Fisherman's Wharf. alcatrazcruises.com. © **415/981-7625.** Admission (includes ferry trip and audio tour) $37 ages 12–61, $35 seniors 62+, $23 children 5–11, free for kids 4 and under; family package (2 adults, 2 kids ages 5–11) $113 (must be purchased in person or by phone, not available for night tour). Night and special tour prices slightly higher. Arrive at least 20 min. before departure time. Streetcar: E/F. Cable car: Powell-Mason.

**Aquarium of the Bay** ★ AQUARIUM   While this nonprofit aquarium is pricy and fairly small, it does provide a pleasant change of pace from the noise and crowds of the bustling streets outside, and knowing that you'll be helping to fund its conservation work and sustainable practices may make paying the ticket price a bit less painful. With over 20,000 sea creatures swimming about, you'll see the usual eels, octopuses, and jellyfish; you can pat bat rays and leopard sharks at the touch pool, or check out the otter exhibit. The highlight for most kids, aside from getting to touch the sea stars and rays, is the conveyor-belt floor that moves you along a clear tube through a 700,000-gallon tank while sharks, rays, and all sorts of fish swim beside you and over your head. If you buy your tickets online, you'll save a few bucks.

Pier 39, the Embarcadero at Beach St. aquariumofthebay.org. © **415/623-5300.** Aquarium admission $25 adults, $20 seniors 65+, $15 children 4–12, free for kids 3 and under; family package (2 adults, 2 kids) $70. Behind-the-scenes and feed-the-sharks tours for an additional fee. Open daily; hours vary but generally 10am–7pm. Closed Christmas. Parking: Pier 39 Garage across the street. Bus: 8X, 39, or 47. Streetcar: E/F. Cable car: Powell-Mason.

**Boudin at the Wharf** ★ FACTORY TOUR   After more than 30 years of being simply a bread shop in the heart of Fisherman's Wharf, Boudin Bakery super-sized into this swank, 26,000-square-foot flagship baking emporium, creating a place to eat *and* learn. Nearly half a block long, it houses a demonstration bakery, museum, gourmet marketplace, cafe, espresso bar, *and* restaurant. You can see the bakery by taking a free, self-guided tour (call ahead to make sure there are no special events happening that might close the tour). The Boudin family has been baking sourdough French bread in San Francisco since the gold rush, using the same simple recipe and original "mother dough" for more than 150 years. About 3,000 loaves a day are baked within the glass-walled bakery. Visitors can watch the entire process from a 30-foot observation window along Jefferson Street or from a catwalk suspended directly over the bakery (which is fun). You'll smell it before you see it: The heavenly aroma emanating from the bread ovens is purposely blasted out onto the sidewalk.

160 Jefferson St. (btw. Taylor and Mason sts.). boudinbakery.com. © **415/351-5561.** Tours daily 11:30am–9pm. Bus: 19, 30, or 47. Streetcar: E/F. Cable car: Powell–Mason.

**Ghirardelli Square** ★ SHOPPING MALL   This National Historic Land-mark property dates from 1864, when it served as a factory making Civil War uniforms, but it's best known as the former chocolate and spice factory of Domingo Ghirardelli (pronounced *Gear*-ar-dell-y), who purchased it in 1893. The factory has since been converted into a three-level mall containing 30-plus stores and five dining establishments. Street performers entertain regularly in the West Plaza and fountain area. Incidentally, the **Ghirardelli Chocolate Company** ★ still makes chocolate, although its factory now is on the other side of the bay. Still, if you have a sweet tooth, you won't be disap-pointed by the company's fantastic (and very expensive) old-fashioned soda fountain here at the mall; their "world famous" hot-fudge sundae is good, too.

900 North Point St. (btw. Polk and Larkin streets.). www.ghirardellisq.com. Stores gen-erally open daily 10am–9pm in summer; rest of year Sun–Fri 10am–6pm, Sat 10am–9pm. Ghirardelli chocolate store and ice cream parlor: ✆ **415/474-3938;** Sun–Thurs 10am–11pm, Fri–Sat 10am–midnight. Bus: 19, 30, or 47. Streetcar: E/F. Cable car: Powell–Hyde.

**Musée Mechanique** ★★ ARCADE   Less of a traditional museum and more a source of classic interactive amusement, this old-fashioned penny arcade (with some modern video games thrown in for good measure) has been one of my favorite places to go since I was a child. Once located at the Cliff House, this mechanical-minded warehouse of more than 200 antique, coin-operated penny arcade diversions is guaranteed fun. Because it's located among the pap of the Wharf, it's easy to confuse this one as a tourist trap, but in fact, the lack of an admission fee (you'll part only with whatever change you deposit into the machines of your choice) prove that's not the case.

Most of the machines require a few quarters to reveal their Coney Island–era thrills, and almost all of the machines are representatives of a form of mechanical artistry rarely found in working condition anywhere. My favorite machines are the Opium Den, a morality tale in which a diorama of smoking layabouts comes alive with serpents and demons, and the Bimbo Box, in which seven monkey puppets respond to your loose change by playing "Tijuana Taxi." There are also newer, yet still classic arcade games, like Whack-a-Mole. But the standout machine is creepy old Laffing Sal, a fun-house figure that roars with laughter (and horrifies small children) upon the dropping of a coin. Don't miss the photo booths, which produce the old-fashioned, quality black-and-white shots that make everyone look good.

Ensuring that guests have as much fun now as they did in the 1930s, when a guy named George Whitney was his generation's leading impresario of cheap entertainment, descendent Daniel Zelinsky—a true aficionado of such amusements—can be found on hand every day but Tuesday, repairing and polishing his beloved machines; he wears a badge reading "I work here."

Pier 45 at Taylor Street. museemecaniquesf.com. ✆ **415/346-2000.** Free admission. Open daily 10am–8pm. Bus: 19, 30, or 47. Streetcar: E/F. Cable car: Powell–Hyde.

**Pier 39** ★★ MALL/NATURE AREA   Anchoring the eastern boundary of Fisherman's Wharf, Pier 39 is a multilevel waterfront complex constructed on an abandoned cargo pier. It is, ostensibly, a re-creation of a turn-of-the-20th-century street scene, but don't expect a slice of old-time maritime life here: Today, Pier 39 is a bustling mall welcoming millions of visitors per year. Still, don't let that put you off; touristy as it is, Pier 39 is a lot of fun and offers something for everyone. You will find more than 50 stores (personal favorites include **Lefty's,** where you can buy things like left-handed scissors and coffee cups; **Krazy Kaps,** where more people spend time trying on ridiculous hats than actually buying them; and **Candy Baron,** which offers barrels and barrels of candy, with adult-themed candy hidden at the back right), as well as 13 full-service restaurants, a two-tiered Venetian **carousel,** bungee jumping, the **Aquarium of the Bay** (see p. 121), **Magowan's Infinite Mirror Maze** (see p. 144), and a stage for street performers who juggle, ride unicycles, and tell corny jokes. Kids love **Trish's Mini Donuts,** where you can put your nose on the glass and watch a machine drop blobs of batter into boiling oil and make tiny, fat, sugar-powdered rings.

Best of all, Pier 39 has the **California sea lions.** Decades ago, hundreds of them took up residence on the floating docks, attracted by herring (and free lodging). They can be seen most days sunbathing, barking, and belching in the marina—some nights you can hear them all the way from Washington Square. Weather permitting, naturalists from Aquarium of the Bay offer educational talks at Pier 39 daily from 11am to 4pm (Memorial Day through mid-October) that teach visitors about the range, habitat, and adaptability of the California sea lion.

Pier 39 is *the* place that some locals love to hate (present company excluded), but kids adore it. Considering that Fisherman's Wharf, including Pier 39, is rated one of the top tourist attractions in the world, my advice to you is: Don't listen to the naysayers. Go check it out for yourself, and grab a bag of donuts.

On the waterfront at the Embarcadero and Beach St. pier39.com. ⓒ **415/705-5500.** Shops daily 10am–9pm, with extended summer/weekend hours. Restaurant hours vary. Parking: Pier 39 Garage across the street (1 hr. parking free with validation for diners at full-service Pier 39 restaurants). Bus: 8X, 39, or 47. Streetcar: E/F. Cable car: Powell-Mason.

**San Francisco Maritime National Historical Park** ★ HISTORIC SITE/MUSEUM    Since 1962, the Hyde Street Pier has been lined with one of the world's best collections of rare working boats, maintained by the National Park Service's San Francisco Maritime National Historic Park. They include the Glasgow-built *Balclutha,* a gorgeous 1886 three-masted sailing ship that, most famously, appeared in the classic Clark Gable movie *Mutiny on the Bounty*; the *Eureka,* an 1890 paddlewheel ferryboat that was once the largest of its kind on earth; the *Hercules,* a 1907 tugboat that worked towing logs up the West Coast; and the lumber schooner *C.A. Thayer* from 1895. The *Alma,* built in 1891, was once one of many schooners that plied the waterways of the Bay Area; today, it's the only one left.

Although it's free to admire the boats from the dock, $10 will get you aboard the *Balclutha,* the *Eureka,* and the *Hercules* as much as you want for a week (National Park Service annual passes also get you on for free). All of the vessels are designated National Historic Landmarks and it's worth seeing them—particularly the *Balclutha,* a 300-foot square-rigger cargo ship that moved goods like grain and coal between San Francisco, England, and New Zealand from 1886 to 1939. Especially interesting are the tiny crew bunkbeds up front, compared to the lavish captain's quarters farther back. In 1899, the wife of *Balclutha*'s Captain Durkee gave birth to a baby girl while aboard the ship; they named her India Frances as they were sailing between India and San Francisco at the time. For more tidbits of history, use your cellphone as an audio guide by dialing ☎ **415/294-6754** and entering one of the 28 tour codes found at nps.gov/safr; click "Plan Your Visit," "Things To Do," and then "Cell Phone Audio Tour."

Before heading to the boats, be sure to pop into the park's signature **Maritime Museum,** technically the **Aquatic Park Bathhouse Building,** on Beach Street at Polk Street. Shaped like an Art Deco ship, it's filled with seafaring memorabilia, and entry is free. Check out the maritime murals. Next stop is the **Visitor Center** (also free) at Hyde and Jefferson Streets, where you can look at "The Waterfront," a surprisingly impressive, informative, and interactive exhibit about San Francisco's waterfront history, including a map and photos of some of the literally dozens of ships buried beneath the wharf and parts of the financial district. Even if you don't usually like history museums,

---

### GoCar Tours of San Francisco

If the thought of walking up and down San Francisco's brutally steep streets has you sweating already, considering renting a talking **GoCar ★** instead. The tiny yellow three-wheeled convertible cars are easy and fun to drive and they're cleverly guided by a talking GPS (Global Positioning System), which means that the car always knows where you are, even if you don't. The most popular computer-guided tour is a 2-hour loop around the Fisherman's Wharf area, out to the Marina District, through Golden Gate Park, and down Lombard Street, the "crookedest street in the world." As you drive, the talking car tells you where to turn and what landmarks you're passing. Even if you stop to check something out, as soon as

you turn your GoCar back on, the tour picks up where it left off. Or you can just cruise around wherever you want (but not across the Golden Gate Bridge). There's a lockable trunk for your things, and the small size makes parking a breeze. Keep in mind, this isn't a Ferrari—two adults on a long, steep hill may involve one of you walking (or pushing). Tours range from 1 to 5 hours and cost $59 to $225. You'll have to wear a helmet, and you must be a licensed driver, at least 18 years old. GoCar has two rental locations: at Fisherman's Wharf (431 Beach St.), and Union Square (321 Mason St.). For more information call ☎ **800/91-GOCAR** (46227) or 415/441-5695, or log onto their website at gocartours.com.

you'll find this one compelling and so will your kids; allow a good 40 minutes to explore.

**Visitor Center:** Hyde and Jefferson sts. nps.gov/safr. ℭ **415/447-5000.** Admission free. Tickets to board ships $10, free for children 15 and under. Daily 9:30am–5pm. **Maritime Museum:** Polk and Beach sts. ℭ **415/561-7100.** Admission free. Daily 10am–4pm. Park open daily except Thanksgiving, Christmas, and New Year's Day. Bus: 19, 30, or 47. Streetcar: E/F. Cable car: Powell–Hyde.

**USS Pampanito** ★ HISTORIC SITE   This sub has been through a lot—it sank six Japanese ships during four tours of the Pacific in World War II. The vessel has been painstakingly restored to its 1945 condition by admirers, who also run a smart, war-themed gift shop on the dock alongside. Tours inside the sub are available (though not recommended for the claustrophobic). She's still seaworthy, although sadly, the last time she was taken out into the ocean was to film the abysmal 1996 Kelsey Grammer film, *Down Periscope*. How glory fades . . . .

Pier 45, Fisherman's Wharf. maritime.org. ℭ **415/775-1943.** Adults $20, seniors 62+ and students $12, children 6–12 $10, free for ages 5 and under. Open daily at 9am; call for seasonal times. Bus: 19, 30, or 47. Streetcar: E/F. Cable car: Powell–Hyde.

# SOMA (SOUTH OF MARKET)

Once a somewhat desolate industrial corner of the city, SoMa is now the city's cultural hub after decades of development. In successive waves, the area has seen the arrival of world-class museums and hotels, the dot-com startups in the 1990s, the Giants' baseball stadium (see p. 221), and most recently, tech companies such as Twitter and luxury high rises such as Salesforce Tower. At its heart lies the **Yerba Buena** cultural complex, which takes up a few city blocks across the street from the San Francisco Museum of Modern Art (see p. 127); the underground Moscone Convention Center lies beneath. SoMa is also home to the oldest public park in the city: the small but charming **South Park** (64 South Park Ave.).

**The Bay Lights** ★★ LIGHT SHOW   If you stand at the waterfront anywhere along the Embarcadero, your natural tendency will be to look left, toward our beautiful Golden Gate Bridge. If it's after sunset, however, look right—at the much-less-fussed-over Bay Bridge that connects San Francisco to Oakland and Berkeley. To celebrate 75 years of connecting San Francisco to the East Bay, artist Leo Villareal was commissioned to cover the bridge with the world's largest LED-light sculpture, creating a light spectacle that appears to dance on the bridge's cables. Now a permanent installation, it's a sight that perfectly showcases San Francisco's blend of art and technology.

Nightly dusk–2am. thebaylights.org.

**Children's Creativity Museum** ★ MUSEUM/AMUSEMENT CENTER In Yerba Buena Gardens you'll find this innovative, hands-on multimedia, arts, and technology museum for children of all ages. Kids howl tunes to the

# A (nearly) CITYWIDE ATTRACTION

With long lines to board, few seats, and a slow pace, San Francisco's **cable cars** ★★★ are not the most practical means of transportation. But they're certainly the most beloved (even for locals), and a visit to San Francisco just wouldn't be complete without hopping a ride on one.

Designated official "moving" historic landmarks by the National Park Service in 1964, the cable cars clank up and down the city's steep hills like mobile museum pieces, tirelessly hauling thousands of tourists each day to Chinatown, Ghirardelli Square, Fisherman's Wharf, and parts in between. The best view is from a perch on the outer running boards—but be sure to hold on, especially around corners.

As the story goes, London-born engineer Andrew Hallidie was inspired to invent the cable cars after witnessing a heavily laden carriage, pulled by a team of overworked horses, slip and roll backward down a steep San Francisco slope, dragging the horses behind it. Hallidie resolved to build a mechanical contraption to replace horse-drawn carts and carriages, and in 1873, the first cable car line was up and running.

Promptly ridiculed as "Hallidie's Folly," the cars were slow to gain acceptance. One early onlooker voiced the general opinion by exclaiming, "I don't believe it—the damned thing works!" Indeed they do—and have for nearly 150 years.

The cars, each weighing about six tons, run along a steel cable enclosed under the street on a center rail. You can't see the cable unless you peer straight down into the crack, but you'll hear its characteristic hum and click-clacking sound whenever you're nearby. The cars move when the gripman (they don't call themselves drivers) pulls back a lever that closes a pincerlike "grip" on the cable. The speed of the car, therefore, is determined by the speed of the cable, which is a constant 9½ mph—never more, never less. The two types of cable cars in use hold a maximum of 90 and 100 passengers.

Hallidie's cable cars were imitated and used throughout the world, but all others have been replaced by more efficient means of transportation. San Francisco planned to do so, too, but met with so much opposition that the cable cars' perpetuation was actually written into the city charter in 1955. The mandate cannot be revoked without the approval of a majority of the city's voters—an unlikely prospect, given the love locals tend to feel for these cars.

San Francisco's three existing cable car lines form the world's only surviving system. The Powell–Hyde and Powell–Mason lines begin at the base of Powell and Market streets; the California Street line begins at the foot of Market Street at the Embarcadero. The fare is $7 per ride. For more information on riding them, see "Getting Around By Public Transportation" in chapter 12 (p. 273).

***The secret to catching cable cars:*** Don't wait in line with all the tourists at the turnaround stops at the beginning and end of the lines; waits can be as long as 2 hours in the summer. Instead, walk a few blocks up the line (follow the tracks) and do as the locals do: Hop on, when space permits, at any of the stops indicated by a brown and white "Cable Car Stop" sign. Hang on to a pole and have your $7 ready to hand to the brakeman.

On really busy weekends, however, if your heart is set on a cable car ride, you might just want to brave the crowds at the turnarounds: The cable cars can fill up and often don't stop to pick up passengers en route.

karaoke machine and make art projects from boxes and scraps of material. One of the most popular stations is the Claymation area where visitors make clay figures and learn all about stop-motion animation by making a quick movie, *Wallace and Gromit*–style. Next door is the fabulous 1906 carousel that once graced the city's bygone oceanside amusement park, Playland-at-the-Beach; there's also a Children's Garden, a cafe, and a fun store.

221 Fourth St. (at Howard St.). creativity.org. © **415/820-3320.** Admission $13; free for ages 2 and under. Tues–Sun 10am–4pm. Carousel: Daily 10am–5pm; $4 per ride ($3 with paid museum admission). Bus: 14, 30, or 45. Streetcar: F. BART: Powell St. or Montgomery St.

## Contemporary Jewish Museum ★ MUSEUM

Set in the heart of the Yerba Buena cultural hub, this museum is dedicated to the celebration of *L'Chaim* ("To Life"). Inside, under the skylights and soaring ceilings designed by celebrated architect Daniel Libeskind, are displays of art, music, film, and literature that celebrate Jewish culture, history, and ideas. Past exhibit subjects have been as varied as Curious George, Gertrude Stein, and Allen Ginsberg. When you're ready for a culture break, nosh on bagels and lox, matzo ball soup, or pastrami on rye at the on-site Wise Sons Jewish Deli.

736 Mission St. (btw. Third and Fourth sts.). thecjm.org. © **415/655-7800.** Adults $14, seniors/students $12, ages 18 and under free. $5 for all Thurs after 5pm; free 1st Tues of the month. Mon–Tues 11am–5pm, Weds closed, Thurs 11am–8pm, Fri–Sun 11am–5pm. Closed Passover, July 4, Rosh Hashanah, Yom Kippur, Thanksgiving, and New Year's Day. Bus: 5, 9, 14, 15, 30, or 45. Streetcar: F. BART: Powell St. or Montgomery St.

## Pier 24 Photography ★★ MUSEUM

At over 90,000 square feet, this former warehouse-turned-museum is one of the largest galleries in the world devoted exclusively to photography and video. But even with this amount of space, the main worry here seems to be that it will get too crowded. So, in an eccentric move (hey, this is San Francisco, after all), the Pilara Foundation, which owns the institution, allows only 30 people in at a time. That means you must make advance reservations online (entry is free), but these exhibits tend to be so dazzling that the advance planning is worth it. In the past, they've featured iconic works by Diane Arbus, Man Ray, and Walker Evans—though you might never know those were the photographers: In an attempt to make the viewers' experience of the art more immediate and unfettered, the gallery posts no wall text whatsoever. Instead, viewers can borrow a loosely organized gallery guide to lead them through the mazelike space. It's rather like an art scavenger hunt.

At Pier 24 (near Harrison St. and the Embarcadero). pier24.org. © **415/512-7424.** Admission free, advance reservations required. Mon–Fri 9am–5:15pm. Streetcar: E.

## San Francisco Museum of Modern Art (SFMOMA) ★★★

MUSEUM  I'll be honest: Until now, I was disappointed in our MOMA. Small, with cramped museum spaces and a design that seemed more about itself than about showcasing art, it wasn't world-class enough for a destination city. But in 2016, after a 3-year closure for renovation and expansion, SFMOMA

When asking for directions in San Francisco, be careful not to confuse numerical avenues with numerical streets. Numerical avenues (Third *Avenue* and so on) are in the Richmond and Sunset districts in the western part of the city.

Numerical streets (Third *Street* and so on) are south of Market Street in the eastern and southern parts of the city. Get this wrong and you'll be an hour late for dinner.

is a positively spectacular museum. It begins with 45,000 square feet of art-filled public space, all free of charge. But pay the (admittedly steep) entry fee, and you'll be able to explore a maze of rooms and floors featuring ongoing, temporary, and showcase exhibitions. You'll typically find at least one multimedia or experiential exhibit. Adults and children alike will enjoy PlaySFMOMA, a museum initiative supporting the creation of artist-made games—recent examples range from a pop-up virtual reality arcade to experimental art games and an art game laboratory. As in the past, the gift shop holds finds worth buying, but the cafe has taken a turn for the better, transformed into a ground-level Manhattan-chic lounge with a menu designed by chef Cory Lee of nearby **Benu** ★★ (see p. 93), plus a light-washed upstairs restaurant that reminds me of the dining room at NYC's MOMA—and that's a good thing.

151 Third St. (across from Yerba Buena Gardens). sfmoma.org. ✆ **415/357-4000.** Adults $25, seniors 65+ $22, ages 19–24 (with ID) $19, 18 and under free. Thurs 10am–9pm, Fri–Tues 10am–5pm, closed Wed. Bus: 14, 30, or 45. Streetcar: F. BART: Powell or Montgomery.

**Yerba Buena Center for the Arts** ★ ARTS COMPLEX    The **YBCA,** which opened in 1993, anchors the sprawling Yerba Buena complex, with two buildings that offer music, theater, dance, and visual arts programs and shows. It's a bit of an architectural showpiece in its own right as well: James Stewart Polshek designed the 755-seat theater, and Fumihiko Maki designed the Galleries and Arts Forum, which features three galleries and a space designed especially for dance. Exhibits range from architecture to activism as well as traveling versions of shows for other museums. *Tip:* For the cost of viewing YBCA's curated monthly series of video or film screenings—mostly experimental film and documentaries—you can get into YBCA's galleries for free.

701 Mission St. www.ybca.org. ✆ **415/978-2700.** Gallery admission $10 adults; $8 seniors, teachers, and students; free ages 5 and under. Free to all 1st Tues of month. Tues–Sun 11am–6pm, Thurs open until 8pm; closed Mon and major holidays. Contact YBCA for times and admission to theater. Bus: 14, 30, or 45. Streetcar: F. BART: Powell St.

**Yerba Buena Gardens** ★ GARDENS    This 5-acre patch of grass and gardens is the centerpiece of Yerba Buena's cultural activity, and a great place to relax in the grass on a sunny day. The most dramatic outdoor piece is an emotional mixed-media memorial to Martin Luther King, Jr. Created by sculptor Houston Conwill, poet Estella Majozo, and architect Joseph De Pace, it features 12 panels, each inscribed with quotations from King, sheltered behind a 50-foot-high waterfall. There are also several individual garden areas, including a Butterfly Garden, the Sister Cities Garden (highlighting flowers from the city's 13 sister cities), and the East Garden, blending Eastern and Western styles. Don't miss the view from the upper terrace, where old and new San Francisco come together in a clash of styles that's fascinating. May through October, Yerba Buena Arts & Events puts on a series of free outdoor festivals featuring dance, music, poetry, and more by local musicians and performers.

Bounded by Mission, Folsom, Third, and Fourth sts. yerbabuenagardens.com. Admission free. Daily 6am–10pm. Contact Yerba Buena Arts & Events, © **415/543-1718** or ybgf.org, for details about free outdoor festivals. Bus: 14, 30, or 45. Streetcar: F. BART: Powell St.

# FIDI (FINANCIAL DISTRICT)

Bordering Union Square and South of Market, most of the area known as the Financial District is a sterile forest of concrete office buildings mingling with a few business-oriented hotels. Yet the area offers more than a sea of suits. Alongside a smattering of destination restaurants (see chapter 5, p. 87) and some gorgeous historical landmarks like the **Sentinel Building** (916 Kearny St.) and the oddly stunning modern **Transamerica Pyramid** (600 Montgomery St.), the Financial District also offers the simple pleasure of walking down a corridor of bustling urbanity to the end of Market street, where it hits the Embarcadero right by the Ferry Building. Suddenly the sky opens up and you can get a wide panorama of the bay and the Bay Bridge—an opportunity to see the forest for the trees, so to speak.

**The Exploratorium** ★★★ MUSEUM    Relocated in 2013 to hip concrete-and-glass digs on Pier 15, the "world's greatest science museum"—according to *Scientific American* magazine—is cooler than ever, though it's also annoyingly crowded. This hands-on museum is all about demonstrating scientific concepts in such a sneaky way that kids think they're just playing. They learn about the properties of motion by swinging a pendulum through sand or watch a chicken's heart beating through a microscope focused on an egg yolk. (*Warning:* That exhibit may put them off scrambled eggs.) With myriad rooms loaded with things to play with, you can spend an entire afternoon here—and may want to plan on it, since you'll likely need to wait your turn to play with bubbles or discover how sound travels.

If anyone needs to refuel, there's the Seismic Joint Café for grab-and-go fare or the Seaglass Restaurant if you're in the mood to sit down and enjoy a meal. Also, if you're looking for something unique to do at night, there's an adults-only event every Thursday evening. My favorite is Pairings nights (every second Thursday of the month), when the focus is all about science and food.

Pier 15 (on the Embarcadero). exploratorium.edu. © **415/528-4444.** Adults $30, seniors/students/visitors with disabilities $25, ages 4–12 $20, free for ages 3 and under. Sat–Thurs 10am–5pm, Thurs also open 6–10pm (for 18+), Fri 10am–9pm. (Some shorter hours in winter.) Parking across the street $10 per hour. Streetcar: F.

**Ferry Building Marketplace** ★★★ HISTORIC SITE/MARKET    Completed in 1898, the Ferry Building was, in its heyday, a travel hub serving as many as 50,000 people a day. After the Bay Bridge and Golden Gate Bridge opened in the late 1930s, however, cars quickly replaced ferries as the preferred mode of transport. It would take until 2003 for the building and its iconic clock tower be opened to the public once more, after a four-year renovation that reimagined its ground floor as an epicurean marketplace. Conveniently located at the foot of Market Street, this shrine to gourmet living features shops and restaurants and high-end take-out eateries run by popular local food vendors. Fresh-baked bread, exotic mushrooms, fancy chocolates, killer hamburgers, and the best Vietnamese fast food you'll ever have—it's all here. A thrice-weekly **farmers' market** (Tues and Thurs 10am–2pm; Sat 8am–2pm) surrounding the building is one of the city's best local scenes, where everyone from chefs to hungry diners converge to load up on fresh produce for the week, not to mention indulging in everything from Korean tacos to Arab street food to freshly made pies and pastries.

Ferry Bldg., the Embarcadero (at Market St.). ferrybuildingmarketplace.com. Ⓒ **415/983-8030.** Most stores daily 10am–6pm; restaurant hours vary. Bus: 2, 12, 14, 21, 66, or 71. Streetcar: F. BART: Embarcadero.

**Wells Fargo History Museum** ★ MUSEUM    Far from being just a corporate PR site, the Wells Fargo Museum paints a surprisingly vivid portrait of early California life by using the company's once-vital stagecoaches as a centerpiece. For generations, the Wells Fargo wagon was the West Coast's primary lifeline; if you didn't want to or couldn't afford to use it (a ticket from Omaha to Sacramento was $300), then you'd be forced to take a long boat trip around Cape Horn. The curators have done a good job of bringing this past to life. You'll read biographies of some of the grizzled drivers of the 1800s, pore over old advertisements, climb aboard a nine-seat wagon, read a reproduction of a "mug book" of highway robbers from the 1870s, and even follow a sort of "CSI: Stagecoach" re-creation, investigating how the company would catch thieves after the fact. Especially after recent financial scandals, Wells Fargo has lost a lot of its cachet in American culture; the Western theme that so fascinated kids in the 1950s faded long ago. This well-assembled, two-story museum (budget about 45 min. to see it all) helps restore some of that magic. There's a free audio tour, too, although the signage is so thorough you won't need it.

420 Montgomery St. (at California St.). wellsfargohistory.com. Ⓒ **415/396-2619.** Admission free. Mon–Fri 9am–5pm. Closed bank holidays. Streetcar: F. Cable car: California St. BART: Montgomery St.

# NORTH BEACH/TELEGRAPH HILL

As one of the city's oldest neighborhoods and the birthplace of the Beat generation, North Beach has a history as rich as the Italian pastries found in the numerous shops along Columbus Avenue. Take a stroll down Columbus and pop into one of the many cafes for espresso, biscotti, and people-watching, or find a bench in Washington Square and take in the scene. (See p. 173 for a detailed walking tour of the neighborhood.)

**Coit Tower** ★ HISTORIC SITE   In a city known for its great views and vantage points, Coit Tower is one of the best. Located atop Telegraph Hill, just east of North Beach, the round stone tower offers panoramic views of the city and the bay. Completed in 1933, the tower is the legacy of Lillie Hitchcock Coit, a wealthy eccentric who left San Francisco a $125,000 bequest "for the purpose of adding beauty to the city I have always loved." Though many believe the tower is a fire hose–shaped homage to San Francisco firefighters (Coit had been saved from a fire as a child and became a lifelong fan and mascot for Knickerbocker Engine Co. #5), the tower is merely an expression of Coit's esteem; an official memorial to firefighters lies down below in Washington Square Park. Inside the base of the tower are impressive and slightly controversial (by 1930s standards) murals entitled "Life in California" and "1934," which were completed under the Depression-era Public Works of Art Project. Depicting California agriculture, industry, and even the state's leftist leanings (check out the socialist references in the library and on the newsstands), the murals are the collaborative effort of more than 25 artists, many of whom had studied under Mexican muralist Diego Rivera. The only bummer: The narrow street leading to the tower is often clogged with tourist traffic. If you can, find a parking spot in North Beach and hoof it. The Filbert and Greenwich steps leading up to Telegraph Hill are one of the most beautiful walks in the city (p. 5).

Telegraph Hill. ✆ **415/362-0808.** Admission free; elevator ride to top $9 adults, $5.50 seniors/ youth 12–17, $2.25 children 5–11 (discounted prices for SF residents). Daily 10am–6pm. Closes 5pm in winter. Closed major holidays. Bus: 39.

# NOB HILL

When the cable car started operating in 1873, this hill, previously known as California Hill, became the city's most exclusive residential area, soon dubbed "Nob Hill" after the newly wealthy residents who'd struck it rich in the Gold Rush and the railroad boom. (See "The Big Four & the Bonanza Kings" on p. 133.) These tycoons built their mansions here, but the homes were almost all destroyed by San Francisco's disastrous 1906 earthquake and fire. Today, the sites of former mansions hold the city's grandest luxury hotels—the **Inter-Continental Mark Hopkins** (p. 69), the **Stanford Court** (p. 68), the **Scarlet Huntington Hotel** (p. 68)—while the spectacular **Grace Cathedral** (see below) occupies the former site of the Crocker mansion.

Although there are few formal attractions here, Nob Hill is well worth a visit, if only to stroll around delightful **Huntington Park** with its cherubic fountain (a copy of the Tartarughe fountain in Rome), attend a Sunday service at the cathedral, visit the **Cable Car Museum** (see below), or ooh and ahh your way around the Fairmont's spectacular lobby. Nob Hill's incredibly steep streets are also great for a workout—some are so steep, the sidewalks have steps!

**Cable Car Museum** ★★ MUSEUM   This museum doesn't just offer an inside look at the inner machinations of the cable car system, it is the hub of the entire actual operating system, with four mighty winding machines working the underground cables that propel the entire system. If there's a cable break, this is where engineers splice it back together using some seriously medieval-looking implements. From decks overlooking the roaring machines, you'll see the cables shoot in from the streets, wind around huge wheels, and disappear back underground to carry more tourists up the city hills. You'll learn how the whole system works, plus get a look at the gripping mechanism that every car extends below the street level. I find it remarkable to think that nearly every larger American city once had systems just like this, but now only San Francisco maintains this antique but highly functional technology.

Don't miss the chance to go downstairs, under the entrance to the building, where, in the darkness, you can peer at the whirring 8-foot sheaves that hoist in the cables from their various journeys around the city. Now and then, a real cable car will stall as it attempts to navigate the intersection outside, where drivers have to let go of one cable and snag another, and a worker will have to drive out in a cart and give it a nudge.

1201 Mason St. (at Washington St.). cablecarmuseum.org. © **415/474-1887.** Admission free. Apr–Oct daily 10am–6pm; Nov–Mar daily 10am–5pm. Closed Thanksgiving, Christmas, and New Year's Day. Cable car: Powell-Mason and Powell-Hyde.

**Grace Cathedral** ★ RELIGIOUS SITE   Although this French Gothic cathedral, the third-largest Episcopal cathedral in the nation, appears to be made of stone, it is in fact constructed of reinforced concrete beaten to achieve a stone-like effect. Construction began on the site of railroad magnate Charles Crocker's ruined mansion in 1927, but work was stalled during the Great Depression and not completed until 1964. Grace Cathedral offers a veritable feast for the eyes; its iconic faceted rose window is only one of 68 stained glass windows, which include such unexpected subjects as Albert Einstein and John Glenn. Adults and children alike will enjoy walking the cathedral's labyrinths; there is one outside and a larger one just inside the cathedral. If you want to dive in and learn more about Grace, take the Grace Cathedral Grand Tour (90 min.; $25) or take a shorter, free, docent-led tour. There's also a free cellphone app, GraceGuide.

Where Grace really stands out is in the compassion of its congregation, in no finer display than in the Interfaith AIDS Memorial Chapel that's located to the right as you enter. Two weeks before his own death from the disease in 1990, pop artist Keith Haring completed a triptych altarpiece called *The Life of Christ.* The final 600-pound work in bronze and white gold patina sits in the chapel's place of honor.

Along with its unique ambience, Grace lifts spirits with services, musical performances (including organ recitals and *evensong,* or evening prayer,

# THE big four & THE bonanza kings

Nob Hill earned its nickname in the late 19th century when millionaire businessmen raced to see who could build the largest, most lavish mansion atop this high ground. Sadly, their fortunes could not protect them from the devastation of the great 1906 earthquake, when most of those showplaces were destroyed. Their legacy, however, lives on.

A powerful quartet known as **"The Big Four"**—Leland Stanford, Collis P. Huntington, Mark Hopkins, and Charles Crocker—was also called The Central Pacific Railroad group after the railroad they financed, running from the Mississippi River all the way to the Pacific Ocean.

The first to build on Nob Hill was limelight-loving **Leland Stanford,** president of the group, who also served as governor of California and as a U.S. Senator. At one point, he could brag his mansion had the largest private dining room in the West, and it's on this site that you'll find the **Stanford Court Hotel** ★ (see p. 68). His name lives on elsewhere, too: After his 15-year-old son passed away, Stanford converted his horse farm in Palo Alto into a university named for the boy, and now Stanford University is a world-famous institution widely considered the Harvard of the West.

While Stanford loved to spend money, **Mark Hopkins,** the group's treasurer, was much more frugal; he was happy living in small, rented quarters on Sutter Street, but his social-climber wife had other ideas. At a cost of $3 million, she commissioned a Gothic-style wooden fairytale castle, complete with towers and spires. Hopkins died just before it was completed and his wife lived there only a few years before moving to the East Coast. On the castle's site today is the **InterContinental Mark Hopkins** ★★ (p. 69).

Known for his ruthlessness, **Collis P. Huntington** spent time behind the scenes greasing palms and lobbying politicians for favorable treatment of the group's interests. The site of his mansion is now **Huntington Park** (at California and Taylor sts.). The last of the Big Four, **Charles Crocker** was the group's construction supervisor, which makes it ironic that he unwisely chose to build his mansion out of wood. After the 1906 fire, the Crocker family donated the entire city block where their home once stood to the Episcopal church, which built the beautiful **Grace Cathedral** (see p. 132) on the site.

While the Big Four made history, the **Bonanza Kings**—four Irish buddies who made their fortunes from a silver mine in Nevada—were much wealthier at the time, although their names have since faded from popular memory. **John William Mackay** and **William S. O'Brien** left little mark on San Francisco, but the mansion of partner **James C. Flood** can still be seen today at 1000 California St. on top of Nob Hill as home to the private **Pacific-Union Club.** Because it was built using Connecticut sandstone, it was one of the few structures in the area to survive the 1906 earthquake and fires. You can't go inside, but you can see the facade and admire the original bronze fence, which still exists on three sides of the property.

The last Bonanza King partner, **James Fair,** died before he could build his mansion on Nob Hill. His daughters, Tessie and Virginia, decided to build a hotel to honor their father, but they got in a little over their heads financially and had to sell it to the Law brothers. The property changed hands on April 6, 1906, less than 2 weeks before the great quake. The hotel burned, but the bit of the structure that survived was completely rebuilt with the help of architect Julia Morgan of Hearst Castle fame, and reopened in 1907, exactly 1 year after the quake, as the **Fairmont San Francisco** ★★★ (p. 69).

# CHINATOWN

The first Chinese immigrants—fleeing famine and the Opium Wars—came to San Francisco in the early 1800s to work as laborers and seek their fortunes in America, or "Gold Mountain," as they called it. By 1851, some 25,000 Chinese people were working in California, and most had settled in San Francisco's Chinatown. For the majority, the reality of life in California did not live up to the promise. First employed as workers in the gold mines during the Gold Rush, they later built the railroads, working as little more than slaves and facing constant prejudice. In spite of their challenges, this segregated community of mostly southern Chinese people thrived. Of necessity, however, they remained in this tight-knit neighborhood—Chinese people were unable to buy homes outside the Chinatown ghetto until the 1950s, when the Chinese Exclusion Act was repealed and they began to face less prejudice.

Today, San Francisco's Chinatown, bordered by Broadway, California, Kearny, and Powell streets, is the oldest in North America and the largest outside of Asia. Although frequented by tourists, the area continues to cater to local Chinese shoppers, who throng the vegetable and herb markets, restaurants, and shops. (For a list of suggested Chinatown restaurants, see box on p. 99.) Tradition runs deep here, and if you're lucky, through an open window you might hear women mixing mahjongg tiles as they play the centuries-old game. (*Be warned:* You're likely to see lots of spitting around here, too—it's part of the culture.)

With dragons at its base, the ornate, jade-roofed **Chinatown Gate** at Grant Avenue and Bush Street marks the entry to Chinatown. Red lanterns hang across the street and dragons slither up lampposts. The heart of the neighborhood is **Portsmouth Square,** where you'll find locals practicing tai chi in the mornings, playing lively games of cards, or just sitting quietly. On the beautifully renovated Waverly Place, a street where the Chinese celebratory colors of red, yellow, and green are much in evidence, you'll find three **Chinese temples:** Jeng Sen (Buddhist and Taoist) at no. 146, Tien Hou (Buddhist) at no. 125, and Norras (Buddhist) at no. 109. If you enter, do so quietly so that you do not disturb those in prayer. A block west of Grant Avenue, **Stockton Street,** from 1000 to 1200, is the community's main shopping street, lined with grocers, fishmongers, tea sellers, herbalists, noodle parlors, and restaurants. Explore at your leisure. For a Chinatown walking tour, see p. 164, and visit sanfranciscochinatown.com for more information.

## The Secret Life of Waverly Place

Ironically, temple-lined Waverly Place was also once the site of two infamous brothels owned by Ah Toy, a Cantonese woman who arrived during the Gold Rush and became the first Chinese prostitute and madam in San Francisco. She lived from 1828 to 1928, ending her days in comfort and wealth in San Jose.

**Golden Gate Fortune Cookie Factory** ★★ FACTORY TOUR  Not much has changed at this tiny Chinatown storefront since it opened in 1963. Workers sit at a conveyer belt, folding messages into thousands of fortune cookies—20,000 a day—as tourists line up to watch the cookies being made and buy a bag of 40 for about $3. You can purchase regular fortunes, unfolded flat cookies without fortunes, or, if you bring your own fortunes, they can create custom cookies.

56 Ross Alley. © **415/781-3956.** Admission free. Daily 9am–6:45pm. Photos 50¢. Bus: 8, 30, 45. Cable car: Powell-Mason.

# UNION SQUARE

Technically, Union Square is a landscaped plaza bounded by Stockton, Post, Powell, and Geary streets, but to the locals, the entire surrounding area is referred to as "Union Square." It boasts one of the nation's most concentrated collections of boutiques, department stores, flagship chain stores (imagine the largest Victoria's Secret you've ever seen) and art galleries. (See chapter 8 for our recommended stores in the area.) When you tire of consuming, or your credit cards max out, grab a latte—or a glass of wine—at one of the cafes in the square. Sit outside, relax, and people-watch—the show is free, and always entertaining.

**Glide Memorial United Methodist Church** ★★ RELIGIOUS SITE Back in the 1960s, Glide Memorial's now legendary pastor, Texas-born Cecil Williams, took over this downtown church and began his famed, 90-minute "celebration" services, preaching diversity, compassion, brotherhood, and acceptance. Williams has since retired the pastorship but he is sometimes on hand anyway, like a kindly high school principal. He's a solid American institution, counting Oprah Winfrey and Quincy Jones among his fans, and having appeared as himself in the Will Smith movie *The Pursuit of Happyness*. His wife, Janice Mirikitani, San Francisco's second Poet Laureate, has also been working at the church since 1969. Glide's Sunday morning services are a little like a late-night TV talk show, accompanied by a skilled six-piece jazz band (Leonard Bernstein was a fan) and backed by a 100-plus-voice choir (the Glide Ensemble, and man they're good). Don't miss an opportunity to attend a service here if you can; there's nothing else like it, and it's impossible to feel unwelcome. Services are at 9 and 11am, but don't show up with less than 15 minutes to spare or you will almost certainly have to participate by TV from a nearby fellowship hall, and that would be a shame. It's not just about Sunday mornings, however: Glide Memorial is also the largest provider of social services in the city, offering help with housing and healthcare and jobs training.

330 Ellis St. (at Taylor St.). glide.org. © **415/674-6000.** Services Sun 9 and 11am. Bus: 27. Streetcar: F. BART: Powell.

# MISSION DISTRICT

This vibrant neighborhood gets its name from the oldest (standing) building in San Francisco, the haunting **Mission Dolores** (facing page). Once inhabited almost entirely by Polish and Irish immigrants, the area saw a large influx of Mexican immigrants beginning in the 1940s, when they were displaced from other parts of the city. In the 1960s, immigrants from Central America began to arrive, recognizing that the neighborhood was becoming a center for the Latino community. Today, however, many Latino families who've lived here for generations are being priced out by young tech workers who can afford higher rents. What draws them here? The Mission, as gritty as it is, has some of the best weather in this city of mini-climates and is by far the hippest place to live in San Francisco, alive at night with casual-chic restaurants, bars, and nightclubs that overflow onto the busy streets—especially on warmer evenings. For a detailed walking tour of the area, see p. 184.

On the map, it's an oblong area stretching roughly from 14th to 30th streets between Potrero Avenue on the east and Dolores Avenue on the west. The heart of the Latino community still lies along 24th Street between South Van Ness and Potrero avenues, where dozens of excellent Mexican, Nicaraguan, Salvadoran, Guatemalan (and more!) restaurants, bakeries, bars, and specialty stores attract people from all over the city. The area surrounding 16th Street and Valencia Street is a hotbed for impressive vintage stores, artisan coffee shops, and restaurants and bars catering to the city's hipsters. While the area has been undergoing gentrification for years, the neighborhood can still be a little sketchy, especially around BART stations located at 16th and 24th streets.

For insight into the community, visit **Precita Eyes Mural Arts Center,** 2981 24th St., between Harrison and Alabama streets (precitaeyes.org; ✆ **415/285-2287**), to take the 2-hour neighborhood tour (Sat and Sun at 1:30pm). You'll start by watching a slide show covering the history of the murals that cover many walls in the area and the mural painting process. After the slide show, your guide will show you murals on a 6-block walk. Group tours are available during the week by appointment. The tour costs $20 adults, $10 seniors (65+) and college students, $6 youth (12–17), $3 for kids under 12.

**Dolores Park** ★★ PARK   If it's a sunny day and you want to hang with the locals, head to this hilly 16-acre park. Blanketed with lush green lawns and dotted with palm trees, a soccer field, tennis courts, a basketball court, a playground, and great views, it can be quite the scene of modern bohemia, with picnickers lounging on blankets covering nearly every open patch of grass and the occasional beloved marijuana-edibles dealer happily offering goods at cash prices. It's a fantastic place to relax and take in good San Francisco vibes. And with lots of great food to be found along 18th street, a picnic can be thrown together in a snap.

Bounded by Church, Dolores, 18th, and 20th sts. sfrecpark.org/destination/mission-dolores-park. Bus: 22. Streetcar: J.

**Mission Dolores** ★★ RELIGIOUS SITE   The history of this church, more formally known as Misíon San Francisco de Asís, is the history of the early city, and there is no other surviving building that is more intrinsic to the early days of the town's formation. The tale goes back to the storied summer of 1776, when this site, then an uninhabited grove, was selected for a mission in a network that ran up and down the coast. Its first Mass was celebrated under a temporary shelter. The current adobe-walled building, which dates from 1791, is the oldest in town, and a rich representative of a city that has lost so much of its history, offering a rare glimpse into the not-so-distant past and the troubled origins of California. With its 4-foot-thick walls and rear garden, this precious survivor from California's colonial days is a hushed and transporting place indeed. It's also almost entirely original, having survived the 1906 earthquake by dint of good old-fashioned craftsmanship—its trusses, lashed together with rawhide, are made of redwood, although in 1916, after the quake, they were reinforced with steel. As you roam around the place, you'll encounter gorgeous altars brought from Mexico during the days of the Founding Fathers.

Following the chapel and the sanctuary, the tour's path visits a modest museum in the back before proceeding outside. In its heyday, the mission was home to some 4,000 people, but of course, most of that land was long ago sold off; look for the diorama, built in 1939, for a clearer picture of how it was all laid out. The back garden contains the graves of California's first governor and the city's first mayor, as well as, shockingly, the bodies of at least 5,000 Indians who died "helping" (read: working as slaves for) the mission. Sad to say, while few people know about the mass extinction, the mission is famous for the one grave that isn't there: The headstone of Carlotta Valdes, which Kim Novak visits in the movie *Vertigo* (1958), was a prop. Around the same time (1952), the compound was named a Basilica, an honorary Church of the Pope, and in 1987, Pope John Paul II swung by for a visit.

16th St. (at Dolores St.). missiondolores.org. ✆ **415/621-8203.** Suggested donation $5 adults, $3 seniors and children. May–Oct 9am–4:30pm; Nov–Apr 9am–4pm. Closed Thanksgiving, Easter, Christmas, and New Year's Day. Bus: 22. Streetcar: J. BART: 16th St. Mission.

# ALAMO SQUARE

**The Painted Ladies of Alamo Square** ★   San Francisco's collection of Victorian houses, known as the **Painted Ladies,** is one of the city's most famous assets. Most of the 14,000 extant structures—rare survivors of the 1906 earthquake—date from the second half of the 19th century and are private residences. Many have been beautifully restored and ornately painted. They are spread throughout the city, but one of the greatest concentrations of Painted Ladies are located in the small area bordered by Divisadero Street on the west, Golden Gate Avenue on the north, Webster Street on the east, and Fell Street on the south, about 10 blocks west of the Civic Center. One of the most famous views of San Francisco—seen on postcards and posters all around the city—depicts sharp-edged Financial District skyscrapers behind a row of Victorians. This fantastic juxtaposition can be seen from Alamo Square, in the center of the historic district, at Fulton and Steiner streets. A **Victorian Homes Historical Walking Tour** (p. 158) is a great way to stroll past, and learn about, more than 200 restored Victorian beauties.

Steiner, btw. Hayes and McAllister sts. Bus: 5, 21.

# CIVIC CENTER

The Civic Center is a study in contrast. While filled with dramatic Beaux Arts buildings, showy open spaces, one of the best museums in the city, and a number of performing arts venues, the neighborhood is also filled with homeless people, and it is sometimes necessary to step around panhandlers and makeshift shelters while en route to the area's attractions.

**Asian Art Museum** ★★ MUSEUM   The largest collection of Asian art in the United States, this stellar museum boasts over 18,000 treasures from Asian countries as varied as China, Tibet, India, and nations in the Middle East. With items spanning a 6,000-year history, it's also the largest museum of its kind in this hemisphere. The concept of a museum devoted solely to Asian culture began in 1960 when Chicago industrialist Avery Brundage agreed to donate his personal collection of Asian art to the city of San Francisco. Over time, the collection outgrew its space in a wing of the **de Young Museum** (see p. 148), and Italian architect Gae Aulenti (famed for the Musée d'Orsay in Paris and the Palazzo Grassi in Venice) was hired to convert San Francisco's former main library into a contemporary showcase. Skylights, glass, and concrete hold three stories of treasures sorted by country. To better understand what you're seeing, I highly recommend taking a free docent-led tour, on which you'll learn about the role of the elephant as the ancient SUV of India, the reason jade can't be chiseled, and, while looking at a Koran from the 14th century, find out what the word "Koran" means. A highlight: one of the only collections of Sikh art in the world. With items of different mediums—including furniture, statues, clothing, paintings, jewelry, and sculpture—the pieces are varied and intriguing, even for kids. The collections change regularly, there is usually a visiting exhibition, and you can borrow an iPad Touch for a free self-guided tour. The museum store has handsome gifts for surprisingly good prices, and Café Asia serves a fabulous Asian chicken salad and a wide-ranging selection of teas.

200 Larkin St. (btw. Fulton and McAllister sts.). asianart.org. ✆ **415/581-3500.** Admission $15 adults; $10 seniors, students (with college ID), youths 13–17, free for children 12 and under. Free 1st Sun of the month. Tues–Sun 10am–5pm; Thurs and Fri evening 5pm–9. Closed Thanksgiving, Christmas, and New Year's Day. Bus/streetcar: All Market St. lines. BART: Civic Center.

**City Hall** ★★ HISTORIC SITE   San Francisco's Beaux Arts City Hall was not built to be just another city hall. After its predecessor crumbled during the '06 quake, residents wanted to show the world that San Francisco was still an

# free CULTURE

To beef up attendance and give indigent folk like us travel writers a break, almost all of San Francisco's art galleries and museums are open free to the public one day of the month, and several never charge admission. You can use the following list to plan your week around the museums' free-day schedules; see the individual attraction listings in this chapter for more information on each museum.

## FIRST TUESDAY

- Yerba Buena Center for the Arts (p. 128)
- de Young Museum (p. 148)
- Legion of Honor (p. 154)

- Contemporary Jewish Museum (p. 127)

## FIRST SUNDAY

- Asian Art Museum (p. 138)

## ALWAYS FREE

- Cable Car Museum (p. 132)
- City Hall (p. 138)
- Glide Memorial United Methodist Church (p. 135)
- Grace Cathedral (p. 132)
- Musée Mechanique (p. 122)
- Maritime National Historical Park & Museum ($5 to board ships; p. 123)
- Wells Fargo History Museum (p. 130)

American powerhouse. In 1913, the new City Hall was designed to be as handsome, proud, and imposing as any government capitol building; it was finished in 1915, just in time for the World's Fair. Most visitors are shocked to learn that its mighty dome is 42 feet *taller* than the one atop Congress in Washington, DC. (Only four domes in the world are bigger: the Vatican, Florence's Duomo, St. Paul's Cathedral in London, and Les Invalides in Paris.) Should another horrible earthquake strike, a 1999 seismic retrofit saw to it that the structure can swing up to 27 inches in any direction; if you look closely at the stairs entering the building, you'll notice they don't actually touch the sidewalk because the entire building is on high-tech springs that had to be slipped, two by two, beneath a structure that already existed and was conducting daily business.

City Hall's most imposing attraction is indeed its fabulously ornate rotunda, a blend of marble (on the lower reaches) and painted plaster (high up), swept theatrically by a grand staircase where countless couples pose daily for their "just married" shots right after tying the knot (Friday is the busiest day for that). You've probably seen this staircase before—it is featured in one of the final shots of *Raiders of the Lost Ark* (1981) as a stand-in for the U.S. Capitol. It was here, in 2004, that thousands of gay couples queued to sign up for their weddings; the first couple in line was an octogenarian lesbian couple who had been together for 51 years. Also, in 1954, Joe DiMaggio and Marilyn Monroe were married here and posed for photos on these steps. Not all the famous happenings at City Hall have been so hopeful. In 1978, the infamous assassination of mayor George Moscone and city supervisor Harvey Milk occurred in two places on the second floor; the resulting trial, in which their killer got a light sentence because, as his lawyers argued, he was high on junk food (the so-called "Twinkie Defense") became a lynchpin of outrage for the gay rights movement. In the rotunda, look up: Sculptures of Adam and Eve can be seen holding up the official seal of the city.

Across the hall at the top of the grand staircase, the sumptuous Chamber of the Board of Supervisors is worth a peek if it's open; its walls of Manchurian oak, plaster ceiling created to mimic wood, and doors hand-carved by French and Italian craftsmen make this one of the most opulent rooms in the city. Laws dictate that it must be open to the public unless in a special session, so pop in for a gander.

Also check out the Light Court off the main rotunda on the ground floor, where you'll find the head of a statue of the Goddess of Progress; she was atop the prior City Hall, in fuller figure, but this is all that survives. The light bulb sockets in her hair were later additions. One-hour tours (Mon–Fri at 10am, noon, and 2pm) are free. Reservations are not needed for groups of fewer than eight people.

1 Dr. Carlton B. Goodlett Place (Polk St. btw. McAllister and Grove sts.). sfgov.org/cityhall. ☎ **415/554-6139.** City Hall open to public daily Mon–Fri 8am–8pm, closed major holidays. Parking: metered or CityPark lot. BART: Civic Center.

# RUSSIAN HILL

Despite the name, you won't find babushkas peddling piroshki here, or even a sizeable Russian community. Many locals don't know this, but the neighborhood got its name when settlers during the Gold Rush discovered a small Russian cemetery at the top of this hill. Apparently, Russian ships passing through San Francisco during the 1800s chose this spot to bury crew members who hadn't survived the voyage. Today, this quiet residential area with stunning views of the bay and quaint neighborhood restaurants is most famous for being home to one of the best-known streets in the world.

**Lombard Street** ★LANDMARK   Known (erroneously) as the "crookedest street in the world," this whimsically winding block of Lombard Street between Hyde and Leavenworth streets draws thousands of visitors each year

---

### This City's for the Birds!

If you're walking around San Francisco—especially Telegraph Hill or Russian Hill—and you suddenly hear lots of loud squawking and screeching overhead, look up. You're most likely witnessing a fly-by of the city's famous green flock of wild parrots. These are the scions of a colony that started out as a few wayward house pets—mostly cherry-headed Conures, which are indigenous to South America—who found each other and bred. Years later they've become hundreds strong, traveling in chatty packs through the city (with a few parakeets along for the ride), and stopping to rest on tree branches and delight residents who have come to consider them part of the family. To learn just how special these birds are to the city, read the book *The Wild Parrots of Telegraph Hill*, or see the heartwarming movie of the same name.

(much to the chagrin of neighborhood residents, most of whom would prefer to block off the street to tourists). The angle of the street is so steep that the road has to snake back and forth to make descent possible. The brick-paved street zigzags around the residences' bright flower gardens, which explode with color during warmer months. This short stretch of Lombard Street is one-way, downhill, and fun to drive. Take the curves slowly, in low gear, and expect a wait during the weekend and in summer. Save your snapshots for the bottom where, if you're lucky, you can find a parking space and take a few quintessential pics. You can also take staircases (without curves) up or down on either side of the street. In truth, most locals don't understand what the fuss is all about. But it is a classic photo op. *Fun fact:* Vermont Street, between 20th and 22nd streets in Potrero Hill, is even more crooked, but not nearly as picturesque.

# JAPANTOWN

The first Japanese arrived in San Francisco, or Soko, as they called it, in the early 1860s. After the 1906 earthquake uprooted the Japanese community that had settled South of Market, they moved to the Western Addition neighborhood and began building churches, shrines, and businesses. By 1940, "Japantown" had grown to cover 30 blocks. Then came World War II. The U.S. government froze Japanese bank accounts and, in 1942, President Roosevelt signed Executive Order 9066, ordering the removal of 112,000 Japanese Americans—two-thirds of them legal U.S. citizens—to camps in California, Utah, and Idaho.

Upon their release in 1945, the Japanese returned to find their old neighborhood occupied. Most of them resettled in the Richmond and Sunset districts; some returned to Japantown, but it had shrunk to an area of around 10 blocks. It wasn't until 1960 that today's Japantown began to take shape, when the city razed the 3-square-block section that had been Japantown and sold the land to a Japanese corporation whose goal was to build a "Japan Center."

Today, the community's sights include the **Buddhist Church of San Francisco,** 1881 Pine St. at Octavia St.; the **Konko-Kyo Church of San Francisco,** 1909 Bush St. (at Laguna St.); the **Sokoji, Soto Zen Buddhist Temple,** 1691 Laguna St. (at Sutter St.); the **Nihonmachi Mall,** on the 1700 block of Buchanan Street between Sutter and Post streets, which contains two steel fountains by renowned local artist and sculptor Ruth Asawa; and the above-mentioned **Japan Center,** a Japanese-oriented shopping mall. There is often live entertainment on summer weekends and during spring's Cherry Blossom Festival—Japanese music and dance performances, tea ceremonies, flower-arranging demonstrations, martial-arts presentations, and other cultural events.

**Japan Center** ★ SHOPPING MALL   Locals head here for its numerous authentic restaurants, teahouses, shops, and the crazy-expensive Sundance

# URBAN renewal

Relaxation and rejuvenation are raised to an art form in the City by the Bay. Here are six spas you may want to try for a massage, facial, or soak.

**Imperial Day Spa,** 1875 Geary Blvd. (imperialdayspa.com; ℂ 415/771-1114), is my hands-down favorite place to unwind, thanks to wonderful Korean-spa-style treatments, clean facilities, and extremely reasonable prices. Its men-only and women-only areas offer clay sauna rooms, a steam room, hot and cold pools, as well as massage. Then there's my favorite scrub treatment, where spa attendants literally scour off your dead skin and leave you baby-smooth. Admission is $25 for 4 hours of R&R, but the entry fee is waived if you get a treatment ($60–$140).

**Kabuki Springs & Spa,** 1750 Geary Blvd. (kabukisprings.com; ℂ 415/922-6000), was once an authentic traditional Japanese bathhouse. After the Joie de Vivre hotel group bought and renovated it, it became more of a Pan-Asian spa with a focus on wellness. You can still get access to the deep ceramic communal tubs (offering co-ed, women-only, and men-only days, for $25 per person) as well as private baths and shiatsu massages. The spa is open from 10am to 10pm daily; joining the baths is an array of massages and Ayurvedic treatments,

body scrubs, wraps, and facials, which cost from $75 to $200.

**Onsen,** 466 Eddy St. (onsensf.com; ℂ 415/441-4987), is a unique package: Pass through the restaurant to the absolutely "om"-inspiring bath house and indulge in a soak and a treatment before returning to the front to dine on Japanese-inspired fare, healthy yet luscious. Date night, anyone?

**International Orange,** 2044 Fillmore St., second floor (internationalorange.com; ℂ 415/563-5000) offers a more posh and modern experience. The self-described spa yoga lounge offers just what it says in a chic white-on-white space on the boutique-shopping stretch of Fillmore Street. They've also got a great selection of clothing and facial and body products, including one of my personal favorites, locally made In Fiore body balms.

**Remède Spa,** 125 Third St. in the St. Regis Hotel (remede.com; ℂ 415/284-4060), has two whole floors dedicated to melting away all your cares, worries, kinks, and knots. Expect wonderful massage, facials, manis and pedis, waxes, and more.

**Bliss Spa,** 181 Third St. in the W Hotel (blissworld.com; ℂ 877/862-5477), an outpost of the hip New York spa, offers a similar treatment menu to Remède's, including wedding specialties.

Kabuki multiplex movie theater. At its center stands the five-tiered **Peace Pagoda,** designed by world-famous Japanese architect Yoshiro Taniguchi "to convey the friendship and goodwill of the Japanese to the people of the United States." Surrounding the pagoda, through a network of arcades, squares, and bridges, you can explore dozens of shops featuring everything from TVs and *tansu* chests to pearls, bonsai, and kimonos. There are also tons of food options here, from quick snack shacks to sit-down meals. Check out **Kinokuniya** (ℂ 415/567-7625; open daily 10:30am–8pm), the enormously popular and extensive bookstore that offers a wide selection of manga, graphic novels, cookbooks, and much more, in both Japanese and English.

Bounded by Post, Geary, Laguna, and Fillmore sts. sfjapantown.org. ℂ 415/922-7765). Open daily 10am–midnight (most shops close earlier). Bus: 2, 3, 22, or 38.

# HAIGHT-ASHBURY

Few of San Francisco's neighborhoods are as varied—or as famous—as Haight-Ashbury. Walk along Haight Street, and you'll encounter everything from drug-dazed drifters begging for change to an armada of funky-trendy shops, clubs, and cafes. Turn anywhere off Haight, and instantly you're among the clean-cut, young urban families who can afford the steep rents in this hip 'hood. The result is an interesting mix of well-to-do professionals and well-screw-you aging flower children, former Deadheads, homeless people, and throngs of tourists who try not to stare as they wander through this human zoo. Some find it depressing, others find it fascinating, but everyone agrees that it ain't what it was in the free-lovin' psychedelic Summer of Love. Is it still worth a visit? Not if you are only here for a day or two, but it's certainly worth an excursion on longer trips, if only to visit the trend-setting vintage and absolutely wild clothing stores on the street (see p. 191), where the "burners" go to get their outfits before they set off on the famous annual desert festival of arts, music, and free expression that is Burning Man.

# THE CASTRO

Castro Street, between Market and 18th streets, is the center of what is widely considered the world's largest and best-known gay community. It's a lovely neighborhood teeming with shops, restaurants, bars, and other institutions that cater to the area's colorful residents. The Castro's landmarks include **Harvey Milk Plaza** (at the intersection of Castro and Market streets), **The GLBT History Museum** (see below) and the **Castro Theatre** (429 Castro St.; castro theatre.com), a 1930s movie palace with a Wurlitzer organ that hosts sing-a-longs to old musical favorites like *The Sound of Music.*

The gay community began to move here in the late 1960s and early 1970s from a neighborhood called Polk Gulch, which still has a number of gay bars. The main drag (so to speak), **Castro Street,** is one of the liveliest streets in the city and the perfect place to shop for gifts and revel in free-spiritedness. Go to **mycastro.com** for local events and **castromerchants.com** for a list of specialty shops. Also, check out **sanfrancisco.gaycities.com**, another resource for local gay bars, restaurants, and events.

**The GLBT History Museum** ★ MUSEUM   North America's first full-fledged gay history museum, set in a former storefront in the Castro, is tiny but formidable, and ultimately quite moving. Recent exhibits have included quirky recaps of 25 years of queer history, with profiles of the first lesbians to marry legally in California (including the pantsuits they wore); a section on the importance of gay bars for the community (illustrated by a marvelously decorative collection of matchbooks); an exhibit on the gay-rights movement (with Harvey Milk's sunglasses and the kitchen table at which he politicked); and displays about gays in the military, hate crimes, AIDS, and gays of color, among other topics. The museum is not appropriate for children—"We want

Looking for something to do that's a little outside of the norm? Here are a few suggestions:

Deemed "the most psychedelic place one can legally reach within the city limits" by *SF Weekly,* **Magowan's Infinite Mirror Maze** (magowansinfinitemirror maze.com; ℂ **415/835-0019**) at Pier 39 (p. 122) will have you completely dazed and confused within minutes. And the entrance fee of $5 (5 and under free) lets you come and go all day.

Climbing through pitch-black tunnels, rooms, and chutes with only your sense of touch to guide the way may not have been how you'd planned to spend your time in San Francisco, but it's definitely a one-of-a-kind experience and especially fun if you go with a bunch of friends.

**The Tactile Dome** at the Exploratorium (p. 129) is a hot commodity, so plan ahead and make a reservation by calling ℂ **415/528-4444** (exploratorium.edu/visit/west-gallery/tactile-dome).

Slides are typically the domain of the elementary school set, but these two small parks' offerings please adults and kids alike. The long, steep concrete slides at **Seward Mini Park** (30 Seward St.) are not for little ones—you can really build up speed! Don sturdy jeans, grab a piece of cardboard, and head to the top. While less imposing, the slightly shorter metal slides at **Esmeralda Slide Park** (at the corner of Winfield St. and Esmeralda Ave.) will still have you giggling as you swoop down the hill.

to show how the erotic pleasure can become political power," co-curator Amy Sueyoshi divulges—but should intrigue anyone with an interest in contemporary history.

4127 18th St. (btw. Castro and Collingwood sts.). glbthistory.org. ℂ **415/621-1107.** Adults $5, California students with ID $3, free 1st Wed of month. Mon–Sat 11am–6pm, Sun noon–5pm. Bus: 24, 33, and 35. Streetcar: F.

# GOLDEN GATE PARK ★★★

Golden Gate Park visitors may be surprised to learn that this beautiful, lush park's land was once mostly sand and labeled part of the "great sand waste" on area maps in Gold Rush times. Today, everybody loves **Golden Gate Park,** and it shows—more than 13 million people each year visit its 1,000-plus acres of public space, which stretches from the middle of the city all the way out to the Pacific Ocean.

Conceived in the 1860s and 1870s, as large urban parks open to the public were just beginning to catch on, this landmark finally began to take shape in the 1880s and 1890s thanks to the skill and effort of John McLaren. Arriving from Scotland in 1887 and armed with a vision, he began landscaping the park. Faced with the aforementioned daunting amounts of sand, McLaren used a new strain of grass called "sea bent," which he had planted to hold the sandy soil along the Firth of Forth back home. Every year the ocean eroded the western fringe of the park, and ultimately he solved this problem, too, though it took him 40 years to build a natural wall, setting out bundles of sticks that the tides covered with sand. He also built the two windmills that stand on the western edge of the park to pump water for irrigation. Under his brilliant eye, the park took shape.

Today the park consists of hundreds of gardens and attractions connected by wooded paths and paved roads. While many worthy sites are clearly visible, there are infinite treasures that are harder to find, so stop first at **McLaren Lodge and Park Headquarters** (at Stanyan and Fell sts., at the east end of the park; © **415/831-2700**) if you want to find the hidden gems. It's open daily 8am to 5pm and offers park maps for $3. Of the dozens of special gardens in the park, the most widely recognized are **McLaren Memorial Rhododendron Dell,** the **Rose Garden,** the **Japanese Tea Garden,** the **San Francisco Botanical Garden,** and, at the western edge of the park, a springtime array of thousands of tulips and daffodils around the **Dutch windmill.** In addition to the highlights described in this section, the park contains lots of recreational facilities: tennis courts; baseball, soccer, and polo fields; a golf course; riding stables; and fly-casting pools. The Strawberry Hill boathouse handles boat rentals. The park is also the home of the **de Young Museum** (see p. 148) and, across from the de Young, the **California Academy of Sciences** (p. 146), which includes the **Steinhart Aquarium.**

To get around inside the park on weekends and public holidays, a free shuttle service is provided. For a complete list of maps, attractions, gardens, and events, visit **golden-gate-park.com.** You can enter the park at Kezar Drive, an extension of Fell Street; bus riders can take no. 5, 28, 29, 33, 37, or 71.

## MUST-ATTEND music festivals

If you want to experience the best of San Francisco's inclusive, feel-good culture—not to mention take in some awesome music—attend one of our local music festivals, which combine a penchant for quality entertainment, food, and drink with the warmer climes of late summer and early fall, and do-whatcha-like attitude (often shrouded in marijuana clouds). Don your favorite Coachella attire or come as you are. Everyone's welcome and people-watching is as captivating as the on-stage performances.

o **Outside Lands** (sfoutsidelands.com) is a 3-day extravaganza held in Golden Gate Park each August where veteran stadium headliners like Metallica and The Who and more of-the-moment talents like St. Lucia, Lorde, Little Dragon, and a smattering of comedians play on multiple stages. With dozens of bands, an abundance of local food and drink tents, and lots of grassy areas on which to sprawl, it's part never-ending picnic, people parade, and all-out blast—all backed by outstanding music. Tickets are expensive ($150 per day or $375 for all 3 days in 2017), and totally worth it. They also sell out fast.

o **Hardly Strictly Bluegrass** (hardly strictlybluegrass.com) has the same venue and happy-go-lucky Golden Gate Park party vibe as Outside Lands, but it's free to all. Held around the beginning of October each year, it features nearly 100 acts on various stages scattered through the Northwestern part of the park. There is some bluegrass involved, but as the name suggests, there's a lot more to be seen and heard.

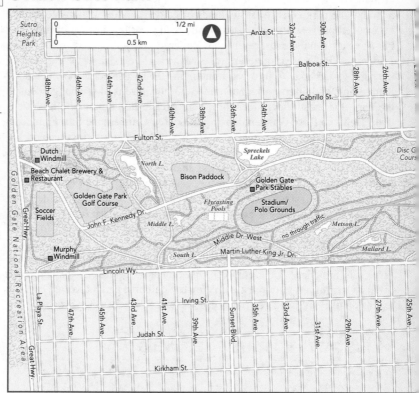

## Park Highlights

**California Academy of Sciences** ★★★ MUSEUM   A Golden Gate Park tenant for over 150 years and stunningly renovated in 2008, this fantastic—and yes, shockingly pricy—family-friendly museum is a spectacular mélange of aquarium, planetarium, natural history museum, and more, with plenty of cool, hands-on things for kids to do and see. The planetarium, access to which is included in admission, is the largest digital planetarium in the world. In the nature section, by the entrance, the main attraction is Claude, a formidable albino alligator. Up a circular ramp, four stories high, is a rainforest where brightly colored frogs play peek-a-boo while butterflies flit around your head. Below, an impressive collection of jellyfish glides its way around large, circular tanks. Topping it all off, literally, is a 2½-acre rooftop garden with 1.7 million plants and flowers.

55 Concourse Dr., Golden Gate Park. calacademy.org. ✆ **415/379-8000.** Adults $36; $31 seniors 65+, youth 12–17, and students with ID; $26 children 4–11; free for ages 3 and under. Free admission on random Sun, watch the website. Mon–Sat 9:30am–5pm; Sun 11am–5pm. Closed Thanksgiving and Christmas. Bus: 5 or 44. Streetcar: N.

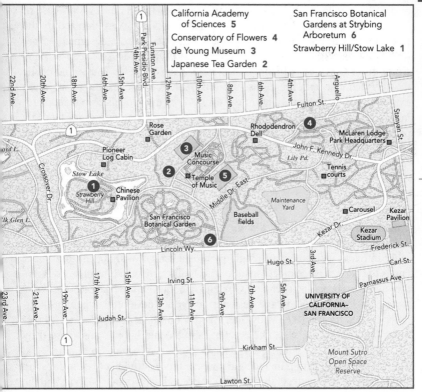

| | |
|---|---|
| California Academy of Sciences **5** | San Francisco Botanical Gardens at Strybing Arboretum **6** |
| Conservatory of Flowers **4** | |
| de Young Museum **3** | Strawberry Hill/Stow Lake **1** |
| Japanese Tea Garden **2** | |

**Conservatory of Flowers ★★ CONSERVATORY** Opened to the public in 1879, this glorious Victorian glass structure is the oldest existing public conservatory in the Western Hemisphere. But it's not just a place of historic interest: The Conservatory is a cutting-edge horticultural destination with over 1,700 species of plants, including rare tropical flora of the Congo, Philippines, and beyond. In fact, this is one of only four public institutions in the U.S. to house a highland tropics exhibit. Its five galleries also host species from the lowland tropics, aquatic plants, the largest Dracula orchid collection in the world, and special exhibits. It doesn't take long to visit, but make a point of staying awhile; outside there are good sunny spots for people-watching as well as paths leading to impressive gardens. If you're around during summer and fall, don't miss the Dahlia Garden to the right of the entrance in the center of what was once a carriage roundabout—it's an explosion of colorful Dr. Seuss–like blooms.

100 John F Kennedy Dr., Golden Gate Park. conservatoryofflowers.org. ℂ **415/831-2090.** Adults $8; $6 seniors 65+, youth 12–17, and students with ID; $2 for children 5–11; free for ages 4 and under; free admission 1st Tues of month. Tues–Sun 10am–6:30pm. Bus: 5, 21, 44, or 71.

**de Young Museum** ★★ MUSEUM   Founded in 1894 for the California Midwinter International Exposition, the de Young evolved from what was originally an eclectic collection of exotic oddities into a quality showcase of fine arts from around the world (many pieces of which were donated by the Rockefeller family), and moved into a world-class custom-designed permanent home in 2005. Permanent displays featuring North American art, and works from Oceania and Africa, have helped make the de Young one of the most-visited fine arts museums in North America, and exciting temporary exhibits and evening wine-and-music events keep even locals coming back for more. Be sure to climb the 144-foot tower to the observation floor for fantastic panoramic views of the city. As a bonus, your de Young admission ticket can be used for same-day entrance at the Legion of Honor (p. 154).

50 Hagiwara Tea Garden Dr., Golden Gate Park (2 blocks from park entrance at Eighth Ave. and Fulton). deyoung.famsf.org. ⓒ **415/750-3600.** Adults $15; seniors 65+ $10, students with ID $6, ages 17 and under free. Tues–Sun 9:30am–5:15pm, open late Fri in summer. Closed New Year's Day, Thanksgiving, and Christmas. Bus: 5, 21, 44, or 71.

**Japanese Tea Garden** ★★ GARDEN   While the aquarium across the way is the obvious draw for families with children, this park, with its charmingly intricate pathways and jungle gym of a bridge, will appeal to all ages and is the perfect place to let the little ones toddle around a bit. John McLaren, the man who began landscaping Golden Gate Park, hired Makoto Hagiwara, a wealthy Japanese landscape designer, to further develop this garden originally created for the 1894 Midwinter Exposition. It's a peaceful, albeit sometimes crowded, place with cherry trees, shrubs, and bonsai, crisscrossed by winding paths and high-arched bridges over pools of water. Focal points and places for contemplation include the massive bronze Buddha (cast in Japan in 1790 and donated by the Gump family), the Buddhist wooden pagoda, and the Drum Bridge, which, reflected in the water, looks as though it completes a circle. After you've toured the garden, take some time for tea and traditional Japanese snacks at the tearoom.

75 Hagiwara Tea Garden Dr. Golden Gate Park. japaneseteagardensf.com. ⓒ **415/752-1171.** Daily 9am–6pm (4:45pm in winter). Mon, Wed, Fri free admission with entrance before 10am, otherwise $9 adult, $6 senior 65+ and youth 12–17, $2 child 5–11, free for ages 4 and under. Bus: 5, 21, 44, or 71.

**San Francisco Botanical Garden** ★ GARDEN   With more than 8,000 plant species on 55 acres, among them some ancient plants in a special "primitive garden" and a grove of California redwoods, this place is as lovely as it is peaceful. And it's one of the few places you'll be able to wander through a Mesoamerican Cloud Garden without actually climbing a mountain in Central or South America. Check the website for a variety of free docent-led tours.

Entrance at 9th Ave. and Lincoln Way, Golden Gate Park. strybing.org. ⓒ **415/661-1316.** Adults $8; $6 seniors 65+ and youth 12–17; $2 children 5–11; free for ages 4 and under; $17 family (2 adults and all children under 17); free 7:30–9am and 2nd Tues of month. Daily 7:30am–6pm (5pm in winter). Bus: 5 or 44. Streetcar: N.

# ESPECIALLY for kids

San Francisco is one of the best cities in the world to visit with children. While some kids will be up for visiting our fine arts museums and cultural sights, the rest will prefer things like a haunting visit to Alcatraz, burping sea lions, an interactive aquarium, and a fortune cookie tour. The following attractions rank tops with most kids:

o **Alcatraz Island** (p. 119)
o **Aquarium of the Bay** (p. 121)
o **Cable Car Museum** (p. 132)
o **Cable Cars** (p. 126)
o **California Academy of Sciences** (p. 146)
o **Chinatown Walk** (p. 164)
o **The Exploratorium** (p. 129)
o **Ghirardelli Ice Cream** (p. 122)
o **Golden Gate Bridge** (p. 150)

o **Golden Gate Park** (p. 144)
o **Golden Gate Fortune Cookie Factory** (p. 134)
o **Fisherman's Wharf** (p. 115)
o **Maritime National Historical Park** (p. 123)
o **Musée Mechanique** (p. 122)
o **Pier 39 and the California Sea Lions** (p. 123)
o **Ripley's Believe It or Not** (p. 118)
o **San Francisco Zoo** (p. 155)
o **Walt Disney Family Museum** (p. 151)
o **Children's Creativity Museum** (p. 125)

The website sfrecpark.org is an excellent resource for recreation centers, pools, and parks.

**Strawberry Hill/Stow Lake** ★ NATURE AREA   One of the sweetest ways to spend a few hours is to rent a boat and cruise around circular Stow Lake, watching painters dab at canvasses, joggers pass along the grassy shoreline, ducks waddle around waiting to be fed, and turtles sunbathe on rocks and logs. At the center of Stow Lake sits 430-foot-high Strawberry Hill, an artificial island that's the highest point in the park. It's a perfect picnic spot, with a bird's-eye view of San Francisco and the bay; it also has a waterfall and a peace pagoda. At the Stow Lake Boat House, you can rent rowboats ($22/hour), pedal boats ($28/hour), or electric boats ($38/hour); there's a snack shop, too.

50 Stow Lake Dr., Golden Gate Park. stowlakeboathouse.com. ℂ **415/702-1390.** Daily 10am–6pm, weather permitting.

# THE PRESIDIO

In October 1994, the Presidio passed from the U.S. Army to the National Park Service and became a National Historic Landmark and park. The 1,491-acre area incorporates a wide (and wild!) variety of terrains—coastal scrub, dunes, and prairie grasslands—that shelter many rare plants and more than 200 species of birds.

This military outpost has a history that spans centuries: from its founding in September 1776 by the Spanish, to 1821 when Mexico won independence and Presidio soldiers switched alliances, to its occupation by the U.S. military in 1846. When San Francisco's population exploded during the Gold Rush, the U.S. government installed battalions of soldiers and built Fort Point to protect the entry to the harbor. By the 1890s, the Presidio was no longer a frontier post but a major base for U.S. expansion into the Pacific. The Presidio expanded again during the 1920s, when Crissy Army Airfield (the first airfield on the West Coast) was established. It saw major action during World War II, after the attack on Pearl Harbor—soldiers dug foxholes along nearby beaches, and the Presidio became the headquarters for the Western Defense Command. Some 1.75 million men shipped out from nearby Fort Mason to fight in the Pacific, and many returned to the Presidio's hospital.

Today, the area encompasses more than 470 historic buildings, a scenic golf course, a national cemetery, the **Walt Disney Family Museum** (facing page), several good restaurants, an inn, miles of hiking and biking trails, scenic overlooks, beaches, picnic sites, and a variety of natural habitats. (It is also home to **Industrial Light & Magic**, George Lucas's groundbreaking special effects and film production company, which is behind much of the special effects in all the *Star Wars* films; that facility, however, is not open to the public.)

The National Park Service offers docent- and ranger-led tours, as well as a free shuttle called **PresidioGo.** The newly renovated **Presidio Visitor Center** (nps.gov/prsf; ✆ **415/561-4323**) open 7 days a week, 10am to 5pm, is the perfect place to start, offering several interactive historical exhibits as well as a large-scale model of the entire park. To reach the visitor center, take bus no. 28, 29, or 43.

**Golden Gate Bridge** ★★★ LANDMARK   Few cities possess an icon that so distinctly pronounces, "I'm here." Truly, nothing makes you sigh "San Francisco" like the elegant profile of the stupendous **Golden Gate Bridge,** which links the city peninsula to the forests of Marin County.

And it's not just an emblem. It's also an epic engineering feat that, when it was completed in 1937, forever transformed San Francisco from a clunky, ferry-dependent city to a mecca of the motor age. President Franklin Roosevelt, in Washington, pushed a button and opened it to traffic, and what was then the world's longest suspension bridge went into service, as it has been reliably ever since (although now it's the second-longest in the country). On opening day, cars paid 50¢ and pedestrians surrendered a nickel to thrill to the sight of the deadly swirl of rushing currents far below. In an era when advances in steel and engineering measured a country's worth, this was a potent symbol of power.

The bridge is not named for its color—it's red, after all, not yellow—or even after the miners of old, but for the channel below, which was originally named by knowing sailors after the treacherous Golden Horn in Turkey. Depending on the weather or the time of day, the stately bridge presents a different personality. That mutable color, known to its 38 ever-busy painters as "international orange," can appear salmon in daylight or clay red as the sun goes down. (It was originally going to be gunmetal grey, like the Bay Bridge, but folks fell in love with the red hue of the primer coat.) Wisely, the architects figured out how to integrate the bridge with the landscape and not obliterate everything that led up to it, as usually happened in the 1930s. Consequently, getting a good snap of the thing isn't as easy as you'd think.

There's a pathway across the bridge's eastern side for pedestrians (open 5am–9pm in summer, 5am–6pm in winter) that is on the best side for fantastic city views (the other side takes in the Pacific), but as you can imagine, it gets crowded on weekends and is nearly always incredibly windy. Unfortunately, the bridge isn't easy to reach on foot, as its entry on the San Francisco side is tangled up among the confusing roadways of the Presidio. The six-lane bridge, built to 1937 proportions, isn't the easiest or safest place to take photographs from your car, either, although plenty of tourists snarl traffic in the effort. Instead, planners constructed a **viewing deck,** complete with a restroom, at the bridge's northern end that is accessible no matter which direction you're coming from on Highway 101. I prefer using it on the way into town, because visitors from southbound traffic get to use a walkway that goes underneath the bridge, offering a unique perspective of its structural underpinnings. Try to show up earlier in the day, when the sun is unlikely to ruin your shots. If you do go onto the bridge, for an extra thrill try to stand in the middle when a boat goes underneath; freighters are exhilarating when seen from above, and the regular tourist sightseeing boats bob helplessly for an amusing moment as they turn around in the teeming waters; sometimes, you can hear their passengers shout in alarm.

*A sad but hopeful note:* After many years of suicides committed by jumping off the bridge, the city is finally moving forward with construction of a "suicide net" that would extend 20 feet out over the water, preventing people from plummeting the nearly 750 feet to the water below.

Hwy. 101 N. goldengatebridge.org. No toll northbound; $7.75 electronic toll when driving south, cash not accepted. Bridge-bound Golden Gate Transit buses (© **511**) depart hourly during the day for Marin County.

**The Walt Disney Family Museum** ★ MUSEUM   While this museum features the expected collection of Walt Disney memorabilia, it's is really more of a tribute to the life of the man behind the mouse. It takes a serious look at Walt Disney's personal life, including his childhood in Kansas City, his move to California with nothing but $40 in his pocket and a dream, and explains how he and his brother, Roy, decided to launch the Disney Brothers Studio. The most moving room is the gallery filled with thoughts and condolences from around the world when Mickey's creator passed away in 1966. But it's not a downer, and children will enjoy the visit. How could they not, with all of the character sketches on display, including the earliest known drawings of Mickey Mouse, and original art from feature films like *Fantasia* and *Dumbo*?

In the Presidio, Main Post, 104 Montgomery St. (at Sheridan Ave.). waltdisney.org. © **415/345-6800.** Adults $25; $20 seniors 65+ and students with ID; $15 children 6–17; free for ages 5 and under. Wed–Mon 10am–6pm, closed Tues. Bus: 28 or 43.

# GOLDEN GATE NATIONAL RECREATION AREA

The largest urban park in the world, GGNRA makes New York's Central Park look like a putting green. It covers three counties along 28 miles of stunning, condo-free shoreline. Run by the National Park Service, the Recreation Area wraps around the northern and western edges of the city, and just about all of it is open to the public with no access fees. The Muni bus system provides transportation to the more popular sites, including Aquatic Park, the Cliff House, Fort Mason, and Ocean Beach (see below for more on all these sights). For more information, contact the **National Park Service** (nps.gov/goga; ✆ **415/561-4700**). See also the "Getting Outside" section of this chapter (p. 161) for tips on hiking, biking, jogging, and beachgoing in the GGNRA.

Here is a brief rundown of the salient features of the park's peninsula section, starting at the northern section and moving westward around the coastline:

**Fort Mason Center for Arts & Culture,** from Bay Street to the shoreline, comprises several buildings and piers used during World War II (for details, see the walking tour on p. 180). Today, they house hostels, museums, theaters, shops, and the much-loved **Greens** vegetarian restaurant (p. 104), which affords views of the Golden Gate Bridge. For information about current museum exhibits and events, visit fortmason.org or call ✆ **415/345-7500.** See p. 180 for a walking tour of the Fort Mason area.

Farther west along the bay, at the north end of Laguna Street, **Marina Green** is a favorite local spot for kite flying, jogging, and walking along the Promenade. South of Marina Boulevard, just past the St. Francis yacht harbor, you can spot the iconic **Palace of Fine Arts** (built for the Panama Pacific Exhibition of 1915), a richly sculptured neoclassical rotunda overlooking a graceful lagoon. The curving building behind it, rebuilt in the 1960s, is now an exhibit hall and event space.

Next comes the 3.5-mile paved **Golden Gate Promenade,** San Francisco's best and most scenic biking, jogging, and walking path. It runs along the shore past **Crissy Field** (crissyfield.org) and ends at Fort Point under the Golden Gate Bridge. Be sure to stop and watch the gonzo windsurfers and kite surfers, who catch major wind here, and admire the newly restored marshlands. The **Warming Hut Café and Bookstore** (✆ **415/561-3042**) is open daily from 9am to 5pm (9am–7pm summer weekends) and offers yummy, organic soups, salads, sandwiches, coffee drinks, and a good selection of outdoor-themed books and cards. Kids go crazy for **House of Air** (houseofair.com; ✆ **415/345-9675**), a warehouse packed with trampolines, a dodgeball court, and places to climb and jump off of. But be warned: There's a reason they make you sign a waiver and show an explicit video about safety and playing at your own risk; with a ton of kids (and adults!) wildly hopping about and bouncy surfaces, somebody's bound to get hurt—and plenty of them do.

Set on the outermost point of land under the Golden Gate Bridge, **Fort Point** (nps.gov/fopo; © **415/556-1693**) affords stunning views of the ocean to the west, the bay to the east, and Golden Gate Bridge overhead. (You may even see a few thrill-seeking surfers trying to ride the turbulent waves while avoiding the treacherous rocks that surround the fort.) The fort actually predates the bridge, having been built between 1853 and 1861 to deter entrance to the harbor, protecting the valuable commercial and military infrastructures within the bay. Designed to house 500 soldiers manning 126 muzzle-loading cannons, the fort never saw active battle, and by 1900, the fort's soldiers and obsolete guns had been removed. Check the website for current operating hours, as they change with the seasons. Guided tours and cannon demonstrations are given once or twice a day on open days, depending on the time of year.

Lincoln Boulevard sweeps around the western edge of the bay to **Baker Beach,** where the waves roll ashore—a fine spot for sunbathing, walking, or fishing. (Unless you're looking to shed your clothes, be aware that the northern portion of the beach is considered one of the largest urban "nude beaches.") A short distance from Baker Beach, **China Beach** is a small cove where swimming is permitted. Changing rooms, showers, a sun deck, and restrooms are available. Meanwhile, hikers can follow the **California Coastal Trail** from Fort Point along this part of the coastline to **Lands End** (visit presidio.gov/trails/california-coastal-trail), where you can look out to offshore Pyramid Rock. At Lands End, a lower and an upper trail offer hiking amid windswept cypresses and pines on the cliffs above the Pacific. A little more inland from Lands End, at the western end of California Street, **Lincoln Park** contains a golf course and the spectacular **California Palace of the Legion of Honor Museum** (see p. 154).

Still farther along the coast lie **Point Lobos** and the **Cliff House** (1090 Point Lobos Ave.; cliffhouse.com; © **415/386-3330**), a total tourist trap that's still worth visiting due to its incredible ocean and beach views (weather permitting). The Cliff House has been serving refreshments to visitors since 1863; the current building was erected in 1909 and renovated in 2004. It's famed for its views of Seal Rocks (a colony of sea lions and many marine birds) and the Pacific Ocean. Immediately northeast of the Cliff House you'll find traces of the once-grand **Sutro Baths** (sutrobaths.com). Built by mayor Adolph Sutro in 1896 as a saltwater bathing facility for the smelly masses without indoor plumbing, the baths turned into a major summer attraction accommodating up to 24,000 people. It burned down in 1966, but the ruins, clinging picturesquely to the cliffs, have become a destination in their own right.

Around the point, you come to San Francisco's largest beach, 4-mile long **Ocean Beach.** Stop by the Ocean Beach bus terminal at the corner of Cabrillo and La Playa streets to learn about San Francisco's history in local artist Ray Beldner's whimsically historical sculpture garden. Though technically not inside the GGNRA, the **San Francisco Zoo** (p. 155) is located across the

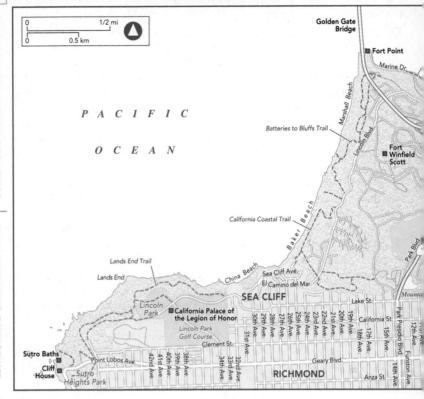

street from Ocean Beach, where Sloat Boulevard meets the Great Highway. At the southern end of Ocean Beach, **Fort Funston** (© **415/561-4323**) has an easy loop trail across the cliffs, where you can watch hang gliders take advantage of the high cliffs and strong winds. It's also one of the city's most popular dog parks. Check out the webcam at flyfunston.org/newwebcam.

The GGNRA extends into Marin County, where it encompasses the Marin Headlands, Muir Woods National Monument, and Olema Valley behind the Point Reyes National Seashore. See chapter 10 for information on Marin County and Muir Woods.

**California Palace of the Legion of Honor ★★** MUSEUM    The most beautiful museum in San Francisco sits perched high on the headlands with a stellar view of the Golden Gate Bridge, so come camera-ready for stunning "wish you were here" shots. Built in 1924 in the Beaux Arts style, the Legion of Honor is a ¾ replica of the Palais de la Legion d'Honneur in Paris, and serves as a memorial to the 3,600 California soldiers who lost their lives fighting on the battlefields of France in World War I. Though the setting alone makes this beaut a must-visit, the collections and ever-changing exhibits of art

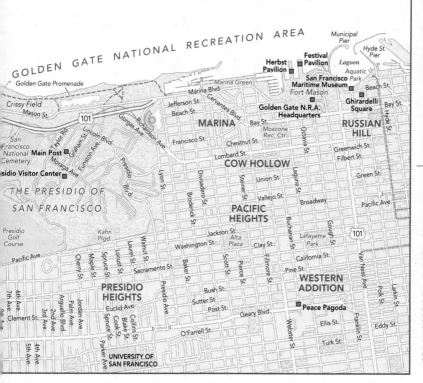

and artifacts are sure to please the fine arts connoisseur. Movie buffs might also recognize it as the setting for pivotal scenes in Alfred Hitchcock's *Vertigo*. Filled with 4,000 years' worth of treasures, the focus is on classical and European art and paintings. Auguste Rodin's 1904 cast bronze sculpture *The Thinker* can be admired in the Court of Honor. Saturdays and Sundays at 4pm, visitors can hear Ernest Skinner's 1924 pipe organ reproducing the sounds of a full orchestra; it is considered one of the finest pipe organs in the world. As an added bonus, if you would like to see more fine arts treasures, your ticket is valid for same-day entrance to the **de Young Museum** ★★ (p. 148) in Golden Gate Park.

100 34th Ave. (at Clement St.), Lincoln Park. legionofhonor.famsf.org. ✆ **415/750-3600.** Admission $15 adults; $10 seniors 65+; $6 students with ID; free for ages 17 and under. Additional fees may apply for special exhibitions. Free admission 1st Tues of month. Tues–Sun 9:30am–5:15pm. Closed Thanksgiving, Christmas, and New Year's Day. Bus: 1, 18, or 38.

**San Francisco Zoo** ★ Located between the Pacific Ocean and Lake Merced in the southwest corner of the city, the San Francisco Zoo has come a long way in recent years and is packed with things to do and opportunities to learn about wildlife conservation. Though grown-ups who are into wildlife will enjoy the visit, it's really aimed at kids, who get a kick out of attractions like the hands-on Children's Zoo, the flock of shockingly pink flamingos, the giant anaconda, the recently restored Carousel, and the ageless Little Puffer train.

Founded at its present site near the ocean in 1929, the zoo is spread over 100 acres and houses more than 2,000 exotic, endangered, and rescued animals, including some 245 species of mammals, birds, reptiles, amphibians, and invertebrates. Exhibit highlights include the **Lipman Family Lemur Forest,** a forest setting for five endangered species of lemurs from Madagascar; **Jones Family Gorilla World,** a tranquil haven for a family group of western lowland gorillas; **Koala Crossing,** which connects to the Australian Walkabout exhibit with its kangaroos, wallaroos, and emu; **Penguin Island,** home to a large breeding colony of Magellanic penguins; and the **Primate Discovery Center,** home to rare and endangered monkeys. **Puente al Sur (Bridge to the South)** has a pair of giant anteaters and some capybaras. The **Lion House** is home to rare Sumatran and Siberian tigers and African lions— if you want to hear some really ear-splitting roars, stop by at feeding time. **African Savanna** is a 3-acre mixed-species habitat with giraffes, zebras, antelopes, and birds. Check the website for a daily schedule of animal feeding times.

The 6-acre **Children's Zoo** offers kids and their families opportunities for close-up encounters with rare domestic breeds of goats, sheep, ponies, and horses in the Family Farm. Touch and feel small mammals, reptiles, and amphibians along the Nature Trail and gaze at eagles and hawks stationed on Hawk Hill. Don't miss a visit to the fascinating Insect Zoo or the Meerkat and Prairie Dog exhibit, where kids can crawl through tunnels and play in sand, just like these amazing burrowing species.

There's a coffee cart by the entrance as well as two decent cafes inside, definitely good enough for a bite with the kids (but beware marauding seagulls, who aren't above snatching food out of unsuspecting hands).

Great Highway btw. Sloat Blvd. and Skyline Blvd. sfzoo.org. ✆ **415/753-7080.** Admission $20 ages 15–64, $17 seniors 65+, $14 children 4–14, free for ages 3 and under. San Francisco residents receive a discount. Daily 10am–5pm. Parking $10 weekdays, $12 weekends and holidays. Bus: 23 or 18. Streetcar: L.

# ORGANIZED TOURS

## Segway Tours ★

Segways are those weird-looking upright scooters you've probably seen on TV. The two-wheeled "human transporter" is an ingenious electric-powered transportation device that uses gyroscopes to emulate human balance. Riding a Segway is fairly intuitive: lean forward, go forward; lean back, go back; stand upright, stop. Regardless, don't worry, there's a free 45-minute training session before you get on your way. The **San Francisco Electric Tour Company** offers Segway-powered narrated 2-hour tours—choose from Wharf and Waterfront, Golden Gate Park, Chinatown at Night tours, and more. There's even a Hills & Crooked Streets tour for advanced riders. For $75, it's not a bad deal, and it's the closest you may ever come to being a celebrity (*everyone* checks you out). Just FYI, you must be at least 12 years old, weigh between 100 and 250 lb., and can't be pregnant to join the tour. No heels, sandals, or flip-flops. For more information, log onto sfelectrictour.com or call *©* **415/474-3130.** (There are many other companies offering Segway tours, but this one consistently gets the best reviews.)

## Walking Tours

Do not miss the opportunity to take one of the 80-plus absolutely free walking tours offered in rotation by **San Francisco City Guides ★★★** (sfcityguides. org; *©* **415/557-4266**), a simply terrific volunteer organization that runs up to a dozen tours a day, from 9:30am to 2pm, plus occasional night tours, all around town. You don't need to make a reservation; just show up at the place and time listed online on its home page, where the weekly schedule is kept up-to-date by the group's single paid employee. (Call ahead for groups of eight or more.) Tours include City Scapes and Public Places, on which you'll discover hidden rooftop gardens and little-known financial museums downtown; a retelling of the history of the Mission Dolores neighborhood, one of the city's most historic; and Gold Rush City, which takes in the stomping grounds of the original '49ers. Most of the city's great attractions, from Coit Tower to Fisherman's Wharf, will have a dedicated tour. These tours are probably the city's best bargain, and they're an inviting way to see some windswept places you may not want to go to alone, including the walkway of the Golden Gate Bridge and the Fort Mason complex. Some 21,000 people a year take advantage of this terrific service, and frugal city buffs could easily fill their vacations with two or three a day. Tours are free, but at the end, your guide, someone who loves and studies the city and wants to share that love, will pass around an envelope and hope for a few bucks.

**Cruisin' the Castro** (cruisinthecastro.com; *©* **415/550-8110;** $30 adults, $25 children 5–12) is an informative historical tour of San Francisco's famous gay neighborhood, focusing on the contribution of the gay community to the city's political maturity, growth, and beauty. This fun and easy walking tour is for all ages, highlighting gay and lesbian history from 1849 to the present. Stops include America's only Pink Triangle Park and Memorial; the original site of the AIDS Quilt Name Project; the residence of Harvey Milk (the first openly gay elected official in California) and also the place where his store, Castro Camera, used to be; the Castro Theatre; and the Human Rights Campaign and Action Center. Tours run Monday through Saturday from 10am to noon and meet at the Rainbow Flag at Harvey Milk Plaza on the corner of Castro and Market streets above the Castro Muni station. Reservations are required.

The **Haight-Ashbury Flower Power Walking Tour** (www.haightashbury tour.com; ☎ **415/863-1621;** $20, free for kids 9 and under) explores hippie haunts with expert local guides who've seen it all. You'll revisit the Grateful Dead's crash pad, Janis Joplin's house, and other reminders of the Summer of Love in 2½ short hours. Tours begin at 10:30am on Tuesdays and Saturdays, and on Fridays at 2pm. Reservations are advised and you can buy tickets online.

To explore Chinatown's less-touristy side, with its many hidden nooks and crannies, sign up with **Wok Wiz Chinatown Walking Tours & Cooking Center,** 250 King St., Ste. 268 (wokwiz.com; ☎ **650/355-9657**). Founded in 1984 by beloved late author and cooking instructor Shirley Fong-Torres, its guides today are all Chinatown natives, who speak fluent Cantonese and are intimately acquainted with the neighborhood's history, folklore, culture, and food. Tours run daily from 9:45am to 1pm and include a hosted, multi-course dim sum lunch (a Chinese meal made up of many small plates of food). There's a less expensive tour that does not include lunch, but even after your guide pops into bakeries to retrieve piping hot pork buns and custard tarts, you'd be surprised by how ready you'll be for the grand finale sit-down meal. Since groups are generally held to a maximum of 15, reservations are essential. The tour (with lunch) costs $50 for adults and $35 for ages 6 to 10; without lunch, it's $35 and $25, respectively. Tickets can be purchased online. My personal favorite is Wok Wiz' I Can't Believe I Ate My Way Through Chinatown tour, which starts with breakfast, moves to a wok shop, and stops for various nibbles at a vegetarian restaurant, dim sum place, and a market-place, before taking a break for a sumptuous authentic Cantonese luncheon. It's offered Saturdays, takes 3½ hours, and costs $90 per person, food included. The city mourns the loss of Shirley, who passed away in 2011.

Finally, for a tour of the areas where tour buses are forbidden, try Jay Gif-ford's **Victorian Homes Historical Walking Tour** (victorianhomewalk.com; ☎ **415/252-9485**). As you might guess, the tour concentrates on architecture, although Jay, a witty raconteur and San Francisco resident for more than 2 decades, also goes deeply into the city's history—particularly the periods just before and after the great earthquake and fire of 1906. You'll stroll through Japantown, Pacific Heights, and Cow Hollow. In the process, you'll see more than 200 meticulously restored Victorians, including the sites where the movie *Mrs. Doubtfire* and the TV series *Party of Five* were filmed. Tours run Monday, Friday, and Saturday at 11am, rain or shine; cost is $25 per person (cash only).

## Bike Tours

Several Fisherman's Wharf companies compete for biking business, and frankly, there doesn't seem to be much difference between the ones listed below, either in price or quality of the rental equipment. They are **Bay City Bike Rentals** (baycitybike.com; ☎ **415/346-2453**), **San Francisco Bike Rentals** (bikerentalsanfrancisco.com; ✆ **415/922-4537**) and **Wheel Fun** (wheelfun rentals.com; ✆ **415/770-1978**). Along with rentals, the first two offer identical guided bike tours over the Golden Gate Bridge and down into Sausalito. The guided portion of the tour ends in Sausalito, and you are then free to ride more, eat lunch, browse the shops, and take the ferry back at your leisure. (*Note:* The $11 ferry ride back to Pier 39 is not included in the price, but the two companies can sell you the ticket if you want one—or you can ride back!) Tours start at 10am and take about 3 hours; helmets, locks, maps, and a safety training class are all included. On the other hand, Wheel Fun offers a GPS-guided audio bike tour along the same route, with the added bonus that you can drop off your bike at the Sausalito Bike Return and ride the ferry back, unencumbered.

## Boat Tours

One of the best ways to look at San Francisco is from a boat bobbing on the bay, where you can take in views of the skyline and the dramatic topography. There are several cruises to choose from. Regardless of which you take, dress in warm layers; it can be freezing cold on the bay.

**Blue & Gold Fleet,** Pier 39, Fisherman's Wharf (blueandgoldfleet.com; ✆ **415/705-8203**), offers a range of options including a 60-minute tour of the bay that traces the historic waterfront; a 90-minute cruise around Alcatraz Island; and a "guaranteed to get soaked" bay adventure on the flame-covered RocketBoat. Prices for tours range from $31 for an adult on one of the cruises to $42 for a combo ticket of a cruise plus the RocketBoat. Ferries are available to Sausalito, Tiburon, and Angel Island for $20 to $24 roundtrip (adults), $11 to $15 (kids and seniors), and free for ages 5 and under.

The **Red & White Fleet,** established in 1892, departs daily from Pier 43½ (redandwhite.com; ✆ **415/673-2900**), offering a variety of bay cruise options including the 90-minute Bridge 2 Bridge ($40 adults, $28 kids 5–17, free 4 and under), 2-hour California Sunset Cruise ($68 adults, $46 kids 5–17, free 4 and under), and Golden Gate tour ($32 adults, $22 kids 5–17, free 4 and under).

## Bus Tours

San Francisco's public transportation system can be hard to master for new-bies, so these hop-on, hop-off tours fill a niche, especially for those just look-ing to see the more popular sights. Before you book, think about what you want to see: Do you want a funky old trolley or an open double-decker bus? A tour that crosses the Golden Gate Bridge and visits Sausalito? Look, too, at how many stops are en route and how often the buses start. In the off-season, that might be just twice a day, making a hop-on, hop-off tour more of a "stay on," so study the bus schedules before booking. Companies to compare include **Big Bus Tours** (bigbustours.com), **City Sightseeing San Francisco** (city-sightseeing.us), and the **San Francisco Sightseeing Company** (san franciscosightseeing.com). Prices vary depending on the tour. *Tip:* A second

# A whale OF A TALE

Not many people outside of California know about the Farallon Islands, nor do many people get to visit up close. These islands, which lie 30 miles outside the Golden Gate Bridge, are home to more than 250,000 seabirds, including tufted puffins and the rhinoceros auklet, once locally extinct but now beginning to thrive again. The entire Gulf of Farallones National Marine Sanctuary is off-limits to civilians, so visitors must gaze from the deck of a fishing or whale-watching boat if they want a peek firsthand.

**SF Bay Whale Watching**, a veteran eco-tourism company, offers trips (starting at $99) out to this outcropping of rock off the coast of San Francisco that is also home to sea lions, seals, dolphins, and the ever-present great white shark. Typically on the search for migrating gray, humpback, or blue whales, expeditions leave from Pier 39 at 8am sharp and pass underneath the majestic Golden Gate Bridge on the 27-mile trip out to the islands. A crew of trained naturalists accompany each voyage, and will stop at the first sign of water spouts on the 5- to 6-hour trips. For more information, visit sfbaywhalewatching.com or call ✆ **415/331-6267.**

day of hopping on and off can often be added for only a few more dollars, though many people find that one day on these buses is more than enough.

## Air Tours

**San Francisco Seaplane Tours** (seaplane.com; ✆ **415/332-4843**), the Bay Area's only seaplane tour company, is a perfect choice for thrill-seekers. For more than 60 years, this locally owned outfit has provided its customers bird's-eye views of the city, flying directly over San Francisco at an altitude of about 1,500 feet. Sights you'll see during the narrated excursions include the Golden Gate and Bay Bridges, Alcatraz, Tiburon, and Sausalito. Half the fun, however, is taking off and landing on the water, which is surprisingly smooth. Trips depart from Mill Valley; the company offers complimentary shuttle pickup at Pier 39. Prices range from $149 per person for the 20-minute SF City Sites Tour to $289 for the 60-minute Norcal Coastal Tour. There's also the 40-minute Sunset Champagne Tour, which includes a bottle of bubbly and a cozy backseat for two. Children's rates are typically about $20 less, and cameras are most welcome.

Equally thrilling (and perhaps more so if you've never been in a helicopter) is a tour of San Francisco and the bay via **San Francisco Helicopters.** The Vista package ($195 ages 13 and up, $150 ages 2–12) includes free shuttle pickup from your hotel or Pier 39, and a 20-minute tour that takes you over the city, past the Golden Gate and Bay Bridges, and Alcatraz Island. After takeoff, the pilot gives a narrated tour and answers questions while the background music adds a bit of a Disney-ride quality to the experience. *Tip:* The view from the front seat is the best, so you may have to yell "shotgun!" as soon as you spot your ride. Picnic lunch and sunset dinner packages are available as well. For more information or reservations, visit sfhelicopters.com or call ✆ **650/635-4500.**

# GETTING OUTSIDE

San Francisco is surprisingly nature-filled for a city, and thanks to the year-round mild weather, residents are all about soaking up the great outdoors. So don some layers, grab your water bottle and sunscreen, and head outside.

**BEACHES**   Most days it's too chilly to hang out at the beach, but when the fog evaporates and the wind dies down, locals love to hit the sands. On any truly hot day, thousands flock to the beach to worship the sun, build sand castles, and throw a ball around. Without a wet suit, swimming is a fiercely cold endeavor and is not recommended. In any case, dip at your own risk—there are no lifeguards on duty and San Francisco's waters are cold and have strong undertows. **Baker Beach** is ideal for picnicking, sunning (be aware that the northern end of the beach is clothing-free), walking, or fishing against the backdrop of the Golden Gate (most fisherman do catch-and-release here, due to pollution in the Bay). **Ocean Beach,** at the end of Golden Gate Park, on the westernmost side of the city, is San Francisco's largest beach—4 miles long, to be exact. Just offshore, at the northern end of the beach, in front of the Cliff House (see p. 153), are the jagged Seal Rocks, inhabited by various shorebirds and a large colony of barking sea lions (bring binoculars for a close-up view). Ocean Beach is ideal for strolling or sunning, but please don't swim here—tides are tricky, and each year bathers drown in the rough surf.

**BIKING**   The San Francisco Parks and Recreation Department maintains two city-designated bike routes. One winds 7.5 miles through Golden Gate Park to Lake Merced; the other traverses the city, starting in the south, and continues over the Golden Gate Bridge. These routes, however, are not restricted to bicyclists, so you must exercise caution to avoid crashing into pedestrians. A bike map is available from the San Francisco Visitor Information Center, at Powell and Mason streets, for $4 (p. 288), and from bicycle shops all around town. Another scenic option is the **Golden Gate Promenade** (see p. 152), which runs for 3.5 miles along the city's northern coast. Ocean Beach also has a public walk- and bike-way that stretches along 5 waterfront blocks of the Great Highway between Noriega and Santiago streets. It's an easy ride from Cliff House or Golden Gate Park.

Convenient to Golden Gate Park, **Avenue Cyclery,** 756 Stanyan St. at Waller St., in the Haight (avenuecyclery.com; *©* **415/387-3155**), rents bikes for $8 per hour or $30 per day. It's open daily 10am to 6pm. For cruising Fisherman's Wharf and the Golden Gate Bridge, check out one of the cycleries listed earlier (p. 158). *Hint:* Reservations are usually not necessary, but most places offer discounts of up to 20% if you reserve online.

**BOATING**   At the **Stow Lake Boathouse** (stowlakeboathouse.com; *©* **415/386-2531**) on Stow Lake, Golden Gate Park's largest body of water, you can rent a boat by the hour and steer over to Strawberry Hill, a large, round island in the middle of the lake. There's usually a line on weekends. The boathouse is open daily 10am to 6pm, weather permitting. Rowboats ($22/hour), pedal boats ($28/hour), and electric boats ($38/hour) are available.

**GOLF**   San Francisco has a few beautiful golf courses. One of the most lavish is the **Presidio Golf Course,** 300 Finley Rd. at the Arguello Gate (presidio golf.com; ✆ **415/561-4661**). Greens fees for non-residents range from $49 (5pm start, no cart) to $145 (weekend morning with a cart). There are also two decent municipal courses in town. Skirting the shores of Lake Merced, the 18-hole **Harding Park,** 99 Harding Rd. (at Skyline Blvd.; tpc.com/tpc-harding-park-golf; ✆ **415/664-4690**), charges greens fees of $127 and up for non-residents. Opened in 1925, and part of the PGA Tour's Tournament Players Club Network, it was completely overhauled in 2002 and has been getting rave reviews ever since. The course is a 6,743-yard par 72. You can also play the easier Fleming 9 Course at the same location. San Francisco's prettiest municipal course, the 18-hole **Lincoln Park Golf Course,** 300 34th Ave. (at Clement St.; lincolnparkgolfcourse.com; ✆ **415/221-9911**) is the oldest course in the city and one of the oldest in the West. The par-68 5,181-yard layout offers terrific views and fairways lined with Monterey cypress and pine trees, and the 17th hole has a glistening ocean view. It charges greens fees of $41 per person Monday through Friday before noon, $45 per person after noon and on weekends and holidays; it opens daily at 7am.

> ### City Stair Climbing
>
> Many health clubs have stair-climbing machines and step classes, but in San Francisco, you need only go outside. Several city stairways will give you not only a good workout, but seriously stunning neighborhood, city, and bay views. Check sisterbetty.org/stairways for a list of stairways—with photos—all over the city.

**PARKS**   In addition to **Golden Gate Park** (p. 144) and the **Golden Gate National Recreation Area** (p. 152), San Francisco boasts more than 2,000 acres of parkland, most of which is perfect for picnicking or throwing around a Frisbee, as long as you don't mind a bit of fog and wind.

Smaller city parks include **Buena Vista Park** (Haight St. btw. Baker and Central sts.), which affords fine views of the Golden Gate Bridge and the area around it and is also a favored lounging ground for gay trysts; **Corona Heights Park** (Roosevelt and Museum ways), which offers 360-degree views of the city and sunny hiking trails; and **Sigmund Stern Grove** (19th Ave. and Sloat Blvd.) in the Sunset District, which has a nice playground and is the site of a famous free summer music and arts festival (sterngrove.org). One of my personal favorites is **Lincoln Park,** a 270-acre green space on the northwestern side of the city at Clement Street and 34th Avenue. The Legion of Honor is here (p. 154), as is a scenic 18-hole municipal golf course (see "Golf," above). But the best things about this park are the 200-foot cliffs that overlook the Golden Gate Bridge and San Francisco Bay. To get to the park, take bus no. 38 from Union Square to 33rd and Geary streets, and then walk a few blocks.

**RUNNING** When the annual **Bay to Breakers Race** ★ (baytobreakers. com; ℭ **415/231-3130**), a 7½-mile run from downtown to Ocean Beach, is held every third Sunday in May, about 40,000 people register to race—and more than 150,000 watch them go. Why so many looky-loos? Every year, many participants come up with zany costumes, making the race part sporting event, part parade. The more serious **San Francisco Marathon** takes place annually at the end of July or first weekend in August. For more information, visit thesfmarathon.com or call ℭ **888/958-6668.** Great **jogging paths** include the entire expanse of Golden Gate Park, the shoreline along the Marina, and the Embarcadero.

**TENNIS** The **San Francisco Parks and Recreation Department** maintains 132 courts throughout the city. Almost all are available free, on a first-come, first-served basis. For an interactive map with addresses, directions, parking, and restroom info, check out sfrecpark.org/recprogram/tennis-program. An additional 21 courts in **Golden Gate Park** cost $6 for 90 minutes, and require reservations on weekends. Check the park's website for details on rules for reserving courts (golden-gate-park.com/tennis.html).

**WALKING & HIKING** The **Golden Gate National Recreation Area** offers plenty of opportunities for getting your walk on. One incredible trek is along the Golden Gate Promenade, from Aquatic Park to the Golden Gate Bridge, a 3.5-mile paved trail along the northern edge of the Presidio out to Fort Point, passing the marina, Crissy Field's restored wetlands, a small beach, and plenty of athletic locals. You can also hike the Coastal Trail all the way from the Fort Point area to the Cliff House. To pick up a map of the Golden Gate National Recreation Area, stop by the park service headquarters at Fort Mason; enter on Franklin Street (ℭ **415/561-4700**). A number of PDF maps are available at nps.gov/goga/planyourvisit/maps.htm.

Farther south along Route 280, **Sweeney Ridge** affords sweeping views of the coastline from the many trails that crisscross its 1,000 acres. From here, the expedition led by Don Gaspar de Portolá first saw San Francisco Bay in 1769. It's in Pacifica; take Sneath Lane off Route 35 (Skyline Blvd.) in San Bruno.

Although most people drive to this spectacular vantage point, a more rejuvenating way to experience **Twin Peaks** is to walk up from the back roads of the U.C. Medical Center (off Parnassus Ave.) or from either of the two roads that lead to the top (off Woodside or Clarendon aves.). The best time to trek is early morning, when the air is crisp and sightseers haven't crowded the parking lot. Keep an eye out for cars, however, because there's no real hiking trail. Walk beyond the lot up to the highest vantage point to really make the best of the view.

# CITY STROLLS

Taking a walk through San Francisco is like passing through a dozen different cities and time periods within the space of a few hours. The views, the food, and the diverse culture will seduce you, and the hills will prove that all of those Chinese dumplings, Italian pastries, and Mexican burritos *are* necessary fuel for powering up and down the steep streets. Yes, there are some killer hills, but the steeper the climb, the better the view at the top. Don't worry too much about strenuousness—only the Russian Hill tour involves some truly steep streets. Plus, what you forego in the comforts of ogling the city from a tour-bus seat, you gain in intimate, up-close experience. Try even one of these recommended strolls and you'll discover why so many artists, poets, and musicians have fallen in love with the City by the Bay.

## WALKING TOUR 1: CHINATOWN: ANOTHER WORLD INSIDE THE CITY

| | |
|---|---|
| START: | **Corner of Grant Avenue and Bush Street** |
| PUBLIC TRANSPORTATION: | **Bus no. 2, 3, 30, 38, or 45** |
| FINISH: | **Commercial Street between Montgomery and Kearny streets** |
| TIME: | **2 hours, not including museum or shopping stops** |
| BEST TIMES: | **Daylight hours, when the streets are most active** |
| WORST TIMES: | **Early or late in the day, when shops are closed and no one is milling around. *Note:* Some destinations on this tour are closed Mondays and Tuesdays.** |
| HILLS THAT COULD KILL: | **None** |

This small but magical section of San Francisco, bounded loosely by Broadway, Stockton, Kearny, and Bush streets, isn't just home to the largest Chinese community outside of Asia, it's also the oldest Chinatown in North America. And that's what makes this place so compelling—its history is visible in the architecture, food, and crowds of Chinese residents who flock to the herb stores, vegetable

# Chinatown & North Beach Walking Tours

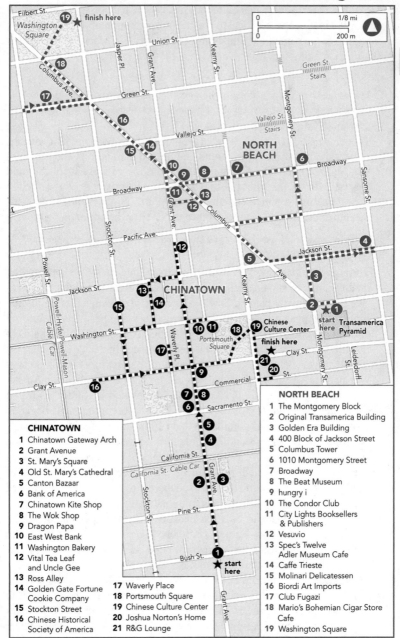

## CHINATOWN

1 Chinatown Gateway Arch
2 Grant Avenue
3 St. Mary's Square
4 Old St. Mary's Cathedral
5 Canton Bazaar
6 Bank of America
7 Chinatown Kite Shop
8 The Wok Shop
9 Dragon Papa
10 East West Bank
11 Washington Bakery
12 Vital Tea Leaf
    and Uncle Gee
13 Ross Alley
14 Golden Gate Fortune
    Cookie Company
15 Stockton Street
16 Chinese Historical
    Society of America
17 Waverly Place
18 Portsmouth Square
19 Chinese Culture Center
20 Joshua Norton's Home
21 R&G Lounge

## NORTH BEACH

1 The Montgomery Block
2 Original Transamerica Building
3 Golden Era Building
4 400 Block of Jackson Street
5 Columbus Tower
6 1010 Montgomery Street
7 Broadway
8 The Beat Museum
9 hungry i
10 The Condor Club
11 City Lights Booksellers
   & Publishers
12 Vesuvio
13 Spec's Twelve
   Adler Museum Cafe
14 Caffe Trieste
15 Molinari Delicatessen
16 Biordi Art Imports
17 Club Fugazi
18 Mario's Bohemian Cigar Store
   Cafe
19 Washington Square

markets, restaurants, and businesses. So much more than a top tourist destination, this densely populated section of the city is a bustling world unto itself, and its Portsmouth Square marks the original city center. On this walk, you'll learn how Chinatown was critical to the original formation of the city and why it continues to be a major destination—not to mention where to grab some delicious food along the way.

To begin the tour, make your way to the corner of Bush Street and Grant Avenue, 4 blocks from Union Square and all the downtown buses, where you can't miss the:

## 1 Chinatown Gateway Arch

This gateway, also called "The Dragon Gate," was built in 1970 with the same materials used in the ceremonial arched entrances of thousands of villages in China. The lion statues flanking the gate are there to guard against evil spirits. The gate has three passageways; if you're feeling important, make sure you enter through the larger, central one—it's meant for dignitaries while the other two are for the common folk.

Once you cross the threshold, you'll be at the beginning of Chinatown's portion of:

## 2 Grant Avenue

Through the gateway, you'll see the street flanked with shops selling quality imports, such as delicately carved jade figurines and less expensive but still lovely painted bowls, alongside cheap souvenirs (think San Francisco mugs and T-shirts). There are also a number of stores selling outlandishly huge and glitzy statues, sculptures, and other "art" that is in no way obviously Chinese but was perhaps made there.

Chinatown's beginnings can be traced to the first three immigrants—two men and one woman—who arrived from China in 1848 on an American ship called *The Eagle*. Gold was discovered at Sutter's Mill in Coloma, California in 1849, and in the 1850s, more immigrants began to arrive from China—predominantly men from southern China's Guangdong province. They toiled building the railroad and working in the shipyards, but despite their hard work (or maybe even because of it), they were despised, overtaxed, and excluded. The Chinese Exclusion Act of 1882 banned immigration of Chinese laborers to the U.S. and prohibited all Chinese immigrants from becoming naturalized citizens.

The great earthquake of 1906 changed everything when the whole district was wiped out—saloons, brothels, homes, and schools burned to the ground. Chinatown was quickly rebuilt, and this time the area saw more benevolent societies and churches than opium dens and saloons. A local businessman named Look Tin Eli recognized that the squalor of the old Chinatown gave his neighbors an image problem, so he arranged to make buildings more tourist-friendly, decorating them with false pagodas and sloping roofs. At a time when the vast majority of Americans never left their home country, coming here felt like venturing to the Orient. The ruse worked, and today, Chinatown retains its stage-set appearance—and its fascination for visitors.

Tear yourself away from the shops and turn right at the corner of Pine Street. Cross to the other side of Pine and on your left you'll come to:

## 3 St. Mary's Square

This small park features a 14-foot metal-and-granite statue of Dr. Sun Yat-sen, leader of the rebellion that ended the Qing Dynasty and founder of the Republic of China. The work of Italian sculptor Beniamino Bufano, who in 1920 travelled to China and met Sun Yat-sen, the statue is in a fitting location; during Sun Yat-sen's exile in San Francisco (before the revolution in 1916), he often whiled away the hours in this square. Visit early in the morning and you may see locals practicing tai chi here.

Walk to the other end of the square, toward California Street, turn left, cross California Street (right over the whirring cable car tracks) at Grant Street, and you'll be standing in front of:

## 4 Old St. Mary's Cathedral

Completed in 1854, this was the state's first building expressly designed to be a cathedral. Since then, it has been through a lot. In 1891, it was superseded by a larger cathedral and demoted to a parish church; later, it was gutted by two catastrophic blazes, one being the 1906 post-earthquake fire. Before you step inside, look up at the tower's clock and read the words beneath—I won't give them away, but they were meant to deter men from visiting the area's many brothels. The shell of the building is original, although its somewhat run-down interior dates to the late 1960s. In 1902, America's first mission for indigent Chinese immigrants was established here; food was served, English was taught, and everyone was welcome.

Step inside to find a written history of the church, striking photos of the destruction the building has endured over the years, and turn-of-the-20th-century photos of a developing San Francisco.

Upon leaving the church, take a right, walk to the corner of Grant Avenue and California Street, and go right on Grant. Here you'll find a shop called:

## 5 Canton Bazaar

Of the knickknack and import shops lining Grant Avenue, this one (at no. 616) is one of the largest—and the kitschiest. You'll find everything from souvenir T-shirts to shot glasses to chopsticks to teapots to Chinese pajamas for adults and children. You should also check out its sister store, Old Shanghai, directly across Grant. It's got great deals on colorful Chinese slippers, an entire upper floor dedicated to women's clothing, and more authentic art pieces at the very back of the store.

Continue in the same direction on Grant Avenue and cross Sacramento Street to the northwest corner of Sacramento and Grant. You'll be at the doorstep of the:

## 6 Bank of America

This building is best appreciated from across the street so you can look up and admire the architecture. Even chain banks use traditional Chinese architectural features here. Notice the dragons subtly portrayed on many parts of the building.

Head in the same direction (north) on Grant to 717 Grant Ave. and head into the:

## 7 Chinatown Kite Shop

A popular neighborhood fixture, owned by the same family since 1969, the Kite Shop offers an assortment of flying objects, including lovely fish kites, nylon or cotton windsock kites, hand-painted Chinese paper kites, wood-and-paper biplanes, pentagonal kites, and even design-it-yourself options. In this wind-filled city, you'll have plenty of places to fly a kite, including the Great Meadow in Fort Mason (p. 152).

Cross Grant to 718 Grant Ave. where you'll find:

## 8 The Wok Shop

This culinary marvel is literally jam-packed with just about any cleaver, wok, cookbook, or vessel you might need for Chinese-style cooking in your own kitchen. And yes, they sell woks—piles and piles of them.

When you exit the shop, go right. Walk past Commercial Street and stop at 752 Grant for:

## 9 Dragon Papa

In the window of this unusual confectionary, you'll find Shing or Derek Tam (father and son) making "dragon's beard" candy by gently wrestling a thick rope of malt syrup, pulling and twisting until it forms millions of white, filmy strands, which they then carefully wrap around a combination of sesame seeds, peanuts and toasted coconut. The beauty of this candy is its subtle, mildly sweet flavor and unusual texture. Try some and carry on.

Continue north on Grant Avenue to Washington Street. Turn right and at 743 Washington St. you will be standing in front of the former Bank of Canton, now the:

## 10 East West Bank

This building boasts the oldest (dating back to 1909) Asian-style edifice in Chinatown. After the earthquake, the city fathers were contemplating moving Chinatown to the outskirts of the city. The construction of this three-tiered pagoda-style building (it once housed the China Telephone Exchange) convinced these powerful men that the neighborhood had the potential to attract tourists and so Chinatown remained where it was.

You're probably thirsty by now, so follow Washington Street a few doors down (east); on your right-hand side, at 733 Washington St., you will come upon:

## 11 Washington Bakery & Restaurant

While the service can be abrupt, this Hong Kong–style diner offers tasty rolls and pastries (the traditional egg custard tarts are good) and exotic, delicious beverages worth stopping for. The lengthy drinks menu is filled with things that may be new to you: red bean ice, jelly grass, and hot melon milk tea, to name a few. There's also Hong Kong–style milk tea, which is black tea with condensed milk or evaporated milk and sugar. Grab a light snack, if you're hungry. There's still much to see.

Head back to Grant Avenue, cross Washington Street, and follow the east side of the street 2 blocks to 1044 Grant Ave.:

## 12 Vital Tea Leaf

(If you already visited the Vital Tea Leaf shop at 509 Grant, you could skip this one.) Step inside to peruse this tea shop's monumental selection of loose and bagged teas. If you're lucky, Uncle Gee, the grouchy owner, will be there to greet you with good-natured insults and jokey threats (along with the occasional fortune cookie) before he introduces you to dozens of varieties of tea. And yes, tastings are part of the experience. You'll come in a stranger, but you leave feeling like part of the family (I promise).

Leave Vital Tea Leaf, make a left, head west up Jackson on the left side of the street to Ross Alley, and make a left into the alley.

## 13 Ross Alley

These alleys, in the bad old days, were rife with gambling, brothels, drug dealing, and worse. St. Louis alley, also off Jackson (you'll pass it as you head to Ross Alley), was known for its slave market, where naked girls were auctioned off to pimps. Thankfully, it's hard to picture today, and there are new memories to be made, including the edible ones at your next stop.

As you continue along the alley headed south, on the left side of the street, at no. 56, you'll encounter the:

## 14 Golden Gate Fortune Cookie Company

You'll probably see the line of tourists or smell the aroma of baking cookies wafting down the alley before you arrive at this tiny storefront. It's worth visiting if only for the glimpse of workaday Chinatown that is so rarely afforded to outsiders. Once inside, you'll see women sitting at a conveyer belt, folding messages into warm cookies as the manager invariably encourages you to try a sample and buy a big bag of the fortune-telling treats. You can purchase regular fortune cookies, unfolded flat cookies without fortunes, or, if you bring your own fortunes, pay extra to have them make custom cookies just for you (I've done this for parties a number of times). Photos inside the factory cost 50¢.

As you exit the alley, cross Washington Street, take a right heading west on Washington, and walk to:

## 15 Stockton Street

This is my favorite part of Chinatown, and the part that most closely resembles a typical urban street in an older Chinese city, with sidewalk produce stands, fish markets, and bakeries. Some of the greasy spoons display the roasted meats of the day in their windows, head and all—the sight repulses some Westerners, but many Chinese customers know how to tell at a glance whether the quality of the inventory is high. You'll also notice that the signs in the shop windows aren't in English as often as they are on Grant Avenue; that's because this is an active shopping street for everyday sundries, particularly for older, Chinese-born residents.

Take your time and wander into the groceries to see how much of the produce and other food items you can identify. You'll find durian, starfruit, fresh lychee, and Chinese broccoli (at excellent prices), as well as salted duck eggs and dried cuttlefish, and you'll have to swim through crowds of assertive Chinese grandmas to get to them. Happily, shopkeepers, though displaying a businesslike manner, are generally willing to explain any product for which you can't read the label.

A quick note about the culture: While some Westerners may find local shoppers (and some shopkeepers) abrupt and pushy, rest assured that it's not about you, but simply a part of the everyday culture here. When you live in a very crowded area, it's often customary to push your way to the front to get what you need, much like native New Yorkers do when navigating the crowds blocking the food case at their favorite deli.

A noteworthy part of this area's history is **Cameron House** (up the hill at 920 Sacramento St., near Stockton St.), which was named after Donaldina Cameron (1869–1968). Called Lo Mo, or "the Mother," by the Chinese, she spent her life trying to free Chinese women who came to America in hopes of marrying well but were forced into prostitution and slavery. Lo Mo is believed to have personally rescued 3,000 Chinese girls who were bound for a life of slavery. Today, Cameron House provides services to thousands of low-income and immigrant children and families.

At 1068 Stockton St. you'll find **AA Bakery & Café,** an extremely colorful bakery with Golden Gate Bridge–shaped cakes, bright green and pink snacks, moon cakes, and a flow of Chinese diners chatting over pastries. **Gourmet Delight B.B.Q.** (1045 Stockton St.) is another recommended stop; here, barbecued duck and pork hang alongside steamed pig feet and chicken feet. Everything's to go, so if you grab a snack, especially their popular pork ribs, don't forget napkins. Head farther north along the street and you'll see live fish and fowl awaiting their fate as the day's dinner.

Meander south on Stockton Street to Clay Street and turn west (right) onto Clay. Continue to 965 Clay St., being sure to plan your visit during the museum's open hours (see below):

16  Chinese Historical Society of America Museum

This is the place to go to really learn about the history and personal experiences of Chinese immigrants in America. In 2016, the museum (chsa.org; ✆ **415/391-1188**) opened a new permanent exhibit, "Chinese American:

Exclusion/Inclusion," which explores the Chinese American experience, from the first immigrants to today. Diving deeply into the lives of Chinese immigrants across the U.S., it is the largest exhibition of its kind in America to date.

The museum also boasts some fascinating artifacts, including a shrimp-cleaning machine, 19th-century clothing and slippers of the Chinese pioneers, Chinese herbs and scales, historic hand-carved and -painted shop signs, and a series of photographs that document the development of Chinese culture in America. The museum is open Wednesday through Sunday from 11am to 4pm. Admission is $15 for adults; $10 for seniors, kids 13 to 17, and college students with ID; and free for kids 12 and under.

Retrace your steps, heading east on Clay Street back toward Grant Avenue. Turn left onto:

## 17 Waverly Place

Also known as "the Street of Painted Balconies" (mostly on your left), Waverly Place is probably Chinatown's most popular side street or alleyway. At 125 Waverley, you'll find the tiny **Tin Hou Temple.** Founded in 1852, it's the oldest Chinese temple in America. It's also on the top floor, and there's no elevator. Visitors are welcome, but be sure to remove your shoes when you go inside to inspect its carvings, traditional architectural details, and altar, portions of which survived the 1906 blaze; it's also customary to leave a few dollars in a red envelope found on the front table. You'll want to step out onto the balcony to catch the view, but do heed the safety signs recommending that no children under the age of 10 venture out—the railings are low and a bit creaky with age. (By the way, this kind of house of worship isn't so common here; there are more Chinese Christians in Chinatown than there are Buddhists.)

Once you've finished exploring Waverly Place, head back to Clay Street (turning right as you leave the temple), making a left onto Clay from Waverly Place. Walk past Grant Avenue, and continue until you come upon the block-wide urban playground that is also the most important site in San Francisco's history.

## 18 Portsmouth Square

This very spot was the center of the region's first township, Yerba Buena, settled by Spanish explorers in the 1770s. Before any semblance of a city had taken shape, this plaza lay at the foot of the bay's eastern shoreline, which in those days was less than a block from here. In 1846, when California was claimed as a U.S. territory, the marines who landed here named the square after their ship, the USS *Portsmouth*. (Today a bronze plaque marks the spot where they raised the U.S. flag.) There were fewer than 50 non–Native American residents in the settlement, and no substantial buildings to speak of.

Yerba Buena—which was renamed San Francisco in 1847—remained a modest township until the Gold Rush of 1849. Over the next 2 years, the population grew from less than 1,000 to over 19,000. When the square became too crowded, long wharves were constructed to support new buildings above the bay. Eventually, landfill expanded the entire area.

That was almost 150 years ago, but as you can see, these days the square is still hopping. By mid-afternoon most days, it's a hive of activity. While you will see children running around the playground, the real games are playing out around upturned cardboard boxes, where groups of elderly men and women are absorbed in games of cards.

It is said that when Robert Louis Stevenson lived in San Francisco in 1880, he loved to sit on a bench here and watch life go by. At the northeast corner of the square, you'll find a monument to his memory, consisting of a model of the *Hispaniola,* the ship in Stevenson's novel *Treasure Island,* and an excerpt from his "Christmas Sermon."

Once you've had your fill of the square, exit to the east at Kearny Street. Directly across the street, at 750 Kearny St., is a Hilton hotel. Cross the street, enter the hotel, and take the elevator to the third floor, where you'll find the:

## 19 Chinese Culture Center

This lively community center (© **415/986-1822**) offers a revolving series of guided tours, art installations, and exhibits, with new events and exhibitions every month. It's free to visit the exhibits, and the knowledgeable staff is happy to offer suggestions for things to do and see in the area. The center is open Tuesday through Saturday, 10am to 4pm.

When you leave the Hilton, take a left on Kearny Street and go 3 short blocks to Commercial Street. Take a left onto Commercial and note that you are standing on the street once known as the site of:

## 20 Joshua A. (Emperor) Norton's Home

Every town has its eccentric local celebrities, and San Francisco likely has had more than its share. But few are as fondly remembered as "Emperor" Joshua Norton.

Details about Joshua Norton's life are a bit foggy until his arrival in San Francisco in 1849. He was born around 1818 somewhere in the British Isles and sailed as a young man to South Africa, where he served as a colonial rifleman. He arrived in San Francisco with $40,000 and proceeded to double and triple his fortune in real estate. With significant funds in the bank, he next chose to go into the rice business. While Norton was busy cornering the market and forcing prices up, several ships loaded with rice arrived unexpectedly in San Francisco's harbor. The rice market was suddenly flooded and Norton was bankrupt. He disappeared for several years and upon his return, proclaimed himself "Norton I, Emperor of the United States and Protector of Mexico." He took to walking the streets in an old brass-buttoned military uniform, sporting a hat with a large, dusty feather.

Instead of ostracizing him or sending him off to a mental hospital, San Franciscans embraced him and gave him free meals. When Emperor Norton died in 1880 (he collapsed at the corner of California St. and

7

Walking Tour 1: Chinatown: Another World Inside the City

CITY STROLLS

Grant Ave.), members of Nob Hill's tony Pacific Club bought a coffin for him; it's said that as many as 30,000 people participated in the funeral procession. In 2013, locals formed the Emperor's Bridge Campaign, a non-profit dedicated to getting a proposition on the state ballot to change the name of the Bay Bridge to "The Emperor Norton Bridge." His legacy lives on!

From here, if you've still got an appetite, you should go directly to 631 Kearny St. (at Clay St.), home of the R&G Lounge.

## 21 R&G Lounge ☕

For decades, the **R&G Lounge** has drawn everyone from neighbors to top chefs for its tasty salt-and-pepper crab, chicken with black-bean sauce, and gorgeously tender and tangy R&G Special Beef. They also offer a variety of vegetarian "meat" dishes, including vegetarian abalone and vegetarian goose. If you're ready for a full Chinese meal, this is the place to indulge.

Otherwise, you might want to backtrack on Commercial Street to Grant Avenue, take a left, and follow Grant back to Bush Street, the entrance to Chinatown. You'll be at the beginning of the Union Square area, where you can catch any number of buses (especially on Market Street) or cable cars, or do a little shopping. Or you might backtrack to Grant, take a right (north), and follow Grant to the end. You'll be at Broadway and Columbus, the beginning of North Beach, where you can venture onward for our North Beach tour (see below).

# WALKING TOUR 2: NORTH BEACH: BEATS, BROADS, AND LITTLE ITALY

| | |
|---|---|
| START: | **Intersection of Montgomery Street, Columbus Avenue, and Washington Street** |
| PUBLIC TRANSPORTATION: | **Bus no. 10, 12, 30, or 41** |
| FINISH: | **Washington Square** |
| TIME: | **3 hours, including a stop for lunch** |
| BEST TIMES: | **Monday through Saturday between 11am and 4pm** |
| WORST TIMES: | **Sunday, when some shops are closed** |
| HILLS THAT COULD KILL: | **The Montgomery Street hill from Broadway to Vallejo streets; otherwise, this is an easy walk** |

You won't see any beaches here today, but North Beach got its name because before the addition of landfill, the area was actually a large beach marking the northeast side of San Francisco. Its shoreline extended to what are now Taylor and Francisco streets. (As a result, there are many ships buried under parts of downtown San Francisco—visit the **Maritime National Historical Park,** covered on p. 123, to learn all about them and see a map of where they're buried.)

To get an idea of what the area looked like during the Gold Rush, before much of the shoreline was filled in the late 1800s, picture a wooden shantytown leading down to a bustling, curved wharf. Over time, the settlement grew and in the 1860s became known as the Barbary Coast, after the pirate-prowling North African coast of the same name.

North Beach (especially Pacific Avenue) was a den of sin, pleasure, and crime. Routinely, after a night of carousing at the saloons and opium dens, young men would pass out and wake up the next day on a ship already well out to sea, where they'd be forced to join the crew for months on end until they could raise enough money to buy passage home. This impression-by-kidnapping method was called being "shanghaied," and it often involved drugs slipped surreptitiously into beer. It was so common in those days that the police barely kept track of the incidents. The brilliant underworld journalist Herbert Asbury, famous today for his book *Gangs of New York,* wrote in his book *Barbary Coast* that the period was "the nearest approach to criminal anarchy that an American city has yet experienced."

North Beach became the city's Italian district when Italian immigrants moved "uphill" in the early 1870s, crossing Broadway from the Jackson Square area and settling in. Once the 1906 earthquake demolished the Barbary Coast's flimsy buildings and infrastructure, new buildings began to spring up, and more Italian immigrants moved in, quickly establishing restaurants, cafes, and bakeries.

The Beat Generation also helped put North Beach on the map, with the likes of Jack Kerouac and Allen Ginsberg holding court in the area's cafes during the 1950s. Although most of the original Beat poets are gone, their spirit lives on in North Beach, which is still a haven for bohemian artists and writers. The neighborhood, thankfully, retains its Italian village feel; it's a place where residents from all walks of life enjoy taking time for conversation over pastries and frothy cappuccinos.

If there's one landmark you can't miss, it's the familiar building on the corner of Montgomery Street and Columbus Avenue (take bus 30 or 41 to get there):

## 1 Transamerica Pyramid

Technically in the Financial District, but just a few blocks south of North Beach, the Transamerica Pyramid is nearly as iconic as the Golden Gate Bridge. Petitions and protests greeted the plan to build this unusual skyscraper, but once it was completed it immediately became a beloved fixture of the skyline. Noted for its spire (which rises 212 feet above the top floor) and its "wings" (which begin at the 29th floor and stop at the spire), this pyramid was San Francisco's tallest building until July 2017, with the opening of South of Market's Salesforce Tower (at an impressive 1,070 feet, it's now the 11th-highest building in the U.S.). The beloved pyramid, now dwarfed, instantly turned into a quaint reminder of San Francisco's more small-town, charming past.

Still, it's a wonder. There's a small, bland visitor's center in the lobby that offers a bit of the history of the building, but the real draw is the exterior and the sweet little park around to the right. A bit more history: the 600 block of Montgomery Street, occupied by the Transamerica

Pyramid today, once held the Montgomery Block, the tallest building in the West (when it was built in 1853). San Franciscans called it "Halleck's Folly" because it was built on a raft of redwood logs that had been bolted together and floated at the edge of the ocean (which was right at Montgomery St. at that time). The building was demolished in 1959 but is remembered as the power center of old San Francisco.

From the southeast corner of Montgomery and Washington streets, look across Washington to the corner of Columbus Avenue. At 4 Columbus Ave. you'll see the:

## 2 Original Transamerica Building

A Beaux Arts flatiron-shaped building covered in terra cotta, this old-fashioned beauty was built in 1909 as a bank. Today, the building houses an outpost of the well-funded Church of Scientology, which may explain why it's so well maintained. Directly across Columbus, you'll see an odd, yet tragically hip row of storefronts, including the quirky Space Between Gallery; Iron and Resin, a men's clothing store geared toward the weekend warrior set; and Blades Co., an upscale yet old-school barbershop.

Cross Washington Street and continue north on Montgomery Street to no. 730:

## 3 Golden Era Building

Erected around 1852, this San Francisco historic landmark building is named after the literary magazine *The Golden Era,* which was published here. Some of the young writers who worked on the magazine were known as "the Bohemians" and included Mark Twain and Bret Harte (who began as a typesetter here but later became famous for his stories about the Gold Rush). Backtrack a few dozen feet and stop for a minute to admire the exterior of the annex at no. 722, a historic landmark which after years of neglect and lawsuits has been restored to its former glory. Fittingly, Filson, an outdoorsy men's clothing store that got its start outfitting miners during the Gold Rush, has taken over the space.

Continue north on Washington Street and take the first right onto Jackson Street, where you'll find the:

## 4 400 Block of Jackson Street

Here you'll find some of the only commercial buildings to survive the 1906 earthquake and fire. Stop in to peruse some of the very high-end shops that now line this block of Jackson Street, or simply admire the architecture. The Hotaling Building (no. 451), built in 1866, features pediments of cast iron applied over the brick walls. At no. 441 is another building that survived the disaster of 1906; constructed between 1850 and 1852, with ship masts for interior supporting columns, it served as the French Consulate from 1865 to 1876. The building at 415 Jackson St., which dates back to 1853, served as headquarters for the Ghirardelli Chocolate Company from 1855 to 1894.

Cross the street and backtrack on Jackson Street. Continue toward the intersection of Columbus Avenue and Jackson Street. Turn right on Columbus, walk halfway up the block, and look across the street for the small triangular building at the junction of Kearny Street and Columbus Avenue.

## 5 Columbus Tower

Also known as the Sentinel Building, this structure survived the earthquake by virtue of being under construction at the time (it was completed in 1907). In the late 1940s it was the original site of the legendary nightclub hungry i. The building went to seed in the 1960s, although the basement contained a recording studio where the Grateful Dead recorded its second album. Director Francis Ford Coppola owns the building now, and most of it houses the offices of his film production company American Zoetrope (now co-owned by his son Roman and his daughter Sofia). Downstairs, he sells his Napa and Sonoma county wines, and there's also a slightly overpriced but good European-style bistro, Café Zoetrope.

Continue north on Columbus Avenue, turn right on Pacific Avenue, then left on Montgomery Street, crossing Broadway, to:

## 6 1010 Montgomery Street

This is where Allen Ginsberg lived when he wrote his legendary poem, "Howl." First performed on October 7, 1955, during the Six Gallery reading—when poets, including Ginsberg, presented their poems in front of a rapt but rowdy crowd in a converted auto-repair shop at 3119 Fillmore St.—"Howl" became the manifesto of the Beat Generation. By the time Ginsberg finished reading, he was crying and the audience was going wild. Jack Kerouac, who refused to read his own work but was drunkenly cheering his friends on, proclaimed, "Ginsberg, this poem will make you famous in San Francisco." It did, of course, make him famous, and its graphic language resulted in poet and publisher Lawrence Ferlinghetti's arrest, leading to a landmark trial (Ferlinghetti won) that saw many literary giants coming forward to defend Ginsberg's work.

Now head back to:

## 7 Broadway

As you walk along this part of Broadway between Montgomery and Columbus, you'll see that the Barbary Coast's risqué business hasn't completely died out. It's usually fairly quiet during the day because the barkers and dancers aren't standing outside in the sunlight trying to lure men (and couples) inside, but the X-rated stores and "gentlemen's clubs" (aka seedy strip clubs) continue to attract men at all hours. Strange to think of a pornshop block as having historical significance, but this one really does.

Keep walking west on Broadway and a little farther up you'll find the current location of:

## 8 The Beat Museum

While it is located amid porn shops and strip clubs, this bookstore and museum is a diamond in the rough and a must for Beat fans. You can purchase "Howl" and other Beat works, as well as memorabilia as priceless as a first edition of Kerouac's *On the Road*. The museum even has a replica of Kerouac's 1949 Hudson, featured in Walter Salles's 2012 film version of *On the Road* (the car is on permanent loan from Salles). The store is open every day from 10am to 7pm; you can wander around the store for free but tickets to the museum are $8 ($5 students and seniors). The museum screens a series of Beat-centric documentaries, most running 90 minutes or so.

Continue along Broadway to:

### 9 hungry i

Now a strip club (at 546 Broadway), the hungry i has switched locations and identities at least four times. Originally located in the basement of Columbus Tower (p. 176), it was owned and operated by Eric "Big Daddy" Nord, a man whose personality was even bigger than his 6-foot 7-inch stature. He sold the club to impresario/producer Enrico Banducci in 1951, who moved it to a cavernous room at 599 Jackson St. three years later. A who's who of nightclub entertainers performed at the hungry i, including Lenny Bruce, Billie Holiday (who sang "Strange Fruit" there), Richard Pryor, and Woody Allen. Incidentally, my mom, local jazz singer Faith Winthrop, was the house singer there in its '50s heyday, as evidenced in the historically accurate major motion picture *Big Eyes* (2014), which features the club and her name on its marquee. In 1963, the as-yet-unknown Barbra Streisand convinced Banducci to let her perform, and the series of concerts she gave there helped launch her career. My mom was there for that, too.

At the corner of Broadway and Columbus Avenue, you will see:

### 10 The Condor Club

Whether or not you approve (I'm on the fence, myself), the Condor Club deserves recognition as part of San Francisco's history. The city's topless scene got its start right here in 1964. The owner, looking for something to liven up his club, asked the chief of police if his waitresses could loosen their bikini tops. They did, and toplessness wasn't far behind. The mayor at the time tolerated it by saying "fun is part of our city's heritage." Within days, every club in the vicinity had also gone topless.

But the person who gets the most credit, to this day, is the voluptuous Carol Doda, who danced a dozen shows nightly at the Condor and was profiled in Tom Wolfe's *The Pump House Gang*. Doda remained a fixture on the San Francisco scene for many years, as a chanteuse and the owner of a store in the Marina district that sold—you guessed it—bras. She passed away in 2015.

Note the bronze plaque claiming the Condor Club as BIRTHPLACE OF THE WORLD'S FIRST TOPLESS & BOTTOMLESS ENTERTAINMENT.

Cross to the south side of Broadway. You'll see a mural of jazz musicians painted on the entire side of the building directly across Columbus Avenue. Diagonally across the intersection is:

### 11 City Lights Booksellers & Publishers

Founded in 1953, initially as the nation's first all-paperback bookstore, this is one of the best and most historic bookstores in the country: a triangular building stuffed with volumes, including many hard-to-find books by fledgling presses. Back in the 1950s, its owner, poet Lawrence Ferlinghetti, decided that good books didn't have to be expensive, and he set about publishing new and unknown writers whose voices he felt needed to be heard. As mentioned earlier, one of his choices was *Howl and Other Poems* by Allen Ginsberg. The book's homoerotic overtones scandalized some, and the resulting obscenity trial made Ferlinghetti's bookstore internationally famous. What stands out to this day, however, is the fact that this small publisher continues to produce at least a dozen new titles every year (open daily, 10am–midnight).

Upon exiting City Lights bookstore, turn right, cross aptly named Jack Kerouac Street, and stop at 255 Columbus Ave., where you'll find:

## 12 Vesuvio

Ah, Vesuvio! There's still nothing quite like this dark little bar, opened in 1948, which somehow manages to feel simultaneously historic and timeless. Because of its proximity to City Lights bookstore, this bar became a favorite hangout of the Beats. Dylan Thomas used to drink here, as did Jack Kerouac, Lawrence Ferlinghetti, and Allen Ginsberg. The building dates from 1913, but maintains the same quirky decor it had during the Beat era. Grab a drink and make your way to a tiny upstairs table for the best view of the bar and the streets.

Facing Vesuvio across Columbus Avenue is another favorite spot of the Beat Generation:

## 13 Spec's Twelve Adler Museum Cafe

Located at 12 Saroyan Place, this is one of the city's funkiest bars, a small, dimly lit watering hole with ceiling-hung maritime flags and exposed brick walls crammed with memorabilia. One of the first nine businesses in San Francisco to be officially designated as a "legacy business," the bar is also a mini-museum—there are a few glass cases filled with mementos brought by seamen who frequented the pub from the '40s on—but the real legacy is the ambience.

From here, walk back up Columbus Avenue across Broadway to Grant Avenue. Turn right on Grant and continue until you come to Vallejo Street. At 601 Vallejo St. (at Grant Ave.) is:

## 14 Caffe Trieste

Opened in 1956 by Giovanni Giota, Caffe Trieste makes a mean espresso—in fact, it claims to be the first espresso purveyor on the West Coast. Many locals linger for hours inside or at one of the sidewalk tables, sipping and chatting. Francis Ford Coppola is said to have written most of the screenplay for *The Godfather* here. Stop by for a coffee or just a peek; if you're not ready to take a break, there are more cafe options farther along your route.

Look across Columbus, where you'll see the famed:

## 15 Molinari Delicatessen

This deli, located at 373 Columbus Ave., has been selling its pungent, air-dried salamis since 1896. Ravioli and tortellini are made in the back of the shop, but it's the sandwiches and the mouthwatering selection of cold salads, cheeses, and marinades up front that captures the attention of most folks. One Italian sub is big enough for two hearty appetites, and their mouth-watering pecorino cheese studded with pistachios will keep if you want to grab a wedge and save it for later.

Continue in the same direction on Columbus until you reach 412, home of:

## 16 Biordi Art Imports

This store has carried imported hand-painted majolica pottery from the hill towns of central Italy for more than 50 years, and it welcomes browsers just as eagerly as serious shoppers. With such a wide selection of brightly painted ceramics at nearly every price point, you may quickly find yourself with the perfect gift for someone back home—and the staff is happy to ship it for you. Biordi handpicks its artisans, and the extensive catalog includes biographies of current artists.

Walk north to the lively intersection of Columbus and Green Street and go left to no. 678, the home of:

## 17 Club Fugazi

For more than 40 years, Fugazi Hall has been staging the zany and whimsical musical revue *Beach Blanket Babylon.* The show evolved from Steve Silver's Rent-a-Freak service, which consisted of a group of partygoers who would attend parties dressed as any number of characters in outrageous costumes. The fun caught on and soon became *Beach Blanket Babylon,* now the longest-running musical revue in the nation.

The show changes regularly, and is often based on current events—think political and pop culture spoofs combined with fantastical costumes. If you get tickets and they're in an open seating section, you should arrive fairly early because you'll be seated around small cocktail tables on a first-come, first-served basis. (Two sections have reserved seating, four don't, and all of them frequently sell out weeks in advance; however, sometimes it is possible to get tickets at the last minute on weekdays.) You'll want to be as close to the stage as possible. And yes, this supercharged show (p. 208 for more information) is definitely worth seeing.

Head back along Green Street and cross Columbus Avenue, turning left on Columbus, proceeding 1 block northwest to 566 Columbus Ave.:

## 18 Mario's Bohemian Cigar Store Cafe ☕

Don't let the name put you off; they haven't sold cigars in over 20 years. This tiny cafe is the perfect stop for breakfast, lunch, or a little evening nosh. Open daily from 10am to 11pm, Mario's offers an unusual Italian specialty: Cappuccino con Vov, which puts today's hazelnut lattes to shame. A traditional zabaglione liqueur, Vov adds a sweet kick reminiscent of eggnog. It's the perfect treat to follow one of their famous sandwiches, made with fresh focaccia from right across the park at Liguria Bakery (1700 Stockton St.).

Once you're ready to move on, cross the street to:

## 19 Washington Square

Established in 1847, Washington Square is one of the city's first parks and has been the heart of North Beach since the 1860s. Today you'll find it at the center of the annual North Beach Festival (held in June) and host to community events throughout the year. The statue of Benjamin Franklin was donated in 1879 by temperance crusader Henry Cogswell. An avid teetotaler, he built similar statues (although usually of himself, not Franklin), fitted with fountains, across the country in an effort to get people to drink water instead of alcohol.

The Roman Catholic Church on the square's northern side on Filbert Street, Saints Peter and Paul Church (1924), is most often cited as the background of some shots of Marilyn Monroe and Joe DiMaggio after their wedding at City Hall in 1954. DiMaggio married his first wife at this church, but could not marry Marilyn there because he never annulled his first marriage. In true literary North Beach style, the Italian motto on the facade quotes not the Bible but Dante's "Paradise," from *The Divine Comedy*.

Your walking tour is over, but there are still dozens of shops, bakeries, and restaurants to explore. *Divertiti!*

# WALKING TOUR 3: RUSSIAN HILL AND FORT MASON: HIKE TO DIVINE VIEWS

| | |
|---|---|
| START: | **Hyde and Union streets** |
| PUBLIC TRANSPORTATION: | **Bus no. 45 or 41, or Powell-Hyde cable car** |
| FINISH: | **Fort Mason Center** |
| TIME: | **1½ to 2 hours** |
| BEST TIMES: | **Friday afternoons for Off the Grid, Sunday mornings for Farmers' Market, or any time of day** |
| WORST TIMES: | **Nighttime** |
| HILLS THAT COULD KILL: | **While sometimes quite steep, this route is mostly downhill. Hyde Street has a slight incline, and you'll have quite a hike if you decide to go down and back up Lombard Street.** |

If you haven't already guessed, this tour is all about spectacular views. Be sure to wear comfortable shoes and an extra layer—you're likely to experience sun and milder temperatures on Russian Hill, followed by chilly wind at Fort Mason. One of the more posh neighborhoods in the city, this tree-lined stretch of Hyde Street is a charming thoroughfare with a cable car line and classic Victorian architecture. From there, the tour winds through lesser-known city parks and gardens to historic Fort Mason. Words can't quite describe how stunning this walk is, but trust me, it's all that and more.

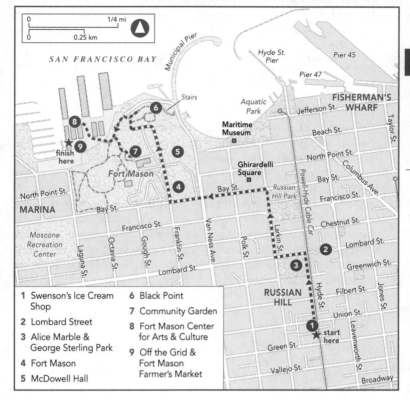

**1 Swenson's Ice Cream Shop**
**6 Black Point**
**2 Lombard Street**
**7 Community Garden**
**3 Alice Marble & George Sterling Park**
**8 Fort Mason Center for Arts & Culture**
**4 Fort Mason**
**9 Off the Grid & Fort Mason Farmer's Market**
**5 McDowell Hall**

## 1 Swenson's Ice Cream Shop

Earle Swenson opened this shop in 1948 after learning to make ice cream while serving in the U.S. Navy. He started with vanilla, his favorite flavor, and went on to develop more than 150 varieties, including Turkish Coffee, which is still available today. Over the years, the Swenson's franchise grew worldwide, and you can now get a "Gold Rush" sundae in a dozen countries, including Saudi Arabia and Taiwan, but this quaint shop is the original and still a local favorite. Grab a cone for the road!

Continue north up Hyde Street to Lombard Street. (As you reach the intersection of Hyde and Greenwich streets, on clear days you'll get a spectacular view of Alcatraz.)

## 2 Lombard Street

Built in 1922 to ease the effects of the steep 27% grade, this curvy one-way street lined with elegant homes is a true San Francisco icon. While you'll see carloads of people queued up to slowly maneuver down the twists and turns at the recommended speed limit of 5mph, you'll get a much better view (and many more photo ops) on foot. You may have heard this block of Lombard called "the crookedest street in the world," but that isn't exactly accurate—the less picturesque Vermont Street in the Potrero Hill neighborhood boasts an even curvier block. From the top of Lombard, you'll get an excellent view of Coit Tower rising above Telegraph Hill.

If you've made the descent down the steepest part of Lombard Street, make the climb back up. Either way, from the top, head west on Lombard Street 1 block to Larkin Street, where you'll find the:

### 3 Alice Marble & George Sterling Park

This small park at the corner of Lombard and Larkin streets is named for George Sterling, the unofficial poet laureate of San Francisco and an instrumental figure in establishing the city's bohemian culture in the early 20th century. According to California historian Kevin Starr, Sterling's friends referred to him as the "King of Bohemia," and his lifestyle at the turn of the century put the free-loving antics of the 1960s to shame. At the entrance, a plaque commemorates one of the many poems he wrote about the "cool, grey city of love." If you're up for another climb, head up the park steps, where you'll find benches and spectacular views of the Golden Gate Bridge. Just above are the Alice Marble Tennis and Basketball Courts, where locals play ball while trying not to get distracted by the incredible 360-degree views.

Head northeast on Larkin Street. At Francisco Street, keep walking straight down the hill where, halfway down, you'll find a staircase. Take the stairs down to Bay Street. On the way down, notice Aquatic Park and Fisherman's Wharf to your right and Ghirardelli Square straight in front. Turn left on Bay Street, crossing Van Ness Avenue, and continue on to the intersection of Bay and Franklin streets, where you'll find the main entrance to:

### 4 Fort Mason

One of the oldest military posts in San Francisco and a National Historic Landmark since 1985, Fort Mason was first called Point San Jose by the U.S. Army when they established the area as a military reservation in 1851. With the population explosion and housing shortage created by the Gold Rush, local real-estate developers swooped in and built private homes once they noticed that the military wasn't occupying the land. For roughly a decade, the area became known as "Black Point" and was home to a group of wealthy civilians, many of them committed members of the anti-slavery movement. When the Civil War began, the army finally evicted the residents, moved into their homes, and reestablished the area as Point San Jose. It wasn't until 1882 that the post was dubbed Fort Mason, in honor of Colonel Richard Barnes Mason, the second military governor of California. If you want to learn more about the fort's history, check out the many detailed signs and maps for more historical highlights, or join one of the tours offered by San Francisco City Guides (p. 157).

Walk straight into Fort Mason along Franklin Street. Just past the chapel, on your right you'll see:

## 5 McDowell Hall

Built in 1877 for General Irvin McDowell, the building remained a general's residence until 1906 when, having survived the earthquake fully intact, it became the army's emergency relief headquarters literally overnight. Today the building is a favorite location for weddings, thanks to unobstructed views of the bay.

Continue north along Franklin Street. You'll notice private residences with some of the best real estate in the country. Along the left, the building with the long porch is the site of Fort Mason's first hospital. Continue straight onto the path to:

## 6 Black Point

This sweet spot is right on the edge of the bluff, jutting out over the bay. On a clear day, Alcatraz will seem close enough to touch. This is a great place to watch the sailboats while enjoying a picnic among fragrant bay trees. The lone cannon perched on the western side of the park was once one of many, strategically placed to protect against an attack from Confederate soldiers during the Civil War. The guns never saw any action.

Head back up the path to Franklin Street, where it hits Funston Road. Turn right onto Funston, then left on Pope Road. Follow Pope and on your left you'll see the:

## 7 Community Garden

Step through the gates of this delightful and surprisingly large community garden and you'll see why there's an 8-year waiting list! Established in 1975, the garden was initially designed to include plots for students of nearby Galileo High School in addition to those set up for community members. Today there are 125 plots where members grow mostly organic vegetables, flowers, and herbs (pesticide use is forbidden).

Head over to the Great Meadow (with five palm trees in the middle) and down the path to the junction of Laguna Street and Marina Boulevard to arrive at:

## 8 Fort Mason Center for Arts & Culture

The waterfront section of this 13-acre former military outpost offers plenty to do and see. Depending on your energy level after your hike, you can peruse the stock at **Readers Bookstore** (open daily, 9:30am–5:30pm), shop for art supplies in every color imaginable at **Flax Art & Design** (open daily, 10am–6pm) or visit the **SFMOMA Artists Gallery** (open Monday–Friday, 10am–5pm) to see what local artists are creating these days. You can also rest your feet and grab a coffee or an excellent artisanal cocktail (read the cocktail menu, even if you don't order one) at **The Interval** (open daily, 10am–midnight), try a vegetarian lunch at the excellent **Greens** restaurant (see p. 104), or see if you can snag a ticket to a weekend show at **BATS Improv Theater** (p. 208). Depending on what time of year you visit, you may also stumble upon annual art and maker fairs, which require you to pay admission but are completely worth the expense.

## 9 Off the Grid

Off the Grid is the city's roaming epicurean extravaganza, not to mention one heck of a good time. Every Friday, from 5 to 10pm (Mar–Oct), food trucks set up shop in the Fort Mason Center parking lot. The trucks converge to create a unique night market, featuring inventive cuisine, live music, and arts and crafts. If you've yet to catch up with the food-truck craze, this is the way to do it; some of the city's best restaurants and most popular food movements (like Mexican-Indian fusion) started here. The same location sees a lively farmers' market every Sunday (9:30am–1pm), where you can start your day the San Francisco way with fresh coffee, produce, and local goods from nearby farms.

From here you can continue along the shoreline to pass through the beautiful Marina Green and restored waterfront marshlands that lead to the base of the Golden Gate Bridge, walk up to Chestnut Street for some shopping and dining, or head to your next adventure.

# WALKING TOUR 4: THE MISSION: AN INTERSECTION OF LATINO AND HIPSTER CULTURE, WITH AMAZING EATS

| | |
|---|---|
| START: | **24th and Alabama streets** |
| PUBLIC TRANSPORTATION: | **Bus no. 12, 27, 48 BART to 24th Street** |
| FINISH: | **Mission and 17th streets** |
| TIME: | **2 hours** |
| BEST TIMES: | **Afternoons** |
| WORST TIMES: | **Nighttime** |
| HILLS THAT COULD KILL: | **None** |

Once known as "the Mission Lands," referring to the land surrounding Mission San Francisco de Asís (p. 137), this warm, sunny neighborhood was originally home to the Yelamu Indians of the Ohlone Nation, until the arrival of the Spanish missionaries. After the Gold Rush of the late 1800s, the area became home to a variety of immigrants, primarily of German, Irish, and Italian descent. Beginning in the 1940s, the Mexican immigrant population grew here as they were displaced from their old neighborhood by the construction of the western base of the Bay Bridge. Since the 1970s, the urban-industrial area has been best known for its colorful Latino culture. But starting around the first dot-com boom of the late 1990s, the gritty area has seen dramatic change again, with Latino culture increasingly giving way to hipsters who have commandeered the houses, apartments, storefronts, and even its plethora of late-night taco joints (some of which are the best north of Mexico). Now, colorful produce markets, *taquerias,* and dollar stores stand alongside hipper-than-hip bars, chic boutiques, trendy restaurants, and artisanal coffee houses.

# Mission District Tour

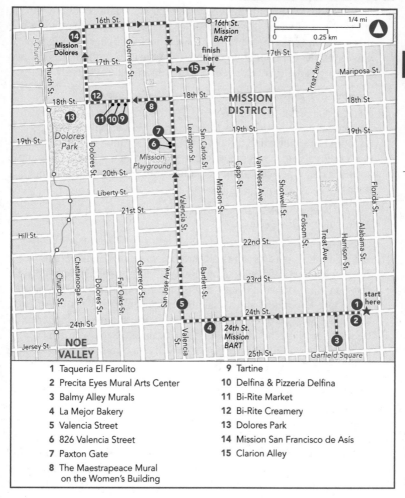

1 Taqueria El Farolito
2 Precita Eyes Mural Arts Center
3 Balmy Alley Murals
4 La Mejor Bakery
5 Valencia Street
6 826 Valencia Street
7 Paxton Gate
8 The Maestrapeace Mural
   on the Women's Building
9 Tartine
10 Delfina & Pizzeria Delfina
11 Bi-Rite Market
12 Bi-Rite Creamery
13 Dolores Park
14 Mission San Francisco de Asís
15 Clarion Alley

In fact, come at night and long stretches of the area feel more like Manhattan's West Village than anything else in San Francisco. If you like your culture and history served with a dash of eccentricity, this stroll is for you!

Start at 24th and Alabama streets, the heart of the Mission's Latino neighborhood. On the northwest corner, you'll find:

## 1 Taqueria El Farolito

There's much debate on which local Mexican joint serves the best burrito (San Franciscans' unofficial favorite food), but this veteran joint always makes the handful of top picks. El Farolito ("little lighthouse") is a local institution that has perfected this beloved local delicacy, according to *Business Week, Bon Appétit*, and residents at large. Taste for yourself and you'll see there's nothing quite like their gargantuan logs of savory meat, spicy rice, and tangy salsa wrapped in a large tortilla—giant all-in-one meals which some say were first created to feed hungry firefighters. If you're not hungry enough to down a full burrito, a fantastic taco or two will give you the fuel you need to get the most out of your adventures.

Cross the street and walk half a block west toward Harrison Street to:

## 2 Precita Eyes Mural Arts Center

This community-based organization (see p. 136), established in 1977, is awash with bright-colored local art. Besides running mural workshops and children's art classes, it organizes guided mural walks. Pick up a souvenir mural postcard or poster at the store and prepare to see the real thing!

Continue west past Harrison Street and turn left down Balmy Alley.

## 3 Balmy Alley Murals

One of the things that makes the Mission District so colorful—literally and figuratively—is its street art and hundreds of murals. Some of the area's oldest murals are along Balmy Alley, a block-long corridor between Harrison and Folsom streets. The murals started in the '80s, as a response to political and social abuses happening in Central America, and many more have appeared in recent years, addressing the influx of "techies" driving rents up and longtime locals out. See if you can spot the references to several internet giants, as well as a certain ubiquitous coffee chain. It's actually quite heartbreaking.

Return to 24th Street and continue walking west, crossing Mission Street, to 3329 24th St.

## 4 La Mejor Bakery

If you haven't already visited one of the many Mexican bakeries lining 24th Street, pop into this one for a quick bite of authentic Mexican pastry goodness. A cream-filled horn, a wedding cookie, or any of their freshly baked rolls and turnovers will sustain you on your journey. Prices are very reasonable, but be sure to bring cash.

Continue west on 24th Street until you get to Valencia Street. Turn right on Valencia to start your stroll.

## 5 Valencia Street

As you'll see, Valencia is the area's hipster hub. Wander in and out of funky, vintage clothing and housewares stores or stop into one of the lively bars (many of which are featured in our Nightlife chapter, beginning on p. 218) if you need a people-watching break. I love **Wonderland** (1266 Valencia St.); it sells art, clothing, and trinkets made by Bay Area artists, and the quirky T-shirt selection has something for everyone.

Continue to walk north on the west side of the street until you come to:

# 6 826 Valencia

Yes, you have indeed entered a pirate supply store! While it is packed with nautical knickknacks, it's much more than a captivating store. Author Dave Eggers (perhaps best known for his screenplays and his memoir *A Heartbreaking Work of Staggering Genius*) started this writing center to help local students with their reading and writing skills. Because of zoning issues, the space needs to operate as a store, which makes for an imaginative setting for the tutoring and classes that take place daily in the back. Check the pamphlets at the front for upcoming readings and meet-ups for the city's bohemian, literary set.

Your next destination is just a few steps away at 824 Valencia.

# 7 Paxton Gate

If you're put off by taxidermied animal heads and other formerly living parts, you might want to skip this stop, but it wouldn't be the Mission without eccentricities to marvel at, and this is a prime example. Oddities inspired by science, taxidermy, and plants fill this mind-bending boutique.

Continue down Valencia Street 1 more block and turn left on 18th Street. On the south side of the street (but the view is better from the north, so you may want to cross), between Valencia Street and Guerrero Street, you'll see:

# 8 The Maestrapeace Mural on the Women's Building

San Francisco has a ton of street art, but this mural is one of the city's largest and most colorful, spanning two sides of the Women's Building. Painted in 1994 (and completely cleaned and restored in 2012), the mural is the work of a multigenerational and multicultural group of seven female artists. Paying homage to women everywhere, the vibrant painting portrays such female icons as Georgia O'Keeffe, Audre Lorde, Quan Yi, Yemeyah, and Coyolxauhqui. Inside the building, you can buy postcards and shirts inspired by the wall.

18th Street boasts one of the hottest food scenes in the city. On just 1 block, between Guerrero and Dolores streets, you'll find some great noshing opportunities, including:

# 9 Tartine

This bakery is a San Francisco (and world!) favorite and it has the lines to prove it. People queue around the block to taste the award-winning cakes, tarts, croissants, and sandwiches. Pastry chefs and married couple Chad Robertson and Elisabeth Prueitt are at the helm of this beloved establishment, earning themselves the James Beard Award for Outstanding Pastry Chef. If you can stand the wait, you'll be rewarded with not only delicious baked goods, but also bragging rights that you've tasted what some consider the best bread in the world. *Tip:* Lines are considerably shorter weekdays before noon.

If it's a full meal you're after, stop in next door at:

## 10 Delfina & Pizzeria Delfina

One of San Francisco's most famous restaurants, hip and relaxed Delfina is the place to go for James Beard Award–winning Italian fare served San Francisco–style (by a polished, professional hipster staff in industrial-chic environs). Run by chef Craig Stoll and his wife, Annie, who is one of the best front-of-house managers around, it has a neighboring pizzeria, which inspired three other locations serving upscale thin-crust pizzas and other deliciously simple provisions.

If the wait is too long at Delfina or you're hoping to enjoy a meal alfresco (there's a great picnicking destination in just two stops), head into Bi-Rite Market half a block away.

## 11 Bi-Rite Market

While this little grocery store is no bigger than most corner stores, meandering through its crowded aisles is like getting a crash course in the bounty that Northern California has to offer. Everything is locally sourced, from the fancy cheese and cured meats to the colorful selection of fruits, veggies, and fresh flowers. There's also a wide selection of prepared food, made fresh daily. Expect to spend a pretty penny here on groceries (a chocolate bar can go for upwards of $10), but if you're a serious foodie, this shop is a worthy stop.

If it's ice cream you crave, cross 18th Street to:

## 12 Bi-Rite Creamery

If the sidewalk looks crowded, it's not because a pop star's in town—that's just the line for the world-famous ice cream stand on the corner of 18th and Dolores streets. The legendary creamery makes small batches of delicious soft-serve and regular ice cream in unique flavors, such as balsamic strawberry, salted caramel, and honey lavender. Prepare to share in order to sample as many as you can, or splurge on one of the creative sundaes.

Now that you've had your fill, you might need to take a load off. On the corner of 18th and Dolores streets you'll find one of the entrances to San Francisco's popular:

## 13 Dolores Park

If San Francisco was a high school, Dolores Park would be the cafeteria—who you are largely dictates where you hang out. It's sort of like a microcosm of the city's young people, making for an entertaining scene. In the Southwest corner, you have what's affectionately referred to as "Gay Beach," where ripped, topless men congregate until the last rays of sun dip behind the hills to the west. As the park slopes down, the families of Noe Valley bring their strollers to the playground. And as you move North, the scene gets younger and rowdier, with spontaneous DJ parties, boozy lawn games, and even costumed theme parties—there's always an occasion in San Francisco!

If you want to take in great views of the city skyline and enjoy a rest, head to the Southwest corner at Church and 22nd streets. Otherwise turn right and walk on the west side of palm tree–lined Dolores Street until you come to:

## 14 Mission San Francisco de Asís

The white building next to the cathedral is the city's oldest structure, dating back to 1791, and is one of few structures not destroyed in the 1906 earthquake. The mission offers a rare glimpse into the origins of the city, and the troubled colonial history of California in general. Take a self-guided tour, starting with the chapel and the small exhibit room. Be sure to take some time wandering through the cemetery, where scenes from Alfred Hitchcock's *Vertigo* were filmed. Of course, you exit through the gift shop, but it's practically a museum in its own right. For more details, see p. 137.

Walk east down 16th Street where bars and tiny, expensive boutiques reign supreme (see the Nightlife chapter and Shopping chapter for recommendations in the area). Continue east on 16th Street until you return to Valencia Street and turn right. Walk 1½ blocks on the east side of the street to come to:

## 15 Clarion Alley

Clarion Alley, bounded by Mission and Valencia streets and 17th and 18th streets, is more art-filled even than Balmy Alley. However, more than Balmy, this alley can be sketchy at times, so trust your gut and don't enter alone if there doesn't appear to be anyone else taking in the art. Most of the alleyway is indeed covered in art, thanks to the Clarion Alley Mural Project (CAMP), which was established in 1992. The group has worked with a diverse number of artists—from folk art painters to impressionists to graffiti artists—to transform the street into a gallery. Many of the masterpieces contain activist messages that speak to the area's extensive history as a center of social consciousness.

Now that you've got a feel for the neighborhood, surely there are some places you want to revisit. You can do that, or hop on the subway at the underground metro and BART stations at 16th and Mission streets to get you downtown or anywhere else you'd like to go.

# SHOPPING

S an Francisco is a little like a consignment shop—if you look in the corners and do a little digging, you're bound to find treasures. Shopping options here represent every style, era, fetish, and financial status—not in sprawling shopping malls, but scattered throughout the city in unique neighborhood boutiques. Whether you're looking for a pair of Jimmy Choo shoes, a Chanel knockoff, or Chinese herbal medicine, San Francisco's got it. Just pick a shopping neighborhood, wear some sensible shoes, and get ready to end up with at least a few take-home treasures.

## THE SHOPPING SCENE

### Major Shopping Areas

San Francisco has many shopping areas, but here's where you'll find most of the action.

**UNION SQUARE & ENVIRONS** San Francisco's most congested and popular shopping mecca is centered on Union Square and spreads out to Bush, Taylor, Market, and Montgomery streets. Most of the big department stores and many high-end specialty shops are here, including **Bloomingdales** (at 4th and Market sts.), **Saks** (Powell St. at Post St.), **Macy's** (at Stockton and O'Farrell), **Neiman Marcus** (at Stockton and Geary), and **Nordstrom** (Market at 5th St.). Be sure to venture to Grant Avenue, Post and Sutter streets, and Maiden Lane. This area is a hub for public transportation; all Market Street and several other buses run here, as do the Powell–Hyde and Powell–Mason cable car lines. You can also take the Muni streetcar to the Powell Street station.

**CHINATOWN** When you pass through the gate to Chinatown on Grant Avenue, say goodbye to the world of fashion and hello to a swarm of cheap tourist shops selling everything from linen and jade to plastic toys and $3 slippers. But that's not all Chinatown has to offer. The real gems are tucked away on side streets, often small, one-person shops selling Chinese herbs, original art, and jewelry. Grant Avenue is the area's main thoroughfare, and the side streets between Bush Street and Columbus Avenue are full of restaurants, markets, and eclectic shops. Stockton Street is best for food shopping (including live fowl and fish). Walking is the way to get around—traffic through this area is slow and parking is next to impossible. Most stores in Chinatown are open longer hours than in the rest of the city (see box p. 192), from about 10am to 10pm. Take bus no. 1, 9X, 15, 30, 41, or 45.

**JACKSON SQUARE**   A historic district just north of the Financial District's Embarcadero Center, this is the place to go for the top names in fine furniture and fine art. More than a dozen dealers on the 2 blocks between Columbus and Sansome streets specialize in European furnishings from the 17th to the 19th centuries. Most shops are only open Monday through Friday from 9am to 5pm and Saturday from 11am to 4pm. Bus: 1, 3, 8, or 10.

**UNION STREET**   Union Street, from Fillmore Street to Van Ness Avenue, caters to the upper-middle-class crowd. It's a great place to stroll, window-shop the plethora of boutiques, try the cafes and restaurants, and watch the beautiful people parade by. Take bus no. 22, 41, 45, 47, 49, or 76.

**CHESTNUT STREET**   Parallel and a few blocks north, Chestnut Street is a younger version of Union Street, with plenty of shopping and dining choices. An ever-tanned, super-fit population of postgraduate singles hangs around the cafes here and scopes each other out. Take bus no. 22, 28, 30, 43, or 76.

**FILLMORE STREET**   Some of the best boutique clothing shopping in town is packed into 5 blocks of Fillmore Street in Pacific Heights. From Jackson to Sutter streets, Fillmore is the perfect place to grab a bite and peruse high-priced boutiques, crafts shops, and contemporary housewares stores. (Don't miss **Zinc Details** ★★; p. 202.) Take bus no. 1, 2, 3, 4, 12, 22, or 24.

**HAIGHT STREET**   Green hair, spiked hair, no hair, or mohair—even the hippies look conservative next to Haight Street's grungy fashionistas. The shopping in the 6 blocks of upper Haight Street between Central Avenue and Stanyan Street reflects its clientele. It offers everything from incense and European and American street styles to furniture and antique clothing. Bus nos. 6, 7, 66, and 71 run the length of Haight Street, and nos. 33 and 43 run through upper Haight Street. Muni N streetcars stop at Waller Street and Cole Street.

**SOMA**   Although this area isn't suitable for strolling, you'll find almost all the discount shopping in warehouse spaces south of Market. You can pick up a discount-shopping guide at most major hotels. Many bus lines pass through this area.

**HAYES VALLEY**   The few blocks of lower Hayes Street, between Octavia and Gough streets, celebrate all things vintage, chic, artistic, and contemporary. It's definitely the most interesting shopping area in town, with furniture and glass stores, trendy shoe stores, and men's and women's clothiers. You can find lots of great antiques shops south on Octavia Street and on nearby Market Street. Take bus no. 16AX, 16BX, or 21.

**THE MISSION**   Where Mexican wrestler masks meet new-age apothecaries meet hip boutiques, the Mission offers an eclectic mix perfect for some entertaining browsing. In just the last few years, a treasure trove of fashionable and

**Store hours** are generally Monday through Saturday from 10am to 6pm and Sunday from 11am to 5pm. Most department stores stay open later, as do shops around Fisherman's Wharf, the most heavily visited area (by tourists).

**Sales tax** in San Francisco is 8.5%, which is added on at the register. If you live out of state and buy an expensive item, you might want to have the store ship it home for you. You'll have to pay for shipping, but you'll escape paying the sales tax. Most of the city's shops can wrap your purchase and ship it anywhere in the world. If they can't, you can send it yourself, either through **UPS** (℃ **800/742-5877**), **FedEx** (℃ **800/463-3339**), or the U.S. Postal Service.

funky stores have popped up on 16th and 17th streets in the Mission, as well as along Valencia Avenue. Find Mexican trinkets, Dia de los Muertos (Day of the Dead) paraphernalia, designer lotions and herbal remedies, cutting-edge fashions, locally designed jewelry, funky art and home decor, and even taxidermy—all in the same quarter-mile stretch. Bus: 12, 14, 22, or 49.

# SHOPPING A TO Z

## Antiques

**Bonhams** ★ Part of a world-renowned chain of auction houses, Bonham's deals in international goodies, from exquisite ancient Japanese screens to Hopi pottery to Art Deco jewelry and more. 220 San Bruno Ave. (at 16th St.). bonhams.com. ℃ **800/223-2854** or 415/861-7500. Open Mon–Fri 9am–5pm.

**McCarney's Furniture** ★ Treasure hunters come here for affordable diamonds in the rough imported from Scotland. Since they carry a wide variety of styles (and lots of "grandma's house"-style pieces), lots of stuff won't appeal. But all you need is one killer find to make a visit here a triumph. 731 Bryant St. mccarneysfurniture.com. ℃ **415/626-0655.** Open Mon, Wed, and Fri 11am–7pm, Tues–Thurs 11am–6pm, Sat–Sun noon–5pm.

**Stuff** ★ If you can't make it across the Bay Bridge to the Alameda Flea market but want to do some digging for "vintage modern" or other antique awesomeness, come to this coop featuring the finds of more than 60 independent curators. The huge Mission-District store is packed with curios and collectables, from furniture to artwork to trinkets to vinyl. 150 Valencia St. stuffsf.com. ℃ **415/864-2900.** Daily 10am–7:30pm.

## Art

For the latest on what artists are showing at the town's galleries, go online to sfbayareagalleryguide.com.

**Catharine Clark Gallery** ★★ Hailed as the first West Coast gallery with a dedicated media room, this gallery's artwork is in a wide range of media, all by exceptional emerging and established contemporary artists. 248

Utah St. (btw. 15th and 16th sts.). cclarkgallery.com. © **415/399-1439.** Tues–Sat 11am–6pm.

**Fraenkel Gallery** ★   Photography is the focus here; world-class artists from around the globe are featured in shows that change every 2 months. 49 Geary St. (btw. Grant Ave. and Kearny St.), 4th floor. fraenkelgallery.com. © **415/981-2661.** Tues–Fri 10:30am–5:30pm, Sat 11am–5pm.

**Hang** ★   Only Bay Area artists are exhibited at Hang, and since many are at the beginning of their careers, prices tend to be more affordable than at other galleries. 567 Sutter St. hangart.com. © **415/434-4264.** Mon–Sat 10am–6pm, Sun noon–5pm.

**Meyerovich Gallery** ★   A blue chip gallery, Meyervoich concentrates on selling the works of such modern masters as Chagall, Matisse, Miró, and Picasso. A Contemporary Gallery, across the hall, features works by Lichtenstein, Stella, Motherwell, and Hockney. 251 Post St. (at Stockton St.), 4th floor. meyerovich.com. © **415/421-7171.** Mon–Fri 10:30am–6pm, Sat 11am–5:30pm

# Books

**Adobe Books & Arts Cooperative** ★★   Yes, they sell books, both new and used at great prices, but to call this beloved Mission District institution just a bookstore would be selling it short. It's also a haven for emerging musicians and artists and a sort of salon for the city's eccentrics. Charming corners to read, art rooms, and regular wine-and-cheese receptions make this store both a vintage-book shopping destination and a cultural hub. 3130 24th St. (btw. Folsom and South Van Ness sts.). adobebooks.com. © **415/864-3936.** Mon–Fri noon–8pm, Sat–Sun 11am–8pm.

**Argonaut Book Shop** ★   When Alfred Hitchcock walked into this bookstore while filming the movie *Vertigo,* he said something to the effect of "This is exactly what a bookstore should look like," and promptly recreated every detail of it on a Hollywood sound stage. This antiquarian book shop specializes in California history, the American West, rare books, as well as maps, prints, and photographs. 786 Sutter St. (at Jones St.). argonautbookshop.com. © **415/474-9067.** Mon–Fri 9am–5pm, Sat 10am–4pm.

**Book Passage** ★★   Run by the ebullient Elaine Petrocelli, this bookstore in the Ferry Building may be small but it's wonderfully well curated, meaning you're sure to find something entertaining to read here. Book Passage is also known for its excellent author events and writer's conferences, both in San Francisco and in its main store in Corte Madera. Ferry Building Marketplace (Embarcadero and Market St.). bookpassage.com. © **415/835-1020.** Mon–Fri 9am–7pm, Sat 8am–6pm, Sun 10am–6pm.

**Books Inc.** ★   Holding the title "The West's Oldest Independent Bookseller," Books Inc., established in 1857, is living proof that an indie book seller can adapt, survive, and even prosper, despite Gold Rush busts and booms, numerous earthquakes, the Great Depression, fires, death, bankruptcy, and, most important (and probably toughest of all), the rapidly changing bookselling climate. Owners Margie and Michael Tucker have created a warm, inviting environment, hosting book clubs, author events, and travel lit groups—everyone is welcome to attend. The chain has three city locations, as well as two **Compass Books** at San Francisco International Airport. Marina: 2251 Chestnut St. (btw. Scott and Pierce sts.). booksinc.net. ✆ **415/931-3633.** Laurel Village: 3515 California St. (at Locust St.), ✆ **415/221-3666.** Opera Plaza: 601 Van Ness (btw. Turk St. and Golden Gate Ave.), ✆ **415/776-1111.** SFO Airport: Terminals 2 and 3. Store hours vary, but generally daily 10am–7pm.

**The Booksmith ★★**  A true gem, with erudite, handwritten recommendations for books dotting the shelves. This Haight store may not be huge, but it is smartly curated and has more than 1,000 different magazines on sale. 1644 Haight St. (btw. Clayton and Cole sts.). booksmith.com. ✆ **800/493-7323** or 415/863-8688. Mon–Sat 10am–10pm, Sun 10am–8pm.

**City Lights Booksellers & Publishers ★**  The city's iconic bookstore (see p. 177)—once owned by Lawrence Ferlinghetti, the renowned Beat Generation poet—is still going strong. The three-level store is particularly good for art, poetry, and political paperbacks, though it also carries more mainstream books. 261 Columbus Ave. (at Broadway). citylights.com. ✆ **415/362-8193.** Daily 10am–midnight.

**Green Apple Books ★★**  A massive purveyor of both new and used books—the store boasts more than 160,000 tomes!—it's an excellent resource for those seeking special books, like modern first editions and rare graphic comics. We also have to give kudos to the knowledgeable and friendly staff, who will help you find whatever you need. *Note:* There's a separate music, fiction, and DVD annex next door. 506 Clement St. (at Sixth Ave.). greenapple-books.com. ✆ **415/387-2272.** Daily 10am–10:30pm.

**Omnivore Books on Food ★★**  Cookbook lovers and chefs know this sweet destination bookstore crammed from floor to ceiling with food tomes. It's the place to come for any and every cookbook and food magazine, plus opportunities to meet famous food authors. Owner Celia Sack knows her stuff. She also buys and sells antique and collectible cookbooks, so if there's something specific you're looking for, she'll either have it or can help you find it. Check the calendar of events to see who's appearing when you're in town. 3885a Cesar Chavez St. omnivorebooks.com. ✆ **415/282-4712.** Mon–Sat 11am–6pm, Sun noon–5pm.

## Cannabis

**Barbary Coast Collective ★**  Marijuana culture is alive and well, if not totally transformed, in the city long known for counterculture. No San Francisco cannabis dispensary better proves the point than this swank Mission

District spot. There's everything you can imagine and more to choose from, but what makes this dispensary really stand out is the luxurious layout, which looks more like a steakhouse than a smokehouse. Some people come to buy and bolt; others come to linger and "partake" on a barstool or at one of the banquettes. *Note:* Until the city works out how to enact the retail part of California's 2018 pot legalization, you'll still need a medical marijuana card to gain entrance and to make a purchase, but if you're determined and have $100 to spend, cards are relatively easy to get—and fast. Just search online for a local option. 952 Mission St. (btw. 5th and 6th sts.). barbarycoastsf.org. © **415/243-4400.** Daily 8:30am–9:30pm.

## Chocolate & Candy

**Dandelion Chocolate** ★★  I eat a lot of chocolate, and I also own and operate a food magazine, so I feel confident in saying Dandelion makes some seriously outstanding chocolate. You can tour and taste for yourself at the "bean-to-bar" factory, cafe, and shop in the Mission, where they transform raw beans to small-batch bars right before your eyes (visible from the cafe during production hours or on one of their $5 factory tours). They also serve chocolate drinks and desserts, and sell—what else—chocolate. Book factory tours well in advance, and wear close-toed shoes to do the tour. 740 Valencia St (at 18th St.). dandelionchocolate.com. © **415/349-0942.** Cafe Mon–Thurs 10am–10pm, Fri–Sat 10am–11pm. Tours Wed–Sat 6:10–6:50pm, 8 guests maximum, for ages 9 and up.

**Z. Cioccolato** ★  This sweet-tooth wonderland offers 40 flavors of fresh fudge, plus saltwater taffy, classic brands of candies of all sorts, and such novelty items as candy bras or G-strings. A decadent North Beach store that's sure to satisfy. 474 Columbus Ave. (at Green St.). zcioccolato.com. © **415/395-9116.** Mon–Thurs 11am–11pm, Fri–Sat 11am–midnight.

## Cigars

**Vendetta Men's Apparel & Vintage Cuban Cigars** ★  Vendetta's motto is "living well is the best revenge." and owner Bruce Rothenberg is all about the finer things in life. At his shop in Nob Hill's Fairmont Hotel, he sells high quality items like fine Italian caps and Persol sunglasses, but Bruce's real specialty is the pre-embargo Cuban cigars he lovingly sells to customers with the reluctance of someone selling his offspring. He knows the history of these babies, dating from 1947 to 1962, and assures you that, like a fine wine, they only get more character with age. It's one of the few stores in the country selling Cubans, and you will pay the price for one of these rare stogies—cigars range from $125 to $250 apiece. Bruce has added a separate smoking room with a cushy sofa where guests can light up and enjoy their purchases. Don't worry, if the Cubans are out of your price range, he carries Dominican and Nicaraguan cigars for a fraction of the price. Fairmont Hotel, 950 Mason St. (btw. California and Sacramento sts.). vendettablu.com. © **415/397-7755.** Tues–Sat 12:30–7pm.

# Fashion

## MEN'S FASHIONS

**Cable Car Clothiers ★**  Since 1939, this gentlemen's store has been helping San Francisco's elite look their most dashing. Selling everything from three-button suits to fedoras to pocket squares, it sources the best from around the world for its clientele, even esoteric buys such as wool hosiery from France and cotton underwear from Switzerland. 200 Bush St. (at Sansome St.). cablecarclothiers.com. ✆ **415/397-4740.** Mon–Fri 9:30am–6pm, Sat 11am–5pm.

## UNISEX

**A-B Fits ★★**  The solution for those who've given up finding a flattering pair of jeans, this North Beach boutique specializes in finding denim that, well, fits. Doing so requires a broad range of options and a dedicated staff. Luckily, A-B Fits has both—the shop carries over 100 styles of jeans and the salespeople are true experts at their highly specialized trade. 1519 Grant Ave. (at Union and Filbert sts.). abfits.com. ✆ **415/982-5726.** Tues–Sat 11:30am–6:30pm, Sun noon–6pm.

**Betabrand ★**  Quirky, functional, hipster, Burner (i.e., Burning Man attendee) . . . this innovative local clothing manufacturer relates to them all, and it's not just due to very clever marketing. They hit their first homerun with "corduround" pants (corduroys with horizontal rather than vertical wales), and there's a strong following for their ultrashiny DiscoLab pants, tuxedos, jackets, and more. Many designs are crowd-sourced—anyone can submit a design, shoppers vote and "pre-buy," and items with traction get produced. Beta really understands millennials' desires and behaviors, which is why new fans continually flock to the store and website. 80 Valencia St. betabrand.com. ✆ **855/694-8766** or 415/400-5995. Mon–Fri 11am–7pm, Sat 11am–8pm, Sun noon–9pm.

**Cary Lane ★**  If you love designer clothes and great deals, beeline to this boutique offering designer apparel for men and women—all up to 80% less than the suggested retail price. Its private label menswear line is relaxed but of solid quality, as is most of the fashion the store carries. Also at 3153 16th St. (✆ **415/896-4564**) and 1262 9th Ave. (✆ **415/592-8731**). 560 Laguna St. (at Hayes St.). carylanesf.com. ✆ **415/ 896-4210.** Mon–Sat 11am–7pm, Sun 11am–6pm.

**Goorin Brothers ★**  Fabulous hats, for both men and women, are the stock in trade of this boutique chain. You'll find porkpie hats, cowboy hats, funky straw fedoras (made by local artists), modern cloth cloches in all colors, and wide-brimmed hats perfect for fashionable garden parties (or gardening). Also near Union Square at 111 Geary St., and in the Haight at 1446 Haight St. 1612 Stockton St. (on Washington Sq.). goorin.com. ✆ **415/426-9450.** Sun–Thurs 10am–8pm, Sat–Sun 11am–9pm.

**MAC ★**  Nope, not the makeup store. The name stands for Modern Appealing Clothing, and that about sums up what's sold here. The owners source attractive and (sometimes) unusual pieces from around the world—Belgium's

Dries Van Noten, Tokyo's Minä Perhonen, and Spain's Sybilla, to name a few—and then help customers arrange them into drop-dead gorgeous outfits. And happily, prices are *slightly* kinder at MAC than they are in the other trendy Hayes Valley shops. Also at 1003 Minnesota St. (at 22nd St.). 387 Grove St. (at Gough St.). modernappealingclothing.com. © **415/863-3011.** Mon–Sat 11am–7pm, Sun noon–6pm.

**Marine Layer ★** Comfort is Marine Layer's *raison d'être*. The firm makes basic, ultrasoft tops that are great for layering—T's, polos, button-downs, cardigans, hoodies—made of a special blend of pima cotton and micro modal that feels already broken-in. Marina: 2209 Chestnut St. Hayes Valley: 498 Hayes St. marinelayer.com. © **415/346-2400.** Daily 10am–7pm.

**Wilkes Bashford ★** The couture boutique that first introduced Armani to the U.S. underwent a total facelift in 2012, making this elegant Union Square temple of commerce even more hoity-toity. The fashions are primarily from France and Italy; services include custom fittings on-site, free wine and coffee, and the advice of a staff of expert stylists. *Tip:* In February there's a warehouse sale, when prices drop by a hair. 375 Sutter St. (at Stockton St.). wilkes bashford.com. © **415/986-4380.** Mon–Sat 10am–6pm.

## WOMEN'S FASHIONS

**440 Brannan Studio Showroom ★** In this massive factory space, local designers sell limited-edition lines to the public; you'll sometimes see one stitching a hem or constructing a jacket in the back. In business since 1998, the Studio's been an incubator for several talented San Francisco designers. While it does carry menswear, the vast majority of these unique and often really fun creations are for women. 440 Brannan St. (near Zoe St.). 440Brannan.com. © **415/957-1411.** Mon–Sat 11am–7pm.

**Dish ★** Don't come here without expecting to buy more than you planned. (I've learned this the hard way.) This well-curated selection of women's wardrobe essentials in the middle of oh-so-chic Hayes Valley sells tops, bottoms, dresses, jewelry, shoes, and purses—all sophisticated, relaxed, and high-quality. They also tend to be things I wear for years, which makes me feel okay about the occasional splurge. Expect to find labels like Rag & Bone, Smythe, Ulla Johnson, Frank & Eileen, and more. 541 Hayes St. dishboutique. com. © **415/252-5997.** Mon–Sat 11am–7pm, Sun noon–6pm.

**Hero Shop ★★** Former *Vogue* fashion-news editor Emily Holt is behind this fashion stylists' favorite haunt for easy, chic, wearable everyday clothing, shoes, and accessories. Drop in if you want to wear something you can be sure not everyone else will have, and explore her picks from top local up-and-comers and established designers. Open Tuesday through Friday 11am to 7pm, Saturday 10am to 7pm, and Sunday noon to 5pm. 982 Post St. heroshopsf. com. © **415/829-3129.** Tues–Fri 11am–7pm, Sat 10am–7pm, Sun noon–5pm.

**Sunhee Moon ★** Clothing for the "modern day Audrey Hepburn" is the goal of local designer SunHee Moon, and with her eye for color and fit, I'd say she's doing a fine job. Her dresses come in a variety of streamlined shapes and exuberant colors, and she creates equally flattering separates: sleek pants, tailored and/or draped tops, and quirkily patterned skirts. Prices, while not low, are more than reasonable for clothing this sturdy yet chic. Also at 3167 13th St. (✆ **415/355-1800**). 1833 Fillmore St. (btw. Bush and Sutter sts.). sunheemoon. com. ✆ **415/928-1800.** Mon–Fri noon–7pm, Sat–Sun noon–6pm.

**Therapy** ★   At this fast-fashion boutique, merchandise ranges from the latest garb to housewares to novelty items, at prices just reasonable enough to be dangerous. You may come in for a small splurge on, say, a scented candle, and find yourself leaving with a new pair of Toms, a locally designed dress, a chunky infinity scarf, and a hat. It's also a great place for playful gifts and quirky cards and books. Look at it this way: A little retail therapy can save you hundreds on the real thing. Also in North Beach at 1445 Grant Ave. (✆ **415/ 781-8899**). 545 Valencia St. (btw. 17th and 18th sts.). shopattherapy.com. ✆ **415/865-0981.** Mon–Thurs noon–9pm, Fri–Sat 10:30am–10pm, Sun 10:30am–9pm.

## Consignment & Vintage Stores

**GoodByes** ★★   The style-conscious citizens of San Francisco consign their cast-offs to this shop, meaning the quality of the goods is high, but the prices often surprisingly low (we've seen $350 pre-owned shoes going for just $35 here). goodbyessf.com. Menswear: 3462 Sacramento St., ✆ **415/346-6388.** Womenswear: 3483 Sacramento St., ✆ **415/674-0151.** Mon–Sat 10am–6pm (Thurs until 8pm), Sun 11am–5pm.

**Held Over** ★   Considered one of the premier vintage/consignment clothing stores in San Francisco, this is where to shop for decade-specific duds, with racks organized accordingly. Also at 1711 Haight St., ✆ **415/668-3744.** 1543 Haight St., near Ashbury; ✆ **415/864-0818.** Mon–Thurs 11am–7pm, Fri–Sun 11am–8pm.

## Food

**Cowgirl Creamery Cheese Shop** ★   One of the farms that pioneered the artisanal cheese craze, the small-production Cowgirl Creamery is headquartered up in Point Reyes, but its city outpost in the Ferry Building Marketplace offers all their signature cheeses, including robust Red Hawk; smooth, creamy Mt. Tam; and famed Humboldt Fog goat cheese. Ferry Building Marketplace, no. 17. cowgirlcreamery.com. ✆ **415/362-9354.** Mon–Fri 10am–7pm, Sat 8am–6pm, Sun 10am–5pm.

**Molinari Delicatessen** ★★   You can't help but pull out your camera when you walk into this North Beach institution dating back to 1896 (see p. 179). It's a food sensory overload. Everywhere you look, shelves, counters, and rafters are filled with jars of colorful sauces, olive oils, cheeses, and imported wines, while all sizes of red and white salamis dangle from strings. Molinari's is the perfect place to grab a thick meat-stuffed sandwich for a picnic at Washington Square Park, 2 blocks away at Columbus and Union

# AMAZING grazing: THE FERRY BUILDING

As much a sightseeing attraction as a place to buy and consume food, the **Ferry Building Marketplace ★★★** and its corollary Farmers' Market (one of the most highly acclaimed farmers' markets in the United States) are tangible proof that people who live in San Francisco lead tastier lives than the rest of the nation (sorry, but it's true!). The produce—organic and sourced from small family farms—looks like it was taken from a still-life painting, the meats and fish are superfresh, and the quality and variety of unusual specialty goods (who knew balsamic vinegar can be clear?) will blow your mind.

Saturday morning is the best time to stop by, when the **Farmers' Market ★★★** is in its full glory, playing host to local meat ranchers, artisan cheesemakers, bread bakers, specialty food purveyors, and farmers. Some are picked for the 10:30am **Meet the Farmer** event, a half-hour interview created to give the audience in-depth information about how and where their food is produced. At 11am, Bay Area chefs give cooking demonstrations using ingredients purchased that morning from the market. (And yes, tastings are given out, as are recipes.) Several local restaurants also have food stalls selling their cuisine—including breakfast items—so don't eat before you arrive. There's also farmers' market activity on Tuesdays and Thursday if you can't get here on Saturday.

The **Marketplace,** open daily, features Northern California's best gourmet food outlets, including Cowgirl Creamery's Artisan Cheese Shop (see p. 198), Recchiuti Confections (amazing chocolate), Acme Breads, Blue Bottle Coffee, Hog Island Oysters, and gluten-free Mariposa Bakery. The famed Vietnamese restaurant the Slanted Door (see p. 90) is here, as is Imperial Tea Court, where you'll be taught the traditional Chinese way to steep and sip your tea, and a myriad of other restaurants, delis, gourmet coffee shops, specialty foods, and wine bars. If you want crazy-good Japanese takeout food, try Delica, and definitely check out Heath Ceramics (see p. 201), a favorite among chefs and food lovers.

The Ferry Building Marketplace is open Monday through Friday from 10am to 7pm, Saturday from 8am to 6pm, and Sunday from 11am to 5pm. The Farmers' Market takes place year-round, rain or shine, on Tuesdays and Thursdays from 10am to 2pm and Saturdays from 8am to 2pm. The Ferry Building is located on the Embarcadero at the foot of Market Street (about a 15-min. walk from Fisherman's Wharf). For more information, visit ferryplazafarmersmarket.com or ferrybuildingmarketplace.com or call ℭ **415/693-0996.**

Streets. 373 Columbus St. (at Vallejo St.). ℭ **415/421-2337.** Mon–Fri 8am–6pm, Sat 7:30am–5:30pm.

## Gifts

**Art of China ★**   Since 1974, this shop has been selling refined Chinese exports—no plastic here! Instead you'll find genuine collectibles, from elegant hand-carved Chinese figurines to cloisonné, porcelain vases, and decorative items (and jewelry) created from ivory, quartz, and jade. 839–843 Grant Ave. (btw. Clay and Washington sts.). artsofchinasf.com. ℭ **415/981-1602.** Hours vary.

**Cost Plus World Market ★**   It sometimes feels like the entire world is on sale at this Fisherman's Wharf store (it's right at the cable car turnaround). You'll find biscuits from Australia, inlaid stools from India, artisanal beers from across the U.S. (they let you build your own six-pack so you can do a tasting), funky shower curtains—you name it, they have it, usually in a foreign brand you haven't seen before and at a price that's more than fair. 2552 Taylor St. (btw. North Point and Bay sts.). worldmarket.com. ✆ **415/928-6200.** Mon–Fri 10am–9pm, Sat 9am–9pm, Sun 9am–8pm.

**Good Vibrations ★**   This female-oriented sex-toy shop is more straightforward and empowering than seedy, thanks to the open, nonjudgmental attitude of the staff (who own the place, incidentally; this is a woman-owned, worker-owned co-operative). Even if you're not in the market for any new gadgets, stop by to see the on-site vibrator museum. Also at 1620 Polk St. (✆ **415/345-0400**), 899 Mission St. (✆ **415/513-1635**), and 189 Kearny St. (✆ **415/653-1364**). 603 Valencia St. (at 17th St.). goodvibes.com. ✆ **415/522-5460** or 800/BUY-VIBE (289-8423) for mail order. Sun–Fri 10am–9pm, Sat 10am–10pm.

**Gump's ★**   Those who need a special item for a special event have been coming here since 1861 when this boutique department store was founded. Gump's carries everything from jewelry to vases to Asian antiques, with many items that can't be found anywhere else, and the service is legendary. It's particularly popular for wedding registries and also has an unusually good collection of Christmas ornaments. 135 Post St. (btw. Kearny St. and Grant Ave.). gumps.com. ✆ **800/766-7628** or 415/982-1616. Mon–Sat 10am–6pm, Sun noon–5pm.

**Nest ★★**   It's hard to categorize Nest—it carries everything from throws and handmade quilts to flowing boho dresses and sleepwear. What ties it all together is the impeccable taste of the owner, and the fact that you won't find a lot of these items anywhere else. This one's fun to just browse, even if the prices stop you from buying. 2300 Fillmore St. (at Clay St.). nestsf.com. ✆ **415/292-6199.** Mon–Fri 10:30am–6:30pm, Sat 10:30am–6pm, Sun 11am–6pm.

**New People ★**   More than just a store, New People is a $15-million complex dedicated to modern Japanese culture, both its Zen side and its over-the-top anime wackiness. In the basement, a THX-certified theater showcases Japanese cinema; the other floors (there are five altogether) feature a nail salon, a crumpet and tea shop (skip it—it's expensive and service is uneven), a boutique dedicated to cute gadget cases, two clothing stores, and more. The fashion stores carry items you likely won't find anywhere else in North America, like Lolita clothes (dresses for grown women made to look like toddler outfits—don't ask) and Sou Sou shoes, the classic form-fitting Japanese shoes with an indent between the big toe and the rest of the toes, here produced in all sorts of wacky, modern patterns. 1746 Post St. (btw. Buchanan and Webster sts.). newpeopleworld.com. No phone. Mon–Sat noon–7pm, Sun noon–6pm.

**Picnic ★★**   We all need a place to dash to for the perfect affordable gift—and for folks living around Russian Hill, Picnic is it. Decor, jewelry, clothing, even adorable San Francisco–themed onesies make this a sure thing for tasteful, modern, on-trend items. 1808 Polk St. picnicsf.com. ✆ **415/346-6556.** Sun 11am–6pm, Mon noon–6pm, Tues–Sat 11am–8pm.

**Rare Device** ★★ A curated collection of chic, modern, well-designed local and international accessories, books, home appointments, and more is the focus at this shop. The owners' exceptional eye promises you'll find something you must have, which explains why it's a favorite stop among San Franciscans. A gallery, located in the shop, changes up local artists monthly. Also in Noe Valley at 4071 24th St. (✆ **415/374-7412**). 600 Divisadero St. rare device.net. ✆ **415/863-3969.** Mon–Fri noon–8pm, Sat 11am–7pm, Sun 11am–6pm.

**SFMOMA Museum Store** ★★ As it should, the remodeled Museum of Modern Art store has one of the city's most spectacular collections of gifts, books, jewelry, toys, home decor, and other *objets d'art*—and at reasonable prices. 151 Third St. (btw. Mission and Howard sts.). museumstore.sfmoma.org. ✆ **888/357-0037.** Daily 10am–6pm (until 9:30 Thurs; closes at 5pm Wed).

# Housewares/Furnishings

**Alessi** ★ Functional yet whimsical—that about describes the kitchen utensils of Italian designer Alberto Alessi (love his spiderlike lemon squeezer), and this is his North American flagship. It's a great place to find a gift, though most shoppers end up getting something for themselves, too, like a silver beaver-shaped pencil sharpener or one of their oh-so-cute kettles. 424 Sutter St. (at Stockton St.). alessi.com. ✆ **415/434-0403.** Mon–Sat 10am–6pm.

**Biordi Art Imports** ★★ Exquisite Italian majolica pottery is the lure here. Some use it to eat off of, but it's so pretty, my guess is most buyers take these plates, bowls, and other items and stick them on the wall for decoration. The owner has been importing these hand-painted collectibles since 1946. 412 Columbus Ave. (at Vallejo St.). biordi.com. ✆ **415/392-8096.** Mon–Fri 11am–5pm, Sat 9:30am–5pm.

**Heath Ceramics** ★★ If you're in the culinary scene, you know that Heath is the tableware provider of choice for chefs, artists, and pretty much anyone around the city with a healthy home-decorating budget. Check out this brand-new showroom, tucked in a quiet area of SoMa right next to the factory, and you'll see why. These plates, platters, and bowls are works of art, in enough colors to complement any environment. The company's good taste extends to its curated selection of glassware and cookware, plus an adjoining cafe, Tartine Manufactory (associated with the famed Mission District restaurant **Tartine,** see p. 187). Want to see how they make their wares? Working factory tours are held the first and third Fridays each month at 2pm, and weekend (non-working) tours on Saturdays and Sundays at 11:30am. 2900 18th St. heath-ceramics.com. ✆ **415/361-5552.** Sun–Wed 10am–6pm, Thurs–Sat 10am–7pm.

**March** ★★ Everything is so tastefully designed at this Pacific Heights boutique, even the oven mitts and aprons are chic. Most of the gorgeous floor coverings, furnishings, tabletop and kitchen items, candles, scarves, and totes come with a wince-worthy price tag. But it's always fun to look, and the pantry shelves are stocked with gourmet preserves, beautifully packaged spices, and other more affordable goodies. 3075 Sacramento St. marchsf.com. ✆ **415/931-7433.** Mon–Fri 10am–6pm.

**The Wok Shop ★★** Every implement ever created for Chinese cooking is available in a store that goes well beyond woks. Cleavers, circular chopping blocks, dishes, oyster knives, bamboo steamers, strainers, aprons, linens, and baskets . . . they're all here at great prices and all imported from China. 718 Grant Ave. (at Clay St.). wokshop.com. ✆ **415/989-3797.** Daily 10am–6pm.

**Zinc Details ★★** This high-style furniture and accessories store just about defines the San Francisco aesthetic, with alternately hip, colorful, and quirky pieces to dress up any home. While many of the furniture comes from international brands like Knoll, a portion are made specifically for the store. 1633 Fillmore St. (btw. Post and Geary sts.). zincdetails.com. ✆ **415/776-2100.** Mon–Sat 11am–6pm, Sun noon–6pm.

## Jewelry

**Love and Luxe ★** There's jewelry and then there's wearable art: The highly curated conversation-starters at this Mission District jewelry atelier are the latter. A tad on the edgy side, necklaces, rings, earrings, and accessories are all handmade by a rotating crop of emerging artists, giving you a sense of the local aesthetic. Guaranteed you'll find a few off-beat, beautiful pieces to commemorate your trip. Even if you're not in the market, this store is still worth a browse. 1169 Valencia St. (btw. 22nd and 23rd sts.) loveandluxesf.com. ✆ **415/648-7781.** Wed–Fri noon–6pm, Sat 11am–7pm, Sun noon–5pm.

**Union Street Goldsmith ★** Locally made contemporary jewelry is the focus here, and many of the pieces feature vibrantly colorful stones. The staff will also create custom designs upon request. 1909 Union St. (at Laguna St.). unionstreetgoldsmith.com. ✆ **415/776-8048.** Tues–Sat 11am–5:30pm.

## Pirate Supplies

**826 Valencia/Pirate Supply Store ★★** When *A Heartbreaking Work of Staggering Genius* author Dave Eggers wanted to set up a literary salon to inspire under-resourced young people to write, the city said his Mission District space was zoned for retail. Naturally, he opened a pirate supply store as a front for the tutoring, mentoring, and writing. Pick up a bottle of "Scurvy be Gone" or tattoo remover. Stock up on eye patches or glass eyes. When you order your custom hook, make sure to specify whether it is for the right or left hand. All proceeds from the store support up-and-coming young writers who hone their craft in the classroom in the back. 826 Valencia St. (btw. 19th St. and Cunningham Lane). 826valencia.org. ✆ **415/642-5905.** Daily noon–6pm.

# shopping CENTERS & COMPLEXES

**Ghirardelli Square** ★ This former chocolate factory is one of the city's quaintest shopping malls and most popular landmarks. Though now dotted with tourist-centric shops, it's the former chocolate and spice factory of Domingo Ghirardelli (say "Gear-ar-dell-y"), and dates back even further to 1864, when the factory made Civil War uniforms. A clock tower, an exact replica of one at France's Château de Blois, crowns the complex. Inside the tower, on the mall's plaza level, is its most popular attraction—the fun yet way-pricey Ghirardelli soda fountain, an old-fashioned ice-cream parlor that also makes and sells small amounts of chocolate. Other stores range from a children's club to a women's clothing boutique, cards and stationery to a doggie boutique. The main plaza shops and restaurants are open daily 11am to 9pm (except Sun when it closes at 6pm). The square has free Wi-Fi, too. 900 North Point St. (at Polk St.). www.ghirardellisq.com. ✆ **415/775-5500.**

**Pier 39** ★ To residents, Pier 39 is an expensive spot where out-of-towners buy souvenirs and greasy fast food. But it does have some redeeming qualities—fresh crab (when in season), stunning views, playful sea lions, fun street performers, and plenty of amusement for the kids. If you want to get to know the real San Francisco, skip the cheesy T-shirt shops and limit your time here to one afternoon, if that. At Beach St. and the Embarcadero. pier39.com.

**Westfield San Francisco Centre** ★ This ritzy 1.5-million-square-foot urban shopping center is one of the few vertical malls (multilevel rather than sprawling) in the United States. Its spectacular atrium is topped with a century-old dome that's 102 feet wide and 3 stories high. Along with Nordstrom (p. 190) and Bloomingdale's (p. 190) department stores and a Century Theatres multiplex, there are more than 170 specialty stores, including Abercrombie & Fitch, Zara, H&M, J. Crew, Kate Spade New York, and Lucky Brand Jeans. The bottom level is sprinkled with probably the best food-court fare you've ever had (don't miss the amazing array of grab-and-go eats at Bristol Farms grocery store). 865 Market St. (at Fifth St.). westfield.com/san francisco. ✆ **415/512-6776.**

## Shoes

**Bulo** ★ Fashion-forward footwear from designers like Donald J. Pliner, Yuko Imanishi, and Bed Stu draws shoppers to this small, hip store. In addition to shoes, Bulo sells belts, socks, wallets, jewelry, and shoe-care products. 418 Hayes St. buloshoes.com. ✆ **415/255-4939.** Mon–Sat 11am–7pm, Sun 11am–6pm.

**Paolo Shoes** ★ Paolo is short for Paulo Iantorno, the owner who designs the store's colorful wedges and towering stilettos for women and funky purple suede ankle boots for men—and then sends his designs to Italy to be handcrafted. But what makes these shoes unique that is they're not only creative and colorful, they're actually comfortable—even the pumps! 524 Hayes St. paoloshoes.com. ✆ **415/552-4580.** Mon–Sat 11am–7pm, Sun 11am–6pm.

## Toys

**The Chinatown Kite Shop** ★ This delightful Chinatown classic sells all sorts of kites, from ones you design yourself to color-saturated fish kites, windsocks, hand-painted Chinese paper kites, wood-and-paper biplanes, pentagonal kites, and more. All of it makes great souvenirs and decorations. 717 Grant Ave. (btw. Clay and Sacramento sts.). chinatownkite.com. ✆ **415/989-5182.** Daily 10am–8pm.

## Travel Goods

**Flight 001** ★ The store for jetsetters, it sells the coolest of luggage tags, TSA-friendly manicure sets, sleek travel pillows, and all sorts of gadgets to make your flight home that much more comfortable and/or fun. 525 Hayes St. (btw. Laguna and Octavia sts.). flight001.com. ✆ **415/487-1001.** Mon–Sat 11am–7pm, Sun 11am–6pm.

## Wine & Sake

**True Sake** ★ Some 150 different brands of sake are available at this specialty store, many of which, owner Beau Timken claims, are available at no other retail store in the U.S. Don't be intimidated if you know nothing about sake: The informed staff will help you make the best decision to suit your tastes and won't just push the pricier varieties (in fact, many of the bottles here are surprisingly affordable). 560 Hayes St. (btw. Laguna and Octavia sts.). truesake. com. ✆ **415/355-9555.** Mon–Fri noon–7pm, Sat 11am–7pm, Sun noon–6pm.

**Wine Club San Francisco** ★ The Wine Club is a discount warehouse that offers excellent prices on more than 1,200 domestic and foreign wines. If you can't find your favorite on sale, the well-informed staff should be able to find you a similar tipple. 953 Harrison St. (btw. Fifth and Sixth sts.). thewineclub.com. ✆ **415/512-9086.** Mon–Sat 10am–7pm, Sun 10am–6pm.

# NIGHTLIFE

San Francisco's nightlife is varied and colorful, just like its population. There's no single nightlife district—activity is scattered throughout the city, which gives you an opportunity to experience the distinctive flavor of more areas. Whether you linger downtown or in SoMa, where most of the city's theater and dance clubs cluster; head to Civic Center for symphony, opera, or ballet; go to the Mission for music, bar-hopping, or cult cinema; or venture to the many attractions tucked into the city's outer nooks and crannies, there's always something fun to do. Bonus: Unlike Los Angeles or New York, in San Francisco you won't have to pay outrageous cover charges to be a part of the scene. It's also unlike New York in one other way: Bars close at 2am, so get an early start if you want a full night on the town here.

For ideas on what's up, check out *Where* (wheresf.com), a free tourist-oriented monthly that lists programs and performance times; it's available in most of the city's finer hotels. The Sunday edition of the *San Francisco Chronicle* features a Datebook section, with information on and listings of the week's events. If you have Internet access, it's a good idea to check out www.citysearch.com, www.sfstation.com, or www.7x7.com for the latest in bars, clubs, and events. For information on local theater, check out **theatre bayarea.org**. If you want to secure seats at a hot-ticket event, either buy well in advance or contact the concierge of your hotel and see if he or she can swing something for you.

**GETTING TICKETS** Goldstar (goldstar.com/san-francisco) offers discounted tickets for everything from Segway tours of Golden Gate Park to lectures and musical and theatrical performances. If you don't know what to do at any given time while visiting San Francisco, this website may have the perfect thing, at an affordable price to boot. Ditto **Eventbrite.com**, which sells tickets to all kinds of city fun and adventure.

**Tix Bay Area** (also known as **TIX;** tixbayarea.org; ✆ **415/430-1140**) sells half-price tickets on the day of performances (as well as full-price tickets in advance) to select Bay Area cultural and sporting events. Tickets are primarily sold in person, with some half-price tickets available on the website. Call or go on line to find out which shows are available that day. A service charge, ranging from $1.75

to $5, is levied on each ticket, based on its full price. The TIX office, located in Union Square on Powell Street between Geary and Post streets, is open Sunday through Thursday from 8am to 4pm and Saturday from 11am to 5pm. *Note:* Half-price tickets go on sale at 11am the day of the performance.

You can also get tickets to most theater and dance events through **City Box Office** (www.cityboxoffice.com; ✆ **415/392-4400**), 180 Redwood St., Suite 100, between Golden Gate and McAllister streets off Van Ness Avenue. It's open weekdays from 9:30am to 5pm and Saturdays noon to 4pm.

**Tickets.com** (tickets.com; ✆ **800/225-2277**) sells computer-generated tickets (with a hefty service charge of $3–$20 per ticket!) to concerts, sporting events, plays, and special events. **Ticketmaster** (ticketmaster.com; ✆ **415/421-TIXS** [8497]) also offers advance ticket purchases (also with a service charge).

# THE PERFORMING ARTS

**San Francisco Performances** ★★ (performances.org), has brought acclaimed artists to the Bay Area since 1979. Shows run the gamut from chamber music to dance to jazz and are held in several venues, including the Herbst Theater and the Yerba Buena Center for the Arts. The season runs from late September to June. Tickets cost from $15 to $96 and are available through **City Box Office** (see above) or through the San Francisco Performances website.

## Classical Music and Opera

**San Francisco Opera** ★★★  The second largest opera company on the continent, this opera company is also one of the most courageous. Along with presenting the classics in lavish, huge productions, the SFO commissions new works each year, and sometimes these new operas can be quite controversial, such as the fall 2013 adaptation of Stephen King's novel *Dolores Claiborne* by American composer Tobias Picker. 2018 welcomes the new production *Girls of the Golden West,* which is based on letters describing the turmoil of living through the Gold Rush. All productions have English supertitles. The performance schedule is a bit odd: The season starts in September and runs for 14 weeks, then takes a break for a few months before starting again in June for 2 months. It's usually possible to get less-coveted seats as late as the day of performance, although prime seats can go months in advance. War Memorial Opera House, 301 Van Ness Ave. (at Grove St.). sfopera.com. ✆ **415/864-3330** (box office). Tickets $30–$398; standing room $10 cash only; student rush $30; active military and seniors $35–45.

**San Francisco Symphony** ★★★  Michael Tilson Thomas, perhaps the most celebrated living American conductor, holds the baton here. Thanks in part to his leadership, the roster is full of world-class soloists, world-premiere pieces, and high-quality performances. Davies Symphony Hall, 201 Van Ness Ave. (at Grove St.). sfsymphony.org. ✆ **415/864-6000** (box office). Tickets $15–$186; rush tickets on select performances $20 (call rush hotline ✆ **415/502-5577** night before for next-day ticket availability).

# Theater

**American Conservatory Theater (A.C.T.)** ★★★ This is, quite simply, one of the best theater companies in the U.S., with peerless acting, design and show-selection. Since its debut in 1967, a number of big names have "trod the boards" here, including Annette Bening, Denzel Washington, Danny Glover, and Nicolas Cage. The A.C.T. season runs September through July and features both classic and contemporary plays. Its home is the stupendously beautiful (and viewer-friendly) **Geary Theater,** built in 1910, a national historic landmark. Geary Theater, 415 Geary St. (at Mason St.). act-sf.org. ✆ **415/749-2ACT (2228).** Tickets $20–$150.

> ### Free Opera
>
> Every year, the **San Francisco Opera** stages a number of free performances. It kicks off the season every September with Opera in the Park, held in Golden Gate Park, followed by occasional free performances throughout the city as part of the Brown Bag Opera program. Schedule details can be found on the company's website at **www.sfopera.com.**

**Berkeley Repertory Theater** ★★★ Across the bay, this theater was founded in 1968 and has been mopping up awards ever since. It rivals A.C.T. (see above) in the quality of its shows, sometimes skewing a bit more avant-garde. Contemporary plays are offered throughout the year, usually Wednesday through Sunday. 2025 Addison St., Berkeley. berkeleyrep.org. ✆ **510/647-2900.** Tickets $57–$135.

**The Magic Theatre** ★★ Sam Shepard was a longtime artist-in-residence at the Magic, premiering his plays *Fool for Love* and *True West* here. That should give you an idea of the high quality of productions by this company, which has been performing since 1967. Building D, Fort Mason Center, 2 Marina Blvd. (at Buchanan St.). magictheatre.org. ✆ **415/441-8822.** Tickets $35–$80; discounts for students, educators, and seniors.

**San Francisco Playhouse** ★ The city's oldest off-Broadway company is located in the intimate upstairs theater of a charming old theater district hotel. Located a quick stroll from Union Square hotels, it's a wonderful way to enjoy San Francisco culture without leaving the downtown area. 450 Post St., in Kensington Park Hotel (btw. Powell & Mason sts.). sfplayhouse.org. ✆ **415/677-9596.** Tickets $20–$135.

**Theatre Rhinoceros** ★ Founded in 1977, this was America's first theater created to address LGBT themes and stories. It's still going strong. The theater is 1 block east of the 16th Street/Mission BART station. The Gateway Theatre, 215 Jackson St. (btw. Battery and Front sts.). therhino.org. ✆ **866/811-4111.** Tickets $10–$45.

# Dance

Top traveling troupes like the Joffrey Ballet and American Ballet Theatre make regular appearances in San Francisco. Primary modern dance spaces include **Yerba Buena Center for the Arts,** 701 Mission St. (www.ybca.org;

*C* 415/978-2787); the **Cowell Theater,** at Fort Mason Center, Marina Boulevard at Buchanan Street (www.fortmason.org; *C* **415/345-7575**); and the **ODC Theatre,** 3153 17th St., at Shotwell Street in the Mission District (www.odcdance.org; *C* **415/863-9834**). Check local papers for schedules or contact the theaters' box offices for more information.

**San Francisco Ballet ★★★**   This venerable company (founded in 1933), is the oldest professional ballet company in the United States and is still regarded as one of the country's finest. Along with its beloved annual *Nutcracker,* it performs a varied repertoire of full-length contemporary and classic ballets. The season generally runs February through May, with *Nutcracker* performances in December. War Memorial Opera House, 301 Van Ness Ave. (at Grove St.). sfballet.org. *C* **415/865-2000** for tickets and information. Tickets $37–$385.

# COMEDY & CABARET

**9**

NIGHTLIFE | Comedy & Cabaret

**BATS Improv ★**   Born out of the improvisational comedy craze that swept the U.S. in the '80s, BATS Improv is the longest-running improv theater in Northern California, and every weekend it serves up new plays, competitions, and even musicals. The award-winning theater focuses on "long form" improv, which means shows are geared toward creating a coherent story line, rather than just 2-minute bursts of weirdness (though the audience is encouraged to yell out ideas throughout the performance). On some nights, teams compete for trophies and bragging rights. Main Company shows are Fridays and Saturdays at 8pm; student performance ensemble shows are Sundays, at varying times each week. Reservations and discount tickets are available through the website; remaining tickets are sold at the box office the night of the show. Bayfront Theatre, Fort Mason Center, Building B # 350, 3rd floor. improv.org. *C* **415/474-6776.** Tickets $5–$22.

**Beach Blanket Babylon ★★★**   The longest-running musical revue in America, and by far one of the most "San Francisco" things to do, this beloved cabaret-style show—playing since 1974—continues to be a riveting 90-or-so minutes of hilarious and outrageous costumes, bawdy humor, campy sexual flirtation, and political and cultural commentary.

   The show's name doesn't describe what you'll see, except possibly the "Babylon" part; it's left over from its debut incarnation, when the theater was filled with sand and audience members had their hands slapped with Coppertone lotion. Some 16,000-plus performances and 6-million-plus tickets later, the show's toothless political commentary and mild sexual innuendo hit just the right spot for a hilarious evening out. Everything about it is pleasingly silly, from the plots to the songs (mostly radio standards in 1-minute bursts) and the impersonations (Donald and Melania Trump, Vladimir Putin, Beyoncé, Lady Gaga, Steve Bannon, and Taylor Swift recently made appearances). The show's main claim to fame, besides its longevity, are its huge wigs and hats, as tall as the proscenium will allow. The climactic bonnet, an illuminated and mechanized city skyline, requires a hidden scaffolding to support.

208

There's a family-friendly option on Sunday afternoons, though the content is still mildly eyebrow-raising (much to the delight of my 'tween daughter, who loves this show as much as I do). Performances are Wednesday and Thursday at 8pm, Friday and Saturday at 6 and 9pm, and Sunday at 2 and 5pm; check the website for additional Tuesday shows in July. Club Fugazi, 678 Beach Blanket Babylon Blvd. (Green St. at Powell St.). beachblanketbabylon.com. (✆ **415/421-4222.** Tickets $25–$155.

**Cobb's Comedy Club ★★**   Since 1984, some of the hottest names in comedy—Louis C.K., Sarah Silverman, Dave Chappelle—as well as up-and-coming local comics have been performing at Cobb's. With cabaret seating and higher stools along the back bar, there's not a bad seat in the house. Cover charges vary by act. Shows are held Wednesday, Thursday, and Sunday at 8pm, Friday and Saturday at 8 and 10:15pm. 915 Columbus Ave. (at Lombard St.). cobbscomedyclub.com. (✆ **415/928-4320.** Cover $16–$60. 2-beverage minimum.

**Feinstein's at the Nikko ★**   Union Square's Hotel Nikko is doing its part to keep quality cabaret and jazz alive in the city with this plush, intimate, 140-seat venue. A wide range of entertainers grace the stage (Kathleen Turner, Darren Criss, Lea Salonga, Melissa Manchester, Jane Lynch, Bernadette Peters, Liza Minnelli, and club founder Michael Feinstein, to name a few). Expect a $20 food-and-beverage minimum per person, which is best spent on a cocktail or a nibble from the small plates menu. Hotel Nikko San Francisco, 222 Mason St. (at Ellis St.). feinsteinsatthenikko.com. (✆ **866/663-1063.** Tickets $18 and up.

**Martuni's Piano Bar ★★**   Open 7 nights a week, this friendly watering hole is the best place in the city to catch casual cabaret–style performances from talented singers and piano players. Patrons range in age from 20s to 60s, but everyone enjoys the strong drinks and convivial atmosphere. Come for the performance or join in yourself with piano karaoke on Monday nights, but be warned: Some serious talent takes the mic. 4 Valencia St. (at Market St.). (✆ **415/241-0205.** Cover and hours vary.

**Punch Line Comedy Club ★**   As San Francisco's longest-running comedy club, Punch Line has played host to celebrity comics such as Ellen DeGeneres and Robin Williams, and continues to bring established and emerging stars to its stage, which features a mural of San Francisco as a backdrop. Showcase night is Sunday, when 15 local comics take the mic to try out new material. You must be 18 or over to attend. 444 Battery St. (btw. Washington and Clay sts.), plaza level. punchlinecomedyclub.com. (✆ **415/397-7573** (recorded information). Cover $14–$20, up to $50 for more popular comics. 2-beverage minimum.

# THE CLUB & MUSIC SCENE

The greatest legacy from the 1960s is San Francisco's continued tradition of live entertainment and music, which explains the great variety of clubs and music here. The hippest dance places are south of Market Street (SoMa), in former warehouses; the artsy bohemian scene centers are in the Mission; and the most popular cafe culture is still in North Beach.

Drinks at most bars, clubs, and cafes follow most big-city prices, ranging from about $7 to $14, unless otherwise noted.

## Rock, Jazz, Blues & Dance Clubs

**Amnesia ★★**    Live performances by local musicians and craft brews are the selling points at this often-cramped, dimly lit, totally awesome Mission District hot spot favored by pretty much everyone, especially given its varied lineup; jazz, swing, bluegrass, comedy, and more are on the calendar here. There's a $2 to $10 cover, depending on the night and performers. 853 Valencia St. (btw. 19th & 20th sts.). amnesiathebar.com. No phone.

**Bimbo's 365 Club ★★**    Family-owned-and-operated since 1931, this intimate, retro-stylish North Beach performance venue still manages to be hip, with its wide variety of fresh musical acts (I've seen Beck here), while maintaining its old dance-hall feel. Lavish Art Deco details, cabaret seating, and swagged curtains transport patrons to a bygone era, while the large dance floor in front of the stage plays host to young revelers and those who want to relive their glory days. Grab tickets in advance at the box office, open Monday through Friday 10am to 4pm. 1025 Columbus Ave. (at Chestnut St.). bimbos365club.com. ✆ **415/474-0365.**

**The Boom Boom Room ★★**    To get a sense of what San Francisco was like when Fillmore Street was the most important scene for West Coast blues, head to this little venue that packs a big sound. Opened by the venerated Mississippi bluesman John Lee Hooker, in the last years of his life it wasn't just his business but his hangout. Today, though it still maintains street cred as a blues hall, it plays host to root music as well, ranging from New Orleans funk to trance jazz. The monthly Soul Train Revival draws a big crowd of weekday warriors who want to shake it on a Wednesday. Open Sunday and Tuesday through Thursday from 4pm to 2am and Saturday and Sunday 4pm to 3am. 1601 Fillmore St. (at Geary Blvd.). boomboomblues.com. ✆ **415/673-8000.** Cover varies from free to $15. Tickets $18–$45.

**Bottom of the Hill ★**    One of the few places in town to offer a ton of all-ages shows, this Potrero Hill venue's savvy programming (and excellent sound system) bring in the crowds. You'll hear everything from indie punk to rockabilly to hard funk, and all of it is top-notch. Doors open nightly around 8:30pm, music starts around 9:30pm; bar closes a tad before 2am. Kitchen open until around the time the band plays. 1233 17th St. (at Missouri St.). bottomofthehill.com. ✆ **415/621-4455.** Cover $10–$50.

**The Chapel ★★**    Named 2013's best new live venue by *SF Weekly*, this bar/restaurant/venue is still an incredible place to catch dinner and a show in the Mission District. You don't even need to change locations! Sister restaurant The Vestry, housed in the same complex, serves upscale comfort food in a loud, lively setting—a contrast to its Gothic church theme. After enjoying cocktails and food at the rustic wood tables or on the back twinkle-lit patio, head into the music venue in a separate high-ceilinged room that was once a mortuary chapel. Make your way to the front to see the band in action, or head to the mezzanine for a bird's-eye view and an up-close look at the arched ceiling. There are two bars in the performance space, but it's just as easy to refill drinks in the restaurant area, where the lines are generally shorter. Indie punk rock acts as well as 19-piece orchestras and everything in between have been on the bill. Check the website for bookings. 777 Valencia St. thechapelsf.com. ☏ **415/551-5157.** Cover varies by act $15–$35.

**DNA Lounge ★**   After a wild nightclub scene? DNA Lounge, host of the famous mash-up party Bootie SF, is where it's at. While Bootie is now in several cities around the country, San Francisco is where it originated, and this SoMa hangout continues to be voted Best Dance Club and Best Theme Night year after year. There's not much ambience to speak of, except what's created from the DJ booth, but when last call is ringing in the rest of the city, this party is just getting started. (Just don't expect to buy more drinks after 2am.) 375 Eleventh St. (btw. Folsom and Harrison sts.). dnalounge.com. ☏ **415/626-1409.** Cover $10 before 10pm; $15 after.

**The Fillmore ★**   Though concert halls around the nation are now called the Fillmore, this is the original, and it's a treasure of San Francisco history. In the 1960s it was the heartbeat of San Francisco counterculture, where legendary promoter Bill Graham booked the Grateful Dead, Jefferson Airplane, Janis Joplin, and Led Zeppelin. While it's no longer a crucible of what's next, it's still an excellent place to see a great show (recent acts have included Sheryl Crow, The B-52s, and Blues Traveler) and small enough (1,250 capacity for most shows) that you can stand in the back, near the bar, and still be satisfied. 1805 Geary Blvd. (at Fillmore St.). thefillmore.com. ☏ **415/346-6000.** Tickets $23–$75.

## DRINKING & SMOKING laws

The drinking age is 21 in California, and bartenders can ask for a valid photo ID, no matter how old you look. Some clubs demand ID at the door, so it's a good idea to carry it at all times. Once you get through the door, forget about cigarettes—smoking is banned in all California bars—and that includes marijuana, whose possession and use is permitted (in limited amount) if you have a medical marijuana card. (In 2018, recreational marijuana use is set to become legal in California, although that still won't mean you can smoke it in bars.) The laws are generally enforced, and though San Francisco's police department has not made bar raids a priority, people caught cigarette smoking in bars can be—and occasionally are—ticketed and fined. Music clubs strictly enforce the law and will ask you to leave if you light up. Last call for alcohol usually rings out at around 1:30am, since state laws prohibit the sale of alcohol from 2 to 6am every morning. A very important word of warning: Driving under the influence of alcohol is a serious crime in California, with jail time for the first offense. You are likely to be legally intoxicated (.08% blood alcohol) if you have had as little as one alcoholic drink an hour. When in doubt, take a taxi.

**Great American Music Hall** ★★  Acts and audiences alike revere this saloon-like ballroom in the Tenderloin that recalls San Francisco's scandalous past. Opened by a crooked politician as Blanco's Café, at one time it was an elegant bordello catering to the hedonism of the emerging metro. (If only the frescoed ceilings, baroque details, ornate balconies, and marble columns could talk.) Over the years, acts who've played here have ranged from Duke Ellington and Sarah Vaughan to Arctic Monkeys, the Radiators, and She Wants Revenge. All shows are all ages 6 and up, so you can bring your family, too. Purchase tickets online, over the phone (📞 **888/233-0449**) for a $4 to $5 service fee, or via fax (download form from the website) to 📞 **415/885-5075** for a $2 service fee per ticket. Stop by the box office to buy tickets directly the night of the performance (assuming the show isn't sold out). 859 O'Farrell St. (btw. Polk and Larkin sts.). musichallsf.com. 📞 **415/885-0750.** Ticket prices and show times vary; call or check website.

**The Independent** ★★  The wonderful Nopa restaurant is not the only reason to head to gritty Divisadero Street, which bisects upper and lower Haight. This long-standing small music hall regularly hosts an eclectic collection of seriously fantastic bands (think the Breeders, Deer Tick, or George Clinton & Parliament Funkadelic). Prices range from $15 to $60 (you'll save a few bucks if you buy beforehand rather than pay at the door), and popular shows sell out quickly, so check the website if you're interested in catching a show while in town. 628 Divisadero St. (btw. Grove and Hayes sts.). theindependentsf.com. 📞 **415/771-1421.**

**SFJAZZ** ★★  The only structure in the U.S. built just for jazz, this $64-million building, which debuted in 2013, is a must-visit for music fans. The lineup consists mostly of jazz, though everything from gospel brunches to Ethiopian blues bands has been on the bill. The main hall's circular stadium seating ensures that there are no bad seats in the house. Be sure to head upstairs and check out the ceramic tile murals created for the center by Southern California artist couple Sandow Birk and Elyse Pignolet. If you want to eat first, you can grab a bite at the center's cafe. Last-minute tickets are often available. 201 Franklin St. (at Fell St.). sfjazz.org. 📞 **866/920-5299.** Tickets $25–$200.

# THE BAR SCENE

Finding your kind of bar in San Francisco has a lot to do with which district it's in. The following is a general description of what types of bars you're likely to find throughout the city:

o **Marina/Cow Hollow** bars attract a yuppie post-collegiate crowd who often get very rowdy.

o Young, trendy hipsters who would turn their noses up at the Marina frequent the **Mission District** haunts. Look out for plaid, skinny jeans, and beanies.

o **Haight-Ashbury** caters to eclectic neighborhood cocktailers and beer lovers.

o The **Tenderloin,** though still dangerous at night (take a taxi), is now a hot spot for serious mixologists and has its fair share of dark, cozy dives.

- Tourists mix with conventioneers at **downtown** pubs.
- **North Beach** serves all types, mostly tourists and post-collegiate crowds.
- **Russian Hill**'s Polk Street has become the new Marina/Cow Hollow scene.
- The **Castro** caters to gay locals and tourists.
- **SoMa** offers an eclectic mix from sports bars to DJ lounges.

The following is a list of a few of San Francisco's more interesting bars. Unless otherwise noted, these bars do not have cover charges.

## SoMa, Downtown, Tenderloin & FiDi

**Bar Agricole ★★**   In mixology circles, the name Thad Vogler carries major weight. He's the drink master behind this chic, sleek cocktail bar, which opts for a look of modern sophistication with clean industrial lines and reclaimed wood. The heated outdoor patio is also a rare draw. As for the cocktails, they're created from hard-to-source small-batch liquors; the food—which goes far beyond bar snacks with offerings like burgers, spaghetti, and baked salmon—is darn good too, a mix of Northern European and Californian cuisine. 355 11th St. (near Folsom St.). baragricole.com. ✆ **415/355-9400.** Mon–Thurs 5–11pm, Fri–Sat 5–midnight, Sun 11am–2pm and 6–9pm.

**Bix ★★★**   Though it's mostly a restaurant, longtime San Franciscans like me rank this dining room's mahogany bar high on the "favorite local bar" list, satisfying our cravings for a taste of old-school San Francisco. The atmosphere is grand and retro-posh, with a piano man tickling the keys (or perhaps a jazz trio, depending on the night) and classic drinks expertly made. Its supper club sophistication makes one drink feel like a special occasion; two drinks will have you notably tipsy, especially if you partake in the generous, perfect martinis. 56 Gold St. (in alley off Montgomery St. btw. Pacific and Jackson sts.). bixrestaurant.com. ✆ **415/433-6300.** Open Mon–Thurs 4:30pm–close (around 9 or 10pm), Fri–Sun 5:30–close (around 10 or 11pm).

**Bourbon & Branch ★★**   Meet San Francisco's modern-day speakeasy, right down to the password you have to give at the door to get in. The folks behind Bourbon & Branch are determined to create an authentic Prohibition-era atmosphere, which means only those who have reservations are admitted, and cellphone use is strictly forbidden. Those who get in the unmarked door (look for the address) choose from an extensive and creative cocktail list, sitting in one of the sexiest lounges in town. There's even a speakeasy *within* the speakeasy (even harder to get into!) called Wilson & Wilson, which offers a $39 tasting flight of three cocktails. 501 Jones St. (at O'Farrell St.). bourbonand-branch.com. ✆ **415/346-1735.** Daily 6pm–2am.

**Burrit Room ★★**   If you want a Prohibition-era cocktail without the fussi-ness and exclusivity of Bourbon & Branch, pop into this stylish upstairs bar in Union Square's Mystic Hotel. Some of the city's best bartenders, clad in suspenders and vests, serve up classic and new-age cocktails without a hint of pretention. A film-noir aesthetic provides a sexy, vintage vibe; delicious (and substantial) bar bites add to the lure, and there's live jazz Thursday through

Saturday from 7pm to 10pm. 417 Stockton St. (btw. Sutter and Bush sts.). mystic hotel.com. ℰ **415/400-0555.** Daily 5pm–1am.

**Cold Drinks** ★★ One of the hottest new bars in town, the masculine, swank, "hidden" upstairs bar in China Live (p. 99) is no secret to anyone. But it is everything you want an upscale bar to be—comfy-chic with clustered seating areas, lighting that makes everyone look good, a heavy dose of glamour, and a knowledgeable, attentive staff. Scotch lovers should make a point of visiting; the full bar has a spectacular collection of the libation as well as cocktails featuring the regional whisky. 644 Broadway (btw. Columbus and Stockton). chinalivesf.com. ℰ **415/788-8188.** Sun–Thurs 5–10pm, Fri–Sat 5pm–midnight.

**Downstairs@Black Cat** ★★ Yet another joint harking to days of yore, this Tenderloin supper club's downstairs bar is spacious, mood-lit, and comfy, with couches, tables, and barstools, all with solid views of the small performance area where live jazz or cabaret is played nightly. You can order food here, too, which makes it easy to make a night of it. *Note:* the friendly wait staff will add a cover charge to your bill if you stay late enough for the live music; they'll also warn you first. 400 Eddy St. (at Leavenworth St.). blackcatsf.com. ℰ **415/358-1999.** Tues–Sat 5pm–1am, Sun 5:30pm–midnight.

**Edinburgh Castle** ★ An oldie but a goodie (founded in 1958), this Scottish pub has the finest selection of single-malt scotches in the city as well as a number of unusual British ales on tap. Beloved of ex-pats (and Britophiles), the decor is filled with U.K. bric-a-brac, and the bar menu, naturally, features fish and chips, delivered from a nearby restaurant until 9pm. Enjoy a pool table, a smoking room with an old piano, large wooden booths, and a balcony area that's great for people watching. Friday and Saturday nights, this divey, no-fuss pub hosts DJs and the crowd gets younger and rowdier. 950 Geary St. (btw. Polk and Larkin sts.). thecastlesf.com. ℰ **415/885-4074.** Daily 5pm–2am.

**Jones** ★★ Think of this large, tucked-away, and notably sexy bar and restaurant just off Union Square as a rooftop bar at ground level. The steep prices correspond with the chic-rooftop notion (and the bar is cash-only), but you're sure to find the young and the beautiful convened at the courtyard's wooden tables on temperate nights. Even blustery eves see plenty of action at the long bar and lounge area. Because it's as much a restaurant as it is a place-to-be bar, it's easy to find yourself popping by for a drink, making new friends, and staying for dinner. That said, food is not the main draw here. 620 Jones St. (btw. Colin Pl. and Geary St.). 620-jones.com. ℰ **415/496-6858.** Tues–Thurs 5pm–midnight, Fri–Sat 5pm–2am, Sun 11am–3pm.

**Local Edition** ★★★ Hidden in the bowels of the historic Hearst Building on Market Street, this subterranean bar pays homage to San Francisco's newspaper history, while its craft cocktails nod to the current mixology craze. Inspired by the newspaper business of the '50s and '60s, the decor features vintage presses, typewriters, and archived clippings from San Francisco periodicals; guests sit in rolling desk chairs from the *Mad Men* era. The bar attracts an after-work crowd, and often gets crowded on weekdays around happy hour. Make a reservation for a table or try your luck at the bar. 691 Market St (at 3rd St.). localeditionsf.com. ☏ **415/795-1375.** Mon–Thurs 5pm–2am, Fri 4:30pm–2am, Sat 7pm–2am.

**Smuggler's Cove ★★**   Behind a nondescript Gough Street exterior lies this pirate-y tiki bar which also happens to be one of the world's best bars. The space is transformed into a vintage pirate ship a la *Pirates of the Caribbean,* complete with a roped-off balcony area that resembles a ship's crow's nest. Exotic Caribbean cocktails, Prohibition-era Havana libations, and more than 400 rare rums ensure you'll taste something you've never had before. And with a fair share of flaming cocktails and punch bowls, the cocktails are serious but the atmosphere is not. The space is small, so expect a line on Friday and Saturday nights. 650 Gough St. (at McAllister St.). smugglerscovesf.com. ☏ **415/869-1900.** Daily 5pm–1:15am.

**Terroir Natural Wine Merchant ★★**   With its rustic wooden beams and a library loft—not to mention a selection of wines to rival any Napa or Sonoma store—this is the oenophile's Shangri-La. Sit at the bar and get an education about the art, science, and soul of the winemaking process—owners Luke, Billy, and Dagan will be happy to tell you everything you ever wanted to know about wine. Not in the mood for a lesson and prefer to simply relax? Head upstairs to the lounge and flip through a book, or play a game (board games are available), while you savor the nectar of the gods. Add in cheese and charcuterie and you can probably skip dinner. 1116 Folsom St. (btw. 7th and 8th sts.). terroirsf.com. ☏ **415/558-9946.** Mon–Thurs 5pm–midnight, Fri 4pm–2am, Sat 5pm–2am, Sun 4–9pm.

# Fisherman's Wharf, Russian Hill, Nob Hill & North Beach

**15 Romolo ★★**   Opened in the late '90s by Jon Gasparini and Greg Lindgren, the duo widely known for serving up expertly made cocktails in compelling environments, this hidden North Beach watering and dining hole has become a San Francisco classic. Mood-lit with a jovial, relaxed vibe, it's one of my favorite places to come when I'm in the 'hood and have a craving for cocktails without pomp. 15 Romolo Place (btw. Broadway and Fresno Pl.). 15romolo. com. ☏ **415/398-1359.** Open Mon–Fri 5pm–2am; Sat–Sun 3pm–2am.

**Buena Vista Café ★**   It's become a modern tradition to visit Buena Vista Cafe to order a $10.50 Irish Coffee, said to have been conceived here in 1952 by a local travel writer. This punch-packing quaff lures hordes of tourists before they wobble toward the cable car turnaround across the street. You may not want to hear how the bartender gets the cream to float—it's aged for 2 days before use. Some 2,000 are served each day in high season, which means you will probably have to wait for a table on a weekend afternoon (better, probably, to come at night; it's open until 2am). These beverages are indeed delicious, and the publike setting is classic without being snooty. 2765 Hyde St.

(at Beach St.). thebuenavista.com. ℭ **415/474-5044.** Mon–Fri 9am–2am, Sat–Sun 8am–2am.

**The Saloon** ★ A true dive, this is supposedly the oldest bar in the city and it certainly looks (and smells) like it. Floors are but worn planks, staff are grizzled and hairy, and the story goes that this place managed to survive the conflagration of 1906 by offering the firefighters free booze. There's live music every night—mostly blues and jazz. Don't come expecting a cruisey scene; come for down-and-dirty music and cheap whiskey. 1232 Grant Ave. (at Columbus Ave.). ℭ **415/989-7666.** Daily noon–2am. Music cover $5–$15 Fri–Sat.

**The Tonga Room & Hurricane Bar** ★★ This sublime, vast, one-of-a-kind bar and restaurant is the pinnacle of classic San Francisco kitsch. In this dim Polynesian-themed fantasia, decorated with rocks and 12-foot tikis, every half-hour lightning strikes, thunder rolls in, and rain falls above the pond in the middle of it all (once the hotel's indoor pool). If you're lucky, you'll be here late enough to see the band playing on a raft right in the middle of the thing. Yes, it's gimmicky, and yes, you'll pay a lot for a cocktail here, but it's pure fun anyway. During happy hour (Wed–Fri 5–7pm), there's a list of strong tropical drinks sold at a discount, and for just $10 you get the run of a heat-lamp-lit buffet of egg rolls and other grub, served beneath the rigging of an imaginary ship's deck. There's a full menu, too, but people tend to take advantage of that later in the night. In the Fairmont Hotel, 950 Mason St. (at California St.). tongaroom. com. ℭ **415/772-5278.** Wed–Thurs and Sun 5–11:30pm, Fri–Sat 5pm–12:30am.

**Vesuvio** ★★★ You haven't fully experienced San Francisco's literary history without a trip to this famous, trinket-stuffed watering hole. It was opened in 1948, just in time to catch all the dissolute Beat writers as they staggered in and out of City Lights, located directly across Jack Kerouac Alley from its front door. In fact, this is where Kerouac and other Beat writers nursed their alcoholism and creative endeavors. Snag a table in the cozy, secluded balcony area overlooking the bar, providing a prime people-watching view. 255 Columbus Ave. (at Broadway). vesuvio.com. ℭ **415/362-3370.** Daily 6am–2am.

## The Marina, Cow Hollow

**Nectar Wine Lounge** ★ Few places in the city, or in North America for that matter, have as copious a menu when it comes to wine: 50 are available by the glass (from all around the globe) and a good 800 by the bottle. Just as impressive is the handsome crowd this hip, industrial-chic watering hole draws. It's a nice place to linger. 3330 Steiner St. (at Chestnut St.). nectarwinelounge. com. ℭ **415/345-1377.** Mon–Wed 5–10:30pm, Thurs–Sat 5pm–midnight, Sun 5–10pm.

**Perry's** ★ Made famous by Armistead Maupin's *Tales of the City,* this nightspot is not the crazy pick-up scene it was in the book. Still, locals and visitors alike enjoy chilling at the dark mahogany bar. An attached dining room offers up all sorts of simple food (think burgers or grilled fish) should you be feeling peckish. 1944 Union St. (at Laguna St.). perryssf.com. ℭ **415/922-9022.** Mon–Wed 7:30am–10pm, Thurs–Sat 7:30am–11pm, Sun 8:30am–10pm.

# cocktails WITH A VIEW

**Harry Denton's Starlight Room ★★★** There are few better places to raise a stylish drink with an unspoiled panorama of one of the world's greatest cities. Most customers stay for dinner and dancing, but it's possible to simply come and enjoy a drink at the bar (though on nights when there's live music, you'll pay a cover charge). *Tip:* Come dressed to impress (no casual jeans, open-toed shoes for men, or sneakers), or you'll be turned away at the door. Atop the Sir Francis Drake Hotel, 450 Powell St., btw. Post and Sutter sts., 21st floor. harrydenton.com. ✆ **415/395-8595.** Tues–Thurs 6pm–midnight, Fri–Sat 5pm–2am, Sun 11am–3:30pm. Cover $10.

**Top of the Mark ★★★** A 19th-floor bar doesn't sound like much, but considering it's in a building atop Nob Hill—and one of the most famous bars in the country—both the view and the mood are high. Floor-to-ceiling windows take in the kind of panorama that makes people want to move to this city: Golden Gate Bridge, Coit Tower, Alcatraz, and beyond, all in a smart, swanky setting. The operators regularly close the space for private parties, so call ahead to make sure it's open. From Wednesday to Saturday, musical acts are booked—mostly jazz or other nice background styles—and cover charges are surprisingly cheap. Dinner is pricey, so we recommend just coming by for the tipple. In the Mark Hopkins InterContinental, 1 Nob Hill Place (btw. California and Mason sts.). topofthemark.com. ✆ **415/616-6199.** Sun 10am–2pm (brunch) and 5–11:30pm, Mon–Thurs 4:30–11:30pm, Fri–Sat 4pm–12:30am. Cover on entertainment nights $5–$15.

**Press Club ★** Come here if you can't get to the wine country this trip but still want a wine-tasting experience. Calling itself an "urban wine-tasting bar," this huge space features eight separate bars which are often manned by reps from regional Northern California wineries (the list of wineries rotates). These sellers are always happy to ship home cases for you, should you enjoy your glass. A mellow soundtrack, elbow room, and gourmet small bites (including Cowgirl Creamery cheese plates) make the Press Club quite popular among the 35-plus crowd. 20 Yerba Buena Lane (near Market St.). pressclubsf.com. ✆ **415/744-5000.** Mon–Tues 4–10pm, Wed–Thurs 4–11pm, Fri 2pm–midnight, Sat 4pm–midnight, Sun 4–8pm.

**Tipsy Pig ★** This cozy (and noisy) gastropub is a great starting point for a Chestnut Street bar crawl. The heated back garden patio, leather booths in the front window, and famous Strawberry Fields cocktails lure a crowd of all ages. For a neighborhood with the reputation of being a bit frat-tastic, this bar is diverse enough to resist the stereotype (most of the time), while still embracing the lively, convivial atmosphere the Marina is known for. The food is good too, if you need something to soak up the heavy pours—*San Francisco Chronicle* food critic Michael Bauer included it in his list of top 100 restaurants in the Bay Area. Plus it has a dedicated kid's menu for family-friendly imbibing. 2231 Chestnut St. (btw. Pierce & Scott sts.). thetipsypigsf.com. ✆ **415/292-2300.** Mon–Thurs 5pm–2am, Fri–Sun 11am–2am.

# The Mission

**El Rio** ★   Just a few blocks south of the most hopping stretch of Mission-area bars, you'll come to this gem that bills itself as a neighborhood bar with "heck of a lot to offer." And it delivers: There's a garden patio, space for regular live shows, juke box, pool table, shuffle board, and some of the best happy hour deals in the city—$1 beers for 7 hours every day. Come here to mingle with friendly locals who care more about neighborhood community than the latest trendy scene. Cash only. 3158 Mission St. (at Precita Ave.). elriosf.com. ℰ **415/282-3325.** Daily 1pm–2am.

**Elbo Room** ★   Not sure whether you want a dive, a lounge, or a dance floor? Veteran nightlife hub Elbo Room offers all three in one playful two-story saloon. Cozy up with no-fuss, strong well cocktails or a PBR-and-shot deal in one of the big booths, try your luck at a classic arcade game in the back, or head upstairs to dance to a live show or DJ set in an intimate setting (there's usually a cover for live shows). The vibe is pure fun, right down to the photo booth. It can get crowded and the bartenders are all business, so know your poison when you catch their attention. 647 Valencia St. (at Sycamore St.). elbo.com. ℰ **415/552-7788.** Open daily 5pm–2am.

**Southern Pacific Brewing Company** ★★   In a city of narrow, hole-in-the-wall bars, it's rare for beer to get such a grand setting. Two floors, a front patio, and 10,000 square feet doesn't necessarily mean it won't be crowded, but your chances of snagging a table near one of the twinkle-light-lit trees inside the warehouse space are pretty good. Sip on unique, small-batch brews made in-house or a curated selection of interesting guest beers. Beer-inspired pub fare almost steals the show—the Brussels sprouts and sage fries are to-die-for! 620 Treat Ave. (btw. 18th and 19th sts.). southernpacificbrewing.com. ℰ **415/341-0152.** Sun–Wed 11am–midnight, Thurs–Sat 11am–2am.

**Trick Dog** ★★   Ask locals to name their favorite bars, and this small, well-known neighborhood haunt is sure to be on several lists. Its award-winning status is due to the thoughtfulness that goes into everything, from the decor (warm, unpretentious industrial-chic) to the bar menu (designed to look and read like a children's book) to the excellent craft cocktails (poured by a friendly staff). It can be crowded here, but you may want to be on your feet anyway, thanks to the choice music selections—the best of the '70s and '80s. There's also a limited snack-y menu to help soak up the alcohol and perhaps make way for a second round. 3010 20th St. (btw. Alabama and Florida sts.). trickdogbar.com. ℰ **415/471-2999.** Daily 3pm–2am.

**Zeitgeist** ★★   It used to be a rough biker bar, but these days you'll likely see more fixed-gear bicycles than Harleys locked up in front. Zeitgeist serves more than 20 types of German beer, most of them dead cheap, making the dive a favorite among the Mission's hipster crowd. But it's the relaxed, gritty environment, somehow untouched by gentrification, that's the real attraction,

NIGHTLIFE | The Bar Scene

especially on sunny days when the mellow beer-garden vibe is in full force in the spacious and very urban backyard. Zeitgeist's Bloody Mary is the best in the city. Cash only. 199 Valencia St. (at Duboce Ave.). ✆ **415/255-7505.** Daily 9am–2am.

## Haight-Ashbury

**Alembic** ★★★   The highly curated drink menu at this Haight Street bar is divided into two parts: One pays homage to the classic cocktail canon, the other offers inventive, new-school concoctions you can't get anywhere else. Gin lovers who need a pick-me-up will love the Nine Volt—gin mixed with green tea and mint makes for a refreshing buzz, while the white Szechuan pepper leaves a slightly tingly mouth-feel. Another creative favorite is Vasco de Gama, which blends Islay Scotch and Buffalo Trace bourbon with an apple syrup spiked with garam masala spices. The heavily tattooed bartenders do well by such classics as Manhattans and Old Fashioneds, too. The surprisingly good bar food has made a name for itself, prompting the owners to expand the kitchen and seating space next door. The menu is in flux and relies on seasonality, but the house-cured salmon and bone marrow are mainstay musts! 1725 Haight (at Cole St.). alembicbar.com. ✆ **415/660-0822.** Mon–Tues 4pm–midnight, Wed–Fri 4pm–2am, Sat 2pm–2am, Sun 2pm–midnight.

**Madrone Art Bar** ★★   San Francisco's bar scene can be a bit quiet during the work week, but that's not the case at this favorite in the Lower Haight area, where a rotating crop of DJs and bands draw crowds every night of the week. Monday nights are the new Saturday with cult-favorite theme night, Motown Monday. People line up around the block to dance to retro mash-ups among paintings from local artists. Come early and you could even enjoy a pre-dancing neck-and-shoulder massage. Cash only. 500 Divisadero St. (at Fell St.). madroneartbar.com. ✆ **415/241-0202.** Mon–Sat 4pm–2am, Sun 3pm–1:30am.

### Hidden Gem Off the Beaten Path

Dog Patch—the gritty but increasingly popular artistic and industrial hub south of AT&T Park—is San Francisco's most exciting up-and-coming neighborhood, and **Third Rail** ★★, at 628 20th St. (btw. 3rd St. and Illinois St.; thirdrail barsf.com; ✆ **415/252-7966**), is the ultimate example why. Its railroad theme, simple industrial design, and relaxed atmosphere pay homage to the area's history, while unusual craft cocktails embrace the city's artisanal cocktail trend. Instead of nuts, nosh on home-made jerky by the ounce, while sipping creative cocktails like the Mount Tam, named for the local gin used in the refreshing concoction—it smells and tastes like the moist pine needles (in a good way!) from the nearby mountain. Other libations, like the Fireside Sour and Bone Machine, experiment with texture and lesser-used liquors. Tell the bartenders what kind of flavors you like, and they'll skillfully deliver without a hint of pretention. It's open Sunday through Wednesday, 3pm to midnight; Thursday to Saturday 3pm to 2am.

# GAY & LESBIAN BARS & CLUBS

For listings of events and happenings around town, check *San Francisco Weekly* and the gay-oriented *Bay Area Reporter,* both free papers that are distributed weekly on Wednesday or Thursday—you can find them stacked at the corners of 18th and Castro streets and Ninth and Harrison streets, as well as in bars, bookshops, and other stores around town. See p. 283 in chapter 12 for further details on gay-themed guides. Also check out the rather homely but very informative site "Queer Things to Do in the San Francisco Bay Area" at sfqueer.com.

**440 Castro** ★★  At this warm and fuzzy bear bar for the Levis-and-leather crowd, most cruise between the video bar downstairs to the dark intimate bar up a few stairs in the back. Always popular, Monday is Underwear Night; Tuesday features $2 beers all day and night. No matter the day, drinks are always strong and cheap. Regular contests like the Battle of the Bulge are a great way to meet new friends. 440 Castro St. (btw. 17th and 18th sts.). the440.com. ℂ **415/621-8732.** Open daily until 2am.

**Diva's Nightclub and Bar** ★  Located in the Tenderloin, all is not as it appears at this transgender-friendly dance and drag bar. Want to go back to school? Naughty schoolgirls appear each Wednesday at 10pm. The Diva Darlings take center stage each Thursday at 10pm. With dance floors, regular shows, and numerous bars, this three-story club filled with beautiful girlz can best be described as a party palace. *Note:* There's a $10 cover Wednesday through Sunday after 10pm. 1081 Post St. (btw. Polk and Larkin Sts.). divassf.com. ℂ **415/928-6006.** Open 6am–2am.

---

### Have a Cigar

Smoking is generally prohibited in San Francisco bars and restaurants, but if you are looking for a fine stogie with a tumbler of rare scotch—and a legal smoking room in which to enjoy your treasures—step inside the **Occidental Cigar Club** (471 Pine St., at Kearney St.; occidentalcigarclub.com; ℂ **415/834-0485**). Though the name implies it is a private club, Occidental is open to the public. A varied selection of premium cigars make good souvenirs to remember your time in the Sin City of the West. It's open daily from noon to 1am.

---

**The Lookout** ★  With two walls of glass and a massive deck looking down on the heart of the Castro, this karaoke bar is a good place to dance and belt out your best rendition of "I Will Survive." Nightly DJs and a weekly drag show add to the excitement. If you get hungry, you don't have to lose your spot in line for the karaoke machine; the Lookout serves surprisingly good food. 3600 16th St. (at Market St.). lookoutsf.com. ℂ **415/431-0306.** Mon–Fri 3:30pm–2am, Sat–Sun 12:30pm–2am. Kitchen until 10pm (11pm Sat), kitchen closed Tues.

**Twin Peaks Tavern** ★★  Known locally as the gay "Cheers," Twin Peaks was the first gay bar in the country to unblock the floor-to-ceiling windows and let the world see just what was going on inside. It sits at the corner of Market and Castro, the true heart of the gay community. In a culture that often worships youth and beauty, Twin Peaks is an oldie but goodie—and tends to attract an older crowd. The 1880s building survived the earthquake and recently gained historic landmark status. 401 Castro St. (at Market St.). twinpeaks tavern.com. ✆ **415/864-9470.** Hours vary, so call.

# PROFESSIONAL SPORTS TEAMS

The Bay Area's sports scene isn't just about the Giants; it includes several major professional franchises. Check the local newspapers' sports sections and team websites for daily listings of local events. Along with each teams' website, **www.tickets.com** and **www.stubhub.com** are good places to hunt for tickets.

## Major League Baseball

San Francisco's National League team, the **Giants** (sfgiants.com) play at beautiful AT&T Park (see box below) in the southeast corner of SoMa; buses 10, 30, 45, or 47 run there, as well as the N streetcar. The American League's **Oakland Athletics** (athletics.mlb.com) play across the bay in Oakland at the Coliseum, reached via the Hegenberger Road exit from I-880. The stadium holds over 50,000 spectators and is accessible through BART's Coliseum station.

## Pro Basketball

For now, the **Golden State Warriors** (nba.com/warriors) play at the ORA-CLE Arena, a 19,200-seat facility at 7000 Coliseum Way in Oakland. In 2019

---

### AT&T Park ★★

If you're a baseball fan, you'll definitely want to schedule a visit to magnificent **AT&T Park**—home of the San Francisco Giants—which has been hailed by the media as one of the finest ballparks in America. From April through October, an often sellout crowd of 40,800 fans packs the $319-million ballpark; which has prime views of San Francisco Bay. Regular tickets can be expensive and hard to come by; bleacher seats and standing-room tickets are cheaper options. If you can't get bleacher seats, you can always join the "knothole gang" at the Portwalk (located behind right field) to catch a free glimpse of the game through cutout portholes into the ballpark. In the spirit of sharing, Portwalk peekers are encouraged to take in only an inning or two before giving way to fellow fans.

One guaranteed way to get into the ballpark is to take a **guided tour,** going behind the scenes to see the press box, the dugout, the visitor's clubhouse, a luxury suite, and more. All tours run daily (except most game days) at 10:30am and 12:30pm. Ticket prices are $22 adults, $17 seniors 55+, $12 for kids ages 3 to 12, and free for active military (with ID). To buy tickets online, log on to sfgiants.com, click on "AT&T Park" on the top banner, and then select "AT&T Park Tours."

they plan to move to the Chase Center, currently under construction, which is located along the waterfront in the Mission Bay neighborhood close to AT&T Park. The season runs November through April, and most games start at 7:30pm.

## Pro Football

The **San Francisco 49ers** (sf49ers.com) moved to their new Levis Stadium in Santa Clara in 2014, which is a bit of a nightmare to get to, not to mention park at (and at ridiculous prices to boot). Still, the August through December football season brings the fans south. Tickets are generally sold out, but are available at higher prices through ticket agents beforehand. For now, the 49ers' arch enemies, the **Oakland Raiders** (raiders.com), play at the Oakland-Alameda Coliseum, off the I-880 freeway (Nimitz Freeway). But they're slated to move to a brand new home and stadium in Vegas by 2020.

# DAY TRIPS FROM SAN FRANCISCO

As remarkable as San Francisco is, adventure awaits less than 30 minutes away in every direction. You can escape the city to the east, across the Bay Bridge, to explore Oakland and Berkeley, where you can hike, shop, tour a famed college campus, browse top-notch museums, and search for volcanic rock and spectacular city views. To the north, just across the iconic Golden Gate Bridge, you can wander the ever-popular redwood forest and peer up the trunk of a 600-year-old giant tree, or explore the scenic waterfronts of tourist-heavy but charming Sausalito and Tiburon. If the fog's got you shivering, you'll be pleased to find that most of these locations can be significantly warmer than San Francisco. Whether you use public transportation, rent a car for the day, or take a guided tour, here are some great ways to spend a day away from the city.

## BERKELEY

13 miles NE of San Francisco

Despite the gentrification changing the entire Bay Area, the city of Berkeley maintains its well-known character as a vibrant, multicultural salad of people with a decidedly liberal bent. UC Berkeley, or "Cal" as it's often called by locals and alums, continues to inspire and entice applicants (more than 82,000 students applied in 2016, of which a lucky 14,433 were admitted). Despite the media portrayal, the university is more academic than psychedelic, with 29 Nobel Prize winners over the years (seven are currently active on staff). But there's definitely still idealism in the air, and the campus remains the occasional site of protests, both peaceful and less so, especially in the current political climate.

There's loads to do beyond the campus, too; drop into the Berkeley Art Museum and Pacific Film Archive to see a film or do some impromptu drawing in the Art Lab; feed a goat at Tilden Park's Little Farm; or queue up for some world-famous Cheese Board pizza. Whatever you do, you'll see that due to the big money and wealthy young professionals pouring into San Francisco these days, this part of the Bay Area is far more diverse in population and personality than ever.

## Getting There

You'll be surprised how easy it is to get to the east bay from San Francisco. Downtown Berkeley Station—the second Berkeley **Bay Area Rapid Transit (BART)** station if you're coming from the city—is 2 blocks from the university. The fare from San Francisco is about $4 one-way. Call ℂ **511** or visit bart.gov for detailed trip information and fares.

If you are coming **by car** from San Francisco, take the Bay Bridge. Follow I-80 east to the University Avenue exit, and follow University Avenue until you hit the campus. Parking is tight near the university, but there are plenty of parking lots and garages in the area and the prices are lower than what you'll find in San Francisco (not that that's hard to accomplish; city parking rates are insane). In other areas of Berkeley, there is more bountiful street parking; just keep an eye out for signs posting parking time limits in both commercial and residential areas, as parking violations come with steep fees.

## What to See & Do

Prospective students, history buffs, or anyone interested in learning about the town's most profound cultural influence should take advantage of the free campus tours (reservations required), which depart daily at 10am from the **Koret Visitor Center** at 2227 Piedmont Ave. in historic California Memorial Stadium (berkeley.edu/visitors; ℂ **510/642-5215**). Of course, the student-led tours are also used by prospective scholars, so in springtime your group may swell to 200 and your guide may dwell on the school's rivalry with Stanford, but everyone is welcome. You'll get heaps of fascinating historical information about the educational institution that fomented some of the strongest protests of the 1960s and '70s; you may also hear about the many important discoveries Cal is responsible for—including vitamins B, E, and K; plutonium; uranium 238; and the stumpy London plane tree, a hybrid that you'll only see here and in San Francisco.

A noteworthy building you'll only have access to on the tour is **Le Conte Hall,** the home of the Physics Department and the site of the first atom collider. (Keep your eyes peeled for parking signs that read, in total seriousness, RESERVED FOR NL—meaning Nobel Laureate; you know the parking situation is grim if you need a Nobel Prize to get a space.) The **Doe Library** doesn't allow public access to the 10 million books in its stacks, but its lobby area, lined with glass cases filled with priceless manuscripts, is open to all. In a reading room upstairs, you'll also find Emanuel Leutze's 1854 painting *Washington Rallying the Troops at Monmouth,* which was intended to be a companion piece to his *Washington Crossing the Delaware* (now at New York's Metropolitan Museum of Art). In all, the Cal campus has a total of 32 libraries covering more than 12 acres, making it one of the largest library complexes in the world.

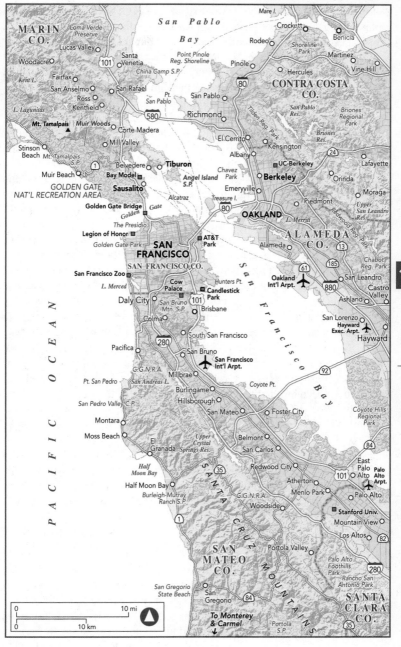

Berkeley has two noteworthy museums. The first is the **Berkeley Art Museum & Pacific Film Archive** ★, 2155 Center St. (bampfa.org; ✆ **510/642-0808**), which reopened in its current space in 2016. The stunning museum grounds integrate a 48,000-square-foot Art Deco building built in 1939 with a new 35,000 square-foot-structure designed by NYC architecture firm Diller Scofidio + Renfro. The space features multiple galleries, two film theaters, a venue for live performances, a reading room, an art lab, a cafe, and more. If you're a film buff, definitely check out the film series calendar, which offers roughly 450 screenings a year, including films from every single cinema-producing country in the world, and silent films accompanied by live music. Film tickets are available online and at the museum, and they include same-day gallery admission, so if you plan ahead of time, you can take in the museum and a movie, all for about what you'd pay at a regular theater. The museum is open Wednesday, Thursday, and Sunday from 11am to 7pm, and Friday and Saturday from 11am to 9pm. Admission is $12 for adults; $10 for seniors, non–UCB students, and visitors with disabilities; and free for ages 18 and under.

If you're traveling with kids, head to the hands-on, kid-friendly **Lawrence Hall of Science** ★ (east of campus at 1 Centennial Dr., lawrencehallofscience.org; ✆ **510/642-5132**). Filled with things to do, this interactive museum will keep everyone busy for at least a couple of hours, especially if the weather's nice and you step outside for Forces That Shape the Bay, an outdoor park that lets you play with soil erosion, direct water flow from simulated Sierra Nevada mountains, and peep through a telescope set up over the sweeping views. It's open daily from 10am to 5pm; admission is $12 for adults, $10 for seniors, students, and children, and free for kids 2 and under.

Cal also boasts the **Hearst Greek Theater,** an 8,500-seat outdoor amphitheater that's been host to the greatest talent and celebrities of the last century, from Elvis to the Grateful Dead to the Dalai Lama to Tom Petty and the Heartbreakers. Chances are there's a fantastic show during your visit, where you'll take in the amazing acoustics while enjoying views of the entire bay and San Francisco skyline. There's not a bad seat in the house, but you may want to pay for reserved seating unless you plan to get there early to claim a spot on the lawn; dedicated fans usually start to line up fairly early. Check the website for the calendar or call the box office (thegreekberkeley.com; ✆ **510/548-3010**) for more information.

## PARKS

Golden Gate Park might have the name recognition, but Berkeley has some of the most extensive, beautiful parks in Northern California, and you can often count on temperatures being about 10 degrees warmer than San Francisco. If you enjoy hiking, swimming, sniffing roses, or just getting a breath of California air, head for **Tilden Park** ★, where you'll find plenty of flora and fauna, hiking trails, an old steam train and merry-go-round, the Little Farm (a farm and nature area for kids), and a chilly tree-encircled lake. If you head to the Little Farm to see the animals, bring some lettuce or celery for the always-hungry goats and sheep—if you're visiting in the spring, you might get a chance to see some baby goats or piglets. The East Bay's public transit system, **AC Transit** (actransit.org; Ⓒ **511**), runs the air-conditioned no. 67 bus line around the edge of the park on weekdays and all the way to the Tilden Visitors Center on Saturdays and Sundays. Call Ⓒ **888/327-2757** or see ebparks.org for more information.

## Shopping

For boutique shopping, head to **College Avenue,** from Russell Street to the Oakland border at Ashby and beyond into Oakland's Rockridge neighborhood. Eclectic boutiques, antiques shops, bookstores, and restaurants line this street, making it a favorite among students and locals. The other, more upscale option is **Fourth Street,** in west Berkeley, 2 blocks north of the University Avenue exit off of I-80. This shopping strip is the perfect place to go on a sunny morning. Grab a cup of java and outstanding pancakes and scones at **Bette's Ocean View Diner,** 1807 Fourth St. (Ⓒ **510/644-3230**). Read the paper at a patio table, and then hit the **Crate & Barrel Outlet,** 1785 Fourth St., between Hearst and Virginia streets (Ⓒ **510/528-5500**), where home furnishings are priced at 30% to 70% off retail. It's open daily from 10am to 7pm. This area also boasts small, wonderful stores crammed with imported and locally made housewares. And don't miss out on a visit to **Castle in the Air** at 1805 Fourth St. (castleintheair.biz; Ⓒ **510/204-9801**), a whimsical shop specializing in all sorts of surprising little trinkets and pieces to add to fairy houses, wreaths, dioramas, and anything else you can dream up.

## Where to Eat

The Bay Area foodie scene these days is more about the East Bay, both Berkeley and neighboring Oakland (see p. 231), than San Francisco itself. Prices are slightly better here, along with more parking and generally larger spaces, which means less wait time for a table; a focus on ethnic food adds diversity to your dining options.

If you want to dine student-style, eat on campus Monday through Friday. Buy something at a sidewalk stand or in the building directly behind the Student Union. Nearby Telegraph Avenue has an array of small ethnic restaurants, cafes, and sandwich shops. Follow the students: If the place is crowded, it's good, super cheap, or both.

You can't get more "Bay Area," however, than opting for a farm-to-table dining experience. Go for the restaurant that shaped an entire generation of chefs with Alice Waters's **Chez Panisse** ★★★ at 1517 Shattuck Ave. (chezpanisse.com; Ⓒ **510/548-5525** for restaurant and Ⓒ **510/548-5049** for cafe); try to reserve a few weeks ahead. Locals go wild for the **Cheese Board Pizza** ★, just two doors down from the mouthwatering baked goods and cheeses at the **Cheese Board Collective** ★ (1504 Shattuck Ave.; cheeseboardcollective.coop; Ⓒ **510/549-3183**). If you happen to be in Berkeley on a Sunday, try something different and delicious and head to **Wat Mongkolratanaram** and its **Thai Community Brunch** (yelp.com/biz/wat-mongkolratanaram-berkeley). Bring

**10**

cash to buy tokens for authentic Thai noodles, soups, curries, and dumplings. This temple fundraiser gets crowded, so it's a good idea to show up a few minutes before it opens (open 10am–1pm).

# OAKLAND

12 miles E of San Francisco

While the fog belt drifts over the Golden Gate and across the bay to parts of Berkeley, the weather in Oakland is more likely to be warm and sunny. The clime, combined with (slightly) lower housing prices and an impressive and rapidly growing food scene, is evolving Oakland from a city known for being one of the nation's most dangerous into a hip, lively, and diverse destination for both visitors and those looking to put down some roots.

Nowadays, proud locals claim that Oakland has more resident artists per capita than any other U.S. city, and it has become a mecca for young, socially conscious individuals fleeing San Francisco's increasingly sterile and exclusive tech scene.

What many don't know is that the city we call Oakland was once inhabited by the Ohlone people before the Spanish colonizers took over the land. (**The Oakland Museum,** p. 229, provides a fascinating and immersive history of the development of this city.) Initially little more than a cluster of ranches and farms, Oakland exploded in size and stature practically overnight, when the last mile of transcontinental railroad track was laid down. Major shipping ports soon followed and, to this day, Oakland remains one of the busiest industrial ports on the West Coast. The price for economic success, however, has been Oakland's lowbrow reputation as a predominantly working-class city; it is forever in the shadow of chic San Francisco. Still, now that the City by the Bay is so crowded, "Oaktown" is in the midst of a renaissance.

Walk the labyrinths at Sibley Volcanic Preserve, take a behind-the-scenes tour and gorge on ice cream at the famous Fenton's Creamery (where I served up mammoth sundaes while attending Cal), stroll along the scenic Jack London Square waterfront, see a show at the phenomenal Fox or Paramount Theatres, explore the fantastic Oakland Museum—they're all great reasons to hop the bay and spend a fog-free day exploring one of California's largest and most ethnically diverse cities. By the end of your visit, you'll be feeling positively "Oaklandish"!

## Getting There

**BART** (bart.gov; ✆ **511**) connects San Francisco and Oakland through one of the longest underwater transit tunnels in the world. Fares are just under $4 one-way, depending on your station of origin; children ages 4 and under ride free. BART trains operate Monday through Friday 4am to midnight, Saturday from 6am to midnight, and Sunday from 8am to midnight, although timing varies depending on when the last train arrives at a station. Exit at the 12th Street station for downtown Oakland.

**By car** from San Francisco, take I-80 across the San Francisco–Oakland Bay Bridge and follow signs to downtown Oakland or merge right to remain on 580 E for other areas of Oakland. It's a large city, so it's a good idea to bring along a map or a map app if you have a smartphone.

For a calendar of events in Oakland, contact the **Oakland Convention and Visitors Bureau** at 463 11th St. (oaklandcvb.com; ✆ **510/839-9000**). The city sponsors eight free guided tours (Wed and Sat at 10am), including a fascinating African-American Heritage tour. Call ✆ **510/238-3234** or visit www2. oaklandnet.com and click on the "Visitors" tab and then "Walking Tours" at the bottom left. Reservations are recommended, but drop-ins usually work fine unless you've got a large group.

Downtown Oakland lies between Grand Avenue on the north, I-980 on the west, Inner Harbor on the south, and Lake Merritt on the east. Between these landmarks are three BART stations (12th St., 19th St., and Lake Merritt), which are handy for visiting City Hall, the Oakland Museum, Jack London Square, and Old Oakland, where you'll find a farmers' market at 9th Street and Broadway every Friday, 8am to 2pm.

## What to See & Do

The **Oakland Museum of California (OMCA),** 1000 Oak St. (museumca. org; ✆ **510/318-8400**), a favorite of adults and children alike, completed a 4-year gallery-by-gallery renovation in 2013. The stunning 25,000-square-foot Gallery of California Natural Sciences boasts more than 100,000 research specimens and artifacts, showcasing much more than just Oakland—it explores the entire state's biodiversity, from Yosemite to Cordell Bank National Marine Sanctuary to Coachella Valley. I particularly like the Gallery of History, which focuses on "Coming to California," with interesting displays of Native American baskets, the Spanish influence, and, of course, the Gold Rush. There are also some very entertaining "wheels of fortune" you can spin to see what your fate might have been during the Gold Rush and other historic times featured in this gallery. Admission is $16 for adults, $11 seniors and students, $6.95 ages 9 to 17, free for ages 8 and under. The museum is open Wednesday through Sunday, opening at 11am and closing at 5pm Wednesday to Thursday, 10pm Friday, and 6pm Saturday and Sunday.

Also worth visiting is Oakland's **Paramount Theatre** ★, 2025 Broadway (paramounttheatre.com; ✆ **510/893-2300**), an outstanding National Historic Landmark and example of Art Deco architecture and decor. Built in 1931 and authentically restored in 1973, its intricately carved walls, plush carpet, beveled mirrors, and gilded details will transport you to Hollywood's Golden Era. As the city's main performing-arts center, it plays host to the Oakland Ballet and Symphony, as well as big-name performers like Chris Rock and Tori Amos. But it is just as popular for its old movie nights, where guests can see a classic film, complete with a pre-show organ serenade, a cartoon, and a chance to win prizes with "Dec-o-Win," all for a mere $5. Guided tours of the 3,000-seat theater are given the first and third Saturday of each month, excluding holidays. No reservations are necessary; just show up at 10am at the box office entrance on 21st Street at Broadway. The tour lasts 2 hours, cameras are allowed, and admission is $5. Children must be at least 10 years old.

If you take pleasure in strolling sailboat-filled wharves or are a die-hard fan of Jack London, you'll likely enjoy a visit to **Jack London Square** ★ (jack londonsquare.com; ✆ **510/645-9292**), the waterfront area where the famous author spent most of his youth. The square fronts the harbor and features restaurants, entertainment, shops, and a farmers' market. In the center of the square is a small model of the Yukon cabin in which Jack London lived while prospecting in the Klondike during the Gold Rush of 1897. In the middle of Jack London Square (and built in 1883!) is a more authentic memorial, **Heinold's First and Last Chance Saloon** (heinoldsfirstandlastchance.com; ✆ **510/839-6761**), a funky, friendly little bar and historic landmark. Here a clock remains frozen at the exact time the 1906 earthquake shook this little dive, forever making the bar slant at 10 degrees. Watch your step, too, because the 'quake warped the floors, adding even more eccentricity to this topsy-turvy establishment. This is where London did some of his writing and most of his drinking. Jack London Square is at Broadway and Embarcadero. Take I-880 to Broadway, turn south, and drive to the end. Or you can ride BART to the 12th Street station and then walk south along Broadway (about half a mile). Or take bus no. 72R or 72M to the foot of Broadway.

**Lake Merritt** is another favorite among locals. The tidal lagoon, 3½ miles in circumference, was bridged and dammed in the 1860s and is now a wildlife refuge, home to flocks of migrating ducks, herons, and geese. To get out on the water, you can rent a boat from **Lake Merritt Boating Center** ★ (✆ **510/238-2196**), in Lakeside Park along the north shore. Or, perhaps, take a gondola ride with **Gondola Servizio** (gondolaservizio.com; ✆ **510/663-6603**). Experienced gondoliers will serenade you as you glide across the lake. Prices start at $60 for the first couple and $10 for each additional person, depending on the time and gondola style. Also along Lake Merritt's shores you'll find the simple pleasure that is **Fairyland** ★ (699 Bellevue Ave.; fairyland.org; ✆ **510/452-2259**). Before Disneyland or any other childhood fantasy park,

---

## The Insider Scoop

While the rest of the world first heard about **Fenton's Creamery & Restaurant** (4226 Piedmont Ave.; fentonscreamery. com; ✆ **510/658-7000**) when it was featured in the Pixar film *Up*, Oaklanders have been flocking to this historic spot since 1894. In addition to ice cream, it serves lunch and dinner, but the sizable sundaes here are incredibly filling, so you can always skip dinner and go right for dessert. All of the ice cream is made on-site, and the "Arctic Tours" of the ice-cream-making process are a must for all ages. Once you've had your fill, you can stop at **Myrtle's Lodge** across the street for Fenton's memorabilia, handmade candy, and toys. Located north and east of downtown Oakland, Piedmont Avenue is filled with interesting shops—the perfect opportunity to walk off all that ice cream! If you're a comic book fan, check out **Dr. Comics & Mr. Games** down the street, at 4014 Piedmont Ave.

## volcanoes IN OAKLAND?!

If you're interested in all things volcanic, definitely visit **Sibley Volcanic Regional Preserve** (6701 Skyline Blvd.; ℂ **888/327-2757**). Aside from the constantly changing, made-by-locals labyrinths scattered throughout this park in the Oakland hills, Round Top, one of the park's highest peaks, is comprised of lava and volcanic debris left behind by a volcano 10 million years ago—a Pliocene epoch volcanic center, to be exact. Download a map at ebparks.org/parks/sibley.htm before you visit, or pick one up at the (unstaffed) visitors' center.

The park is an interesting place to hike, not just because of the volcanic rock but also the varied terrain and numerous smaller trails that break off from the main ones and meet up again farther along your walk. In 1 hour, you'll hike through forest, up onto ridges that offer up gorgeous 360-degree views, and down into ravines holding intricate labyrinths that will make the hike worth it for little ones and kids at heart. Bring a picnic lunch and a blanket, find a shady spot, and kick off your shoes while enjoying the view. Be sure to bring water, however, as it gets hot on the many exposed parts of the hill. The park is open March through October from 7am to 10pm, and November through February from 7am to 6pm. Another reason to like this park? The restrooms are in good shape and generally clean!

there was this "storybook theme park." Founded in 1950 and featuring fairytale sets, farm animals, and live entertainment, it's an interactive flashback to a simpler time, complete with live puppet shows, tiny toddler rides, play structures, picnic areas, and a chance to walk into a (fake) whale's mouth. Fun interactive fairytale sets feature recorded storytelling boxes that work at the turn of a plastic key you can buy onsite. This spot is so child-focused that adults can't get in without one. So bring a child and a sense of sweet, relaxed adventure to this mellow, charming spot.

To experience the avant-garde and burgeoning Bay Area art scene as the locals do, check out Oakland's **Art Murmur,** a free monthly gallery stroll on the first Friday of every month, in which the galleries and multi-use venues are open to the public for artist receptions (oaklandartmurmur.org). This event takes place throughout Oakland, so be sure to check the website for specific locations. Now a separate but related entity offered on the same day, **Oakland First Fridays** invites you to wander in and out of exhibits while enjoying a lively street festival complete with food trucks, live music, and spontaneous dance circles on Telegraph Avenue between Grand and 27th streets from 6 to 9pm.

## Where to Eat

The city of Oakland has become a dining destination in its own right, and if you really want to start at the top, look no further than **Commis** ★ (3859 Piedmont Ave.; commisrestaurant.com; ℂ **510/653-8902**). Chef James Syhabout, an Oakland native, has garnered two Michelin stars for this tiny yet elegant restaurant that offers a price-fixed, eight-course tasting menu and is opened Wednesday through Sunday. The wine list is fantastic, in case you were wondering.

You really can't go wrong at **Wood Tavern** ★ (6317 College Ave.; wood tavern.net; ✆ **510/654-6607**), a contemporary and convivial spot known for its great selection of wines by the glass and contemporary American food (think seasonal, farm-fresh cooking). Vegetarians won't find tons of offerings on the menu (it veers more toward pork belly and duck but always offers at least one stellar fish dish), but don't let that dissuade you; when asked, the chefs will put together spectacular animal-free dishes. If you want to know where the in-crowd dines, **Duende** ★ (468 19th St.; duendeoakland.com; ✆ **510/893-0174**) is the place to be. With a hip Oakland edge and Spanish flair, the food and cocktails are absolutely delicious. Like its sister Berkeley, Oakland also has a slew of wonderful, spectacularly affordable ethnic restaurants dotting its streets.

# SAUSALITO ★

5 miles N of San Francisco

The first town you'll enter once you cross the Golden Gate Bridge, picturesque Sausalito is extremely touristy, but also very much a home to its fewer than 8,000 residents. With houses scaling the hillside, and a quaint waterfront that includes its famed houseboat communities, Sausalito feels rather like St. Tropez on the French Riviera (minus the beach, bathing suits, and hotter climes). We locals that don't live in the city limits do come here, primarily to sail, kayak, or paddleboard on protected Richardson Bay, or to dine waterfront on nice days (all of which you can do, too). But you won't find us ducking in and out of the very tourist-targeted gift shops.

Next to the pricey bayside restaurants, antiques shops, and galleries are hamburger joints, ice-cream shops, and souvenir shops where it's Christmas all year round. Sausalito's main strip is Bridgeway, which runs along the water; on a clear day the views of San Francisco far across the bay are spectacular. After admiring the view, those in the know make a quick detour to Caledonia Street, 1 block inland; not only is it less congested, it also has a better selection of cafes and shops. Since the town is all along the waterfront and only stretches a few blocks, it's best explored on foot.

## Getting There

The **Golden Gate Ferry Service** fleet (goldengate.org; ✆ **415/923-2000**), operates between the San Francisco Ferry Building (at the foot of Market Street) and downtown Sausalito. Service is frequent, running at reasonable intervals every day of the year except January 1, Thanksgiving, and December 25. Check the website for an exact schedule. The ride takes a half-hour, and one-way fares are $12 for adults; $6 for seniors, youth ages 6–18, and passengers with disabilities; children 5 and under ride free (limit two children per full-fare adult). Ferries of the **Blue & Gold Fleet** (blueandgoldfleet.com; ✆ **415/705-5555**) leave from Pier 41 (Fisherman's Wharf); the one-way cost is $13 for adults, $7.50 for kids 5 to 12, free for kids 4 and under. Boats run on a seasonal schedule; phone or log onto their website for departure information.

**By car** from San Francisco, take U.S. 101 N and then take the first right after the Golden Gate Bridge (Alexander exit); prepare for traffic during summertime, when cars often back up on the bridge while waiting to exit. Alexander becomes Bridgeway in Sausalito. But before hitting town, consider taking a quick detour for a memorable photo-op at the Headlands. To do that, once you merge onto Alexander Avenue, drive under Highway 101 and turn right onto Conzelman Road, right before the ramp heading back to San Francisco. From here, you can pull over along the shoulder (you may have to wait for parking) to get a dramatic vantage point of the red bridge jetting out from tumultuous waters. Drive farther and you'll glimpse the rolling hills of the Marin Headlands and secluded Rodeo Beach to the right. You might be tempted to keep driving on this dramatic, winding road high above the city behind you. If you do, you'll eventually get to Point Bonita Lighthouse, the opposite direction of Sausalito but a wonderfully scenic, undeveloped diversion. You'll find great walking/hiking trails here, too.

## What to See & Do

Above all else, Sausalito has scenery and sunshine; once you cross the Golden Gate Bridge, you're usually out of the San Francisco fog patch and under blue California sky—with more comforting climate to boot. (That said, of all of Marin County's towns, Sausalito is most subject to spillover fog rolling in through the Golden Gate, so if it's sun you're after, check the weather before heading here in shorts and a T-shirt.) Houses cling to the town's steep hills,

# highway 1: THE FAMOUSLY SCENIC DRIVE

California's coastal Pacific Coast Highway 1 is famously scenic, and the stretch just north of the Golden Gate Bridge headed north is no exception. Follow it on a clear day and give yourself a few hours to wind the ocean-view cliffside roads leading to wonderful destinations—many of which are worthy of their own day trip. Along the way, look for **Muir Beach Overlook, Muir Beach, Stinson Beach** (if you want a true California Beach day), **Point Reyes** town (2 blocks of cute shops and restaurants and the nearby amazing **Point Reyes National Seashore, Tomales Bay**), and, a mere 75-minute drive north of S.F. in picturesque Marshall, oyster shucking and eating at **Hog Island Oyster Co.,** 20215 Shoreline Highway, Marshall (hogisland oysters.com/locations/marshall/marshall_picnic_area; (✆) **415-663-9218**)! It's a thing—actually a 3-hour picnic lunch that regularly sells out, so reservations must be made in advance. But you don't need a destination to make this memorable drive. Just make sure you have a full tank of gas, water and snacks, sunscreen, walking shoes, and a sense of adventure and let the road lead the way. You'll find breathtaking vistas and spots to stop and hike or simply snap endless selfies at almost every turn. When you're ready to head back, you can return the way you came or check GPS to see if finding your way to Highway 101 inland will get you home faster.

overlooking a colony of sailboats below. Most of the tourist action, which is almost singularly limited to window-shopping and eating, takes place at sea level on Bridgeway. Sausalito is a mecca for shoppers seeking souvenirs, kitschy clothes and footwear, and arts and crafts. Many of the town's shops are in the alleys, malls, and second-floor boutiques reached by steep, narrow staircases on and off Bridgeway. Caledonia Street, which runs parallel to Bridgeway 1 block inland, is home to more shops.

Younger children (up to 8 years old) will love the **Bay Area Discovery Museum ★★,** East Fort Baker, 557 McReynolds Rd. (bayareadiscovery museum.org; ☎ **415/339-3900;** admission $15 adults; $15 ages 1 to 17; $14 babies 6 to 11 months and seniors 65 and older), which is open daily 9am to 5pm except holidays. Set upon 7½ acres at Fort Baker, close to the base of the Golden Gate Bridge, this indoor-outdoor hands-on learning and play center is like San Francisco's science-based Exploratorium for younger kids, complete with a pirate ship to climb on, art studios, interactive science exhibits, and a room devoted to trains. If you need to occupy young, active minds and want to experience a gorgeous setting yourself, this is the place to spend a few hours. (Bring a jacket; it's often chilly here, even on nice days.) There is a modest but expensive cafe on-site serving wholesome sandwiches, soups, and salads. If you don't want to pay a premium for basic provisions, bring your own snacks or lunch and eat at one of the picnic tables.

For science-minded folks fascinated by the Bay Area's complex geography, visit the wholly original **Bay Model Visitors Center,** 2100 Bridgeway (www. spn.usace.army.mil/Missions/Recreation/Bay-Model-Visitor-Center/; ☎ **415/332-3871**). It's a hangar-like space filled with a working, wet model of the entire Bay Area. Built in 1957 by the U.S. Army Corps of Engineers to help scientists understand the complex patterns of the water currents and the tides, it's capable of duplicating, at a smaller time scale, the way the tides flow in the Bay. Buildings aren't represented, but major landmarks such as bridges are identifiable as you walk around the space, which is about the size of two football fields, or 1½ acres. Water, which is shallow throughout, is studded with some 250,000 copper tabs that help recreate known current patterns. Admission is free; it's typically open Tuesday to Sunday 10am to 4pm, but summer hours vary.

The facility, the only one of its kind in the world, hasn't been used for research since 2000, leaving it to educate school groups about Bay conservation. A visit is quite relaxing; many days, you'll be one of the only guests there, and the only sounds in the enormous room will be the faint sound of the water pumps. The model sits on the site of an important World War II shipbuilding yard, called Marinship ("ma-RINN-ship"). Tucked away to the left of the exit (don't miss it) is a terrific exhibit, full or artifacts and a video, that chronicles the yard, where an astonishing 93 ships were built in 3½ wartime years.

Nearby, you'll find one of my favorite things to do in Marin—head to **Sea Trek Kayak** at Richardson Bay (seatrek.com; ☎ **415/488-1000**), where you can rent a kayak or standup paddleboard and get out on the calm waters. The

If your trip allows for a night away from city noise, Sausalito's Fort Baker boasts one of the most charming upscale getaways in the country in an unforgettable, soothing setting. Called **Cavallo Point Lodge** (601 Murray Circle, Fort Baker; cavallopoint.com; ℂ **415/339-4700**), it's located in the fort's former general's quarters that flank the center green. Situated at the base of the Golden Gate Bridge, just 10 minutes from the city, each room has postcard-perfect views of the famous red arches, San Francisco's Marina district, or the rolling hills of the Marin Headlands. Prices range from $359 to $442 for a standard suite up to $650 for a two-bedroom suite, which sleeps six. The resort's partnership with Lexus means U.S. residents staying at the hotel can borrow a luxury sedan to explore the surrounding areas and city. Even if you can't stay the night, this historic slice of paradise is worth a visit. Have a meal at Murray Circle or Farley Bar, where you can enjoy Californian cuisine on the plush porch seating while soaking up the view. Or snag a rocking chair, the perfect place to enjoy the hosted wine-and-appetizer hour every evening. Take a cooking class in the sunny working kitchen, where local chefs teach guests how to use the organic bounty of the area. Or for a daily fee, enjoy use of the meditation pool, sauna, and Jacuzzi at the hotel's spa.

experience is unbeatable. Don't worry if you've never been in a kayak before or don't have the right attire; these are unsinkable and virtually untippable, and Sea Trek provides waterproof gear you can slip over your clothes. Rent a single-person kayak or a double and paddle your way around the shoreline to get up close and personal with dozens of sea lions and harbor seals, Sausalito's charming and famously bohemian houseboat communities, and shorebirds. Afterward, a walk through the parking lot leads to my favorite lunch spot in Marin—**Le Garage** (see p. 236).

## Where to Eat

The bayfront terrace at **Barrel House Tavern ★★**, 660 Bridgeway (barrelhousetavern.com; ℂ **415/729-9593**), has such magical water and city views, even we locals will forge through traffic, park in the nearby by-the-hour lot, and pull up a barstool at this handsome, relaxed New American restaurant. Find the easy-to-miss entrance and head to the narrow back deck on a nice day to order oysters, ribs, or a gourmet burger. Or settle in at one of the inside tables or bar seats and have what you like. Either way, it's one of the best bets in the area. A few blocks away is **Sushi Ran ★★**, 107 Caledonia St. (sushiran.com; ℂ **415/332-3620**), a spot for quality sushi that has become so expensive, it's priced me out of the market. Still, if someone else is buying, I'll happily head to the main bar and dining room or adjoining room and covered patio for top-quality nigiri and fancy cooked dishes. A more casual option is **Napa Valley Burger Company ★** (670 Bridgeway (napavalleyburgercompany.com; ℂ **415/332-1454**), where gourmet burgers, fries, and salads are accompanied by a good beer menu. The hippest spot on the waterfront, **Bar Bocce ★**, 1250 Bridgeway (barbocce.com; ℂ **415/331-0555**), draws young crowds from San

Francisco on nice days. As its name suggests, you can play bocce ball while sipping your drink (there's not a full bar, but the sangria is yummy). With outdoor seating featuring cushioned benches wrapped around fire pits, and a tiny sandy beach for the kids a few feet away, this is the perfect place to relax and refresh. My all-time favorite spot, however, is **Le Garage ★** (85 Liberty Ship Way #109; legaragebistrosausalito.com; 📞 **415/332-5625**), a marina-front French bistro with indoor and outdoor seating. The fresh, reliable fare is served up with a hearty side of atmosphere and relaxed tranquility. Don't miss the grass-fed burger with perfect fries and aioli, mussels in white wine sauce, or the shrimp or lobster salad. Though off the beaten path, it's an easy stroll from the ferry landing, and you can also drive and park in the restaurant's designated parking lot.

# MARIN ★, MUIR WOODS ★★ & MOUNT TAMALPAIS ★★

N of the Golden Gate Bridge

Don't be tempted by the several bus tours available for these spots; these day trips are an easy drive, though parking can be a hassle once lots fill up. A family of four will save a fortune—and see a lot more—by simply hiring a rental car for about $90 for the day.

## Muir Woods

While the rest of Marin County's redwood forests were devoured to feed San Francisco's turn-of-the-20th-century building spree, Muir Woods, in a remote ravine on the flanks of Mount Tamalpais, escaped destruction. Soaring toward the sky like a wooden cathedral, Muir Woods is unlike any other forest in the world; visiting here is an experience you won't soon forget.

Magnificent California redwoods have been successfully transplanted to five continents, but their homeland is a 500-mile strip along the mountainous coast of southwestern Oregon and Northern California. The coast redwood, or *Sequoia sempervirens,* is one of the tallest living things known to man; the largest known specimen in the Redwood National Forest towers 368 feet. (It has an even larger relative, the *Sequoiadendron giganteum* of the California Sierra Nevada, but the coastal variety is stunning enough.)

In the 1800s, redwoods were so plentiful here that people thought they'd never run out, and pretty much every single building in San Francisco and beyond was built of redwood. You could argue that the trees got their revenge on the city, when anything made of them went up in smoke in the fire after the earthquake. After the quake, in 1908 President Teddy Roosevelt consecrated this park—one of the last groves of the trees in the area—as a National Monument.

Granted, Muir Woods is tiny compared to the Redwood National Forest farther north, but you can still get a pretty good idea of what it must have been like when these giants dominated the entire coastal region. What is truly amazing is that they exist a mere 6 miles (as the crow flies) from San Francisco—close enough, unfortunately, that tour buses arrive in droves on the weekends. You can avoid the masses by hiking up the **Ocean View Trail,** turning left on **Lost Trail,** and returning on the **Fern Creek Trail.** The moderately challenging hike shows off the woods' best sides and leaves the lazy-butts behind.

To reach Muir Woods from San Francisco, cross the Golden Gate Bridge heading north on Highway 101, taking the Stinson Beach/Highway 1 exit heading west, and follow the signs (and the traffic). If you're coming during summer, head out early to avoid the traffic. The park is open daily from 8am to sunset, and the admission fee is $10 per person 16 and over. Advance reservations are required for parking ($8 per car) or seats on the shuttle from Highway 101 parking lots ($3); to reserve, contact the **National Parks Service at Muir Woods** (nps.gov/muwo; ✆ **415/388-2596**).

## Mount Tamalpais

Though Mount Tam—as the locals call it—is just barely tall enough to be considered a mountain, that doesn't keep residents from lovingly referring to

## THE LIVING dead

If you're in or passing through Marin and want a little local flavor Grateful Dead-style, head to **Terrapin Crossroads** in San Rafael (100 Yacht Club Dr., San Rafael. terrapincrossroads.net.; ✆ **415/524-2773**). Tucked behind a bunch of car dealerships along the San Rafael Canal, this restaurant and live music venue is not only owned by Grateful Dead bass guitarist Phil Lesh, it's also frequented by him and his pals. The food is fine, but it's the music and twirling, feel-good vibes you'll want to come for. Most nights there's a live band playing in the bar area, and many nights there's also one jamming in the pay-to-enter, barn-like Grate Room. If you're around during the summer, definitely come for one of their weekend jams in The Backyard, when crowds gather on the back lawn for beer, food, live music. It's a rare convening of the county's groovier residents, who've long been overrun by the well-heeled, multimillionaire set. The restaurant and bar are open Monday through Friday 4pm to 9:30pm, Saturday and Sunday 11am to 9:30pm.

it as "the sleeping lady" for the way the peak and surrounding foothills resemble feminine curves. While it's sunny most days, most evenings the fog from the West alluringly wraps the lady in a blanket of mist. Mount Tam's trails, peaks, and vistas are the Bay Area's favorite outdoor playground, and it's a mission of most active residents to discover their favorite secret trails and overlooks. You don't need inside knowledge, however, to appreciate the scenic beauty. The main trails—mostly fire roads—see a lot of foot and bicycle traffic on weekends, particularly on clear, sunny days when you can see a hundred miles in all directions, from the foothills of the Sierra to the western horizon. It's a great place to escape the city for a leisurely hike and to soak in towering redwood groves and breathtaking views of the bay. Follow the windy roads to the west and you'll ultimately end at **Stinson Beach,** a dreamy, quiet coastal community with down-home residents, multimillion-dollar beachfront second homes, and a beautiful, expansive sandy shoreline.

To get to Mount Tamalpais by car, cross the Golden Gate Bridge heading north on Highway 101, and take the Stinson Beach/Highway 1 exit. Follow the signs up the shoreline highway for about 2½ miles, turn onto Pantoll Road, and continue for about a mile to Ridgecrest Boulevard. Ridgecrest winds to a parking lot below East Peak. From there, it's a 15-minute hike up to the top, where you'll find a visitor center with a small exhibit and a video, plus a helpful staff. Visitor center admission is free; it is open weekends 11am to 4pm. Park hours are 7am to sunset year-round. For a list of guided hikes, see **friendsofmttam.org.** You are welcome to hike in the area on your own; it is safe, great for little ones, and the trails are well-marked.

## Where to Eat

Right off Highway 101 at the turnoff to begin the climb to Mount Tam and beyond is **Buckeye Roadhouse ★** (15 Shoreline Hwy., Mill Valley; ☎ **415/ 331-2600**), an extremely popular, historic restaurant serving updated versions of familiar comfort foods in an atmospheric lodge-like setting. It's seriously overpriced, but it's got some of the best atmosphere in all of Marin, a small but fun bar scene, and delicious oysters bingo and chili-lime brick chicken. Because they serve continuously from lunch through dinner, this could be the perfect stopover on your way in or out of the area. Note that if you come during prime dining time without a reservation, you're likely to have a long wait. High up on the mountain, the **Mountain Home Inn ★**, 810 Panoramic Hwy., Mill Valley (mtnhomeinn.com; ☎ **415/381-9000**) offers a swell brunch and panoramic views from the outdoor deck.

If you make it over Mount Tam, just past Muir Woods, look for the **Pelican Inn ★**, 10 Pacific Way, Muir Beach (pelicaninn.com; ☎ **415/383-6000**). Built in 1979 to resemble a 16th-century English cottage, it's a perfect place to grab a beer at the old-fashioned bar—dartboard and all—and sprawl out on the lawn for lunch after a hike.

# ANGEL ISLAND ★ & TIBURON ★

8 miles N of San Francisco

A California State Park, **Angel Island** is the largest of San Francisco Bay's three islets (the others are Alcatraz and Yerba Buena). The island has been, at various times, a prison, a quarantine station for immigrants, a missile base, and even a favorite site for duels. Nowadays, its dark past exists only in the ghosts rumored to haunt the former military buildings. The island is now the domain of visitors who are looking for 360-degree views of the bay, sunshine, trails, grassy picnic grounds, and a scenic beach. Hike, bike, take a tour, or just relax on this picturesque, car-free island.

Connected by ferry to Angel Island, uberwealthy **Tiburon,** situated on a peninsula of the same name, is a living postcard, almost too beautiful to be real. It looks like a cross between a seacoast town and a Hollywood Western set, as Main Street has been preserved to reflect its roots as a Gold Rush train town. Palatial, multimillion-dollar homes perch on the hills, overlooking the proud yachts and sailboats below. The view from the waterfront of San Francisco's skyline and the islands in the bay explain why residents happily pay the precious price to live here. For the visitor, it's a lazy touristy jaunt, mostly worth exploring—especially in summer—if your idea of a good time is perching on a sunny bayfront deck at a pricy restaurant, peering at the stunning city views (provided it's not blanketed in fog, which is often the case), and lingering over brunch and Bloody Marys. It's also a nice stop on your way to Angel Island if you want to drive to Marin and hop a ferry from there.

## Getting There

Ferries of the **Blue & Gold Fleet** (blueandgoldfleet.com; ✆ **415/705-8200**) from Pier 41, Fisherman's Wharf, travel to both Angel Island and Tiburon (but not via the same boat). You can also hop a ferry from The Ferry Building at the foot of Market Street on weekends. Boats run on a seasonal schedule; phone or look online for departure information. The round-trip fare to Angel Island is $20 for adults, $11 for seniors 65+ and kids 5 to 12, and free for kids 5 and under when traveling with an adult. The fare includes state park fees. A one-way ticket to Tiburon is $13 for adults, $7.50 for seniors 65+ and kids 5 to 12, and free for kids 5 and under.

To go directly to Tiburon **by car** from San Francisco, take U.S. 101 to the Tiburon/Highway 131 exit and then follow Tiburon Boulevard all the way downtown, a 40-minute drive from San Francisco. Good luck finding a parking spot in Tiburon; try the lot behind the **Tiburon Playhouse** movie theater at 40 Main St.

The **Tiburon–Angel Island Ferry** (angelislandferry.com; ✆ **415/435-2131**) connects the two destinations, a 15-minute crossing. Tickets cost $15 for adults, $13 for children 6 to 11, $5 for kids 3 to 5, and $1 for bikes. One child 2 or under is admitted free of charge with each paying adult (after that it's $3.50 each). The dock in Tiburon is at Tiburon Boulevard and Main Street.

Boats run on a seasonal schedule, but usually depart hourly from 10am to 5pm on weekends, with a more limited schedule on weekdays. Call ahead or look online for schedules. Tickets can only be purchased when boarding and include state park fees.

## What to See & Do on Angel Island

Passengers disembark from the ferry at **Ayala Cove,** a small marina abutting a huge lawn area equipped with tables, benches, barbecue pits, and restrooms. During the summer season, there's also a small store, a gift shop, the **Cove Cafe** (with surprisingly good grub and a boxed lunch option available for pickup if you order in advance), the seasonal, weekends-only **Cantina** restaurant, where live music makes for a fun afternoon, and an overpriced mountain-bike rental shop. If history is of interest, you can check out **The United States Immigration Station Museum** (if you don't want to walk, you can pay $7 for a shuttle ride).

Angel Island's 12 miles of hiking and bike trails include the **Perimeter Road,** a paved path that circles the island and offers breathtaking views of San Francisco, the Marin Headlands, and the Golden Gate and Bay Bridges. The perimeter path is bike-friendly for all levels, with only slight inclines and clear markers. For more experienced riders, an interior path offers a more strenuous mountain-biking experience. The Perimeter Road winds past World War II military barracks, former gun emplacements, and other historic government buildings that recall the island's various pasts; several turnoffs lead to the top of Mount Livermore, 776 feet above the bay. Sometimes referred to as the "Ellis Island of the West," Angel Island was used as a holding area for detained Chinese immigrants awaiting admission papers from 1910 to 1940. You can still see faded Chinese characters on some of the walls of the barracks where the immigrants were held, sometimes for months.

Besides walking and biking, there are a number of other ways to get around the island, all of which can be booked at angelisland.com. Schedules vary depending on the time of year. The 1-hour audio-enhanced open-air **Tram Tour** costs $17 for adults, $15 for seniors, $11 for children 5 to 11, and is free for children 4 and under. The Tram will stop at vistas and riders can get off for photo ops. A guided 2-hour **Segway Tour** costs $68 per person, and is only available for those 16 years and up. Long pants are recommended; closed shoes are mandatory. For more information about activities on Angel Island, visit **angelisland.com**.

For a more adventurous way to see the entire circumference of the island and take in the surrounding panoramas from a unique vantage point, try a guided **sea-kayak tour ★**, available for paddlers over 16. Offered a few times during high season, tours range from day trips to overnights. All equipment is provided (including a wetsuit, if needed), and no experience is necessary. Rates start at $90 per person. For more information, contact the Sausalito-based **Sea Trek** (seatrek.com; ✆ **415/488-1000**). *Note:* Tours depart from Ayala Cove on Angel Island, not Sausalito.

# What to See & Do in Tiburon

Despite its historic facade, Tiburon is, in reality, a sleepy, luxurious stretch of yacht-club suburbia. Boutiques, souvenir stores, art galleries, and dockside restaurants flank its one tiny main shopping street at the water's edge, housed in color-splashed, turn-of-the-century converted boathouses. The main thing to do in tiny Tiburon is stroll along the waterfront, pop into its handful of stores, and spend an easy $60 on drinks and appetizers. For that reason, I recommend popping by only if you're on your way to Angel Island or somewhere else or simply want a laid-back few hours of alfresco dining with stunning city views (weather permitting). If you do find your way here, stop at **The Candy Store on Main Street** at 7 Main St. (maincandystore.com; ✆ 415/435-0434). With fudge samples, edible Lego bricks, and every imaginable sweet you'd expect to find in Willy Wonka's factory, it's a stop you can't help but love.

## Where to Eat in Tiburon

It's rare that a restaurant with such a tourist-friendly view has solid food to boot, but pricy **Guaymas ★★** (5 Main St.; guaymasrestaurant.com; ✆ 415/435-6300) delivers on both fronts, which is why it remains a favorite in this discerning community. Sit outside mere feet away from bobbing sailboats and indulge in margaritas, guacamole, ceviche, and a number of authentic Mexican dishes from various regions. Add on a stunning panoramic view of the city, and the damage the drinks do to your wallet might be the only reason to leave. On a sunny day, you'll find San Francisco's brunch-time warriors flocking in droves to **Sam's Anchor Cafe ★★** (27 Main St.; samscafe.com; ✆ 415/435-4527) a few doors away. Same stunning view, an even bigger outdoor patio, brunch, and top-quality burgers, Bloody Marys, and beer draw crowds of twenty- and thirtysomethings who linger at the sundrenched tables and get good and tipsy before biking or ferrying their way back into the fog. It gets crowded on nice days, so it's worth getting there early for prime seating.

# WINE COUNTRY

The lush, hilly countryside of this region is so beautiful it's a draw in itself, but of course, the main reason to come here is unparalleled access to world-class food and drink served in pastoral chic elegance. Whether you spend a day or a week, you'll see that wine country is all about the Good Life—so much so that you may want to drop everything and move here to stomp grapes (trust me: I did it, except for the grape-stomping part). But before you sell off your belongings, consider the popular wine country joke that's not a joke: You know what it takes to make a small fortune in wine country? A large fortune. The same could be true for exploring the region: Even the simplest motels are expensive, destination dining rooms can cost well upward of $100 per person when all is said and done, and wineries that used to charge $5 to $10 to taste now ask closer to $25 per person. Still, there's fun to be had here on any budget, especially if you pace yourself and visit no more than two to three wineries in a day; picnicking is a fantastic way to dine here, and some of the sweeter, smaller boutique hotels include breakfast and plenty of snacks in their nightly fee.

Use this chapter as a quick primer for a weekend or day trip into a world that you are sure to fall in love with.

## A QUICK LAY OF THE LAND

Picture the whole area as a long, uppercase U in which the two top tongs are pinched together around a light mountain range. On the "left," or western, tong of the U is widespread **Sonoma County,** where the principal north-south road, U.S. 101, goes straight to the Golden Gate. In **Napa County,** the eastern half, it's the more congested route 29, which, especially around rush hour, can be slow going.

At the bottom of the U, the town of Sonoma is connected to the town of Napa, 30 minutes east, by a long stretch of rural Highway 121/12. A little south of there, Highway 37 links Napa County to Highway 101 and I-80; either road can take you back to the city, although the 101 is probably faster.

# AFTER THE FIRES: wine country update

In October 2017, Napa and Sonoma made international headlines when the most devastating wildfires in the state's history swept through both wine regions for nearly a full week, leaving mass devastation in their wakes. Thousands of structures and 42 lives were confirmed lost. By all accounts, it was horrific and devastating to the communities affected.

Ironically, despite the sensationalistic news coverage, much of the "wine" part of wine country survived relatively unscathed. Yes, some wineries and vineyards experienced damage, but 2 weeks after the fires were finally put out, only a handful of wineries had reported partial or full loss, out of some 400 wineries in Napa Valley and more than 425 wineries in Sonoma. In fact, vineyards, cleared of dry vegetation and regularly irrigated, literally acted as firebreaks in many areas.

The timing was also fortunate for the wine industry. The white-wine grapes and most of the red-wine grapes had already been harvested, so they weren't affected by smoke. Those varieties that were still on the vine when the fires started were protected by their thick skins, and any residual aromas can be removed during the winemaking process.

Cast your eyes into the hillsides as you drive through either valley and you're sure to see evidence of the fire. But all the properties in this book—and 98% of the tourist industry attractions in general—are intact and as glorious to visit as they always were. What's more, they're likely to be happier to see you than ever. A newfound sense of community, strength, and gratitude now beats through the heart of Northern California wine country, and your visit is exactly the support this tourism-based economy needs to speed its recovery.

North from Napa, the principal towns (which gradually grow smaller and quainter), are **Yountville, Oakville, St. Helena** (all adorable), and finally the Main Street town of **Calistoga** (known for hot springs). Not far north from that, 29 turns into 128 and links up with **Geyserville,** at the tippy top of the Sonoma wine region.

From there, heading south on Highway 101 through Sonoma County, you hopscotch between populous towns and quiet hamlets. First is **Healdsburg** (a swanky-sweet weekenders' town square good for strolling), and **Santa Rosa** (bigger and with cheaper motels, but no wineries to speak of within it, though there is an airport here). From there, Route 12, also known as Sonoma Highway, branches off to the east through **Kenwood,** the charming town of **Glen Ellen,** and finally **Sonoma,** the county's historic seat. West and southwest of Santa Rosa, along Route 116, the towns of **Sebastopol** and **Forestville,** and finally, **Guerneville**—where the thick redwood forests begin—are in what's called the Russian River Valley. The vibe here is more laid-back, and in summer the big pastimes are canoeing and swimming. Guerneville is also a well-known gay resort town, particularly in summer, although you won't find it raging often with parties; the visitors tend to be a bit more middle-aged and settled. (For a resource on gay-friendly resorts and restaurants, go to gayrussianriver.com.)

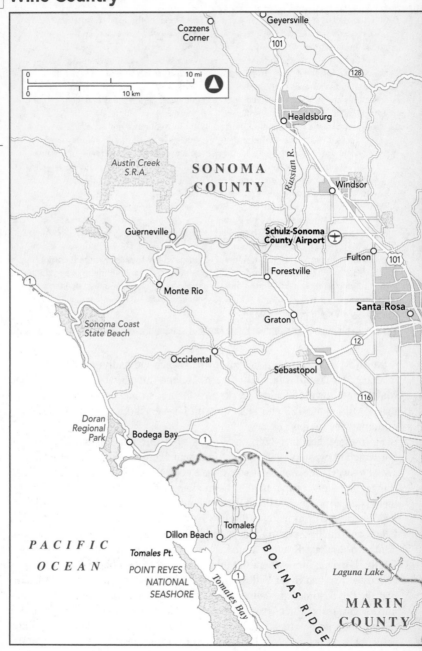

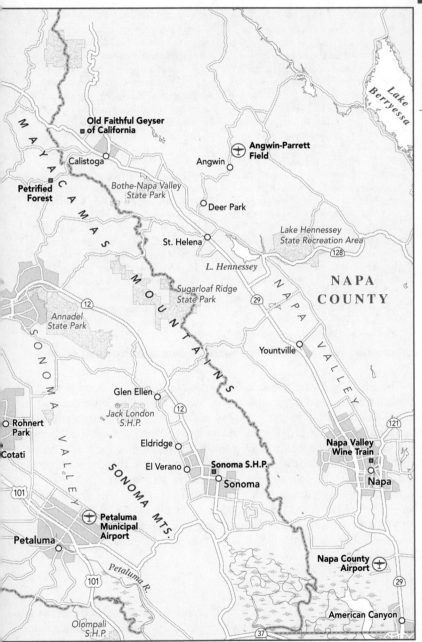

# deciding BETWEEN NAPA OR SONOMA

Choosing which area to visit is a tough call, but the choice can be easy if you consider the strong suits of each.

If world-famous restaurants, super-luxury accommodations, vintage hot springs, and larger brand-name wineries with elaborate facilities and tours sound good to you, aim for **Napa.** You can stay in the town of Napa, Calistoga, or anywhere in between—getting from one end of the valley to the other takes about 40 minutes, so it really doesn't matter. If I were you, I'd plan my accommodations around where I want to dine. Yes, you'll need to hop in and out of the car all day while wine tasting. (Hire a car service or designate a driver; there's no public transportation here.) But trust me: There's nothing worse than gorging yourself silly on a memorable meal and too much wine, and then finding yourself a half-hour's drive from your hotel.

**Sonoma County,** on the other hand, is more pastoral, laid back, and wholesome feeling. Here you'll find more family-owned wineries, where the winemakers themselves are pouring the day's drink. With charming rural roads leading to the next great wine-tasting experience, it's less congested, more spread-out, and has the most attractive square around (in Healdsburg). You can still find luxury and hot springs here, too—famed **Sonoma Mission Inn** (p. 264) is a case in point. There are also noteworthy dining excursions and an abundance of exceptional wines. Should Sonoma be your pick, I highly recommend you choose between spending your time in Sonoma Valley (cute shopping and dining square in the town of Sonoma, and a handful of great wineries, some quite historic) or vast Northern Sonoma, with Healdsburg as its epicenter, a plethora of wonderful wine regions scattered over winding roads, with fun outdoor activities such as canoeing along the Russian River.

Maybe it's not so easy to choose. But the good news is, you really can't go wrong.

The character of the two counties varies slightly. While Napa is mostly verdant farmland and some small towns, Sonoma has a few larger communities (Santa Rosa) and its topography is much more varied, from rolling hills and farms in the east, to deliciously damp redwood forests in the middle west, to wild and undeveloped seashore. (Remember Hitchcock's *The Birds*? It was shot in Bodega Bay, on the Sonoma Coast. It's still just as rustic now, although it's a 30-minute drive through forests from what we consider wine country.)

It really doesn't matter which area you make your base—they're all spectacular. But Sonoma and Napa combined cover a heck of a lot of real estate, so you'd be wise to select just one area to explore—either Napa Valley, Sonoma Valley, or Northern Sonoma. To do them all justice, you'd need at least 2 weeks!

# NAPA VALLEY

Just 55 miles north of San Francisco, 35-mile-long Napa Valley comprises a string of small towns surrounded by vineyards, all of which rely on tourism for most of their livelihoods. At its southern end, the town of Napa is the most cosmopolitan. With no vineyards in sight (other than those in the Carneros region, which you'll hit heading into town, depending on how you get here), Napa has a walkable and slowly-gentrifying downtown, and a continually growing number of restaurants and hotels, making it a hotbed for wine country fun. To the north, off Highway 29, the tiny town of Yountville is home to one of the most renowned foodie strips in the country (thanks to restaurants by Thomas Keller, Michael Chiarello, and more). Oakville and Rutherford are primarily known for the wineries that reside there, while St. Helena has charming shopping and dining along its tiny Main Street. Farther north still is Calistoga, where a cluster of hot springs, motels, B&Bs, shops, and a very relaxed vibe draw laid-back tourists. No matter where you stay, you'll be minutes from dozens of wineries worth a visit.

## Napa Wineries

With more than 400 wineries scattered throughout the valley, you could tour Napa's wineries for months and still not try them all. So don't approach winery circuits the way you might the great museums of Paris or the rides at Disneyland. You can't hit everything, so don't even try. The key is to find places that deliver the experience you want, whether it's a specific wine varietal, a style, dramatic architecture, or a killer view. Relax about tasting—no matter where you choose to go, you can trust that in this competitive region, you won't be served swill. (Frankly, I've always found that during the course of a fun adventure, almost any wine tastes amazing.) Rather than provide a laundry list of Napa's offerings, I'll highlight wineries that have a little something extra—a terrific view, a rich history, an outstanding art collection, or a particularly noteworthy tour. Still, there are other delicious experiences to be found in Napa, so don't hesitate to ask your well-traveled friends, hotel concierge, or people you meet along the way for wineries they recommend.

To make planning your itinerary easier, get the downloadable maps from **visitnapavalley.com**, the website run by the Napa Valley Conference and Visitors Bureau. (It's kind of buried, so if you want a quicker link go to visitnapavalley.com/wineries/winery-map.) If you can't download maps beforehand, don't fret; they're distributed widely and for free, and your hotel or B&B will have more maps than you'll know what to do with. Check out opening hours and tour times, schedule advance tours if required, and chart a path that doesn't require a lot of backtracking. Otherwise, you'll spend more time in the car than the tasting room.

### CALISTOGA

**Castello di Amorosa Winery ★★**   The exuberant, over-the-top European pretensions of some Napa landlords are immoderately on display at this sublime, huge, medieval-style castle completed in 2007. With its basement dungeon outfitted with antique torture devices, 72-foot-long Great Hall with high coffered ceilings, and 107 guest rooms, Castello di Amorosa gets its reputation more for being a tourist attraction than for its quality wines, which are only sold here. The $25 entry fee includes a tasting of five wines; for $30 you taste six wines, including some reserves. Visitors under 21 pay $15.

# HOW TO WINE taste

It doesn't really matter if you don't know the difference between chardonnay and cabernet; trust me, no one cares. But if you want to learn how to wine taste, California's wine country is the perfect classroom. Provided the tasting room you're visiting isn't slammed with visitors, the hosts will certainly show you exactly how to sniff, swirl, and spit. But if you're left to your own devices, follow these tips:

**Look:** It may seem pompous to raise your glass in the air toward the light, but go ahead—then tip it to the side, and admire the wine's color. You can actually tell a lot about the wine by its color, including the varietal, whether it's a "young" or an "aged" wine, or how it was fermented. It takes time to understand exactly what to look for, but if you follow this practice for the wines you taste, you might just begin noticing distinctions between various varietals and vintages.

**Swirl:** Gently swirl the contents of your wineglass. This process aerates the wine and allows you to smell it better. It also creates an opportunity to learn more about the wine. The speed at which its "legs," or drips, roll down the side of the glass can indicate whether the wine is higher in alcohol and/or sweetness (slower legs) or has less alcohol/sugar (quicker legs).

**Smell:** Stick your nose in the tilted glass and take a good whiff. Make up words to describe what you smell: barnyard, strawberries, cotton candy, whatever. Wines have distinctive aromas, and with practice you can begin to identify, but I've found the power of suggestion plays an equal hand. No matter whether you smell pineapple and stone fruit or plain old wine, it's still fun to play the guessing game.

**Sip:** This part is pretty straightforward, but do it like the pros: Take small sips and breathe a little air into your mouth while the wine's in there to further aerate it and spread the flavor across your palate.

**Spit:** Your choice, of course, but wineries keep a little spittoon on the bar that's for your use. I hate this part, even though I spit fairly often, because it requires some finesse to do it right. Otherwise, you'll be like me with a little stream of wine dripping down your chin—or quickly tipsy if you swallow all that you taste. Still, it's another thing that's fun to try.

**Pace Yourself:** Plenty of people saddle up to the bar and gulp down every last drop of every last wine—and you're welcome to do the same (provided you're not driving, of course). But know that even small sips at three or four wineries can add up to a sudden need to splay out on the back seat of your car for an impromptu siesta. So, if you want to have fun and make it to the dinner hour, slow it down.

---

(Prices go up by $5 on holidays or after noon on weekends.) Combined tours and tastings ($40 per person) last 1 hour and 45 minutes and require reservations. Owner Daryl Sattui also runs the V. Sattui Winery in St. Helena, which regularly overflows with picnickers.

4045 N. Saint Helena Hwy., Calistoga. castellodiamorosa.com. © **707/967-6272.** Daily Mar–Oct 9:30am–6pm, Nov–Feb 9:30am–5pm.

**Chateau Montelena** ★ One of the wineries that put Napa Valley on the global map, this pastoral estate won a top honor among white wines at the Judgment of Paris in 1976 (commemorated in the 2008 movie *Bottle Shock*), and continues to hold its head high today. The basic walk-in "current release" tasting is $30 for four wines or $40 if you make an appointment for a "semi-private" experience. If you're deeply interested, set aside 1 hour for its Library Wine Tasting (Sun, Tues, and Thurs 10am and 2pm; $60; reservation required). This isn't a place well laid-out for hordes of casual gawkers, but the ivy-covered, castle-like winery building (1882) is pretty, and the Chinese garden and 5-acre pond, Jade Lake, make a lovely place to sit for a few minutes. The people pouring here (they're in the modern ranch-style building) know their wine, and they're still proud of the victory that put Napa on the serious wine drinker's map. Look carefully for the easy-to-miss driveway; as you're driving to the winery, if the road you're on gives way to hairpins and ever-climbing altitude, you've gone too far, and you're on a mountain pass.

1429 Tubbs Lane, Calistoga. montelena.com. ✆ **707/942-5105.** Daily 9:30am–4pm.

**Schramsberg** ★★★  Yes, it's expensive and you have to reserve a tour and tasting in advance, but this 217-acre sparkling wine estate, a landmark once frequented by Robert Louis Stevenson and the second-oldest property in Napa Valley, is one of the valley's all-time best places to explore. For decades Schramsberg's delicious sparkling wine has been the label U.S. Presidents serve when toasting dignitaries from around the globe. The mystique begins the minute you park in the lot and wander toward the greeting area, where lush, overgrown foliage surrounds picture-perfect ponds (plan time for plenty of selfies!). The sparkling wine caves, which wind 2 miles (reputedly the longest in North America), were partly hand-carved by Chinese laborers in the 1800s; with dangling cobwebs and seemingly endless passageways, the caves have an authentic Tom Sawyer ambience, and you can't help but feel you're on an adventure. The comprehensive tour includes a stop in a formal tasting room, where you'll sample surprisingly varied selections of their high-end bubbly. Tours start at $70 per person. If you'd prefer to sip wine and skip the tour, you can do that by appointment for $50 at their sister property, **Davies Vineyards,** at 1210 Grayson Ave. in St. Helena.

1400 Schramsberg Rd. (off Hwy. 29), Calistoga. schramsberg.com. ✆ **707/942-2414.** Daily 10am–4pm, with 5 scheduled tours. Tours and tastings by appointment only.

**Sterling Vineyards** ★  The highlight of a tour of this big-business winery (with embarrassingly too-cool people on their website) is to ride on its aerial tram ($32; $15 for ages 4–21; under age 4 free), which affords some fantastic views over the area as it takes you to the main building, which sits on a hill some 300 feet above the valley floor. To get the most out of it, budget plenty of time and go on a clear day, especially because the tram can be closed in stormy, windy, or overly hot weather. You have to pay the fee even if you don't ride the tram, but the price also includes a tour (self-guided, not nar-rated) and a current-release tasting. They also offer more extensive tastings, including a food and wine experience for $75 per person. There aren't many places in wine country where kids are welcomed or engaged, so the tram is definitely a top choice if you're traveling with little ones. Picnicking is allowed. Interesting side note: The bells in the tower used to hang in St. Dunstan's of Fleet Street, London, a church that was destroyed in World War II.

1111 Dunaweal Lane, Calistoga. sterlingvineyards.com. ✆ **800/726-6136.** Daily 10am–5pm.

## NAPA

**The Hess Collection** ★★★   A top choice for art lovers, here wine is served in a ground-floor tasting room, with an expertly curated selection of modern art collected by Swiss owner Donald Hess (who regularly loans his works to top museums) displayed in a spacious two-level gallery. Hess grants his support to 20 living artists at a time, saying he'll reassess when they either die or become "well established." (Among his picks: both Robert Motherwell and Francis Bacon—it's fair to say the guy's got an eye.) The art is arresting, the front garden is picture-perfect, and the drive up winding roads to get here is fun, too. Spring through fall, if you feel like splurging you can reserve a spot on a 3-hour "vine to table tour and lunch," which includes an exclusive tour of the vineyards and winemaking practices and a three-course, wine-paired lunch.

4411 Redwood Rd., Napa. hesscollection.com. ✆ **707/255-1144.** Tours and tasting $30–$60 per person; tours with wine and food tastings $65–$175. Visitor center and gallery 10am–5:30pm; winery and vineyard tours 10:30am–3:30pm.

**Quixote** ★★   This hidden, hillside property is the only U.S. structure designed by late great European artist Friedensreich Hundertwasser. Whimsical and captivating even to those who know nothing about design, it's a structural fantasy world with undulating lines, a gilded onion dome, and a fearless use of color. During the $65-per-person, reservation-only sit-down tasting, visitors can sample the winery's current releases. If you're interested in visiting, reserve in advance—due to zoning laws, this truly one-of-a-kind Stags' Leap District winery welcomes up to 10 guests per day, all of whom are likely to find themselves as awestruck by the architecture as they are by the powerful petite sirahs and cabernet sauvignons.

6126 Silverado Trail, Napa. quixotewinery.com. ✆ **707/944-2659.** Tastings by appointment only daily 10am–4pm.

**Shafer Vineyards** ★★   For a truly intimate and educational tour and tasting, make an appointment at this low-key, family-owned winery. Founders John and Doug Shafer, along with winemaker Elias Fernandez, use sustainable farming and solar energy to make truly outstanding wines, and you'll be hard-pressed to find a more relaxed, personal tour and tasting—it highlights the true flavor and passion for quality Napa Valley winemaking. The $75-per-person price, which includes tasting five wines (including their famed $265-per-bottle Hillside Select), is significant, but for wine lovers, the 1½-hour experience is worth it. These are popular tours—book at least a month in advance.

6154 Silverado Trail, Napa. shafervineyards.com. ✆ **707/944-2877.** By appointment only Mon–Fri 10am and 2pm; closed weekends and holidays.

## OAKVILLE/RUTHERFORD/YOUNTVILLE

**Chandon** ★★ Founded in 1973 by French champagne house Moët et Chandon, this gorgeous, well-manicured estate is the place to go if you want to join revelers basking on a sunny patio with bottles of bubbly and gourmet snacks. There are fun, comprehensive free tours of the process for making their sparkling wine, but what makes this place pop is the scene—unlike other tasting rooms, this one is designed to encourage visitors to kick back and stay awhile. And people happily do, especially since sandwiches, cheese platters, and more are also available for purchase.

1 California Dr. (at Hwy. 29), Yountville. chandon.com. © **707/944-2280.** Daily 10am–4:30pm; hours vary by season, so call to confirm. Call or check website for tour schedules.

**Inglenook** ★★ Wine country experiences don't get more highly produced than a visit to this dramatic, perfectly appointed, incredibly landscaped historic property with an owner who's one of the great filmmaking legends. But Francis Ford Coppola knows how to set a compelling scene—and how to make wine—so it's all good. Come here to wander the gorgeous grounds and treat yourself to a $45 sit-down Heritage Tasting, the $50 Inglenook Experience (includes a chateau tour and tasting in the caves), or make an advance reservation for one of the exclusive "private experiences." You can also shop the boutique for upscale tchotchkes, or grab a bite at the on-site bistro.

1991 St Helena Hwy., Rutherford. inglenook.com. © **707/968-1100.** Tours and tastings $45–$95 per person. Chateau 11am–5pm, bistro 10am–5pm.

**Robert Mondavi** ★★ This Mission-style winery founded by the pioneer of modern-day California winemaking (who died at age 94 in 2008) is one of my top recommendations for visitors who'd like a comprehensive but easily digestible schooling on winemaking and winetasting. Its grounds are beautiful and well-appointed, but the real attraction here is the range of tours. You might want to begin with the wine-tasting basics tour ($25 for a 45-min. review of how to read a wine label and to see, smell, sip, and spit). The 30-minute Discovery Tour, which is a good fast primer, requires no reservations (though they max out at 20 people) and is offered daily in the summer and on weekends the rest of the year; it costs $25 for two tastings, and kids are welcome (under 13 tour free). The year-round 90-minute Signature Tour features a sit-down guided wine tasting (three tastes), requires advance reservations, and costs $40 per person. You'll stroll the vineyards and the cellars; children are welcome but must be at least 13 years old to attend. After your tour, make sure to explore the grounds; you'll encounter a collection of chunky sculptures by Beniamino Bufano (famous for chopping off his trigger finger and mailing it to President Woodrow Wilson rather than fight in World War I—his digital protest didn't seem to affect the power of his art.) The tasting rooms generally offer about 10 wines that are exclusive to the winery, and tastings start at $5. Each summer, the winery hosts outdoor concerts, something it's been doing since 1969, 3 years after Mondavi kicked off Napa's post-Prohibition rise.

# mud BATHS

In the 1800s, the big draw in this region wasn't wine, but hot mud baths. The quake of 1906 shifted the location of many springs, wiping out most of the wells that then existed in Sonoma County as well, so today, the best place for a geothermal treatment is in Calistoga in Napa County.

Like bungee jumping or hot-air ballooning, a mud bath is a once-in-a-lifetime vacation treat. Most day spas mix the mud and hot springs water (which is a little over 100 degrees) with clay, peat, and volcanic ash from the nearby St. Helena volcano—this may stain some swimsuits, so don't wear your best one, or, like most people, don't wear anything at all. These treatments used to be touted as an excellent remedy for arthritis, but modern marketing laws being what they are, they're now promoted mostly as stress relievers (though supporting scientific studies show that arthritis sufferers may, in fact, find some relief).

The following Calistoga day spas all include mud baths—the most "local" treatment—as well as massage and hydrotherapy (check websites for full menus). Some mud baths are thick, others soupy; some start as mineral-water baths before having ash mixed in, and others offer a pre-mixed tub before you begin. The style doesn't matter, but make sure the spa you visit uses mineral water, which means it's been drawn hot from the earth.

**Dr. Wilkinson's Hot Springs Resort** (1507 Lincoln Ave.; drwilkinson.com; ✆ 707/942-4102), set in a delightfully 1950s motel complex, has been a player in Calistoga for generations. It offers a range of treatments, but it's basic in the classically medicinal approach spas once had. The mud bath as described above is $89 and takes a little over an hour.

**Golden Haven** (1713 Lake St.; goldenhaven.com; ✆ 707/942-8000), with its couples-sized tubs, is popular with honeymooners. A treatment costs $94 per person.

**Indian Springs Calistoga** (1712 Lincoln Ave.; indianspringscalistoga.com; ✆ 844/378-3635), one of my favorite getaways, has all volcanic-ash mud baths, which include a eucalyptus steam, plus mineral bath for $95. Pay an additional $25 and you can loll the day away at the enormous outdoor pool and gorgeous, meditative grounds.

Don't miss a chance to attend a concert if you can (plan in advance; they sell out); with wine flowing and people picnicking and dancing to the music of extremely famous names, it's Napa Valley living at its best.

Hwy. 29, Oakville. robertmondaviwinery.com. ✆ **888/766-6328.** Daily 10am–5pm; closed holidays.

## Napa Beyond the Wineries

Don't bother with the touristy wine train that traverses Napa County; it's a trap on which you're required to eat their mediocre food, and you can't get off and on as you wish (though they do have the opportunity to visit a few wineries en route).

**diRosa Preserve ★** Some 2,200 works of art are kept on 900 stunning acres, centering on a 35-acre pond. Though the main gallery is closed for renovation through late 2017, much of the grounds and its works (delightfully fractured, wild, avant-garde experiments, many of the kinetic variety, and every one of them by Bay Area artists) are still accessible. You can pay $5 and browse the collection on your own or take one of three 90-minute tours ($12, including the $5 admission), which give you an overview of the property's highlights, including the Historic Residence and the core of the collection. Students of landscaping and architecture won't want to miss it, nor will fans of eccentric contemporary art. Others may leave scratching their heads. But no one departs without sighing over the greenery at least once.

5200 Carneros Hwy. 121, Napa. dirosaart.org. ℂ **707/226-5991.** Wed–Sun 10am–4pm. Closed holidays. $5 adults, ages 12 and under free.

## Where to Stay in Napa Valley

Accommodations in Napa Valley run the gamut from standard motels and floral-and-lace Victorian-style B&Bs to world-class luxury retreats, all easily accessible from the main highway that stretches across the valley. Most of the romantically pastoral options (think hidden hillside spots with vineyard views or quaint small-town charmers) are on the outskirts of historic St. Helena, which has the best walking/shopping street (at least for now; Napa is on its way to surpassing it), and the equally storied, but more laid-back and afford-able spa town of **Calistoga.** The few commercial blocks of tiny **Yountville** have become a destination thanks to a number of famous restaurants (includ-ing the world-renowned **French Laundry ★★★,** p. 260) as well as a handful of high-end hotels and middle-end B&Bs. The most "reasonably priced" (a relative term in this high-priced area) choices are the B&Bs, small hotels, and national chain options in downtown Napa—the closest thing to a city in these parts—which also has some very of-the-moment restaurants. Vacation house rentals are another option, though they are harder to come by, due to local laws. No matter where you stay, you're just a few minutes (or less) away from world-class wineries.

### CALISTOGA

**Calistoga Ranch ★★★**   One of the most luxurious retreats in the region, this resort is set on an eastern mountainside on 157 pristine hidden-canyon acres, dotted with freestanding accommodations along hilly pathways that accommodate only foot and golf-cart traffic. As the area's newest uberluxe address, its rooms are also the most tricked out—and all are steps away from one of two swimming pools (one is adults-only), a gorgeous state-of-the-art indoor-outdoor spa, and a lakeside restaurant (open only to guests; it's good but not great). You'll also find free yoga and painting classes, stargazing excursions, and, completing the world-class experience, bicycles or Mercedes Benzes (available first-come, first-served) for use, free of charge.

580 Lommel Rd., Calistoga. calistogaranch.com. ℂ **707/254-2800.** 46 cottages. $745–$7,000 double. **Amenities:** Restaurant; concierge; spa; gym; Jacuzzi; outdoor pools; room service; free Wi-Fi.

**The Chanric Inn ★★★**   Art-filled contemporary decor, tons of thoughtful touches, an outdoor pool and hot tub, and hosts who ensure your every wish is granted make this hilltop retreat in a wide-porched, Victorian-style farm-house a fantastic choice in Calistoga. Each morning, hot coffee and biscotti sit outside guest-room doors, followed by a gourmet three-course champagne breakfast. Later in the day, guests are treated to hors d'oeuvres, wine, and a champagne nightcap, which can be enjoying on a garden patio with outdoor fireplace.

1805 Foothill Blvd., Calistoga. thechanric.com. ℂ **877/281-3671** or 707/942-4535. 7 units. $499–$599 double. Rates include breakfast. **Amenities:** Outdoor pool; hot tub; massage room; free Wi-Fi.

### Dr. Wilkinson's Hot Springs Resort ★

At this Calistoga institution, your money buys a simple, immaculately clean and comfy room (some with kitchenettes) along with access to multiple hot-spring pools. Buildings are distinctly 1950s-motel-style (standard room sizes, walls of brick tile, and a vintage neon sign out front), but the resort has gone to extra lengths to upgrade the rooms to a modern standard (think flatscreen TVs, iPod docking stations, nice textiles). The patios and outdoor courtyards are well-groomed, fitting places to unwind before exploring the shops and food along Lincoln Avenue. If you stay here, you can avail yourself of a standard pool plus a pair (indoor and outdoor) of pools fed by mineral water. Then, of course, there's this place's famously medicinal mud bath spa (p. 252). The resort also main-tains a few multi-room cottages nearby, which are terrific for families and well-priced.

1507 Lincoln Ave. (Hwy. 29, btw. Fairway and Stevenson aves.), Calistoga. drwilkinson. com. ℂ **707/942-4102.** 42 units. $249–$350 double; $164–$670 cottages. **Amenities:** Jacuzzi; 3 pools; spa; free Wi-Fi in lobby.

### Indian Springs Calistoga ★★★

With a spectacular spa with mud baths, massage, and other treatments; a geyser-heated Olympic-size pool; stunning meditative grounds; and a solid and well-priced restaurant, Sam's Social Club, this is one of the best places to stay for a resort-style experience without the outlandish price tag of many upscale getaways in the area. Immaculate and spacious contemporary rooms are scattered in freestanding buildings around the expansive property. It's so relaxed here that if you don't want to walk from your room to the spa or to the bar (where you can try house-made beer or a spectacular artisan cocktail), you can simply hop on one of the complimentary bikes—in your soft, comfy robe, if you like. Don't forget to leave a note on the gratitude tree.

1712 Lincoln Ave., Calistoga. indianspringscalistoga.com. ℂ **844/378-3635** or 707/709-8139. 115 units. $339–$589 double. **Amenities:** Restaurant; Jacuzzi; outdoor mineral pool; spa; free Wi-Fi.

### Roman Spa Hot Springs Resort ★

It's clean, not pricey for a double, and well located (just a block off Calistoga's main street), so try not to worry that there's nothing Roman or even remotely chic about this quaint place. There are three mineral pools on site (one's an outdoor whirlpool), and mud baths and massage are available. The two-bedroom units with kitchens are good for families.

1300 Washington St., Calistoga. romanspahotsprings.com. ℂ **800/914-8957** or 707/942-4441. 60 units. $209–$279 double. **Amenities:** 3 mineral pools; sauna; spa; coin-op laundry, free Wi-Fi.

## NAPA

**Best Western Plus Elm House Inn ★★** One of the best values in Napa, this four-building inn has spacious and attractive rooms, with lovely landscaping, a hot tub on the patio, and experts behind the desk (they're helpful in setting up wine tasting itineraries for first timers). There are all sorts of extras, including a good breakfast (with made-to-order items!) and freshly baked cookies in the afternoon. If walking stairs is an issue for you, be sure to ask the staff for a ground-level room or an upstairs room in a building with an elevator. The hotel is within walking distance of Napa's downtown center and close to Highway 29, the region's thoroughfare; wineries are mere minutes away.

800 California Blvd., Napa. bestwestern.com. ℂ **888/849-1997** or 707/255-1831. 22 units. $139–$259 double. Rates include breakfast. **Amenities:** Hot tub; laundry facilities; free Wi-Fi.

**Cedar Gables Inn ★★** In 1892, Edward S. Churchill commissioned the noted British architect Ernest Coxhead to create this magnificent, 10,000-square-foot Tudor mansion as a wedding present for his engaged son. Today it attracts honeymooning couples visiting the area, with romantic rooms, especially the four with fireplaces (five have whirlpool tubs and all come with a bottle of complimentary port). Guests mingle in the evening in front of a roaring fireplace in the English tavern for wine and cheese; breakfast in the mornings is a sumptuous three-course feast.

486 Coombs St. (at Oak St.), Napa. cedargablesinn.com. ℂ **800/309-7969** or 707/224-7969. 9 units. $189–$329 double. Rates include full breakfast. **Amenities:** Free Wi-Fi.

**Napa River Inn ★★** Located on the (sometimes) picturesque Napa riverfront, steps from downtown's best restaurants and shopping, this boutique hotel in a historic building and two annexes hits a homerun by paying attention to the details. That means that, along with a smartly appointed room swathed in tasteful contemporary decor, you get local bath products, breakfast delivered to your room, in-room coffee, nightly wine tastings, and rides to town. Bonus: It's on the same block as impossible-to-resist Sweetie Pies bakery and **Angèle ★★** restaurant (see next page).

500 Main St., Napa. napariverinn.com. ℂ **855/516-1090.** 66 units. $239–$599 double. Rates include breakfast and evening wine. **Amenities:** Spa; free parking; free use of bikes; gourmet market and wine shop; free Wi-Fi.

## YOUNTVILLE

**Maison Fleurie ★★** This charming inn comprises three ivy-covered houses, so the digs vary greatly, depending on whether you're in the Provencal-style main house, in the carriage house, or the bakery-turned-guesthouse. If having a private balcony, patio, or Jacuzzi tub is important, be sure to read the website descriptions carefully. All rooms are cozy, though, with comfortable beds and private bathrooms. The lovingly tended grounds include a pool and a hot tub. A generous breakfast starts the day; end it in style with afternoon hors d'oeuvres and wine as well as evening cookies (also complimentary).

6529 Yount St. (btw. Washington St. and Yountville Cross Rd.), Yountville. maison fleurienapa.com. ⓒ **800/788-0369** or 707/944-2056. 13 units. $269–$399 double. Rates include breakfast and afternoon wine reception. **Amenities:** Jacuzzi; outdoor pool; free use of bikes; free Wi-Fi.

# Where to Eat in Napa Valley

Napa Valley's restaurants draw as much attention to the region as its award-winning wineries. Nowhere else in the state are kitchens as deft at mixing fresh seasonal, local, organic produce into edible magic, which means that menus change constantly to reflect the best available ingredients. Add that to a great bottle of wine, and you have one heck of an eating experience. Here are some picks, from an affordable diner to a once-in-a-lifetime culinary experience, and everything in between.

## CALISTOGA

**Solbar** ★★ CALIFORNIA  There's no greater compliment for a hotel restaurant than to have a loyal local following, and this restaurant at Solage Calistoga resort and spa—the sister property of uberluxury resort Auberge de Soleil—has that and then some. It has exactly the kind of atmosphere you want for literally every meal: plush patio environs (complete with couches!) and inside dining for breakfast and lunch, and cozy-chic indoor evening dining accompanied by optional outdoor fire-pit snuggling. Still, surroundings will take you only so far; the farm-fresh menu here takes you the rest of the way with innovative, flavorful, and flat-out gorgeous courses. Another perk? They serve food continually from breakfast through dinner, allowing you to grab a bite the second you want it.

755 Silverado Trail, Calistoga. solagecalistoga.com. ⓒ **707/226-0850.** Reservations recommended. Breakfast $14–$21; lunch $19–$28; dinner $25–$40. Daily 7am–9:30pm.

## NAPA

**Angèle Restaurant & Bar** ★★ COUNTRY FRENCH  Whether you're seated in the cozy dining room or on the riverfront patio, you can count on Angèle to deliver a delicious downtown Napa experience. It's not just that its design is a case study on how to do a restaurant right (though it is), or that the seasonally inspired menu elevates familiar French fare while holding on to local favorites like crispy roast chicken (it does). It's all of it put together—alongside the pro hospitality of owner Bettina Rouas, who is almost always on hand. Add a bottle of wine and you've got the makings of a beautiful dining memory.

540 Main St. (in the Hatt Building), Napa. www.angelerestaurant.com. ⓒ **707/252-8115.** Reservations recommended. Main courses $17–$32. Sun–Thurs 11:30am–9pm; Fri–Sat 11:30am–10pm.

**Bistro Don Giovanni** ★★ ITALIAN   North of downtown, right where the atmosphere changes from town to country, this beloved Italian restaurant delivers good-time vibes whether you sit inside the huge bright dining room, on the wrap-around terrace, or at the bar (one of the friendliest around). It's good for practically any occasion, from date night to family gatherings to business lunches. (It's also open lunch through dinner, so you can eat at off times if you like.) The pizza and house-made pasta are undeniably delicious, but I'm always seduced by the beet-and-haricot-vert salad and seared salmon with buttermilk mashed potatoes and chive butter. The best part? While there are seasonal changes, most of the menu stays the same—whatever you fall in love with on this trip, you'll likely be able to enjoy again next time you visit.

4110 Howard Lane (on Hwy. 29), Napa. bistrodongiovanni.com. ✆ **707/224-3300.** Main courses $18–$30. Daily 11:30am–10pm.

**Morimoto** ★★ JAPANESE   Continuing the Napa parade of chefs you watch on TV, this shockingly large, industrial-chic restaurant is the offering of Masaharu Morimoto of *Iron Chef* fame. No mere vanity project, Morimoto calls this his flagship, and the food certainly is worthy of that moniker. It can be hard to decide what to order—the menu is very extensive—but specials include tofu made fresh tableside, creative sushi offerings, and salads crafted from ingredients freshly picked on nearby farms. I tend to have the best experience ordering from the appetizers, but, if you're adventurous and well-funded, you may want to put your fate in the chef's hands and opt for the $120 omakase tasting menu. Along with 200 sakes, Morimoto serves a fine selection of wines from nearby vineyards. Late-night diners rejoice: The dining room stays open until 10pm Sunday through Thursday and 11pm on Friday and Saturday, while the lounge stays open a good hour later.

610 Main St., Napa. morimotonapa.com. ✆ **707/252-1600.** Main courses $36–$44. Reservations recommended. Sun–Thurs 11:30am–2:30pm and 5pm–midnight, Fri–Sat 11:30am–2:30pm and 5pm–1am.

**Oxbow Public Market** ★★ ECLECTIC/CONTEMPORARY AMERICAN   Food lovers simply must stop by this co-op gourmet marketplace in downtown Napa. Both a place to eat and drink and a destination for buying local ingredients and edible gifts, this spacious, welcoming hall with centerpiece seating is one of my favorite places to dine, because everything here is so good. Grab an ultrafresh taco from C Casa (they also have insane gluten-free donuts at their gluten-free kiosk). Throw back oysters and bubbly at Hog Island Oyster Co. (on their shaded patio, if desired). Score some fresh spices at Whole Spice. Treat yourself to some of my favorite ice cream at organic Three Twins or a cupcake from Kara's Cupcakes. Along with outstanding food, you'll find some of the best prices in the valley.

610 & 644 First St., Napa. oxbowpublicmarket.com. Daily 10am–9pm; closed Thanksgiving, Christmas, and New Year's Day.

**Torc** ★★ FARM-TO-TABLE CONTEMPORARY AMERICAN   Bright, lively, and relaxed, with high ceilings, rough-hewn-stone-wall environs, and refined contemporary American cooking, this upbeat, sexy spot is a prime dinner haunt for locals in downtown Napa. Perhaps it's because you can sense this is a restaurant with heart, thanks to the ever-involved husband-and-wife owners Sean and Cynthia O'Toole, who oversee the cuisine, wine selection, cocktail menu, and everything in between. But it's also surely the food—like irresistible deviled eggs with pickled onions and bacon, lobster risotto, or Akaushi Beef short rib with blue oyster mushroom, fava beans, Fiddler's Green fennel, and polenta—served alongside an impressive wine list, including unexpected by-the-glass options. *Tip:* Pop in for happy hour (5–6:30pm) for $6 wines and $5 bites.

1140 Main St., Napa. torcnapa.com. © **707/252-3292.** Main courses $29–$34. Wed–Mon 5–9:30pm.

## ST. HELENA

### Farmstead at Long Meadow Ranch ★ AMERICAN FARMHOUSE
A country-chic dining room and contemporary seasonal cuisine make this a favorite locals' spot in St. Helena, especially for brunch. But anytime's a good time to indulge in the generous servings of hearty, locally inspired American fare such as pork hash (at brunch) or blackened trout with green tomatoes. The Heritage St. Louis Ribs with green-apple coleslaw and barbecue sauce is a specialty worth devouring. Happy hour, held from 4 to 6pm Monday through Thursday, is a fun way to kick off the evening, or nosh through a complete meal, with $3.50 beer, $9 to $10 house wines, and a menu of filling nibbles like a fully loaded charcuterie board, wings, and deviled eggs. An adjoining cafe opens earlier for caffeine addicts, and a general store is full of edible mementos.

738 Main St., St. Helena. longmeadowranch.com. © **707/963-4555.** Sun 11am–9:30pm, Mon–Thurs 11:30am–9:30pm, Fri–Sat 11am–10pm.

### Gott's Roadside ★
I can't help but feel offended to fork over 80 bucks for a burger, fries, and shakes lunch for four. But that doesn't stop diners from lining up at this original drive-in (with a popular outpost in San Francisco's Ferry Building) to feast on upscale diner classics at outdoor picnic tables. Formerly called Taylor's Refresher, it's been slinging burgers since 1949 and looks it. But along with classic burgers and fries on the menu, you'll find gourmet salads and fish sandwiches. Beware if it's cold or rainy, because every seat is outdoors and not all are sheltered. A third branch, pressed from the same mold, exists at the **Oxbow Public Market ★★** (see listing above) in central Napa.

933 Main St., St. Helena. gotts.com. © **707/963-3486.** Main courses $7–$15. Open daily 7am–9pm. Summer hours 7am–10pm.

### Terra/Bar Terra ★★ CONTEMPORARY AMERICAN
Casual or dressy dining—you choose, at this quiet two-in-one restaurant. One side (Bar Terra) houses a relaxed bar and dining room with a few tables and terrific (and unusual) small plates and entrees, while the original Terra showcases James Beard Award–winning chef Hiro Sone's awe-inspiring ability to master and borrow from French, Italian, and Japanese cooking traditions and make them

his own. Crudo, pasta, fish, steak, it's all done perfectly here. Cocktails are made from fruits and herbs grown in the owners' garden. Desserts are also primo, so save room.

1345 Railroad Ave., St. Helena. terrarestaurant.com. ℗ **707/963-8931.** Reservations recommended. Bar: Plates $7–$26. Dining room: 4-course menu $89; 5-course $109; 6-course $126; chef's menu changes nightly. Thurs–Mon 6–9:30pm. Closed 2 weeks early Jan.

## YOUNTVILLE

**Ad Hoc ★★** INTERNATIONAL   For those who'd like to try star chef Thomas Keller's cuisine (see **French Laundry ★★★**, next page), but also pay rent this month, Ad Hoc is the solution. Most famous for its fried chicken dinners (served only on Mon), the restaurant offers a daily changing, prix fixe menu, served family style. The fare ranges across the globe for inspiration—one day you might get jambalaya, another day the menu will feature shrimp scampi—the one constant being the high quality of both the ingredients and the cooking. Want to go even more casual? Pop by the adjoining eatery, **Addendum,** on Thursday, Friday, and Saturday between 11am and 2pm to buy a fabulous, homey $17 boxed lunch of ribs, pulled pork, or fried chicken (and sometimes lobster rolls), which you can take to go or eat in a grassy area dotted with picnic tables. (*Tip:* You can also order them online and pop in to pick them up. Hello picnic perfection!)

6475 Washington St., Yountville. adhocrestaurant.com. ℗ **707/944-2487.** Thurs–Mon 5–10pm, Sun 10am–1pm. Prix fixe $55.

**Bottega Ristorante ★★** ITALIAN   Emmy-winning TV host Michael Chiarello was a chef first, and here he goes back to his roots. As at many other restaurants in the area, the ingredients are proudly locavore, but here the cooking is decidedly Italian. When the weather's chilly, there are few more pleasant places to linger than in front of the fireplace in Bottega's dining room, with a glass of local red in your hand and a perfectly plated pasta within your fork's reach. On warmer days and eves, the patio's posh seating (with outdoor fireplaces) is the place to be.

V Marketplace, 6525 Washington St., Yountville. botteganapavalley.com. ℗ **707/945-1050.** Main entrees $15–$25 lunch, more at dinner. Reservations recommended. Tues–Sun 11:30am–3pm and daily 5–9:30pm.

**Bouchon Bakery ★★** FRENCH BAKERY   It's expensive and you'll likely have to wait in line, but you should pop by this Yountville spot, if only to be able to answer "yes" when everyone later asks you if you went to Bouchon Bakery. The attraction: a (relatively) affordable taste of world-famous chef Thomas Keller's greatness in the form of awesome coffee (get iced on hot days), freshly baked breads (and sandwiches), luscious pastries, and salads. Take 'em to go for picnic provisions or sit at one of the few tables outside. *Tip:* For faster service, you can order online and schedule pickup.

V Marketplace, 6528 Washington St., Yountville. thomaskeller.com. ℗ **707/944.2253.** Sandwiches $8–$9.25, pastries $3.50–$6. Daily 7am–7pm.

**The French Laundry** ★★★ FRENCH   Repeatedly recognized as one of the best restaurants in the world for nearly 2 decades, chef Thomas Keller's original flagship culinary shrine is about as far away from an average dining experience as you can get. A multicourse affair that literally takes hours to complete, it consists of plate after plate of bite-size edible works of art. Some hinted at on the menu, many others arriving unexpectedly, all courses are presented to guests by an impeccably well-trained staff that commands attention throughout the meal with elaborate explanations of what you're about to eat. It's A-list dining theater to be sure. Alas, it's hard to leave here without feeling about as overfed as a goose destined to become foie gras. But that doesn't stop French Laundry from being on every foodie's bucket list.

6640 Washington St., Yountville. frenchlaundry.com. ✆ **704/944-2380.** Tasting menu $295. Reservations essential. Daily lunch Fri–Sun 11am–1pm, dinner 5:30–9:15pm.

# SONOMA COUNTY

Less developed than Napa, Sonoma's gaggle of ordinary towns, ranches, and wineries offer a genuine backcountry ambience—and a lower density of wineries, restaurants, and hotels. But that doesn't mean there isn't plenty to do and see. Low-key wine tastings are held at small, family-owned wineries scattered along the woodsy roads of this 17-mile-long, 7-mile-wide valley bordered by the Mayacama mountains to the east and the Sonomas to the west.

## Sonoma Valley Wineries

Unlike Northern Sonoma, Sonoma Valley is relatively condensed: A small cluster of wineries surround Sonoma's town square, with a string of additional stops off the highway as you head south or north along the main highway. While planning your route, get a copy of the Official Visitors Map put out by Sonoma County Tourism Bureau (sonomacounty.com; ✆ **800/576-6662**); online, you can order a variety of information to be sent to you. If you want to range farther afield, see Northern Sonoma County wineries, p. 265.

**Benziger Family Winery** ★★★   A 20-minute drive north of Sonoma, family-run Benziger offers one of the region's better tours, or actually a selection of them. A 45-minute tram tour ($25) whisks you around the property, takes you into wine caves 70 feet under the hillside, teaches about cooperage (barrel making), and of course includes actual tasting of their wines; a more intimate, slower-paced cave tour and tasting ($40) lets you walk through and taste in the atmospheric caves; and a $50 adventure (limited to 10 guests) explores the winery, vineyards, caves, and wines themselves (in other words, there's plenty of sipping going on). Whichever you embark upon, you'll learn how the all-organic, sustainable winery goes about making good wine without despoiling the land. In winter, sheep wander the property, browsing the grass around the vines; all organic waste is recycled, and the winery even runs an "insectary" where beneficial bugs are encouraged to breed. All in all, these are some of most well-rounded tours on the market, and something about the facility—maybe its idealism—gives you a sense that you're not just being herded through. If you want to skip the schooling and go straight for the drink, it's $20 to taste a variety of wines in the tasting room.

1883 London Ranch Rd., Glen Ellen. benziger.com. © **888/490-2739.** Daily 10am–5pm.

**Gundlach Bundschu Winery ★★** The oldest continually running family-operated winery in California, this is the quintessential Sonoma winery—relaxed and playful, yet wine obsessed. It's also got great wines to try and the best picnic grounds in the valley. (Hike to the top of Towles' Hill for a sensational view.) Fantastic additional activities (Midsummer Mozart Festival, film fests, awesome concerts) give even more reason to scope out GB.

2000 Denmark St., Sonoma. gunbun.com. © **707/938-5277.** Daily 11am–5:30pm (closes 4:30pm Nov–Apr). 1-hr. tours by appointment only. Book in advance for groups of 8 or more.

**Robledo Family Winery ★★★** This quiet winery is one of the great personal success stories of the area. The family patriarch came to America from Michoacán, Mexico, in 1968, and, starting as a laborer for the respected Christian Brothers winemakers, worked his way up bit by bit, until he finally owned his own spread. There are "live barrels" in the tasting room, which means they're full of aging wine, and the smell throughout is marvelous. They don't do tours, but one of Mr. Robledo's kids is usually on duty, so you're bound to have a truly interesting and possibly inspiring conversation. Tastings are $15 for six current-release wines, $20 for reserve wines, and $25 for a flight of reserve cabernet sauvignon. Bottles, which you can't buy anywhere else, start at $22. This winery received a huge honor in early 2008 when Mexican president Felipe Calderón, on the first visit to the region by any Mexican president, visited only the Robledo winery. He, too, is from Michoacán.

21901 Bonness Rd., Sonoma. robledofamilywinery.com. © **707/939-6903.** Mon–Sat 10am–5pm, Sun 11am–4pm.

## Sonoma Valley Beyond the Wineries

**Jack London State Historic Park ★** The famous writer's ashes are buried at this historic park, where he spent his final years and where his wife stayed on afterward. London's study, in the cottage ($4 adults, $2 seniors 62+ and students 13–18, free for ages 12 and under), contains artwork from his stories and items he picked up on his travels. Elsewhere on the property is a ruin of a magnificent house London tried to build—it burned down before it was done. There's an easy half-mile trail through the bucolic surroundings, and plenty of spots for a pastoral picnic. On weekends, docents give tours at 11am, 1pm, 2pm, and 3pm, and during summer, an awesome Broadway Under the Stars season features pros from NYC and beyond.

2400 London Ranch Rd., Glen Ellen. jacklondonpark.com. © **707/938-5216.** Daily 9:30am–5pm, museum 10am–5pm; cottage noon–4pm. Park entrance $10 per vehicle, $5 per person for walk-ins.

**Depot Park Museum** ★   Just north of Sonoma Plaza, the Sonoma Valley Historical Society's often-overlooked museum is full of intriguing artifacts, such as a painted stage curtain from the plaza's long-gone Union Hotel, complete with era ads. The staffers in charge are generous and excited; ask to hear the 1850s Swiss music box and they'll tune it up for you. Not all exhibits are labeled, so ask questions—they love telling tales here.

270 First St. West, Sonoma. depotparkmuseum.org. ✆ **707/938-1762.** Fri–Sun 1–4pm.

**Luther Burbank Home & Gardens** ★   Horticulturalists will be drawn here—gardeners revere Burbank for developing more than 800 new varieties of plants, particularly roses. His former home is now a national historic landmark, and the surrounding acre of land contains many of his creations.

Santa Rosa Ave. at Sonoma Ave., Santa Rosa. lutherburbank.org. ✆ **707/524-5445.** Free admission. Open until sunset.

**TrainTown** ★★   Even folks from San Francisco drive north to spend a half-day at this sweet, woodsy play area founded in 1968. The main attraction is a quarter-scale steam train ($6.75 per person), which meanders around 4 miles of track, stopping so you can pet and feed goats (bring quarters for the food dispenser!). There are also six small (and mostly unintimidating) amusement park rides ($2.75 per ride per person, 6-ride coupons $15) and a defunct steam train that's free to all. Every time I come, I feel refreshed by the sheer simple joy this place brings, plus the notion that the family behind the park hasn't sold out or gone glitzy like most of the area. Founder Stanley L. Frank, an Oakland printing magnate and model train enthusiast, continues to meet his original goal to make TrainTown "a 10-acre elaborate tabletop railroad, which

## A PAEAN TO peanuts

Fans of the "Peanuts" comics should try to spend a few hours in happy absorption at the surprisingly lavish **Charles M. Schulz Museum and Research Center** ★★★ (schulzmuseum.org; ✆ **707/579-4452**), at 2301 Hardies Lane in Santa Rosa. Sparky, as he was called, made ungodly amounts of money off the licensing of his creations, and so his estate has the financial wherewithal to burnish his reputation at this two-story gallery-cum-library, which would be worthy of any major artist.

There's lots to see and do here. Of course, there are tons of strips from the entire run of the series—always the original, never copies—and biographical information about Sparky, who died in 2000 (this place opened in 2002). Even more interesting are tributes by other artists, such as a life-size Snoopy made of Baccarat crystal, Christo's *Wrapped Snoopy House*, and a wall mosaic of 3,588 tiles by Yoshitero Otari. The museum preserves Schulz's work room, with its worn drawing board, bottles of Higgins ink, and an unremarkable book selection. Also fun are the non-stop showings of classic TV specials and movies. (Kids will particularly enjoy that, as well as the outdoor play area.) The museum is open daily 11am to 5pm weekdays and 10am to 5pm weekends (closed Tues in low season, fall through spring). Admission is $12 adults, $8 seniors, $5 youth and students.

is outdoors and rideable; where sense of direction is lost, and best appreciated by the under sophisticated and over sophisticated."

20264 Sonoma Ave., Sonoma. traintown.com. ✆ **707/938-3812.** Summer daily 10am–5pm; fall–spring Fri–Sun 10am–5pm. Closed when raining and Thanksgiving and Christmas Day.

## Where to Stay in Sonoma Valley

The biggest choice is whether to stay in downtown Sonoma, with easy access to its walkable shopping and dining square, or anywhere else in the valley, which promises small-town surroundings and a guaranteed drive to any activities. Regardless, you're destined to spend time behind the wheel, as the wineries and attractions are scattered. Keep in mind that in peak season and on weekends, most B&Bs and hotels require a minimum 2-night stay. Of course, that's assuming you can find a vacancy; make reservations as far in advance as possible. If you are having trouble finding a room, call the **Sonoma Valley Visitors Bureau** (sonomavalley.com; ✆ **866/996-1090** or 707/996-1090), which can refer you to lodgings with rooms to spare. The **Bed and Breakfast Association of Sonoma Valley** (sonomabb.com; ✆ **800/969-4667**) can also refer you to a B&B that belongs to the association.

### GLEN ELLEN/KENWOOD

**Beltane Ranch** ★★★   This century-old working ranch just about defines the word bucolic—and throw "charming" in there for good measure. Spacious rooms, each with its own sitting area, are filled with well-chosen antiques. The 105-acre estate is laced with hiking trails, gardens, and a good tennis court for those who want to work up a sweat. Breakfast is superb, with eggs and produce grown right on the ranch. Guests have a tough time leaving Beltane's wide wrap-around porch; it's the perfect place to while away the afternoon-into-evening, glass of vino in hand. *Tip:* Request upstairs rooms for the best views.

11775 Sonoma Hwy./Hwy. 12, Glen Ellen. beltaneranch.com. ✆ **707/833-4233.** 5 units, 1 cottage. $195–$625 double. Rates include breakfast. **Amenities:** Tennis court; free Wi-Fi.

**Kenwood Inn & Spa** ★★   You'll feel like you've landed in Italy when you drive up to this Tuscan-inspired resort with its honey-colored villas, flower-filled flagstone courtyard, and splendid views of vineyard-covered hills. The rooms are just as Italianate, swathed in imported tapestries and velvets, and filled with custom-made imported furniture. Each gets a fireplace, balcony (except those on the ground floor), and spa tub. The lack of TVs is intentional; this is a place to slow down and be in the moment. As for the included buffet breakfast, get ready to skip lunch—you won't need it after the feast served here.

10400 Sonoma Hwy., Kenwood. kenwoodinn.com. ✆ **800/353-6966** or 707/833-1293. 29 units. $372–$589 double. $35 resort fee includes sparkling wine at check-in, breakfast, day pass to Parkpoint Health Club, and wine reception. 2-night minimum weekends. Children 17 and under not encouraged. **Amenities:** Spa; outdoor pool; 2 outdoor hot tubs; concierge; free Wi-Fi.

## SONOMA

**Fairmont Sonoma Mission Inn & Spa** ★★ Located on 12 meticulously groomed acres, this is Sonoma's only world-class resort. Known for its old-world looks—it's a stunning three-story replica of a California mission, built in 1927 and painted pink, plus newer luxury wings—it's even more famous for its unparalleled spa facilities. Along with naturally heated artesian mineral pools and whirlpools, it features a beautiful indoor pool and spa area, a great gym (with yoga), plus access to golf, tennis, and excellent white-tablecloth dining. Rooms are elegant, and many have fireplaces.

100 Boyes Blvd., Sonoma. fairmont.com/sonoma. © **800/441-1414** or 707/938-9000. 226 units. $259–$1,259 double. Rates include free wine tasting (4:30–5:30pm) and free bottle of wine. Valet parking free for day use, $35 for overnight guests. **Amenities:** 2 restaurants; golf course; health club, fitness center, spa; Jacuzzi; sauna; 3 outdoor pools; babysitting; bike rental; concierge; room service; free Wi-Fi.

**Sonoma's Best Guest Cottages** ★★ These adorable little houses were once grubby workmen's cottages for field hands. Today, they've been upgraded to become terrific mini-homes for tourists. Candy-colored and sweet, they're equipped with kitchens, living rooms, big bathrooms, wide-plank wood floors, and outdoor sitting areas. Their location 2 miles east of Sonoma town makes for an ideal home base to explore both counties. Though they're meant as cozy retreats for two, you might be able to squeeze a tot or two in with you, and the maintenance standards couldn't be higher. Bonus: Their small on-premises market cafe offers local cheeses, wines, coffee, and sandwiches and salads. Check the website for last-minute deals on available rooms; they tend to be good.

1190 East Napa St., Sonoma. sonomasbestcottages.com. © **707/933-0340.** 4 units. $203–$399 cottage. **Amenities:** Private garden; full kitchen; BBQ grill on request; free Wi-Fi.

**Sonoma Creek Inn** ★ An excellent value, the Sonoma Creek Inn is sweetly decorated (crisp white bedspreads, fun lampshades, the odd tile mosaic in the wall) and fitted with flatscreen TVs and in-room coffeemakers. Rooms are a tad more spacious than they are at other converted motels in the area, and an extra $20 buys you a balcony or a pleasant walled patio with your own fountain—a nice touch. Boyes Boulevard is a little noisy (well, for Sonoma), and the neighborhood is strictly farm community—it needs some grooming but is safe. That said, there is Creekside Café next door, which serves breakfast and lunch. Check the website's special offers.

239 Boyes Blvd., Sonoma. sonomacreekinn.com. © **888/712-1289** or 707/939-9463. 16 units. $155–$269. Free parking. **Amenities:** Concierge; wine-tasting passes; free Wi-Fi.

## Where to Eat in Sonoma

**Fremont Diner** ★★ DINER This adorable roadside diner with old-fashioned aesthetics and homey, hearty cooking has Bay Area foodies making a special trip. Come here for fluffy omelets, serious coffee, brisket hash, fried chicken, pies, and gourmet milkshakes so thick they need a spoon. When the weather's nice, people eat outside, though the real character here is indoors.

2660 Fremont Dr., Sonoma. thefremontdiner.com. ✆ **707/938-7370.** Main courses $9–$13. Mon–Wed 8am–3pm, Thurs–Sun 8am–9pm.

**The Girl and the Fig** ★★ PROVENÇAL   One of the longest-running Sonoma favorites for top-quality food, this acclaimed restaurant's "girl" is chef/proprietress Sondra Bernstein, known for her charcuterie platters and her talent for mixing Provençal cuisine with local Sonoma ingredients. On warm days and eves, the patio seating is special, and the wine list is always a treat. It's a delightful place to dine, but if you don't make it here, know that you can now buy Bernstein's jams and chutneys (and yes, some are made with figs) at stores around the area; they make a great gift.

110 W. Spain St., Sonoma. www.thegirlandfig.com. ✆ **707/938-3634.** Main courses $17–$26. Mon–Thurs 11:30am–10pm, Fri 11am–11pm, Sat 8am–11pm, Sun 10am–10pm.

**La Bamba** ★★   Usually parked just around the corner from fancy **Sonoma Mission Inn** ★★ (see listing above), this true locals' spot is a taco truck with extremely tasty, classic Mexican grub, catering to many of the people working the land—the ones who prune the vines and make the wine happen, most of them immigrants from Mexico, Colombia, and other Latin countries. Tacos are just $1.50 each and fillings change daily (though you can usually get the delish pastor tacos).

Usually parked at 18155 Sonoma Hwy., Sonoma. Daily noon–midnight. No phone.

# Northern Sonoma County

Northern Sonoma embraces a variety of appellations—Dry Creek Valley, Alexander Valley, Russian River Valley—each with at least one cluster of wineries. Getting from one appellation to another along the rural roads is part of the fun, provided you have a designated driver. Alas, there's no way for us to include all the wineries worth visiting, but the following selection will get you started. Once you head out, you're bound to stumble upon many more.

## NORTHERN SONOMA COUNTY WINERIES
### Geyserville
**Francis Ford Coppola Winery** ★★   Owned by the legendary director, this winery is, not surprisingly, perfectly directed, from its wine tours to its movie memorabilia to its utterly chic and fun swimming pool, where you can reserve four lounge chairs and your own dressing "cabine" for the day ($170 to $215, including cans of sparkling bubbly for adults; rates vary on weekends and holidays). Yes, the price is insane, but when the thermostat hits 110° and your server delivers yet another perfect iced cocktail and a crisp salad as you linger under the shade of an oversize umbrella, it may seem worth every penny. Even if you skip the pool, you'll enjoy a glass case full of Coppola's filmmaking awards, including the Oscars he won for *The Godfather* and a giant bamboo cage used as a prop in *Apocalypse Now*. The 45-minute tour (daily at 11:30am, 1pm, and 2:30pm) is a good deal; for $32, you see the

vineyard, learn about the vintner's grape philosophy, pop into the barrel room to taste wine right out of barrels, and wind up with a sampling of some reserve wines. Without the tour, tastings are free (for two pours), with additional offerings starting at $20. This is also one of the few wineries where you'll find picnic tables that are actually in the vineyards.

300 Via Archimedes, Geyserville. francisfordcoppolawinery.com. ℂ **707/857-1400.** Daily 11am–6pm.

## Guerneville

**Korbel** ★★  One of the best historical tours is at the home of America's best-selling sparkling wine maker—which, for reasons that are still not entirely clear, is permitted to call itself a champagne maker (usually only wineries in the Champagne region of France may do so). Korbel was started here in 1882 by a Czech cigar-box maker who got in trouble back home for political unrest; his mom snuck him out of prison by smuggling civilian clothes under her skirts during a visit. That story is interesting enough, but the place is full of stuff like that—for example, the cleared area in front of the work buildings was once the site of the train line to San Francisco (50-min. tours of the property start in the old railway station). The old winery is now a history center, with lots of period winemaking implements and photographs, including some fascinating snaps of the property when it was full of redwood stumps. (They called Guerneville "Stumptown" then.) Guides keep things witty and fresh; you'll learn a lot about the tools and the process of champagne-making wrapped in a mini-history of the area. Free tours (which include four tastings) run daily, every hour in winter, every 45 minutes in summer. Mid-April to mid-October, daily except Mondays at 1pm and 3pm, there's also a rose garden tour: The rose gardens feature more than 250 varieties of roses, many of them antiques planted by the first Czech immigrants. Interestingly, although 1.3 million cases a year are made here, only eight people work in the factory, which probably means your tour group will outnumber them.

13250 River Rd., Guerneville. korbel.com. ℂ **707/824-7000.** Shop/tasting room open daily 10am–4:30pm.

## Healdsburg

**Armida** ★★★  People come from miles around to sit out on Armida's generous wooden deck overlooking a manmade reedy pond, sipping wine, sharing food they've brought, and enjoying great photo ops. Choose to settle in the sun or in the shade and hang out for as long as you like. The winery just asks that you drink only their wine on property. (If you don't, as they explain it, "it upsets our dog.") The tasting center is relaxed, and the winemakers don't take the scene too seriously; one of its wines is called PoiZin (as in "the wine to die for") and the wine club is called Wino. Six specialty wines (usually three red, three white) can be sampled for $20. It's a warm-hearted place without a slice of pretension, but with very good vino.

2201 Westside Rd., Healdsburg. armida.com. ℂ **707/433-2222.** Daily 11am–5pm. Closed holidays.

**Bella Vineyards & Wine Caves** ★★    Arched doors built into the hillside (and visible from the parking lot) are the entrance to one of the coolest tasting areas you'll ever visit. Zins and Rhône varietals are poured here, in a cave complete with cafe tables and impossibly chic ambience. Tastes go for $15.

9711 W. Dry Creek Rd., Healdsburg. bellawinery.com. ✆ **866/572-3552** or 707/473-9171. Daily 11am–4:30pm. Appointment necessary for groups of 8 or more.

**Ferrari-Carano Vineyards & Winery** ★    One of the more big-business wineries in the area, this is also a place to ogle incredible gardens and views. In spring, wisteria vines burst with blooms and thousands of tulips brighten the already-gorgeous grounds; a formal Asian garden features rhododendron, Japanese arched bridges, boxwood, maples, magnolia, and roses. On sunny weekends you can sip a flight of wines while relaxing at umbrella-shaded tables on a beautiful terrace. Tours are offered daily at 10am, and they require reservations. The $10 tasting charge for four current releases is refunded with a $50 purchase, or for $25 you can enjoy a reserve tasting in the Enoteca Lounge.

8761 Dry Creek Rd., Healdsburg. From Hwy. 101, take Dry Creek Rd. exit west and go 9 miles. ferrari-carano.com. ✆ **707/433-6700.** Daily 10am–5pm. Tours Mon–Sat 10am with reservation.

**Preston of Dry Creek** ★★    One of the most charming wineries in Sonoma, this spacious, bucolic spot overflows with character, from its wisteria-shaded picnic tables to its bocce court (available to play on the weekends) to its farmhouse tasting room. Follow the neon sign's instruction and "drink zin," but also dabble in the Rhone varietals—and sample seasonal produce and bread made on location at the farm store. A $10 tasting, refundable with purchase, is a small price to pay for the fun you'll have. *Note:* No groups over eight.

9282 W. Dry Creek Rd. (about 1 mi w of Yoakim Bridge Rd.), Healdsburg. prestonofdry-creek.com. ✆ **707/433-3372.** Daily 11am–4:30pm.

## NORTHERN SONOMA BEYOND THE WINERIES

**Armstrong Redwoods State Reserve** ★★    This 805-acre reserve, 2 miles north of Guerneville, is a place of peace, silence, and very big redwood trees—some of them more than 300 feet tall and at least 1,400 years old. The moistness of the air means that when the sunlight does break through the dense ecosystem, it can draw steam off the bark of the mighty trees, creating a seriously beautiful environment. Save the entrance fee by parking at the visitor center and walking in. There are a few trails, but overall it's not busy, so it's often pin-drop quiet.

17000 Armstrong Woods Rd., Guerneville. www.parks.ca.gov/?page_id=450. ✆ **707/869-2015.** $8 per vehicle. 8am–1 hr. after sunset.

## WHERE TO STAY IN NORTHERN SONOMA

Santa Rosa, the most densely populated area, also has the most choices—ranging from B&Bs to motels to hotels—though it's not exactly in the middle of the vineyard action. If you want to immerse yourself in a community with true wine country flair, Healdsburg is the best choice, with a variety of places to stay, including some swanky boutique hotels. Laid-back Russian River attracts gay and lesbian Bay Area residents, who spend their days playing in or lounging by the lazy river. In between are many sweet towns and wooded enclaves offering places to lay your head.

## Guerneville

### Creekside Inn and Resort ★★

The thick redwood forests of the Russian River Valley are soothing, and so is the Creekside, a complex of apartments of varying sizes, all built on stilts above the forest floor. There are two options: an individually themed and designed bed-and-breakfast room (the waffles you'll get are marvelous and the rooms are adorable), or cottages with full kitchens (most have dishwashers and gas fireplaces, and all have private decks and screened-in porches). The staff here is genuinely friendly and laid-back, and there's also a pool. The pubs and coffee cafes of downtown Guerneville are a short walk away over a pedestrian bridge.

16180 Neeley Rd., Guerneville. creeksideinn.com. ✆ **707/869-3623.** 28 units. $109–$195 double; pricier cabins (up to $295) will easily house 6 people. **Amenities:** Pool; free Wi-Fi.

## Healdsburg

### Honor Mansion ★★★

Heading to wine country for your honeymoon? This is where you'll want to stay, and it truly is a mansion. With the exception of the Angel Oak room (which features a schmaltzy, off-putting mural of cherubim), the decor here is to die for, with each room decorated differently, featuring sleigh or wrought-iron beds, hand-carved wooden dressers, gazillion thread-count linens, electric fireplaces, and private patios (some rooms have two!). Every morning, coffee and biscotti arrive at your door at a pre-requested time; that's followed by a sumptuous buffet breakfast in the main house (guests choose between main-house rooms and free-standing cottages, including one swank one at the bottom of a historic water tower, with a roof-top spa tub). On-site: a 40-foot lap pool, tennis and basketball courts, a PGA-certified putting green, two competition bocce ball courts, croquet courts, and a quarter acre of zinfandel vines. Sorry, to keep the romantic atmosphere intact, kids under 16 are not welcome.

891 Grove St., Healdsburg. honormansion.com. ✆ **800-554-4667** or 703/433-4277. $355–$700 double. Rate includes breakfast and evening wine reception. **Amenities:** Pool; tennis courts; basketball courts; free Wi-Fi.

### Travelodge Healdsburg ★

While this motel is in a not-so-sexy, industrial part of town, its rates flat-out rock and its rooms do the job. You'll be happy if all you want is a clean room in an expensive area and easy access to the region's bucolic charms, which are less than 3 minutes away.

178 Dry Creek Rd., Healdsburg. travelodge.com. ✆ **800/499-0103** or 707/433-0101. 22 units. $89–$237 double. Free parking. **Amenities:** Free Wi-Fi.

## WHERE TO EAT IN HEALDSBURG

Healdsburg has the highest concentration of outstanding restaurants. Because most of them surround the square, you can easily indulge and then take a stroll to window shop and get a feel for local life.

**Chalkboard** ★★ SEASONAL REGIONAL Epitomizing the hyperlocal farm-to-table passion of Northern California chefs, this relaxed, two-room restaurant features artfully crafted small plates by chef Shane McAnelly. Rather than a specific cuisine, the daily-changing menu is inspired by produce from the restaurant's 3-acre garden as well as local farms. That means the freshly picked salads and crudo are accompanied by vibrant, ultrafresh house-made pastas, salmon, and steak. Fresh pretzels with cheddar cheese sauce, local wines, and creative cocktails round out the reasons why this is now a top choice in downtown Healdsburg. Sunday through Friday, if you don't have a reservation, pop by for a happy hour taste between 4:30 and 6:30pm.

29 North St. Healdsburg. chalkboardhealdsburg.com. ℂ **707/473-8030.** Main courses $16–$26. Reservations recommended. Mon–Fri 5pm–9pm. Sat–Sun 11:30am–9:30pm.

**El Farolito** ★★ MEXICAN There's some incredible authentic Mexican food in these parts, and this charming casual spot is one place to find it—with appealing atmosphere to boot. All the greatest hits are represented here—guacamole, enchiladas, fajitas, carnitas, fish tacos, even chicken or pork with mole—and they're all very good. What's less ordinary is the tequila and mezcal list. With more than 100 offerings, and pros behind the bar, you're destined to experience a fantastic margarita, shot, or both. Why not? You're on vacation!

128 Plaza St. Healdsburg. elfarolito2000.com. ℂ **707/433-2807.** Main courses $8–$18. Sun–Thurs 10am–9:30pm Fri–Sat 10am–10:30pm.

**Jimtown Store** ★★ DELI A gourmet country store with loads of charm, this is the place to stop for fantastic box lunches, gourmet picnic grub, and fun trinkets. A small seating area helps when you realize that what you've just ordered looks so good, you can't wait another minute to try it.

6706 State Hwy. 128, Healdsburg. jimtown.com. ℂ **707/433-1212.** Box lunches $12–$17. Mon–Fri 7am–5pm; Sat–Sun 7:30am–5pm; closes earlier in winter.

**Willi's Seafood & Raw Bar** ★ SEAFOOD There's something for everyone at this longtime festive hot spot; the Latin-inspired menu is large and diverse, comprising numerous small plates. Dozens of local wines are available by the glass, carafe, and full bottle. Outdoor seating is prime on summer evenings, while inside provides much-needed respite when the thermostat reaches for the cloudless skies.

403 Healdsburg Ave., Healdsburg. willisseafood.net. ℂ **707/433-9191.** Small plates $10–$15. Sun–Mon 5–9pm; Tues–Thurs 11:30am–9:30pm; Fri–Sat 11:30am–10pm.

# PLANNING YOUR TRIP TO SAN FRANCISCO

**12**

Spontaneity is fun, but to really get the most out of your NorCal adventure, a little prior planning goes a long way. In this chapter, you'll find a whole slew of travel-planning tips and information, including how to get to San Francisco, how to get around once you're in the city, and how to make the most of your visit. There's also an alphabetical listing of miscellaneous resources and organizations that you can turn to for even more trip-planning assistance.

## GETTING THERE

### By Plane

The northern Bay Area has two major airports: San Francisco International and Oakland International. Fifty major scheduled carriers serve **San Francisco International Airport** (SFO; flysfo.com), 12 miles directly south of downtown on U.S. Route 101. Drive time to downtown during rush hour is about 40 minutes; at other times, it's about 20 minutes. Ten miles south of downtown Oakland, at the Hegenberger Road exit from Interstate 880 (if heading north, take the 98th Avenue exit), **Oakland International Airport** (OAK; oaklandairport.com) has traditionally served passengers with East Bay destinations, but many San Franciscans prefer this less-crowded, more accessible airport; it takes about 35 minutes to get there from downtown San Francisco (traffic permitting). From either airport, you can also ride BART, an aboveground rail and subway system, to downtown San Francisco and the East Bay. For transportation details, see "Getting Into Town," below.

#### ARRIVING AT THE AIRPORT

Wherever you're coming from, international travelers arriving by air should be prepared for the possibility of delays when arriving in the United States. U.S. airports have considerably beefed up security at immigrations checkpoints, and clearing **Customs and Immigration** can take as long as 2 hours. You can try speeding up this process by enrolling in the Global Entry program (globalentry.gov), which allows expedited entry for pre-approved travelers.

## GETTING INTO TOWN
### From San Francisco International

One of the fastest and cheapest ways to get from SFO to the city is to take **BART** (Bay Area Rapid Transit; bart.gov; ✆ **415/989-2278**), which offers numerous stops within downtown San Francisco. This route, which takes about 35 minutes, avoids traffic and costs a heck of a lot less than taxis or shuttles. A BART ticket costs $8.95 (children under 4 ride free) for a one-way ride from SFO to the Embarcadero stop. Just jump on the airport's free shuttle bus to the international terminal, enter the BART station there, and you're on your way to San Francisco. Trains leave approximately every 15 minutes during operating hours (weekdays 4am–midnight, Sat 6am–midnight, and Sun 8am–midnight). See p. 274 for more information about how to ride BART.

> ### Traffic Alert
>
> Call ✆ **511** or visit www.511.org for up-to-the-minute information about public transportation and traffic.

A **taxicab** from SFO to Fisherman's Wharf costs about $60, plus tip, and takes around 30 minutes, traffic permitting. You can also opt for **Uber** and **Lyft**—taxi-like ride-service apps accessed only via cellphone. (If you don't have their apps on your smartphone and you plan on cabbing it, definitely download them, as they'll save you money to and from the airport as well as getting around town.)

**SuperShuttle** (supershuttle.com; ✆ **800/BLUE-VAN** [258-3826]) offers door-to-door airport service in a shared van with a few other passengers. Simply wait at the designated SuperShuttle pick-up spot outside the terminal. They will take you anywhere in the city, charging $17 per person to a residence or business; each additional person going to the same location is usually charged $8. (The same goes for the return trip to the airport.) Reservations are required for the return trip to the airport and should be made 1 day before departure. While the shuttle service usually works well, keep in mind that you could be the first one picked up and the last one dropped off, depending on your destination, so this trip could take a while. For $74, you can charter the entire van for up to 10 people, or reserve an **ExecuCar** private sedan ($65) for up to three people.

The San Mateo County Transit system, **SamTrans** (samtrans.com; ✆ **800/660-4287**), runs two buses between SFO and Mission and 7th streets. Bus 292 costs $2.25 and makes the trip in about 45 minutes. Check the SamTrans site for schedules.

### From Oakland International

The cheapest way to reach downtown San Francisco is to take **BART** from the Oakland Airport to the Coliseum station in Oakland, where you can transfer to any San Francisco–bound train. BART trains leave the airport every 6 minutes from 5am to 11pm on weekdays, 6am to 11pm on Saturdays, and 8am to 11pm on Sundays; between 11pm and midnight, they run every 20 minutes. The Oakland Airport BART station is located right across from the Terminal

1 baggage claim and a short walk from Terminal 2. BART fares vary depending on your destination, but the trip to any of the downtown San Francisco stations costs $10.20 one way (children 4 and under ride free). The entire excursion should take around 45 minutes. See p. 274 for more information about riding BART.

A **taxicab** from OAK to Fisherman's Wharf costs about $70, plus tip, and takes around 40 minutes, traffic permitting.

## By Car

San Francisco is easily accessible by major highways. **I-5,** which runs north-south, connects to I-80 and I-580, which head into San Francisco; **U.S. 101** cuts south-north through the peninsula from San Jose and across the Golden Gate Bridge to points north. If you drive from Los Angeles, you can take the longer coastal route along **Highway 1** (about 455 miles, 10 hours) or the inland I-5 route (381 miles and 6 hours). From Mendocino, the drive to San Francisco is 154 miles and takes just over 3 hours; from Sacramento, 87 miles and 1½ hours; from Yosemite, 210 miles and 4 hours.

If you are driving and aren't already a member, it's worth joining the **American Automobile Association** (**AAA;** csaa.com; © **800/922-8228**). Memberships start as low as $56 per year, and provide roadside and other services, including valuable hotel discounts. **Amoco Motor Club** (bpmotor-club.com; © **800/334-3300**) is another recommended choice.

## By Train

Traveling by train takes a long time and usually costs as much as, or more than, flying. Still, if you want to take a leisurely ride across America, rail may be a good option and the views can't be beat.

San Francisco–bound **Amtrak** (amtrak.com; © **800/872-7245**) trains leave from New York and cross the country via Chicago. The journey takes about 3½ days, and seats sell quickly. At press time, the lowest one-way fare cost $186 from New York (that's a reserved seat with no bed and a transfer in Chicago) and $136 from Chicago. If you're planning a train trip that lasts more than a day, unless you're a human pretzel and can sleep in the train seats, reserving one of the small but expensive rooms is the way to go. You'll arrive refreshed and full of stories from the sights you'll see and the people you'll meet on the journey. Round-trip tickets from Los Angeles start at $59 and involve two buses and a train. All trains arrive in Emeryville, just north of Oakland, and connect with regularly scheduled buses to San Francisco's Ferry Building and the Caltrain station in downtown San Francisco at Fourth and Townsend streets. **Caltrain** (caltrain.com; © **800/660-4287**) operates train service between San Francisco and cities on the eastern side of the peninsula.

# GETTING AROUND

The best way to figure out how to get around San Francisco is www.511.org. Enter your current location and desired destination, and the site will give you all your transportation options, including fares, type of transportation, even when the next bus will reach your stop. For more tips, see box on p. 24.

# By Public Transportation

The **San Francisco Municipal Transportation Agency,** better known as "Muni" (sfmta.com; © **311,** or **415/701-2311** outside San Francisco), operates the city's cable cars, buses, and streetcars. Together, these three services criss-cross the entire city. Fares for buses and streetcars are $2.75 for adults, or $1.35 for seniors 65+, children 5 to 18, and riders with disabilities. Exact change is required on all vehicles except cable cars, which currently make change (there is talk of eliminating cash payment for cable car fares, so be sure to ask before you ride); you can buy tickets in advance on your smart-phone using the **MuniMobile** app (available at sfmta.transitsherpa.com) If you're standing waiting for Muni and have a smartphone, check nextmuni. com to get up-to-the-minute information about when the next bus or streetcar is coming—Muni's NextBus uses satellite technology and advanced computer modeling to track vehicles on their routes, with information constantly updated.

For detailed route information, visit sfmta.com, go to the "Getting Around" drop-down menu, and click "Routes and Stops." Each route has its own map, and when you click on the map, you will see real-time details of bus loca-tions—you can even watch them slowly crawl across your computer screen as they move. For a big-picture look at all Muni routes, click on "Muni System Maps."

**CABLE CAR**  These mobile national treasures are truly fun to ride. While they may not be fast (speeds top out at 9 miles per hour), they'll get you to your destination in style, provided your destination is on their three limited routes, which are concentrated in the downtown area. The most scenic, and exciting, is the **Powell–Hyde line,** which follows a zigzag route from the corner of Powell and Market streets, over both Nob and Russian hills, to a turntable at Victorian Square in front of Aquatic Park. The **Powell–Mason line** starts at the same intersection and climbs Nob Hill before descending to Bay Street, just 3 blocks from Fisherman's Wharf. The third, still scenic but

---

## Muni Discounts

Muni discount passes, called **Passports,** entitle holders to unlimited rides on buses, streetcars, and cable cars. A Passport costs $21 for 1 day, $32 for 3 days, and $42 for 7 consecutive days. There is no discount for children or seniors. Passports are sold at many loca-tions throughout the city (for a list, visit sfmta.com/getting-around/transit).

Another option is buying a **CityPASS** (citypass.com; $89 adults, $66 kids 5–11), which entitles you to unlimited Muni rides for 9 days, and includes admission to four (or five, depending on which you choose) local attractions. These passes are sold online or at any of the CityPASS attractions; for more discount card details, see box on p. 118.

slightly less dramatic, is the **California Street line,** which begins at the foot of Market Street and runs a straight course through Chinatown and over Nob Hill to Van Ness Avenue. All riders must exit at the last stop and wait in line for the return trip. The cable car system operates from approximately 6am to 1am, and each ride costs $7; passes and MuniMobile tickets are accepted.

**BUS** Buses reach almost every corner of San Francisco and beyond—they even travel over the bridges to Marin County and Oakland. Overhead electric cables power some buses; others use conventional gas engines. All are numbered and display their destinations on the front. Signs, curb markings, and yellow bands on adjacent utility poles designate stops, and most bus shelters display Muni's transportation map and schedule. Many buses travel along Market Street or pass near Union Square and run from about 6am to midnight. After midnight, there is infrequent all-night "Owl" service. Unless you're traveling with a large group, it's a good idea to avoid taking buses late at night.

Popular tourist routes include bus number 5, which runs to Golden Gate Park; 41 and 45, which travel along Union Street; and 30, which runs between Union Square, Chinatown, Ghirardelli Square, and the Marina District. A bus ride costs $2.75 for adults, or $1.35 for seniors 65+, children 5 to 18, and riders with disabilities; exact change is required.

**STREETCAR** Six of Muni's seven streetcar lines, designated **J, KT, L, M,** and **N,** run underground downtown and on the streets in the outer neighborhoods. The sleek rail cars make the same stops as BART (see below) along Market Street, including Embarcadero Station (in the Financial District), Montgomery and Powell streets (both near Union Square), and the Civic Center (near City Hall). Past the Civic Center, the routes branch off: The J line takes you to Mission Dolores; the L and M lines run to Castro Street and beyond; and the N line parallels Golden Gate Park and runs all the way to the Embarcadero and AT&T Park. The K-Ingleside/T-Third Street car runs from Balboa Park through downtown to AT&T Park and the San Francisco Caltrain station and then continues south along Third Street.

The seventh, and most recently added, line isn't a newcomer at all; it's an encore performance of rejuvenated 1930s streetcars from all over the world. The beautiful, retro multicolored **F-Market and Wharves** streetcar runs from 17th and Castro streets to the Embarcadero; some cars stop there, but every alternate F-line car continues to Jones and Beach streets in Fisherman's Wharf. This is a quick, charming, and tourist-friendly way to get up and down town without any hassle.

Streetcars run about every 15 minutes, and more frequently during rush hours. They operate daily from about 4am to 2am, with a few exceptions. Because the operation is part of Muni, the fares are the same as for buses, and passes are accepted.

**BART** The high-speed rail network **Bay Area Rapid Transit** (bart.gov; ✆ **415/989-2278**)—usually just called BART—connects the San Francisco peninsula (starting just south of the airport) with the East Bay—Oakland, Richmond, Concord, Pittsburg, and Fremont. Four stations are in downtown

San Francisco along Market Street (see "Streetcar," above). One-way fares range from $1.95 to $12.05, depending on distance. (Children 4 and under ride free.) Machines in the stations dispense tickets that are magnetically encoded with a dollar amount, and computerized exits automatically deduct the correct fare. Trains run every 15 to 20 minutes, Monday through Friday from 4am to midnight, Saturday from 6am to midnight, and Sunday from 8am to midnight. On the BART website, you can download a trip planner for smartphone or tablet.

## By Taxi

This isn't New York, so don't expect a taxi to appear whenever you need one. If you're downtown during rush hour or leaving a major hotel, it won't be hard to hail a cab; just look for the lighted sign on the roof that indicates the vehicle is free. Otherwise, it's a good idea to call one of the following companies to arrange a ride: **National Veteran's Cab** (✆ **415/321-TAXI**), **Luxor Cabs** (✆ **415/282-4141**), **De Soto Cab** (✆ **415/970-1300**), **Green Cab** (✆ **415/626-4733**), or **Yellow Cab** (✆ **415/333-3333**). Unfortunately, despite the call, you still might be left high and dry. What to do? Call back if your cab is late and insist on attention, but don't expect prompt results on weekends, no matter how nicely you ask. For an estimate of fares, including an allowance for traffic, visit taxifarefinder.com.

Due, I suspect, to the historically woeful lack of taxis, San Francisco was an early adopter of ride-sharing technologies, such as **Lyft** and **Uber,** and today, you'll see hundreds of vehicles sporting Lyft and Uber stickers on their windshields—especially since even locals have given up driving (and steep parking prices) in exchange for the ease of hopping a shared or private ride. You don't hail them like you would a cab: You must first download the **Uber** or **Lyft** app onto your smartphone, enter your credit card information, and then, via the app, request a ride from wherever you are. A car will pick you up, usually within minutes. You'll have the option of choosing a shared ride at a lower price or an "express" ride for a bit more; if you've got a group of up to six people, you can also request a larger vehicle, at a larger (but still usually reasonable) fee. And the entire transaction is carried out through your smartphone—no need to carry cash!

## By Car

You don't need a car to explore downtown San Francisco. In fact, with the city becoming more crowded by the minute, a car can be your worst nightmare—you're likely to end up stuck in traffic with lots of frustrated drivers, pay upwards of $50 a day to park (plus a whopping new 14% parking lot tax), and spend a good portion of your vacation looking for a parking space. **Don't bother.**

If you want to venture outside the city, however—perhaps taking a day trip to Napa Valley or Muir Woods—driving is the best way to go. Picking up a car in the city early in the morning and returning it that evening will save a fortune for a family of four. Before heading outside the city, especially in winter, call ℭ **800/427-ROAD (7623)** for California **road conditions.** You can also call ℭ **511** for current traffic information.

**CAR RENTALS** All the national car-rental companies operate in the city and have desks at the airports. Companies include **Alamo** (alamo.com; ℭ 800/651-1223), **Avis** (avis.com; ℭ 800/352-7900), **Budget** (budget.com; ℭ 800/218-7992), **Dollar** (dollar.com; ℭ 800/800-5252), **Enterprise** (enterprise.com; ℭ 855/266-9289), **Hertz** (hertz.com; ℭ 800/654-4173), **National** (national-car.com; ℭ 800/227-7368), and **Thrifty** (thrifty.com; ℭ 800/367-2277). Most car rental agencies have a minimum-age requirement—usually age 25. Some also have a maximum-age limit. If you're concerned that these limits might affect you, ask about rental requirements at the time of booking to avoid problems later.

Car-rental **rates** vary even more than airline fares. Prices depend on the size of the car, where and when you pick up and drop off, the length of the rental period, where and how far you drive it, whether you buy insurance, and a host of other factors. A few key questions can save you hundreds of dollars, but you have to ask—reservations agents don't often volunteer money-saving information:

o Are weekend rates lower than weekday rates? Ask if the rate is the same for pickup Friday morning, for instance, as it is for Thursday night.

o Does the agency assess a drop-off charge if you don't return the car to the same location where you picked it up?

o Are special promotional rates available? If you see an advertised price in your local newspaper, be sure to ask for that specific rate; otherwise, you could be charged the standard rate. Terms change constantly.

o Are discounts available for members of AARP, AAA, frequent-flier programs, or trade unions? If you belong to any of these organizations, you may be entitled to discounts of up to 30%.

o How much tax will be added to the rental bill? Will there be local tax and state tax?

---

## Safe Driving

Here are a few quick tips for safe California driving:

o California law requires that drivers and passengers all wear seat belts.

o California law also requires that any cellphone use while driving, including GPS for navigation, must be completely hands-free.

o You can turn right at a red light (unless otherwise indicated), after yielding to traffic and pedestrians, and after coming to a complete stop.

o Cable cars always have the right of way, as do pedestrians at intersections and crosswalks.

o Pay attention to signs and arrows on the streets and roadways or you might suddenly find yourself in a lane that requires exiting or turning when you want to go straight. San Francisco's many one-way streets can drive you in circles, but most road maps of the city indicate which way traffic flows.

○ How much does the rental company charge to refill your gas tank if you return with the tank less than full? Most rental companies claim their prices are "competitive," but fuel is almost always cheaper in town, so try to allow enough time to refuel the car before returning it. Some companies offer "refueling packages," in which you pay for an entire tank of gas upfront; the cost is usually fairly competitive with local prices, but you don't get credit for any gas remaining in the tank. If a stop at a gas station on the way to the airport will make you miss your plane, then by all means take advantage of the fuel purchase option. Otherwise, skip it.

**INSURANCE** Make sure you're insured. Hasty assumptions about your personal auto insurance or a rental agency's additional coverage could end up costing you tens of thousands of dollars, even if you are involved in an accident that is clearly the fault of another driver.

If you already have your own car insurance, you are most likely covered in the United States for loss of or damage to a rental car and liability in case of injury to any other party involved in an accident. Be sure to check your policy before you spend extra money (around $10 or more per day) on the **collision damage waiver (CDW)** offered by all agencies.

If you use a major credit card (especially gold and platinum cards) to pay for the rental, it may provide some coverage as well. Terms vary widely, so call your credit card company directly, before you rent, to learn if you can rely on the card for coverage. If you are uninsured, your credit card may provide primary coverage as long as you decline the rental agency's insurance. If you already have insurance, your credit card may provide secondary coverage, which basically covers your deductible. However, note that *credit cards will not cover liability,* which is the cost of injury to an outside party and/or damage to an outside party's vehicle. If you don't hold an insurance policy, seriously consider buying the rental company's additional liability insurance, even if you decline the CDW.

**INTERNATIONAL VISITORS** If you're visiting from abroad and plan to rent a car in the United States, keep in mind that foreign driver's licenses are usually recognized in the U.S., but you may want to consider obtaining an international driver's license. Also note that insurance and taxes are almost never included in quoted rental car rates in the U.S. Ask your rental agency about these additional fees—they can add a significant cost to your rental car.

**PARKING** If you want to have a relaxing vacation, don't even attempt to find street parking on Nob Hill, in North Beach, in Chinatown, by Fisherman's Wharf, or on Telegraph Hill. Park in a garage (ideally using one of the many parking-garage-finding apps, which often offer discounts if you buy before you arrive) and use cabs or buses to get around.

If you do find street parking, pay attention to street signs that explain when you can park and for how long, and don't forget to put money in your parking meter, if there is one. If you don't have cash, you can use a credit card. Be especially careful not to park in tow zones during rush hours.

Curb colors indicate parking regulations. *Red* means no stopping or parking, *blue* is reserved for drivers with disabilities who have a disabled plate or placard, *white* is reserved for non-commercial loading zones (there's a 5-min. limit and the driver must stay in the vehicle), *green* indicates a 10-minute limit, and *yellow* and *yellow-and-black* curbs are commercial loading zones reserved for vehicles with commercial plates (yellow zones are often enforced only during business hours, so check for signs or curb stencils that list hours of enforcement). Also, don't park at a bus stop or in front of a fire hydrant, and watch out for street-cleaning signs. *Note:* No parking in red zones means that your car should be *completely* outside of the red; even a few centimeters can result in a ticket or a tow. Residents, already annoyed because their driveways are often partially blocked, can be quick to call a tow truck.

If you violate the law, you might get a hefty ticket or your car might be towed; to get your car back, you'll have to get a release from the nearest district police department and then go to the towing company to pick up the vehicle.

When parking on a hill, **curb your wheels**—turn them toward the curb when facing downhill, away from the curb when facing uphill. Curbing your wheels not only prevents a possible "runaway" but also keeps you from getting a ticket—an expensive fine that is aggressively enforced.

## By Ferry

**TO/FROM SAUSALITO OR LARKSPUR** The **Golden Gate Ferry Service** fleet (goldengateferry.org; ℂ **415/455-2000**) shuttles passengers daily between the San Francisco Ferry Building, at the foot of Market Street, and downtown Sausalito, Tiburon, or Larkspur. Service is frequent, departing at reasonable intervals every day of the year (Tiburon service is weekdays only) except January 1, Thanksgiving Day, and December 25. Phone or check the website for an exact schedule. The ride takes about half an hour. One-way fares to Sausalito or Tiburon are $12 for adults, $6 for seniors 65+, youth ages

---

### Park Smart

In a high-tech city like San Francisco, it only follows there would be a way to use your computer or smartphone to help find parking. **Sfpark.org** is an award-winning website (a mobile app is available too) that collects and displays real-time information about available parking in the city, in an effort to stop people from driving in circles and polluting our city while hunting for a spot. You can look at a map of the city parking garages; get addresses, directions, and hourly prices; and even see how many spots are available inside each garage. If you hit the green "pricing" key, it will show dark green for more expensive garages and light green for the less expensive places. For metered street parking, the map will show red in areas of limited street parking, navy for some availability, and light turquoise for good availability. For both garage and metered parking, prices are regularly adjusted up or down monthly, depending on demand.

## Earthquake Advice

Although San Francisco does lie in an earthquake zone, these are rare events. If an earthquake does happen while you are in the Bay Area, however, don't panic. If you're in a tall building, don't run outside; instead, move away from windows and toward the building's center. Crouch under a desk or table, or stand against a wall or under a doorway. If you're in bed, get under the bed, stand in a doorway, or crouch under a sturdy piece of furniture. When exiting the building, use stairwells, not elevators. If you're in your car, pull over to the side of the road and stop, but wait until you're away from bridges or overpasses, as well as telephone or power poles and lines. Stay in your car. If you're outside, stay away from trees, power lines, and the sides of buildings.

5 to 18, and passengers with disabilities. One-way fares to Larkspur are $11.50 adults, $5.75 seniors, youth, and passengers with disabilities. Children 4 and under travel free when accompanied by a full-fare paying adult (limit two kids per adult).

Ferries of the **Blue & Gold Fleet** (blueandgoldfleet.com; ✆ **415/773-1188** for recorded info) provide round-trip service to downtown Sausalito, Tiburon, and Angel Island. For Sausalito or Tiburon, the one-way fare is $12.50 for adults, $7.50 for seniors 65+ and youth 5–11. The Angel Island ferry costs $9.75 adults one-way, $5.50 seniors and youth. Boats run on a seasonal schedule, so check the website for details. Boats leave from Pier 41, and tickets can be purchased at the pier.

**TO/FROM OAKLAND OR ALAMEDA** The **San Francisco Bay Ferry** fleet (sanfranciscobayferry.com; ✆ **415/705-8291**) runs a daily route that connects Pier 41, the San Francisco Ferry Building, Alameda, and Oakland's Jack London Square; some routes also include AT&T Park. Phone or check the website for an exact schedule, as it changes with the seasons. The rides to Oakland and Alameda take just over half an hour. One-way fares to Oakland and Alameda are $6.80 for adults, $63.40 for seniors 65+, youth ages 5 to 18, and passengers with disabilities.

# BEFORE YOU GO
## What to Bring

Dress in layers, even in the summer. As the saying goes in San Francisco, if you don't like the weather, wait 5 minutes. With offshore breezes, microclimates, and the prevalence of fog in the summer, the temperature changes constantly in San Francisco, particularly if you're on the move. Even if it's sunny and warm at noon, bring a sweater or light jacket just in case—when the fog rolls in, it gets chilly fast.

Pack **prescription medications** in your carry-on luggage, and carry them in their original containers, with pharmacy labels—otherwise they won't

**WHAT THINGS COST IN SAN FRANCISCO**

| | |
|---|---|
| Taxi from SFO to downtown | $60 |
| Inexpensive hotel room, double occupancy | $150 and under |
| Moderate hotel room, double occupancy | $150–$275 |
| Small cup of coffee (Peet's or Starbucks) | $2 |
| One gallon of regular gas | $3.75-$4 |
| Admission to museums | $10–$35 |
| Glass of Napa Valley red wine | $10–$15 |
| Bus or streetcar fare for adults | $2.75 |
| Cable car fare | $7 |

make it through airport security. Visitors from outside the U.S. should carry generic names of prescription drugs.

For more helpful information on packing for your trip, head to Frommers. com and click on the "Tips & News" drop-down section, which contains packing tips and information.

## What It Will Cost

As major U.S. cities go, San Francisco tends to be on the more expensive side. A competitive market keeps hotel prices high, and restaurant meals can be pricy, thanks to a combination of high rents and the high ambitions of this foodie capital. There are bargains, however, and our listings try to steer you to them. Plan your activities carefully and you can get a lot for your tourist dollar in San Francisco.

It's always advisable to bring money in a variety of forms on a vacation: a mix of cash, credit cards, and ATM cards. Credit and debit cards are the most widely used form of payment in San Francisco: You must have a credit card (not a debit card) to rent a car, and hotels and airlines usually require a credit card imprint as a deposit against expenses.

Before you leave home, you should also have enough petty cash upon arrival to cover airport incidentals, tipping, and transportation to your hotel. You can always withdraw money upon arrival at an airport ATM, but you'll still need to make smaller change for tipping (for tipping guidelines, see p. 287).

If you are traveling from overseas, check with your credit or debit card issuer to see what fees, if any, will be charged for overseas transactions. Recent reform legislation in the U.S. has curbed some exploitative lending practices, but many banks have responded by increasing fees in other areas, including fees for customers who use credit and debit cards while out of the country—even if those charges were made in U.S. dollars. Fees can amount to 3% or more of the purchase price. Check with your bank before departing to avoid any surprise charges on your statement.

Frommer's lists prices in the local currency. The currency conversion rates we list here were correct at press time, but rates fluctuate—before you leave on your trip, consult a currency-exchange website such as www.xe.com to get up-to-the-minute rates.

## THE VALUE OF THE U.S. DOLLAR VS. OTHER POPULAR CURRENCIES

| US$ | Can$ | UK£ | Euro (€) | Aus$ | NZ$ |
| --- | --- | --- | --- | --- | --- |
| 1 | 1.29 | 0.75 | 0.86 | 1.30 | 1.45 |

# [FastFACTS] SAN FRANCISCO

**Area Codes**  The area code for San Francisco is **415;** for Oakland, Berkeley, and much of the East Bay, **510;** for the peninsula, generally **650.** Napa and Sonoma are **707.** Within city limits, you don't need to dial the prefix to call other numbers in the 415 area code.

**ATMs**  Nationwide, the easiest and best way to get cash away from home is from an ATM (automated teller machine), also known as a "cash machine" or "cashpoint." In the land of shopping malls and immediate gratification, there's an ATM on almost every block. Major networks include **Cirrus** (mastercard.com; ✆ **800/424-7787**) and **PLUS** (visa.com; ✆ **800/847-2911**). Go to your bank card's website to find ATM locations at your destination. Be sure you know your daily withdrawal limit before you depart.

*Note:* Many banks impose a fee every time you use a card at another bank's ATM, and that fee is often higher for international

transactions (up to $5 or more) than for domestic ones (where they're rarely more than $3). In addition, the bank from which you withdraw cash may charge its own fee. Visitors from outside the U.S. should find out whether their bank assesses a 1% to 3% fee on charges incurred abroad.

*Tip:* One way around these fees is to request "cash back" when making debit card purchases at grocery, drug, and convenience stores. Be sure to ask whether they charge extra usage fees.

**Business Hours**  Most banks are open Monday through Friday from 9am to 5pm as well as Saturday mornings. Many banks also have 24-hour ATMs. (See "ATMs," above.) Store hours are generally Monday through Saturday from 10 or 11am to at least 6pm, with shorter hours on Sunday. Note that stores in Chinatown, Ghirardelli Square, and Pier 39 stay open much later during the tourist season, and large department stores around Union Square

may keep later hours. Most restaurants serve food from about 11:30am to 10pm, sometimes later on weekends. Nightclubs and bars are usually open daily until 2am, when they are legally bound to stop serving alcohol.

**Car Rental**  See "By Car" in "Getting Around" above, p. 275.

**Cellphones**  See "Mobile Phones," p. 284.

**Credit & Debit Cards**  Most establishments in San Francisco accept **Visa** (Barclaycard in Britain), **MasterCard** (Eurocard in Europe, Access in Britain, Chargex in Canada), **American Express,** and **Discover.** These cards provide a convenient record of all your expenses and offer relatively good exchange rates. You can withdraw cash advances from your credit cards at banks or ATMs, but high fees make credit card cash advances a pricey way to get cash.

**Debit cards**—ATM cards with major credit card backing—are now a commonly acceptable form of payment in most stores and restaurants. Debit cards draw money directly from your checking account. Some stores will also let you receive cash back on your debit card purchases. Don't rely on being able to use a debit car to rent a car, however; call ahead to ask if your rental car company accepts debit cards. Even if they do, they may require you to have a very large dollar amount available for them to "hold" until you return the vehicle in perfect shape.

**Crime** See "Safety," p. 285.

**Disabled Travelers** Most disabilities shouldn't stop anyone from traveling. There are more options and resources out there than ever before.

Most of San Francisco's major museums and tourist attractions have wheelchair ramps. Many hotels offer special accommodations and services for wheelchair users and other visitors with disabilities—ramps, extra-large bathrooms, and telecommunication devices for hearing-impaired travelers. Check your hotel website to find out how accessible it is.

Travelers in wheelchairs can request special ramped taxis by calling **Yellow Cab** (✆ **415/333-3333**). Ramped taxis charge the same rates as other taxis. To use public transport, get a free copy of the **Muni Access Guide** (for a printable copy, visit sfmta. com and click on "Accessibility" in the "Getting Around" drop-down menu)

published by the San Francisco Municipal Transportation Agency's Accessible Services Program. You can also stop by its office at One South Van Ness, 3rd floor (✆ **415/701-4485**), open weekdays 8am to 5pm.

As for rental cars, many companies offer equipment for customers with special travel needs, from mobility scooter rentals to specially outfitted cars with swivel seats, spinner knobs, and hand controls. **Alamo** (✆ **800/651-1223**), **Avis** (✆ **800/331-1212**), and **Budget** (✆ **800/314-3932**) have special hotlines to provide accessible vehicles at any of their U.S. locations with roughly 48 hours (sometimes less) advance notice; **Hertz** (✆ **800/654-3131**) requires 24 to 48 hours advance notice at most locations.

Organizations offering a vast range of resources and assistance to travelers with disabilities include: **SATH** (Society for Accessible Travel & Hospitality; sath. org; ✆ **212/447-7284**) and the **American Foundation for the Blind** (afb.org; ✆ **800/232-5463**). You can also visit **Mobility-Advisor. com** to get a variety of travel resources for persons with disabilities (click on the "Accessible Travel" link, under "Recreation").

Two travel agencies that offer customized tours and itineraries for travelers with disabilities are **Flying Wheels Travel** (flyingwheels travel.com; ✆ **507/451-5005**) and **Accessible**

**Journeys** (disabilitytravel. com; ✆ **800/846-4537**).

The online magazine **Emerging Horizons** (emerginghorizons.com) offers destination suggestions and loads of tips for traveling in wheelchairs or with other forms of limited mobility.

**Discounts** For local discounts on attractions and restaurants, visit **groupon. com** and **baycityguide. com/coupons.html**. With Groupon, you purchase the deal ahead of time—deals than can be up to 40% off of a variety of attractions. Make sure to read the fine print for any restrictions before you purchase a Groupon or use a coupon.

**Doctors** See "Hospitals," below.

**Drinking Laws** The legal age for purchase and consumption of alcoholic beverages is 21; proof of age is required and often requested at bars, nightclubs, and restaurants, so bring ID when you go out. Supermarkets and convenience stores in California sell beer, wine, and liquor. While most restaurants serve alcohol, some serve only beer and wine. By law, bars, clubs, restaurants, and stores cannot sell or serve alcohol after 2am; "last call" tends to start at 1:30am. Do not carry open containers of alcohol in your car or any public area that isn't zoned for alcohol consumption. The police can fine you on the spot. And nothing will ruin your trip faster than getting a citation for DUI (driving under the influence).

**Driving Rules** See "Getting Around," p. 272.

**Electricity** Like Canada, the United States uses 110 to 120 volts AC (60 cycles), compared to 220 to 240 volts AC (50 cycles) in most of Europe, Australia, and New Zealand. Converters that change 220–240 volts to 110–120 volts are difficult to find in the United States, so bring one with you.

**Embassies & Consulates** All embassies are in the nation's capital, Washington, D.C., but San Francisco is home to nearly 70 foreign consulates. For a complete list of consulates in San Francisco, with contact information, visit www.embassypages.com/city/sanfrancisco or call for directory information in Washington, D.C. (☎ **202/555-1212**).

**Emergencies** Call ☎ **911** to report a fire, call the police, or get an ambulance anywhere in the United States. This is a toll-free call (no coins required at public telephones).

**Family Travel** San Francisco is a prime family destination, offering some of the country's best attractions for children (see box p. 149), and it has a number of family-friendly hotels (see p. 71).

Recommended family travel websites include: **FamilyTravel.com**, a comprehensive site that offers lots of resources for traveling with kids, plus recommendations for age-specific activities; the online

magazine **Family Travel Network** (familytravel network.com), which offers travel tips and deals; and the parent-written site **TravelWithYourKids** (travelwithyourkids.com), offering sound advice for long-distance and international travel with children.

**Health Insurance** If you worry about getting sick away from home, you may want to consider **medical travel insurance.** To get the low-down on travel insurance offerings, visit frommers.com and click on "Health & Travel Insurance" from the "Tips & News" drop-down menu. In most cases, if you're a U.S. resident, your existing health plan will provide the coverage you need (be sure to carry your insurance ID), but foreign visitors may have to pay medical costs upfront and be reimbursed later.

**Hospitals** **Saint Francis Memorial Hospital,** 900 Hyde St., between Bush and Pine streets on Nob Hill (saintfrancismemorial.org; ☎ **855/565-0287** or 415/353-6000), provides emergency service 24 hours a day. The hospital also operates a **physician-referral service** (☎ **877/650-9611** or 415/353-6566).

**Internet & Wi-Fi** Many cafes have wireless access, as do most hotels. For a huge list of free Wi-Fi hotspots—including every Starbucks and Peet's coffee shop, Barnes and Noble, FedEx office, and McDonald's—visit **wififreespot.com**; log onto **cybercafe.**

**com** for a list of internet cafes in San Francisco. All San Francisco libraries are completely wired, including the San Francisco Main Library (100 Larkin St.; ☎ **415/557-4400**), which in 2015 became the first 10 gigabit library in the country, providing visitors and staff with the fastest internet speeds of any library. San Francisco International Airport has wireless access, and many of the city's public parks have free Wi-Fi (for a list, go to sfgov.org/sfc/sanfranciscowifi).

**Legal Aid** While driving, if you are pulled over for a minor infraction (such as gliding through a stop sign), never attempt to pay the fine directly to a police officer; this could be construed as attempted bribery, a much more serious offense. Pay fines by mail, or directly to the clerk of the court. If accused of a more serious crime, say and do nothing before consulting a lawyer. In the U.S., the burden is on the state to prove a person's guilt beyond a reasonable doubt, and everyone has the right to remain silent, whether he or she is suspected of a crime or actually arrested. Once arrested, a person can make one telephone call to a party of his or her choice. The international visitor should call his or her embassy or consulate.

**LGBTQ Travelers** Gays and lesbians make up a good portion of San Francisco's population, so it's no surprise that clubs and bars all over town cater to them. Since the 1970s, **the Castro** has been the city's center for gay communities and nightlife. With society's changing norms, gay life has become less centralized (some might say less ghettoized) over the years, but for some gay travelers, this is still The Place to Be, especially on a festival weekend, when the streets are filled with out-and-proud revelry. For others, it's a quaint relic of the past to be visited occasionally (while shielding their children's eyes from the sex toys in shop windows). For other San Franciscans and visitors, the Castro is simply a fun area with some wonderful shops and good restaurants.

Although lesbian interests are concentrated in the East Bay (especially **Oakland**), a significant community resides in the **Mission District** (around 16th and Valencia sts.), **Hayes Valley,** and **Bernal Heights.**

Distributed free every Thursday, the **Bay Area Reporter** (ebar.com) has comprehensive listings and a weekly calendar of events; look for stacks at the corner of 18th and Castro streets, at Ninth and Harrison streets, and in gay-oriented bars, bookshops, and stores around town.

**San Francisco Pride** (sfpride.org/travel) is another good resource for LGBTQ-friendly travel in the city. **San Francisco Travel** (sanfrancisco.travel/lgbt) has designed LGBTQ itineraries, and can help you plan your

wedding in the city. Travel agencies that focus on the LGBTQ market include San Francisco–based **Now, Voyager** (nowvoyager.com; ☏ **800/255-6951**) and lesbian-oriented **Olivia** (olivia.com; ☏ **800/631-6277**).

For more general resources, check out the **International Gay and Lesbian Travel Association (IGLTA;** iglta.org; ☏ **954/630-1637**), with its online directory of gay- and lesbian-friendly travel businesses; **Purple Roofs** (purpleroofs.com), which lists gay-friendly hotels, B&Bs, travel agents, and tour operators; and **GayTravel.com** and **OutTraveler.com**, both of which provide information about gay-oriented lodging, dining, sightseeing, nightlife, and shopping establishments. For travel guides that cover the world through an LGBTQ lens, check out the **Spartacus International Gay Guide** (spartacusworld.com) and the **Damron** guides (damron.com).

For more gay and lesbian travel resources, visit Frommers.com.

**Mail**   At press time, domestic postage rates were 34¢ for a regular postcard, 49¢ for a large postcard or a regular letter. Always include zip codes when mailing items in the U.S. (to find correct zip codes, visit usps.com/zip4). For international mail, a postcard costs $1.20.

If you aren't sure what your address will be in the United States, mail can be

sent to you, in your name, c/o General Delivery at the main post office of the city or region where you expect to be. The addressee must pick up mail in person and must produce proof of identity (driver's license or passport). Most post offices will hold mail for up to 1 month, and are open roughly Monday to Friday from 8am to 6pm, and Saturday from 9am to 3pm.

**Mobile Phones**   Just because your cellphone works at home doesn't mean it'll work everywhere in the U.S. (thanks to our nation's fragmented cellphone system). Take a look at your wireless company's coverage map on its website before heading out; some signals may disappear or be very weak in rural areas, such as parts of wine country. If you're heading for a destination where you know your phone won't work, **rent** one that does from **InTouch USA** (intouchusa.com; ☏ **800/872-7626**), but be aware that airtime is pricey.

If you're not from the U.S., your mobile phone most likely uses the **GSM** (Global System for Mobile Communications) **wireless network;** be advised that GSM has poor reach in much of the U.S. Your phone will probably work in major cities, but it may not work in rural areas, and you may not be able to text back home.

**Money**   The most common bills in the U.S. are $1 (a "buck"), $5, $10, and $20 denominations. There are also $2 bills (seldom encountered), $50 bills, and $100 bills. (The last two are usually not welcome as payment for small purchases.)

Coins come in seven denominations: 1¢ (1 cent, or a penny); 5¢ (5 cents, or a nickel); 10¢ (10 cents, or a dime); 25¢ (25 cents, or a quarter); 50¢ (50 cents, or a half dollar); the gold-colored Sacagawea coin, worth $1; and the rare silver dollar.

**Newspapers & Magazines** The city's main daily newspaper is the *San Francisco Chronicle* (sfchronicle.com), which is sold throughout the city. In the *Chronicle*'s Sunday edition, the pink "Datebook" section is a handy preview of the week's upcoming events. The free *San Francisco Examiner* (sfexaminer. com) is published Monday through Friday with a weekend edition. The free weekly *San Francisco Bay Guardian* (sfbg.com) and *SF Weekly* (sfweekly.com) are indispensable for last-minute suggestions for nightlife outings and adventures.

**Passports** Every traveler entering the U.S. is required to show a passport. All persons, including U.S. citizens, traveling by air between the United States and Canada, Mexico, Central and South America, the Caribbean, and Bermuda are required to present a valid passport. *Note:* U.S. and Canadian citizens entering the U. S. at land and sea ports of entry from within the western hemisphere must now also present a passport or other documents compliant with the Western Hemisphere Travel Initiative. Visit www. cbp.gov/travel/us-citizens/ western-hemisphere-travel-initiative for details).

**U.S. Citizens** To find your regional passport office, check the U.S. State Department website (travel. state.gov/content/passports/ en/passports/information/ where-to-apply/agencies. html) or call the **National Passport Information Center** (ⓒ **877/487-2778**) for automated information.

**Police** In an emergency, dial ⓒ **911.** For nonemergency police matters, call ⓒ **415/553-0123.**

**Safety** For a big city, San Francisco is relatively safe, but you should still take common sense precautions (for example, don't leave your purse or phone on the seat of your parked car). In a few neighborhoods, such as Lower Haight, the Mission, the Tenderloin (a few blocks west of Union Square), and Fisherman's Wharf (at night especially), we advise exercising extra caution.

Avoid carrying valuables with you on the street, and don't display expensive cameras or electronic equipment. Hold on to purses and bags, and place your wallet in an inside pocket. In theaters, restaurants, and other public places, keep your possessions in sight.

Remember also that hotels are open to the public, and in a large hotel, security may not be able to screen everyone entering. Always lock your room door.

**Driving safety** is another factor. We don't recommend driving in San Francisco if you can avoid it, but if you must, try to arrive and depart during daylight hours. Use a GPS application on your smartphone, or ask for written directions to your destination or a map with the route clearly marked. If you drive off a highway into a doubtful neighborhood, leave the area as quickly as possible. Always try to park in well-lit and well-traveled areas.

If you have an accident, even on the highway, stay in your car with the doors locked until you assess the situation or until the police arrive. If you're bumped from behind on the street or are involved in a minor accident with no injuries, and the situation seems suspicious to you, motion to the other driver to follow you. Never get out of your car in such situations. Go directly to the nearest police precinct, well-lit service station, or 24-hour store.

If someone attempts to rob you or steal your car, don't resist the thief or carjacker. Report the incident to the police department immediately by calling ⓒ **911.** This is a free call, even from pay phones.

**Senior Travel** Nearly every attraction in San Francisco offers a senior discount; age requirements vary (specific prices are listed in chapter 4). Public transportation and movie theaters also have reduced rates. Don't be shy about asking for discounts, but always carry some kind of identification—driver's license, passport—that shows your date of birth.

Members of **AARP** (travel.aarp.org; ✆ **888/687-2277**) get discounts on hotels, airfare, and car rentals. AARP offers members a wide range of benefits; anyone 50 and over can join. The quarterly magazine *Travel 50 & Beyond* (travel50andbeyond.com) also offers travel resources and discounts for seniors.

**Smoking** Each year, smoking laws in the city become stricter. Smoking is illegal inside most buildings, at entryways, bus stops, public parks, beaches, and at any outdoor public events. Hotels are also increasingly going nonsmoking, though some still offer smoking rooms. You can't even smoke in California bars unless drinks are served solely by the owner. San Francisco International Airport no longer has hazy, indoor smoking rooms; there are a few designated areas outside, pre-security.

**Student Travel** A valid student ID will often qualify students for discounts on airfare, accommodations, entry to museums, cultural events, movies, and more in San Francisco. Check out the **International Student Travel Confederation** (aboutistc.org) for comprehensive travel services, information, and details on how to get an **International**

**Student Identity Card (ISIC),** which qualifies students for substantial savings on all sorts of tickets, as well as providing students with basic health and life insurance and a 24-hour help line. The card is valid for up to 16 months. Apply for the card online at myisic.com/isic-card, or purchase one through **STA Travel** (statravel.com; ✆ **800/781-4040**), the biggest student travel agency in the world. No longer a student but still under 26 years old? The same organizations can give you an **International Youth Travel Card (IYTC),** which entitles you to some discounts. Similar services for both Canadian and U.S. students are provided by **Travel CUTS** (travelcuts.com; ✆ **800/667-2887**); for Irish citizens, there's **USIT** (usit.ie; ✆ **01/602-1906**), an organization for student, youth, and independent travel.

**Taxes** The United States has no value-added tax (VAT) or other indirect tax at the national level, but every state, county, and city may levy its own local taxes on purchases, hotels, air travel, and other line items. Sales tax in San Francisco is 8.5% (not included in price tags). Hotel room taxes range from 12% to 17% around Northern California.

**Telephones** Local calls made from a pay phone cost 50¢—that is, if you can find one. They are a dying breed; only about 200 remain in the city. Public pay phones at airports now

accept American Express, MasterCard, and Visa.

Most long-distance and international calls can be dialed directly from any phone. **To make calls within the United States and to Canada,** dial 1 followed by the area code and the seven-digit number. **For international calls,** dial 011 followed by the country code, city code, and the number you are calling.

For **reversed-charge or collect calls,** and for person-to-person calls, dial the number 0 then the area code and number; an operator will come on the line to assist you. If your operator-assisted call is international, ask for the overseas operator.

Calls to area codes **800, 888, 877,** and **866** are toll-free. However, calls to area codes **700** and **900** (chat lines, bulletin boards, "dating" services, and so on) can be expensive—charges of 95¢ to $3 or more per minute. Some numbers have minimum charges that can run $15 or more.

For **directory assistance** ("Information"), dial ✆ 411 for numbers in the U.S. and Canada. For dedicated long-distance information, dial 1, then the appropriate area code plus 555-1212.

**Time** The continental United States is divided into **four time zones:** Eastern Standard Time (EST), Central Standard Time (CST), Mountain Standard Time (MST), and Pacific Standard Time (PST). (Alaska and Hawaii have their own zones.) San

Francisco is in Pacific Standard Time, which means that when it's 9am in San Francisco (PST), it's 10am in Denver (MST), 11am in Chicago (CST), noon in New York City (EST), 5pm in London (GMT), and 2am the next day in Sydney.

In most of the U.S., **Daylight saving time** is in effect from 2am on the second Sunday in March to 2am on the first Sunday in November. Daylight saving time moves the clock 1 hour ahead of standard time.

For help with time translations, download our convenient Travel Tools app for your mobile device. Go to frommers.com/go/mobile and tap on the "Travel Tools" icon.

**Tipping**   In the U.S., tipping is expected for most service personnel—in fact, they're paid lower wages with the expectation that they'll make it up in tips. Don't stiff the people whose job is to make your trip a success.

In hotels, tip **bellhops** at least $3 ($5–$10 if you have a lot of luggage) and tip the **chamber staff** $5 to $10 per day (more if you've left a big mess for him or her to clean up). Tip the **doorman** or **concierge** only if he or she has provided you with some specific service (for example, calling a cab for you or obtaining difficult-to-get theater tickets). Tip the **valet-parking attendant** $2 to $5 every time you get your car.

In restaurants, bars, and nightclubs, tip **service staff** and **bartenders** 15% to 20% of the check, tip **checkroom attendants** $2 to $5 per garment, and tip **valet-parking attendants** $5 per vehicle.

As for other service personnel, tip **cabdrivers** 15% to 20% of the fare, tip **skycaps** at airports at least $2 per bag ($5 if you have a lot of luggage), and tip **hairdressers** and **barbers** 20%.

**Toilets**   Those weird, olive-green kiosks on the sidewalks of busy areas of San Francisco are self-cleaning public toilets, given to the city for free by French potty-maker JCDecaux (advertising makes up the cost). They charge 25¢ to enter, with no time limit. We don't recommend using them in certain neighborhoods, such as the sketchier parts of the Mission, because they're mostly used by crackheads and prostitutes. Toilets can also be found in hotel lobbies, bars, restaurants, museums, department stores, railway and bus stations, public parks and playgrounds, and service stations. Restaurants and bars in heavily visited areas, however, may reserve their restrooms for patrons.

**Travel Insurance**   For information on traveler's insurance, trip cancellation insurance, and medical insurance while traveling, visit frommers.com and click on "Health & Travel Insurance" from the "Tips & News" drop-down menu.

**Vaccinations**   Unless you're arriving from an area known to be suffering from an epidemic (particularly cholera or yellow fever), inoculations or vaccinations are not required for entry into the United States.

**VAT**   See "Taxes," p. 286.

**Visas**   The U.S. State Department has a **Visa Waiver Program (VWP)** allowing citizens of the following countries to enter the United States without a visa for stays of up to 90 days: Andorra, Australia, Austria, Belgium, Brunei, Chile, Czech Republic, Denmark, Estonia, Finland, France, Germany, Greece, Hungary, Iceland, Ireland, Italy, Japan, Latvia, Liechtenstein, Lithuania, Luxembourg, Malta, Monaco, Netherlands, New Zealand, Norway, Portugal, San Marino, Singapore, Slovakia, Slovenia, South Korea, Spain, Sweden, Switzerland, Taiwan, and the United Kingdom. (**Note:** This list was accurate at press time; for the most up-to-date list of countries in the VWP, consult travel.state.gov/content/visas/en/visit/visa-waiver-program.html.)

Even though a visa isn't necessary, in an effort to help U.S. officials check travelers against terror watch lists, visitors from VWP countries must register online through the **Electronic System for Travel Authorization (ESTA)** before boarding a plane or a boat to the U.S. Travelers must complete an electronic application providing basic personal and travel eligibility information. The Department of Homeland Security recommends filling out the form at least 3 days before traveling. Authorizations will be valid for up to 2 years or until the traveler's passport expires, whichever comes first. Currently, there's a US$14 fee for the online application. Existing ESTA registrations remain valid through their expiration dates. *Note:* Any passport issued on or after October 26, 2006 by a VWP country must be an **e-Passport** for VWP travelers to be eligible to enter the U.S. without a visa. Citizens of these nations also need to present a round-trip air or cruise ticket upon arrival.

E-Passports contain computer chips capable of storing biometric information, such as the required digital photograph of the holder. If your passport doesn't have this feature, you can still travel without a visa if the valid passport was issued before October 26, 2005 and includes a machine-readable zone; or if the valid passport was issued between October 26, 2005 and October 25, 2006 and includes a digital photograph. For more information,

go to travel.state.gov/content/visas/en/visit/visa-waiver-program.html#ESTA.

**Canadian citizens** may enter the United States without visas, but will need to show passports and proof of residence.

Citizens of **all other countries** must have (1) a valid passport that expires at least 6 months later than the scheduled end of their visit to the U.S.; and (2) a tourist visa.

For information about **U.S. visas,** go to travel.state.gov/content/visas/en.html.

For up-to-date visa information, **Australian** citizens can contact the **U.S. Embassy Canberra,** Moonah Place, Yarralumla, ACT 2600 (℡ **02/6214-5600**); or go to au.usembassy.gov/; **British** subjects can call the **U.S. Embassy Visa Information Line** (℡ **(0)20 7499-9000** from within the U.K. or ℡ **703/439-2367** from within the U.S.) or visit uk.usembassy.gov; **Irish** citizens can contact the **U.S. Embassy Dublin,** 42 Elgin Rd., Ballsbridge, Dublin 4 (℡ **353 1 668 8777** from within the Republic of

Ireland; ie.usembassy.gov/); and **New Zealand** citizens can contact the **U.S. Embassy New Zealand,** 29 Fitzherbert Terrace, Thorndon, Wellington (℡ **644/ 462-6000;** nz.usembassy.gov/).

**Visitor Information**
The **San Francisco Visitor Information Center,** on the lower level of Hallidie Plaza, 900 Market St., at Powell St. (sftravel.com; ℡ **415/391-2000**), is the best source for specialized information about the city. You can request the free "Visitors Planning Guide" and the "San Francisco Visitors" kit, which includes a 6-month calendar of events; city history; shopping and dining information; several good, clear maps; and lodging information; both are also available via the website.

To view or download a free state guide and travel planner, log onto the **California Tourism** website at visitcalifornia.com/visitors-guide-request.

**Wi-Fi** See "Internet & Wi-Fi," p. 283.

# Index

See also Accommodations and Restaurant indexes, below.

## General Index

### A
A-B Fits, 196
Accessibility, 282
Accommodations. *See also* Accommodations Index
  best of, 7
  in Castro, 82–84
  in Civic Center and Tenderloin, 81–82
  for families, 71, 78
  free parking, 79
  at Golden Gate Bridge, 235
  in Haight–Ashbury, 84–85
  home exchanges, 60
  in Japantown, 80–81
  in Marina, Pacific Heights, and Presidio, 76–80
  money-saving tips, 56–58
  in Napa Valley, 253–256
  in Nob Hill, 67–70
  in North Beach and Fisherman's Wharf, 73–76
  in Northern Sonoma County, 267–268
  online discounts, 59
  private, 59
  in SoMa and South Beach, 70–72
  in Sonoma Valley, 263–264
  in Union Square, 60–67
Addresses, finding, 25–26, 128
Adobe Books & Arts Cooperative, 193
Ah Toy, 134
Air tours, 160
Airports, 270–272
Alamo Square, attractions, 137–138
Alcatraz Island, 1, 119–121
  one-day itinerary, 11
  one-day itinerary with kids, 18
Alembic, 219
Alessi, 201
Alice Marble & George Sterling Park, 182
American Conservatory Theater (A.C.T.), 207
Amnesia, 210

Angel Island, 239–241
Antiques, shopping for, 192
Anza, Juan Bautista de, 34
Aquarium of the Bay, 9, 19, 121
Architecture, best of, 6
Area codes, 281
Argonaut Book Shop, 193
Armida, 266
Armstrong Redwoods State Reserve, 267
Arrival information, 270–272
Art, shopping for, 192–193
Art Murmur, 231
Art of China, 199
Artspan Open Studios, 55
Asian Art Museum, 6, 138
AsiaSF, 4
ATMs, 281
AT&T Park, 221
Ayala, Juan, 34
Ayala Cove, 240

### B
Baker Beach, 153, 161
Balmy Alley Murals, 186
Bank of America, 38, 168
Banks, 281
Bar Agricole, 213
Barbary Coast, 39
Barbary Coast Collective, 194–195
Bars, 212–219
  Fisherman's Wharf, Russian Hill, Nob Hill, North Beach, 215–216
  Haight–Ashbury District, 219
  LGBTQ clubs, 220–221
  Marina, Cow Hollow, 216–217
  Mission District, 218–219
  SoMa, Downtown, Tenderloin, FiDi, 213–215
BART (Bay Area Rapid Transit), 271, 274–275
Baseball, 221
Basketball, 221
BATS Improv Theater, 183, 208
Bay Area Discovery Museum, 234
The Bay Lights, 125
Bay Model Visitors Center, 234
Bay to Breakers Foot Race, 53, 163

Beach Blanket Babylon, 2, 12, 179, 208–209
Beaches, 161, 233
The Beat Museum, 176–177
Beatniks, 40–41
"Be-in," 41
Bella Vineyards & Wine Caves, 267
Benziger Family Winery, 260–261
Berkeley, 223–228
  attractions, 224–227
  dining, 227–228
  shopping, 227
  transportation to, 224
Berkeley Art Museum & Pacific Film Archive, 226
Berkeley Repertory Theater, 207
Betabrand, 196
Big Brother & the Holding Company, 48–49
"The Big Four," 133
Bike tours, 158–159
Biking, 5, 22, 161
Bimbo's 365 Club, 210
Biordi Art Imports, 179, 201
Birds, wild parrots, 140
Bi-Rite Market, 188
Bix, 213
Black Point, 183
Bliss Spa, 142
Blue & Gold Fleet, 279
Boat tours, 159
Boating, 161
  in Oakland, 230
  on Stow Lake, 23
Bonanza Kings, 133
Bonhams, 192
Book Passage, 193
Books, San Francisco in, 50
Books Inc., 193–194
The Booksmith, 194
Bookstores, 193–194
The Boom Boom Room, 210
Boomtown era, 38–39
Bottle Rock Napa Valley, 53
Bottom of the Hill, 210
Boudin at the Wharf, 121
Bourbon & Branch, 213
Broadway, 176
Buddhist Church of San Francisco, 141
Buena Vista Café, 215
Buena Vista Park, 162
*Bullitt* (film), 49
Bulo, 203
Burning Man, 143

# Photo Credits

# Map List

*Frommer's EasyGuide to San Francisco, 2nd Edition*

Published by
**FROMMER MEDIA LLC**

ISBN 978-1-62887-378-8 (paper), 978-1-62887-379-5 (ebk)

Editorial Director: Pauline Frommer
Editor: Holly Hughes
Production Editor: Erin Geile
Cartographer: Roberta Stockwell
Photo Editor: Meghan Lamb
Cover Design: David Riedy

For information on our other products or services, see www.frommers.com.

FrommerMedia LLC also publishes its books in a variety of electronic formats. Some content that appears
in print may not be available in electronic formats.

Manufactured in the United States of America

5 4 3 2 1

## ABOUT THE AUTHOR

Native San Franciscan **Erika Lenkert** has authored more than two dozen travel guides to San Francisco and California, including several Frommer's guidebooks. During her 25 years in journalism, she's written a restaurant column for *San Francisco* magazine, was a restaurant critic for the *San Francisco Chronicle*, and has authored feature stories on the Bay Area for national magazines, such as *Travel + Leisure, Food & Wine, and InStyle*. Erika now resides across the Golden Gate Bridge, in Marin County, but still considers the city her home.

## ABOUT THE FROMMER TRAVEL GUIDES

For most of the past 50 years, Frommer's has been the leading series of travel guides in North America, accounting for as many as 24% of all guidebooks sold. I think I know why.

Though we hope our books are entertaining, we nevertheless deal with travel in a serious fashion. Our guidebooks have never looked on such journeys as a mere recreation, but as a far more important human function, a time of learning and introspection, an essential part of a civilized life. We stress the culture, lifestyle, history, and beliefs of the destinations we cover, and urge our readers to seek out people and new ideas as the chief rewards of travel.

We have never shied from controversy. We have, from the beginning, encouraged our authors to be intensely judgmental, critical—both pro and con—in their comments, and wholly independent. Our only clients are our readers, and we have triggered the ire of countless prominent sorts, from a tourist newspaper we called "practically worthless" (it unsuccessfully sued us) to the many rip-offs we've condemned.

And because we believe that travel should be available to everyone regardless of their incomes, we have always been cost-conscious at every level of expenditure. Though we have broadened our recommendations beyond the budget category, we insist that every lodging we include be sensibly priced. We use every form of media to assist our readers, and are particularly proud of our feisty daily website, the award-winning Frommers.com.

I have high hopes for the future of Frommer's. May these guidebooks, in all the years ahead, continue to reflect the joy of travel and the freedom that travel represents. May they always pursue a cost-conscious path, so that people of all incomes can enjoy the rewards of travel. And may they create, for both the traveler and the persons among whom we travel, a community of friends, where all human beings live in harmony and peace.

Arthur Frommer